Francisco I. Madero

FRANCISCO INDALECIO MADERO AND SARA PÉREZ DE MADERO

Francisco I. Madero

APOSTLE OF

MEXICAN DEMOCRACY

By Stanley R. Ross

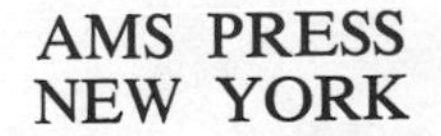

Reprinted with permission of Columbia University Press
From the edition of 1955, New York
First AMS EDITION published 1970
Manufactured in the United States of America

International Standard Book Number: 0-404-05409-9

Library of Congress Card Catalog Number: 79-122591

AMS PRESS, INC.
NEW YORK, N.Y. 10003

TO LEE

Acknowledgments

I AM PARTICULARLY indebted to three members of the staff of Columbia University. Professor Frank Tannenbaum not only suggested the topic of this study, but also was of incalculable assistance through his sympathetic appreciation and penetrating understanding of Mexican history and of the Mexican people. John A. Krout, Vice-President of the University, who created a memorable impression as a teacher, offered understanding, interest, and encouragement to the author. Professor Andrés Iduarte, on leave from the University, displayed continuing interest in a study related to his native land, and his name and friendships opened many doors.

Two trips to Mexico to collect data for this biography demonstrated convincingly that the Mexican people are most hospitable, helpful, and cooperative. Persons in many walks of life placed their time, information, and private material and libraries at my disposal. Since much historical data is concentrated in private hands while the public archives are incomplete and inadequately organized, this study would never have been completed without the cooperation of the individuals involved. The willingness of persons related to Madero or associated with him and of those who had participated in the events described to discuss the various aspects of the subject with the author was most encouraging and most valuable.

José C. Valadés generously placed his extensive private library, particularly rich in documentary and manuscript materials relating to the Díaz period and the Flores Magón movement and including many of Madero's speeches, at my disposal. In addition, Sr. Valadés arranged for access to the material contained in the Archivo de Madero, consisting of some twenty thousand items including the late President's private correspondence from 1906 to 1911 and official papers for the period 1911 to 1913. These papers are located in the home of the late Alfredo Alvarez. Extremely valuable for the period of the Madero armed movement was the archive of the late Federico González Garza, who collected much of the material while serving as Secretary-General of the Madero revolution. Luis Cabrera and Vito Alessio Robles opened the doors of their magnificent private libraries to me, while the late Félix F. Palavicini permitted me to use letters exchanged between him and Francisco Madero. Colonel Octavio Magaña Cerda placed at my disposal part of the documentary collection in his possession including the correspondence of Francisco de la Barra and the archive of Zapata's headquarters.

My research in Mexico advanced pleasantly along a path smoothed by the bonds of acquaintance and friendship. Each person contacted assisted the author and then arranged for him to meet others who might be of further assistance. Rodulfo Brito Foucher, Federico González Garza, Miguel Alessio Robles, and José Rubén Romero expended considerable time and effort to arrange such meetings. The author was most fortunate to be able to talk with Madero's brothers Raúl and Carlos; his cousin Rafael Hernández; and the family attorney, Adrián Aguirre Benavides. The late Sra. Sara Pérez de Madero, widow of the President, left a memorable impression in the interview she granted in her home in Colonia Roma. Valuable data was obtained in conversations with the following persons: Miguel Alessio Robles, Vito Alessio Robles, Juan Barragán Rodríguez, Rodulfo Brito Foucher, Luis Cabrera, Antonio Díaz Soto y Gama, Federico González Garza, Pablo Martínez del Río, Manuel Mestre Ghigliazza, Félix F. Palavicini, Alfonso Taracena, José Vasconcelos, Silvio Zavala, and Rafael Zubarán Capmany.

While engaged in research for this study, I found the staffs of the following institutions most efficient, cooperative, and helpful: the Columbia University Libraries, New York Public Library, and the Library of the University of Nebraska; the National Archives and the Library of Congress, in Washington, D.C.; and in Mexico, the Archivo General de la Nación, La Biblioteca Nacional, La Hemeroteca Nacional, El Museo Nacional de Historia, Arqueología y Etnología de México, La Biblioteca de Guerra de la Secretaría de Defensa Nacional, and the Benjamin Franklin Library. The late Miss Bertha Harris of the last-named institution was particularly helpful in arranging introductions to the directors of the various Mexican research centers.

I am indebted to Columbia University for a fellowship and to the State Department of the United States for a travel grant which permitted me to complete this study.

The maps in this volume were drafted by Raymond Price, and my wife, Leonore, prepared the Aztec symbol for war which decorates the map of Mexico at the beginning of the book.

I wish also to thank members of the staff of Columbia University Press who have aided in the preparation of this book, including Dr. William Bridgwater and Miss Barbara Melissa Voorhis.

These acknowledgments would be incomplete without a word of appreciation for Vica and Carlos Iturbe, who offered my wife and me the hospitality of their home and the warmth of their friendship during our residence in their country. Lastly, I am deeply indebted to my wife who encouraged and assisted me in the accomplishment of this study.

S. R. R.

Lincoln, Nebraska
September, 1954

Contents

Frontispiece:

Maps

Francisco I. Madero

I. Fruit of Parras

NEAR THE END of the eighteenth or early in the nineteenth century an Iberian [1] family named Madero settled in northern Mexico. Evaristo Madero, grandfather of Francisco I. Madero, established the foundation of the family's fortune and prominence. At nineteen he owned and operated a train of wagons, each drawn by six mules, carrying merchandise along the roads and trails linking Parras, Saltillo, Monterrey, San Luis Potosí, and San Antonio. The Civil War in the United States created an unusual opportunity for the alert merchant. Cotton brought out of Texas yielded a handsome return, and thus was begun one of the outstanding family fortunes in Mexico.

Evaristo broadened the family's economic interests to include cotton and guayule haciendas, textile factories, wine distilleries, and copper mines and refineries, together with rolling mills in Monterrey, Tampico, and Mérida. He founded the first bank on the northern frontier, the Bank of Nuevo León in Monterrey. Despite their rivalry with the American concessionaires Guggenheim and Rockefeller over copper and guayule interests, the Madero family prospered under Porfirio Díaz's program of enforced peace, economic development, and selective prosperity. It has been estimated that by 1910 Evaristo Madero had amassed one of the ten largest fortunes in Mexico, exceeding thirty million pesos (approximately fifteen million dollars).

[1] This writer has been unable to discover evidence to substantiate the assertion that the family was ethnically of Jewish origin.

Evaristo Madero also entered politics, serving as governor of Coahuila from 1880 to 1884. His incumbency was well remembered for the stimulation given to elementary education and to cultural projects. However, the return of Porfirio Díaz to the presidency in the latter year resulted in the elimination of Evaristo from the gubernatorial post. This move was inevitable in a system based on provincial government staffed by unconditionally loyal friends of the president, friends selected and sustained by him. The dictator also issued secret instructions to General Reyes to maintain surveillance over the former state head who never again occupied public office.

Evaristo contributed not only to the economic and social prominence of the Madero family but also to its numbers. Twice married, he begot nineteen children, fourteen of whom lived to maturity. When Evaristo died at the age of eighty-two in 1911, he was survived by thirty-four grandchildren and fifty-six great-grandchildren in addition to the fourteen children.

His son Francisco, father of the subject of this study and bearer of the same name, concentrated on economic pursuits. A vigorous business man, he built his personal fortune primarily through mining interests and cattle raising, achieving a capital which exceeded fifteen million pesos. Francisco Madero the elder married Mercedes González Treviño, the youngest of sixteen children of a distinguished and wealthy family of Monterrey. In the front room of the Hacienda of the Rosary in Parras, Coahuila, a town named for the Mediterranean grapevines which proved adaptable to the sandy soil, Francisco Indalecio Madero was born October 30, 1873. He was the first of fifteen children resulting from this marriage.[2]

Mercedes de Madero, very young at the time of Francisco's birth, always remained conscious of her inexperience as a parent and regretted it. The baby cried a great deal and ate poorly. The family felt that this undernourishment accounted for Francisco's small physical stature. His mother remembered him as a sickly, melancholy child, given to repose and contem-

[2] Thirteen children were to reach maturity: Francisco, Gustavo, Emilio, Alfonso, Raúl, Gabriel, Carlos, Mercedes, Angela, Rafaela, and Magdalena.

plation in strong contrast to the friskiness of his younger brother Gustavo.[3] In Parras, a community of some seven thousand inhabitants, Francisco learned his first letters from two religiously inclined ladies, and, later, the husband of one of them gave him rudimentary training in music. Since the youngster (affectionately called Panchito by his family and intimates) showed a marked preference for the country, he was taken frequently to visit family properties. This early experience together with his later close association with agricultural activities prompted him to observe: "I come from the virgin land and in its womb I received my first education; I know, therefore, the innate need . . . of those who suffer [there] . . . remote from education and justice."[4]

However, by the very circumstances of his birth and background, Madero was placed near the apex of the Mexican social and economic pyramid, removed, virtually isolated, from the majority of the Mexican people and their problems. Persons in the upper class of Mexican society maintained almost a separate existence. They enjoyed an overwhelming degree of social prominence based on actual or assumed racial purity, economic position, and prestige founded, most often, on extensive land ownership. Concentrations of land in a few hands meant economic power and political domination as well for the few. Absentee operation, with vacation-like seasonal exceptions, was characteristic. This social element alone had access to education, most frequently in the foreign environment of Europe and occasionally in the even more alien land to the north. If this social background was limiting, Madero's family situation was controlling. The family was large, but very closely knit. The family environment was paternalistic and patriarchal and was dominated by Grandfather Evaristo. Francisco Madero was, to an exceptional degree, a creature of this family structure.

[3] Prof. Hernán Rosales, "La madre del Presidente Madero habla de la infancia de su hijo," *El Universal,* May 17, 1927; Interview with Raúl Madero in July, 1948.

[4] *Ibid.*

The development of the youth was influenced by several emotional experiences of psychological significance. At the age of twelve, in the year 1885, he entered the Jesuit College of San Juan in Saltillo, the capital of Coahuila. An emotional youth not long removed from the elementary religious instruction provided by his mother and the pious ladies of Parras, Pancho Madero was so greatly impressed that he desired to enter the Company of Jesus. "I became convinced that it was for me the only path to salvation." [5] The following year he and Gustavo attended St. Mary's College in a suburb of Baltimore, Maryland. He later recalled that remaining there less than a complete academic year he learned very little English and "nothing else because of not knowing the language." [6] At this second church institution his ardor for a clerical career disappeared. "If I had not attended that college where they made me know religion under such somber and irrational colors, the innocent beliefs which my mother taught me would have lasted a much longer time." [7]

Despite this disillusionment and the admittedly slight educational gain Francisco left this school with vivid impressions and happy remembrances of the friendliness of a tutor, of rides in horse-drawn sleighs and of other rides down hills, at dizzy speed, on small individual sleds. Lastly, Madero recalled a quarter-hour-long fist fight with an American student. Remembering details of the schoolboy struggle, its toll in discolored eyes, bleeding noses, and bruised faces, and the handshake that followed in the washroom, Madero had no unkind thoughts of his rival. On the other hand, the priests who watched the fight and shouted encouragement to the contestants were scathingly denounced by Madero in his memoirs.

During the vacation at Parras which preceded a trip to Europe in order to continue his education, an incident reportedly occurred which in startling fashion foreshadowed the future. A gathering at the home of Francisco's companion,

[5] Madero, "Mis memorias," *Anales del Museo Nacional*, p. 9.
[6] *Ibid.*
[7] Taracena, *Madero: Vida*, p. 10.

Ernesto Fernández Arteaga, turned to the planchette for amusement. The device was manipulated to obtain mediumistic messages foretelling the future of each youth. When Francisco's turn arrived, the planchette spelled the reply that Madero would be president of Mexico. This glimpse of the future and its serious acceptance by Francisco produced great hilarity among the adults present, some of whom undoubtedly had influenced the result. Revealing as this purported incident may be of Francisco as a boy, it is to be doubted that, as some have suggested, the conviction of his presidential destiny dominated Madero's thoughts and actions from that moment. Gustavo and Francisco sailed from New York for France where they were to continue their studies. With the exception of the first and final days of the trip, the older brother was seasick throughout the crossing. Born of his discomfort was the fantastic idea of going home on horseback by way of Siberia to avoid the dreaded return voyage.

Francisco remained in Europe for five years, from 1887 until 1892. He completed his primary education at the Lycée of Versailles (later called Lycée Hoche). His familiarity with the language enabled him to learn a great deal during a little more than a year in attendance. Then Madero began his professional training in the School of Advanced Commercial Studies in Paris. Besides shorthand and accounting, he studied manufacturing (including methods of production, location of raw materials, markets, and cost-price determinations), political economy, commercial geography, applied mathematics, finance, civil and commercial law, and budgetary legislation. In retrospect he regarded the French educational system as excellent, expressing particular approval of the constant examinations which obliged the student to study all through the year. Pleased by the hospitable and courteous reception accorded the foreigner, Madero reacted with typical Latin American partiality for France. "When we [Latins] go to France, we feel more at home than in the United States because our character corresponds more closely with the French than with the Anglo Saxon." A believer in theoretical and practical democracy, Madero recalled with enthusiasm the equality of treatment accorded in the government's colleges to Frenchmen and foreigners alike, including those "from the most backward parts of the globe." [8]

In Paris, Madero underwent a significant emotional experience. In 1891 there accidentally came to his attention some issues of the *Revue Spirite* which had been founded by Allán Kardec.[9] Madero lacked sufficient preparation to develop his own doctrine and did not subject his acquired beliefs to penetrating analysis. The young Mexican student considered himself capable of evaluating spiritism in a dispassionate manner since in that period he had "no religious belief nor any philosophical creed." He obtained the writings of Kardec. These, he said, "I did not read . . . but rather devoured . . . Because their doctrine was so rational, beautiful, and new it captivated me. From that moment I considered myself a spiritist." [10] He attended various spiritualist sessions at which the mediums advised him that he was a "writing" medium. He experimented, but the only result was a small, wavy line which Madero attributed to the weariness of his hand, it having remained for a long time in the same position. Despite his acceptance of this doctrine, it did not immediately influence his life. Rather, it was a seed which would germinate later having found a favorable soil.

The Paris spiritualists introduced him to the study of Oriental religions. The result was a study of the *Bhagavad Gita,* the dialogues which contain teachings basic to Hindu religious belief. The *Bhagavad Gita,* the *Song of Heaven,* glorifies action. Krishna, the god of peace and salvation, speaks to the warrior Arguna on the importance of denying the material and affirming the spiritual, the ultimate truth. Arguna, about to enter combat against some enemies whom he does not hate,

[8] Madero, "Mis memorias," p. 11.

[9] Allán Kardec was the pseudonym of León Hipólito Denizar Revail, author of *The Book of the Spirits* and a high priest of the spiritist movement.

[10] Madero, "Mis memorias," p. 12.

asks Krishna why he must fight when he holds no such sentiment. Krishna tells him that to flee would lead his enemies to charge him with cowardice. If he dies, he will enjoy divinity. If he conquers, the world will be his. There is nothing better than a righteous battle. This must have been a doctrine attractive to the altruistic Madero, who would shortly enter the lists in behalf of the Mexican people. Unlike Ghandi, Madero was literal, not interpretative, in his approach. His commentaries on the Indian classic reveal not only the nature of his new beliefs but also the direction in which they would ultimately lead him. He marveled at the breadth of the spirit of tolerance of the *Bhagavad Gita* and at its agreement with the teachings of Jesus. "The most effective way to worship the divinity is to 'delight in the good of all beings,' or what is the same, to love our brothers as Jesus taught." From his study Madero concluded that it is possible for a human being to achieve the highest degree of virtue in any occupation or profession, politics included. All that is required is for "our acts to have a useful end for humanity . . . [and] to be in harmony with the Divine Plan because they tend to favor the welfare of the human race and its progress."[11]

Vacations, the time of family visits and opportunity for travel, were pleasant interludes for the Mexican youth living and studying in France. Two such vacations were especially memorable. In 1889 the whole family arrived to spend the season in France and, with Francisco, visited the Paris International Exposition and Versailles. During the vacation of 1891 Francisco accompanied his mother, brothers and sisters, and several uncles to Royan, a French resort located at the mouth of the Gironde River. For nearly three months he indulged daily in two favorite pastimes, swimming and extended walks. During that season the youth also accompanied members of the family to Bordeaux, Lourdes, and San Sebastián.

[11] Ferrer de M., *Vida de Madero*, pp. 13-14; *La Opinión*, Oct. 8, 1933. Taracena noted that Madero had prepared a *Spiritist Manual* under the pseudonym "Bhima" and a translation of Denis's *After Death* which he signed "Elisa." Taracena, *Madero: Vida*, p. 124.

And with friends of the family, he visited Brussels, Antwerp, The Hague, Amsterdam, and Poland as well. Five years had elapsed since he had left Mexico, and Madero, homesick, resolved to return as quickly as possible. Therefore, he sacrificed the grand tour of Europe which his father had authorized. Although he planned to make the trip at some later date, responsibilities were to occupy his time and other ideas and dreams were to fill his imagination so that he never did.

After his return to his homeland, Madero spent three months at the Hacienda of the Rosary where a large part of the family sojourned during the summer. A skilled horseman, he passed considerable time in the saddle. Swims and dances also absorbed his energies. These annual vacations in the delightful environs of Parras always left Francisco with the most pleasant of memories, and this one was no exception.

The season ended, Francisco and Gustavo accompanied their father and two of their sisters, Mercedes and Magdalena, to California. While the sisters enrolled in a convent school, the boys entered the University of California at Berkeley. Francisco studied at this institution for eight months perfecting his knowledge of English and acquiring general information about agriculture which later was to prove exceedingly useful. At the end of the school year the brothers toured the California coast and visited Yosemite Valley. This was Francisco's last foreign pleasure trip. His years of formal education had been completed. The major portion of it must be considered training rather than education, for his preparation had been almost exclusively vocational in order to train him for a career in business and agricultural management. Virtually his only intellectual preparation lay in his acquired conviction of the efficacy of Anglo-Saxon democracy, his enthusiastic acceptance of Gallic egalitarianism, and his responsiveness to the spiritist emphasis on human welfare and progress.

In the fall of 1893 the twenty-year-old Francisco returned to Mexico to assume his place in the economic affairs of the Madero family. His father assigned him the task of developing properties in the semiarid area near San Pedro de las Colonias. The elder Madero was responsible for the introduction and popularization of the cultivation of American cotton in the lower region of the Nazas River. The northern variety produced a far superior yield to the cotton grown previously. The son revealed something of his own thinking when he sharply criticized planters who had retained the old variety because of an "inconceivable spirit of routine." [12]

Since there was no water flowing over the beds of the Nazas that year, Francisco busied himself with becoming familiar with his parents' properties. This period represents his first opportunity to become acquainted with the rural people and their problems. However, the rural population of northern Mexico was and is predominantly mestizo, with socio-economic experience and cultural development markedly different from that of the Indian peoples who predominate in the more densely populated regions in the central and southern sections of the country. Consequently, extended application of this experience would not be possible for Francisco. Gustavo and Francisco were guided by Atanasio González, administrator of the lands, who had served as a cavalry captain during the internal fighting of the pre-Díaz period, and Francisco, always an avid student of history, followed the administrator's account of his campaigns with lively interest.

The following year, 1894, Francisco began to cultivate cotton on his father's property. He introduced modern machinery and experimented with American and African cottonseed, which he imported in the search for greater crop yield. His efforts were successful, and, as the region prospered, he encouraged colonists to settle in the area. Among the first to come were Madero's brothers Alfonso and Emilio. Francisco Madero merits recognition as a leading pioneer in the development of the Laguna region which became one of the most productive areas of Mexico. Continuing to administer his father's holdings while renting others in his own interest, he devoted his major efforts to agriculture for sixteen years. Within eight years Madero, by his own skillful efforts and by fa-

[12] Madero, "Mis memorias," p. 15.

vorable opportunity and family resources, had accumulated a personal capital in excess of a quarter of a million dollars.

Madero's reputation as a progressive agriculturalist does not rest on his individual achievements alone. For example, he began to study methods for the most effective utilization of the Nazas River waters which irrigated the Tlahualilo region in Durango and the Laguna region in Coahuila. It was in connection with obtaining data for this study that Madero first had occasion to correspond with Finance Minister Limantour, whom his family esteemed and regarded as a friend. He published the results of his investigations in a folio in which he recommended the construction of a dam in Fernández Canyon to store water for use in years of drought. The study drew favorable comments from many sources including President Díaz.[13] In addition, Madero was active in the organization of a cotton growers syndicate formed to defend the members' interest against the millers who appeared to have leagued together to force the cultivators to sell at low prices. These activities coincided with his growing interest in politics, and the two efforts were probably not without some connection.

Unquestionably disinterested was Madero's energetic promotion of the well-being of his tenants. He carried over the paternalistic, patriarchal tradition of his family into his relations with the workers. Not content with raising salaries and assuring personally the accurate weighing of the cotton harvested, Madero applied his ideas and resources to the problem of bettering the life of these people. He provided his workers with well-ventilated and hygienic living quarters. His personal physician was required to visit the haciendas to care for the

[13] Madero sent copies of his study to both Limantour and Díaz. He wrote to the former about "this work which I judge of great utility for this district and even for the nation." Madero to José Ives Limantour, Nov. 17 and 29, 1907, AdeM.

Although the reply of Gen. Díaz to Madero's letter of Feb. 1, 1908, is not directly known, a letter written by Madero to him implies that the Mexican President wrote an acknowledgment complimenting his efforts. Madero to Gen. Porfirio Díaz, Feb. 2, 1909, AdeM. Madero, *La sucesión presidencial,* pp. 370-75.

sick. With his own funds Madero sustained elementary schools on the properties and required the workers to send their children. Fairness, unostentatious generosity, and an unassumed democratic nature earned for Madero the deep affection of his workers. Even those who later opposed Madero politically admitted that he was an outstandingly progressive hacendado.

His altruism extended beyond the boundaries of his property. During a year of absolute drought food prices soared and ninety percent of the townspeople were jobless. Madero promoted among the wealthier inhabitants the idea of establishing a public dining room to provide food for those in need. Although this institution alleviated the difficulty, Madero, who never had any children of his own, continued to feed daily more than threescore youngsters in his own home. He gathered in his house a number of orphans whom he protected and educated. Charitable institutions could always depend on his moral and financial support. He contributed generously to the establishment and maintenance of a hospital in San Pedro. In the same community he supplied the initiative for the creation of a commercial college. In addition to a substantial monthly contribution to this institution, Madero provided scholarships for a number of students. Included among the recipients was Elías de los Ríos, later stenographer for his benefactor.

Madero was not satisfied to conform to the role of the son of a rich landowner. Philanthropy, even beyond the concept of *noblesse oblige,* did not still the inner compulsion to do good for his fellow men. By chance, in 1896, he obtained some knowledge of homeopathy from a Colonel Carlos Herrera. Homeopathy is a medical theory holding that disease is cured by remedies which produce in a healthy person effects similar to the symptoms of the complaint of the patient. The remedies are usually administered in very small doses. After studying this theory and employing it to tend his own ills, Madero became convinced of its practicality. As eight years later he was to sacrifice fortune and, ultimately, his life in an effort to reform his nation, so in 1901 he surrendered his time and energy to cure suffering humanity. He opened his door to the sick, listened to their complaints, and offered advice and treatment. With his medicine chest he visited the houses of his workers to treat the infirm. In his archives is preserved a ninety-two page "medical" notebook in which the homeopathist patiently entered his observations on the course of the illness and the results of his ministrations for each patient. While some of his notations are medical curiosities, they do provide a remarkable view of the author. Madero revealed in his records an anxiety lest he be deceived in diagnosis. However, once this was completed he prescribed with confidence. His reactions to developments were not those of a scientist, but rather of an extremely emotional, sensitive man. A prolonged, difficult case caused the impromptu doctor to despair of achieving a cure. New prescriptions, in such a case, were noted in a nervous, scrawly hand. When favorable results were obtained, Madero exultantly noted them in a clear, large hand. According to these notes Madero prescribed for over three hundred persons in 1901 alone.[14]

Although a man of affairs, Madero continued to accept the patriarchal paternalism of his family. He was always the exceptional son and brother. Indeed, his exceedingly close ties with his family and the influence its members endeavored to exercise over him were among the most serious handicaps in Madero's political and revolutionary career. Even after he had achieved economic success, his grandfather, parents, and uncles continued to consider him in the subordinate status of a son within the family. Because economic pursuits did not satisfy his soul, because of his excessive enthusiasm, and because he went so far in his altruism and humanitarianism, Madero did not enjoy a reputation for practicality in his own family. The impression persists that his elders, and even Gustavo and his sisters, patronized and used the tolerant, devoted Francisco. Only the younger brothers conceded the eldest son authority and respect.

[14] *La Opinión,* April 22, 1934.

In Madero's archives are hundreds of letters which he wrote to members of his family. While they incidentally reflect on his lack of literary preparation, from these letters emerges the picture of Francisco's relationship with his family. To his younger brothers studying abroad Madero wrote sometimes with presumptive authority but always with great affection. He made them send him their grades. Advice was freely given, and reprimands were not lacking. He complained when they did not write, urged them to work hard at school, and expressed concern about their reported extravagance. Other passages in this family correspondence provide an insight into the author's thinking. When Raúl indicated an interest in a military career, Madero opposed the idea with a penetrating analysis of the disabilities of the military profession. Francisco expressed an optimistic, if unjustified, view of the drift of international conduct when he anticipated that nations would "become more civilized, abate their bellicose instincts and accustom themselves to respect the rights of other nations in order to be able to enjoy peace." [15] When it was a question of marriage for his sister, the eldest brother expressed his conviction that Rafaela's choice should prevail.[16]

Madero's letters to the older members of the family reveal the exceptional, dutiful son. With tenderness, considerateness, and great respect Francisco addressed himself to his grandfather and parents. Weekly, he would write his father, in the greatest detail, of the properties which he was administering for the elder Francisco. He reported to his father the quantity of feed each head consumed and detailed the most trivial expenditures. The letters show him always solicitous of the health of the members of the family, especially of that of his mother. Mercedes must quiet the anxiety of her son by answering persistent queries about her pulse, the manner in which certain foods affected her, and prescriptions received from doctors. Once this information had been obtained, Fran-

[15] Madero to his brother Evaristo E. Madero, July 4, 1906, and to Raúl Madero, Sept. 20, 1906, AdeM.

[16] Madero to Rafaela Madero, July 27, 1906, AdeM.

cisco would send her homeopathic prescriptions and recommend diets to be followed.

When Madero's mother became gravely ill with typhoid fever in 1901, he credited homeopathy with saving her life. It was during this long, serious illness of his mother that the eldest son underwent a moral change of significance. Consider this twenty-eight-year-old, extremely sensitive young man. A small person, of less than one hundred and forty pounds and under five feet three inches tall, Madero was, however, well proportioned. Persons who met him were impressed by the bulging, full forehead and the deep-set, restless, and animated brown eyes. His face was full and would have appeared round but for the very black, pear-shaped beard which with a mustache surrounded a wide mouth. The almost constant smile which illumined his face accentuated the fullness of his cheeks. Francisco had the eyes and expression of his mother. His manner was nervous, his air hurried. When he talked, his hands darted about. His high, thin voice grew shriller as his earnestness increased. In addition to riding, swimming, and hiking, Madero loved to dance. He smoked a great deal, drank beer, and possessed a very fine wine cellar. If his self-indictment is accepted, he was leading a life of dissipation. Reflecting under the emotional stress of his mother's illness, Madero concluded that he had led a useless life.

He resolved to stop smoking and drinking and proceeded to dispose of the contents of his wine cellar. Dancing remained the only form of indulgence retained from his earlier life. Since Madero always adopted ideas with extreme fervor, he became a very vocal advocate of temperance. He further simplified his regimen by becoming a vegetarian. Lastly, he vowed to return to Sarita.

Sara Pérez, daughter of Marcario Pérez, who owned lands in the states of Mexico and Querétaro, had attended school in California with Francisco's sisters. Francisco scarcely knew her then, but her close friendship with Mercedes and Magdalena resulted in their meeting again in Mexico. Madero visited Sarita in Mexico City, and they corresponded regularly. Although they loved each other deeply, Francisco's feelings wandered; for this he blamed "distance and dissipation." "I ended by breaking with her for no reason." [17] An even more active social life could not ease the memory of this love. When, in 1901, Madero redirected his life, he determined to renew the relationship with Sara. Repeatedly he wrote to his cousin Rafael Hernández inquiring about her. "I am anxious to see Sarita . . . with my own eyes in order . . . [to learn] whether she has forgotten everything that happened." [18] He persisted in his purpose and, despite obstacles, apparently including the objection of Sara's father, at last "had the pleasure of embracing the one who was to be my inseparable companion and who was to occupy so predominant a place in my heart." [19] Sara and Francisco were united in a civil ceremony on January 26, 1903, in the Mexican capital. Marcario Pérez did not attend the wedding. A religious ceremony was performed the following morning by the archbishop.

After a brief stay at the Reforma Hotel, Francisco and his bride returned to San Pedro to take up residence in a house facing the principal plaza. Here they lived modestly in conjugal bliss marred only by their mutual disappointment that there was no issue from the union. Francisco proved a considerate, thoughtful husband. Sara, a fragile woman, was a model of tenderness, understanding, and abnegation. She apparently contributed determination and direction to her husband's decision to reorient his life's work. Her steadfast devotion to her husband in the difficult times ahead was accompanied by a talent for submerging her own personality and individuality in the interest of her husband and his cause.

Within a short time Madero was to make politics his sphere of action. Perhaps the discussion of a "final" reelection for dictator Díaz stimulated Madero's thinking along political lines. Assuredly his democratic ideology was a factor. How-

[17] Madero, "Mis memorias," p. 16.

[18] Madero to Rafael Hernández, March 25, 1902, AdeM.

[19] Madero, "Mis memorias," p. 16; Madero to Sr. Pérez, May 11, 1904, *La Opinión*, Feb. 4, 1934.

ever, Madero's entry into the political arena was closely associated also with his belief in spiritism. After his return to Mexico from Europe, Madero remained a devotee of spiritism, organizing a small group for its study in San Pedro, subscribing to a spiritist review, corresponding with its followers in various countries, and ordering copies of Kardec's *Book of the Spirits* and León Denis's *After Death.*

About this time Madero became involved in a discussion with his uncle, Antonio Garza, which provides a key to his religious and spiritist thinking. He wrote his uncle that it was advisable to list the points on which they were in agreement in order to discover the cause of their differences. He noted that both accepted the "existence of an uncreated, eternal, infinitely great and good God." They also agreed that the soul or spirit exists in eternal life and that on leaving the body it experiences joys or pains as merited. Lastly, they agreed that spirits are capable of communicating with the living, although the uncle reserved that for good spirits.

Madero started from these three points in the presentation of his own beliefs. He affirmed that both good and bad spirits can and do communicate with the living. The latter are able to distinguish the good from the bad by various means. "One of His envoys to this world or, as you believe, His own son Jesus Christ, has forewarned us . . . that there are many false prophets, but that by their works . . . we would know them." An additional check, Madero observed, is that in many parts of the world the spirits have made the same revelations simultaneously. Then Madero raised the question of God's object in permitting the spirits of deceased persons to communicate with the living. He believed that the purpose is to aid the living "along the difficult road of virtue." The letter ends on an extremely anticlerical note, since Madero took issue with the "infallibility of the Pope and of the Church" because "those authorities have abrogated reason and free will, a faculty which God gave to us." [20]

Although he had abandoned as unsuccessful experiments in spirit writing in Paris, Madero resumed his efforts during the

[20] Madero to Antonio Garza, Nov. 26, 1901, AdeM.

long hours he nursed his Uncle Manuel Madero, ill with a gastric disorder. He reported that he felt, after a short time, a force, alien to his own will, move his hand with great rapidity. He resolved to continue the experiments. A few days later his hand wrote, in large trembling letters, "Love God above all things and your neighbor as yourself." The next day the incident was repeated. The third day brought a recommendation for prayer. Madero later avowed that he received many messages on philosophical and moral questions and that they were always treated with competence and in beautiful language. To these communications in particular and to the principles of spiritism in general Madero attributed his transformation and his preoccupation with the welfare of his country.[21]

In 1906 he served as a delegate for the Center for Psychological Studies of San Pedro de las Colonias to the First National Spiritist Congress in Mexico City. He actively participated in debate and served on several commissions. One of these groups investigated suitable means to disseminate the spiritist philosophy more effectively. Apparently, Francisco Madero had found his chosen path to spread spiritism and to serve his fellow men. In a letter dated June 26, 1906, he wrote to León Denis in Tours, France, that he was thinking of entering politics "as soon as there would be an opportunity," since that was the arena in which he had "elected to fight for the cause."[22] That same summer he cautioned his brother Evaristo, who was studying abroad, not to "lose sight that you are a Mexican." He also urged his brother to accustom himself to the physical aspects of the military school whether he liked it or not in order that "when you return to your country you may be capable of performing important services. This would be particularly true if you should arrive in time for the great political struggle which is being prepared for the not too distant future."[23] Francisco I. Madero was thinking in terms of service to his nation and its people.

[21] Madero, "Mis memorias," p. 17.

[22] AdeM.

[23] Madero to his grandfather Evaristo E. Madero, Aug. 4 and 26, 1906, AdeM.

II. The Peace of Porfirio

WHEN FRANCISCO MADERO was born, Mexico was on the threshold of a new political era. Within three years Porfirio Díaz had initiated the successful military uprising which marked the beginning of three decades of domination. Madero matured during the dictatorship of Porfirio Díaz and achieved historical significance in the turmoil which accompanied and followed the end of Díaz's long rule.

In 1904 the presidential term had been extended to six years, and Porfirio Díaz had been elected for his sixth term. The regime of Díaz marks a startling change in the rhythm of the life of the Mexican nation. The violent irregularity of political affairs gave way to the steady beat of the seemingly perpetual continuation of Díaz in power. While politics were restrained, the economic development of the nation was accelerated, rapidly and forcibly. The rule of Porfirio Díaz was the political and economic miracle of nineteenth-century Mexico.

Since its achievement of independence Mexico had suffered from chaos. Governments before 1876 lasted less than a year on the average, and only two administrations finished out the constitutionally prescribed period. Government as a dependable, regular institution had virtually disappeared, and economic progress had been limited. Against this background the Díaz regime appeared miraculous. Díaz had achieved power, in conformity with the pattern of Mexican politics since independence, through violence and military might. As had happened so often before, the constitution had served as justification for revolution rooted in ambition for power and political status.

Once in control Díaz strove to give Mexico peace and internal stability. Where presidents had been unable to maintain themselves in office, Díaz proceeded to rule for thirty-one of the succeeding thirty-five years, the last twenty-seven consecutively. Where brigandage, revolution, and warfare had previously been constants, the new era was disturbed only by sporadic outbreaks which were quickly and efficiently eliminated. The second objective, after peace, of Díaz was his theme of *nada de política y mucha de administración* (no politics and plenty of administration). As translated into practice, the phrase warned that no meddling opposition would be tolerated. In exchange was offered the promise of efficient government bringing order, progress, and upper-class prosperity. Indeed, the accomplishment of material progress and prosperity was a noteworthy characteristic of the Díaz period. Political peace and stability were made the basis for economic advancement, for rapid, forced industrialization.

The results of that policy can be read in the statistics of improved governmental finances, tremendous foreign investments, railroad development, and expansion of commerce, industry, and mining. Internal improvements were not neglected. The ports were improved, while coasts were charted and lighthouses constructed. Mexico City was converted into a modern metropolis with broad avenues, electric streetcars, and impressive, if extravagant, public buildings. The capital became a showplace, a solid and silent testimony to the greatness of the Mexican leader who had accomplished so much. A world enamored with order, progress, and prosperity was quick to praise Díaz and his work.

A few voices were vehemently and passionately critical. Dr. Luis Lara Pardo summarized the Díaz policy as one of "extermination, degredation, and prostitution." Another writer labeled the regime a "despotic autocracy." In 1910, the very year of the centenary celebration of Mexican independence,

John Kenneth Turner called Mexico "barbarous."[1] However, most foreigners were impressed by the façade of peace and material progress which obscured the means by which it was created and maintained and the price that had to be paid for it. But the political techniques used by Díaz to obtain and preserve peace and to continue his regime in power are basic to an understanding of the period of his rule as well as to such understanding of the political considerations which colored greatly the opposition initiated toward the close of that period.

Porfirio Díaz received, in 1876, a nation of people weary of anarchy, civil war, and misery. The Mexicans were anxious for stability and peace. The interim regime of Manuel González, from 1880 to 1884, further convinced the nation of the indispensability of the leader who resumed the presidency. To this extent the Díaz regime probably did emanate, at least initially, from the popular will. Most of the subsequent reelections of the President rested to a degree on the tolerance or apathy of the Mexican people, but the duration of the Díaz government would imply that trust and apathy alone do not suffice as explanation. The government of General Díaz though regular in appearance was by function and nature strictly personal.

Díaz abolished the Constitution of 1857, not in word or in writing, but in fact. A federated republic, division of powers between the branches of government, and democracy were among the fictions maintained. Elections were ritual-like. In practice all authority came to be vested in the central government, primarily in the executive branch and specifically in the president. The reelection of this official became a matter of form. From the president down, elective, legislative, and judicial machinery were supplanted by administrative procedures. Personal government as a political method was substituted for political parties and principles. Political relationships were built on the bases of friendship and dependability. The

[1] Turner, *Barbarous Mexico;* Lara Pardo, *Madero,* p. 96; Rubén García, *El Antiporforismo,* p. 101.

cabinet, the Congress, and the governors were bound to the dictator by ties of friendship and interest. A similar relationship existed between the *jefes políticos* (political chiefs) and the governors and between the municipal presidents and the *jefes políticos.* The entire machinery of local, provincial, and national government became dependent upon the will of one man.

These ties of friendship were cemented with the mortar of self-interest. Díaz united politics and interest, bestowing concessions, monopolies, and positions of prestige. Each beneficiary of this system became an ardent supporter of peace and, therefore, of the maintenance of Díaz in power. An established policy of the dictator was to divide and conquer, to play individual against individual, group against group. In this manner Díaz avoided the development of a concentration of strength which might challenge his position. Also, the persons involved tended to strengthen Díaz in order to forestall their opponents, and the nation preferred the retention of Díaz to disagreeable, factious alternatives. Ambitious rivals who dared openly to oppose Díaz received the *pan o palo* (bread or stick) treatment. The choice was to accept material rewards, usually with the loss of political influence, or to be eliminated.

Members of the cabinet were chosen not only for capacity but also for adhesion to the President. Díaz followed a Machiavellian policy of playing ministers against each other. The national congress, carefully selected and regimented, was a decorative body during most of the Díaz period lacking legislative initiative and independence. Similarly, the judiciary was selected in a manner conducive to the dominance of the executive. In spite of the federalist constitution state sovereignty was of necessity a fiction. The same pattern of centralized control was applied in the provinces. The Díaz government frequently intervened in state affairs. The governors were all unconditionally friends of the President, selected and sustained by him. Governor was balanced against governor, and military commanders served to keep them in check. Furthermore, loyalty was maintained by opportunity to exercise local tyranny and to acquire material rewards. The conduct of some provincial authorities made that of Díaz, by contrast, seem exemplary for probity and restraint.

The presidential influence extended to the state legislatures and beyond to the units of local government. *Jefes políticos,* subordinate to the president or his governors, absorbed the authority of the municipal governments. Díaz achieved peace in Mexico generally by achieving it locally in a nation which is essentially parochial. Local chieftains and bandits were tied to the central government by giving them official positions which converted them into instruments of the government. The alternative was liquidation. The superlative example of the conversion of bandit into policeman was the creation of rurales, the renowned mounted constabulary of rural police. Legally sanctioned oppression supplanted irregular brigandage. Mexico became safe for the right people. As the central government grew in strength and prestige, greater control could be exercised over the petty tyrants who had contributed to the attainment of its position.

Irresponsibile and ambitious military personnel had been one of the major elements in the turbulence of Mexican political life. The dictator drew the fangs of the militarists by neutralizing their influence and by giving them a vested interest in his regime.[2] Generals became wealthy men supporting a government generous with economic concessions and land grants, or one willing to countenance the padding of expense accounts by a commander while he was selling supplies to the Indians against whom he was campaigning. Commanders who were suspected of unextinguished ambition or those who had the audacity to challenge Díaz were dealt with severely.

The conflicts of Mexican history sometimes arose for reasons other than mere ambition and avidity for the spoils of office.

[2] The creation of the Depósito de Jefes y Oficiales (Trust of Chiefs and Officers) in the Secretariat of War was an inspiration of pure genius. All persons able to prove military service to the liberal cause were incorporated at half salary tying them to the new regime with gratifying results in terms of public security.

When ideas were the background of strife, two major political groups with divergent ideals could be discerned. One group, the conservative, regretted the consequences of Mexican independence and longed for a return to the institutional patterns of the colonial epoch associated with stability and prosperity. The second, or liberal, group desired to take up the cudgel against the colonial institutions—church, large estates, and army—which had largely survived the passing of Spanish control. The former dreamed of a centralized monarchy, the latter of a federalized republic. Mexico, prior to 1876, was their battleground. Peace between them seemed inconceivable. However, the great compromise of the Díaz regime won him the support of both contending groups. The conservatives bowed to Díaz because he offered peace and stability and the perpetuation of the remaining colonial institutions. The liberals succumbed to the assured benefits of the newly initiated capitalism—progress and the nineteenth-century version of liberalism. This arrangement offered nothing for the mass of the people, but they had played little part in the politics and struggles of Mexican history, and no great change was anticipated.

The Catholic Church contributed another foundation stone to the imposing edifice of national stability which Díaz constructed. Although the dictator had followed the liberal banner, he adopted a policy of conciliation toward the Church. Some writers attribute the development of this policy to the influence of his deeply religious second wife, but it was primarily a matter of politics. The anti-Church legislation of the Reform period remained part of the law of the land, but there was no practical enforcement. There was a noticeable cordiality between officials of the government and dignataries of the Church. With good reason Father Cuevas writing of the period from 1875 to 1896 asserted that "those nineteen years almost without the loss of a single day, with slow but sure activity, were certainly years of reconstruction." [3] It was perhaps inevitable that this Church revival should be accompa-

[3] Cuevas, *Historia de la iglesia,* V, 409.

nied by advances in the economic power of the Church. During the Díaz period the Church managed to recover some of its wealth, influence, and prestige. Although there is some evidence after the turn of the century that the Church was becoming restive in its relationship with the government, for good or ill it had become associated with and committed to the Díaz system.

The very elements which had been the sources of trouble or the objects of contention before Díaz had come to power had been transformed into supports for the regime and contributors to the peace of the nation—the local caciques (chieftains), the army, the liberal and conservative groups, and the Church. To these elements of support must be added the capitalists, primarily foreign, who, encouraged and generously assisted, developed into a mercantile and financial oligarchy committed to the continuance of the dictatorship as the best guarantee of their position of privilege, wealth, and power. Opportunity also attracted the intellectuals. The bureaucracy was expanded nine hundred percent under Díaz, absorbing many educated persons. Others, especially lawyers, found employment with foreign concessionaires. Schools, excepting Church institutions, were sustained by the government and subject to its control. The administration extensively subsidized the press which served to defend its policy, damn its enemies, and swell the chorus of praise for the dictator. Opposition papers were subjected to systematic persecution.[4] There was hardly an intellectual of that generation who was not tied to the regime. Therefore, it is understandable why

[4] *El Imparcial* was the outstanding example of a subsidized paper. Its director, Rafael Reyes Spindola, received about 50,000 pesos annually. Because of its relative cheapness and its abundance of news, this paper was an important element in the support of the regime. The most frequent device used to suppress journalistic opposition, aside from harassment and violence, was imprisonment on the decision of a single magistrate for the crime of "defamation." Long indeed would be the list of independent journalists who suffered imprisonment for this crime. Cabrera, *Obras políticas,* pp. 10 and 36*n.*; *El Debate,* Sept. 11, 1909; *El Imparcial,* Sept. 9 and 10, 1909; A. P. González and Figueroa Domenech, *La Revolución,* p. 47.

the Mexican Revolution suffered a deficiency of intellectual preparation and spokesmen.

The price paid by the Mexican people for the accomplishments of the Porfirian system was high and constitutes a serious indictment of the regime. Opposition was ruthlessly suppressed. Behind the walls of Belem in the capital and in the military prison of San Juan de Ulúa the dictator endeavored to break the spirit of those who dared to oppose him. For more stubborn cases there was the penal colony of Quintana Roo, the most deadly territory in the nation. Persons assigned to jobs as well as those sentenced there rarely returned. Not all the opponents of the regime lived to experience the confines of the prisons. Many persons were victims of the *ley fuga* (law of flight). Summary executions were carried out, and the laconic notation, "Shot while trying to escape," served as acceptable explanation.

Forced conscription into the army, forced migrations, and forced labor were additional methods of persuasion and pacification. When troops were needed, each state had to provide a contingent. Consignment to arms, the *leva* (levy), was not universal or by lot, but by administrative designation. As exercised by local officials the *leva* was developed into an instrument of persecution and vengeance. The Yaqui Indians of Sonora were transported at gun point from their homes to work as forced labor on the henequen (sisal hemp) plantations of Yucatán and in the tobacco fields of the Valle Nacional in Oaxaca as punishment and in the name of pacification. Mexico had peace, but the price included tyranny and suppression.

The peace, opportunity, and prosperity brought by the regime of Porfirio Díaz were reserved for the selected few. The political, social, and economic interests of the bulk of the Mexicans were treated with contemptuous disdain when considered at all. Not only was all political activity suppressed, but Díaz failed to take advantage of his long tenure in office to prepare the people for democratic participation in their government. A political writer of the period observed that the Mexican people had "learned the habit of obedience, but still had to acquire that other fundamental lesson of civilization, consciousness of their own political rights." [5] The people of Mexico also suffered from a lack of equity in the administration of justice. Justice, like security and opportunity, was the prerogative of the few. The state of public education was disgraceful. Schools were built, but the number was inadequate and the distribution uneven. Outside the capital and the key provincial cities facilities were practically nonexistent. Even accepting official statistics the illiteracy rate was shocking and showed only a slight decrease by the end of the period. In 1895 eighty-six percent of the population was unable to read and write, and at the close of the Díaz regime four out of every five persons were still illiterate.[6] Health conditions were equally discouraging. There was a high incidence of enteritis, pneumonia, malaria, and venereal disease.[7]

The heaviest burden of the Díaz era was imposed on the local and rural level involving the overwhelming majority of the people. There the price of the system was highest, creating conditions which were certain to cause trouble. The generalized despotism of local authorities (caciquism) has already been noted. The local chieftain was converted into an instrument of the central government, a local tyrant without initiative and without local support. He had become an enemy of his own people and his own area.[8] The rural area remained isolated, geographically and culturally, from national life. The great cities improved while the rural sections suffered from a lack of transportation and communication facilities and the small towns and villages were neglected. Worst of all, the agrarian policy of the Díaz government reversed the efforts of the mid-nineteenth-century Reform movement to destroy

[5] Calero, *El problema actual,* p. 20.

[6] Sierra (ed.), *México, su evolución social,* II, 570-71, section by Chávez; Pani, *Una encuesta,* p. 154.

[7] Lara Pardo wrote in 1908 that "venereal disease is so common that to reach adult life without contracting it may be considered exceptional." *La prostitución,* p. 179.

[8] Cabrera, *Obras políticas,* pp. 177, 183; Tannenbaum, *Peace by Revolution,* pp. 101, 133, 145.

the feudal pattern of Mexican landholding, with serious consequences for the socio-economic equilibrium of the society.

A persistent theme in Mexican history has been the struggle between the privately owned estate, the semifeudal hacienda, and the communal landholding village. The reformers of the fifties, motivated by ideals of liberalism and individualism, lashed out against the feudal land system. The *Ley de desamortización* (Law of Expropriation) of 1856, later made part of the Constitution of 1857, was more than an attack on the economic holdings of the Church. It was a well-intentioned effort to advance the Indian economically by making him an owner of private property, to develop the ranchero (small-farmer) class as a counterpoise to the large estate owners, and, by achieving both these goals, to make possible real democracy in Mexico. The landholding villages came under the prohibition against corporate holdings, and it was soon apparent that the effects of the law were opposed by the Indians and, where applied, disastrous for the villages. As a result, the application of the law to villages was moderated until Porfirio Díaz came to power.[9]

Starting with a theory that was a concoction of liberalism emphasizing modernization and industrialization and a brand of Spencerian dogma proclaiming survival of the fittest, the ideological architects of the Díaz period manifested disdain for the Indian mass and projected colonization through immigration. The communal village should be destroyed and the Indian reduced as an element in the population and replaced by a more desirable immigrant element.[10] The policies directed to these ends facilitated the victory of the hacienda and generalized a form of agrarian feudalism throughout the country.

Díaz enforced the Reform Laws against the villages. Circulars in 1889 and 1890 decreed that all communal lands must be divided, and it was estimated that over two and a quarter

[9] Phipps, *Agrarian Question in Mexico*, p. 77; Whetten, *Rural Mexico*, p. 86.

[10] Molina Enríquez, "Boletín de . . . Agricultura, parte II," *Revista de economía*, p. 37; Mendieta y Núñez, *El problema agraria*, p. 95.

million acres were allotted to individuals, the major portion of which found its way, ultimately, into the hands of large landowners, speculators, and land companies. A series of colonization laws had similar objectives with the additional justification of an attempt to clarify land titles and to recover illegally alienated public lands. Surveying companies were authorized to search for, locate, and survey *terrenos baldíos* (national lands not legally alienated and considered, therefore, as "empty lands"). The company or individuals, usually government favorites, were entitled to one third of the lands outright as well as to the privilege of purchasing as much of the remainder desired at a ridiculously low price. Land could not be sold in units exceeding twenty-five hundred hectares (about 6,200 acres), and there was a colonization requirement, but the companies could hold the land for speculative purposes and generally ignored their colonization commitment. The modifying law of 1894 permitted sale of tracts without size limitation and extended the area open to survey. The floodgates were thrown open for land absorption on a tremendous scale. The small landholder whose title was not adequate and the landholding village which could not legally hold land suffered. Wholesale denunciations of villages holding lands followed, with the Indians dispossessed or their villages incorporated into large estates.[11] When the inhabitants of the fertile Valley of Papantla in the state of Veracruz resisted the survey of their lands during the winter of 1890, the government responded with a full-scale invasion of the area and proceeded to a systematic extermination of the men, women, and children of the valley.

Indian villages were also deprived of their lands through the manipulation of water rights. By an act of 1888 the president received jurisdiction over water rights with authority to grant monopoly concessions. Control of water meant control of the land. Lastly, Indian tribes—for example, the Yaquis and

[11] In Yucatán, Don Olegario Molina, the Secretary of Agriculture, denounced in his own interest the lands, roads, and town sites of the Mayas. *El País,* May 3, 1909.

Mayos of Sonora and the Mayas of Yucatán—were deprived of their lands as punishment for rebellion. In the name of peace and progress just grievances were ignored, and cruel suppression, dispersal, and peonage awaited the Indians who protested or resisted. The basic element in the Mexican population was to be exploited and possibly eliminated in the name of the exalted goal, material progress.

This wholesale attack on the Indian village upset the equilibrium of native society and, consequently, depressed the well-being of the inhabitants. The principal fate awaiting the majority was a status of peonage on the large estates. By 1910 over ninety percent of the villages in the most heavily populated section of the country, the central plateau, had lost their lands. Through absorption of village lands and tremendous concessions of public domain, the hacienda system was confirmed and extended. The large estate rested on a foundation of debt peonage aggravated by pitifully low wages (twelve to eighteen cents daily), usually paid in kind, token, or credit, and by the exploitive operation of the *tienda de raya* (plantation store). While some of the new extractive plantations showed a degree of rough efficiency, the hacienda lands generally were not fully or effectively employed. Fertility declined, speculation increased, and land prices rose under this modern feudalism.

Although the number of individual landowners increased nearly threefold between 1854 and 1910, the percentage of land ownership was very small. The hacendado, favored by the government and avoiding and shifting the tax burden, enjoyed a distinct advantage over the small landholders. Probably no more than three percent of the total rural population owned any land at the end of the Díaz period. The hacienda, controlling about half the land and rural population and including over four fifths of the rural communities, dominated politically, economically, and socially the rural life of a predominantly rural nation. The fact that there were eight hundred and thirty-four hacendados and perhaps nine million landless peasants living in miserable peonage makes understandable González Roa's assertion that the revolution was agrarian above all. To oppressive conditions was added the humiliation that much of the land had passed into foreign hands.

Foreign capitalism was superimposed on this feudal agrarian base. The forced, accelerated industrialization accentuated the colonial pattern of the Mexican economy, for the emphasis was on the extractive industries, especially mining. Foreigners built railroads under liberal conditions, ignoring the basic economic needs of the country and favoring external over domestic trade. The government, reversing Mexican legal patterns dating from colonial times, gave concessionaires unquestioned title to subsoil mineral deposits. Díaz boasted regularly of the new titles conceded to mining properties, for this was progress. Mexico received only long hours and low wages for her sons. Negligible revenues returned to the government. The foreigners were siphoning off the wealth, and, in the process, the nation's resources lost their nationality. The foreigners were not only exploiting Mexico economically but enjoying influence greatly out of proportion to their numbers. Favorable consideration in the courts was assured. There was daily proof of the charge that Mexico under Díaz had become "the mother of foreigners and the stepmother of Mexicans."

The industrialization of Mexico and the vigorous exploitation of her wealth brought a new labor element on the scene. The growth of an independent industrial labor force free from the old controls and enjoying mobility of movement was of primary importance for the future revolutionary development. Work on the railroads offered an alternative to the restrictive life of the plantation. Railroads facilitated emigration to the United States and contact with new ideas. Workers were made available to those selected to exploit the resources of Mexico, and the power of the government was employed to prevent industrial labor from making itself felt. However, during the last decade of the dictatorship strikes occurred at the Green Consolidated Mining Company in Cananea, Sonora, and at the textile mills in Río Blanco, Veracruz.

While these outbreaks did not represent a serious threat to the regime, they were symptomatic of the increasing discontent. The role assumed by the government in the strife between capital and labor revealed once more, as in the case of the Indian wars, that bloody suppression was the Díaz remedy for the social ills of the people.[12]

The most tragic aspect of the material progress and prosperity of the Porfirian era was the fact that the mass of the people did not participate. On the contrary, the industrial advance was made possible by the construction of tariff walls which raised prices to the Mexican consumer. The inefficient hacendado was protected from outside competition by duties on foodstuffs—at a time when food had to be imported! Food prices in Mexico, in contrast with those in the rest of the world, rose during this period. While industrial wages advanced somewhat, dollar wages of the rural workers remained approximately the same. Declining real wages inevitably meant a declining standard of living.

Francisco Madero, sensitive and altruistic, was disturbed by the spectacle his country presented under "The Peace of Porfirio." His belief in spiritism and democracy contributed to his decision to enter politics. The former appealed to the emotionalism and sentimentalism of this man who seemed to be searching restlessly for his role in life.[13] It provided the moral and philosophical framework for his humanitarian and social impulses. A devotee of democracy, Madero became convinced that prolonged dictatorship was the explanation for the ignominy which engulfed his nation.

[12] Tannenbaum, *Peace by Revolution*, p. 136; Tannenbaum, *Agrarian Revolution*, pp. 137-38, 155.

[13] Madero's enthusiasm for spiritism, like his practice of temperance, vegetarianism, and homeopathy, made him the perfect target for ridicule. Although there is considerable disagreement as to whether or not Madero believed in and practiced spiritism during his presidency, it is possible that spiritism was a contributory factor to his blind confidence and suicidal tolerance once he achieved political power.

III. A Taste of Politics

IT IS DOUBTFUL whether Madero presumed initially to think that he could save his fellow citizens. Rather, his earliest efforts were the result of his belief that he, like other citizens, had a sacred obligation to cooperate in the practice of democracy. He credited an incident in Monterrey in 1903 with shocking him out of his "criminal indifference." On April 2 of that year in the capital of Nuevo León agents of Governor Bernardo Reyes dissolved with gunfire a peaceful demonstration by supporters of an independent challenger for the gubernatorial post. Friends and relatives of Madero witnessed the tragic event, and Francisco was deeply moved by their first-hand accounts.

The sensation which the Monterrey affair produced in the nation convinced Madero that public spirit and a sense of decency were not dead. Although it was evident that the government was determined to suppress any opposition movement, Madero and some friends agreed to organize at the first opportunity a truly democratic movement "to begin the struggle for the reconquest of our liberty." [1]

The gubernatorial election in Coahuila in 1905 presented the desired opportunity. For four years Madero and some

[1] Madero, *La sucesión presidencial,* pp. 11-12.

On Dec. 30, 1904, just prior to beginning his political career, Madero drew up his will in which he designated his wife as sole beneficiary. When he took this precautionary step, he was thirty-one, healthy, and with a promising enconomic future. The will antedated his tragic death by eight years and two months. *La Prensa,* Aug. 30, 1936.

relatives and friends had talked half-heartedly of doing something about the shameful conditions in the state. Reports that the candidacy for governor of Frumencio Fuentes, friend of Vice-President Corral, was about to be announced in Torreón prompted Madero's group to enter the campaign in an effort to block this candidate. They organized a political group in San Pedro, the Benito Juárez Democratic Club, and selected Madero as president of the directive board. They planned to work for the organization of similar clubs throughout the state and then to convoke a convention to select a gubernatorial candidate for the independents.

Shortly before the club in San Pedro was organized, Madero wrote several letters which reveal his thinking at that time. He emphasized his limited, peaceful objectives and was most anxious to reassure those who might misinterpret or be concerned about his purposes. Madero invited Jaime Gurza to be a member of the directive board of the projected group. He felt that the presence of this reputable citizen, known in the capital, would serve as a guarantee that their group had no intention of throwing down the revolutionary gauntlet to Porfirio Díaz. On the contrary, Madero stated, their purpose, without being guilty of "exaggerated servilism," was to obtain from the Mexican President consideration of state public opinion in selecting the governor. If that was not possible, he indicated to his conservative cousin, Rafael Hernández, the group would proceed to assume the opposition role "by all legal means." However, in a letter to Alberto Gurza, Madero wrote of a long-range objective consistent with his democratic orientation, namely, that the people should begin to exercise their rights with a view to effecting the gradual disappearance of tyranny. Lastly, he wrote to his brother Gustavo to dissuade him from the belief which early arose among members of the family that the eldest son's political activities were undesirable and dangerous.[2]

Toward the end of 1904 municipal elections were held in San Pedro. Although related to the general statewide cam-

[2] Taracena, *Madero: Vida*, p. 39.

paign, the local contest was an independent episode for Madero's group because it involved only the San Pedro club. The club members decided to present candidates for the municipal posts. They nominated a respected farmer, Francisco Rivas, for mayor to run on a platform including promises to further education, to improve the town's water supply, to take steps against alcoholism, and to respect the rights, particularly that of suffrage, of all citizens.

Election day found Madero very active, visiting each voting booth and advising people of their rights and how to exercise them. When the board of scrutiny established itself in the plaza, the police formed a semicircle around it. A clash between the authorities and the people seemed inevitable, and, to avoid it, Madero arranged for the board to move to his house to complete its task. Madero charged that the "government used every type of chicanery to nullify our efforts" and to turn deserved victory for the independents' mayoralty candidate into defeat.[3]

Undismayed, the members of the Benito Juárez Democratic Club intensified their preparations for the gubernatorial election. Madero himself corresponded with notable persons in the state, traveled about organizing clubs, and wrote articles.[4] At the time the club chose its directive board it was agreed to establish an aggressive political weekly, *El Demócrata.* On this paper Madero served his apprenticeship as a political writer. The first of his series of articles was entitled "Vox populi, vox dei"; it testified eloquently to his democratic faith.[5] Through the paper the independents spoke to the people of their rights and invited them to participate in the approaching election. A few weeks later the San Pedro group also began publishing a satirical paper called *El Mosco* (The Gnat).

An admirer of American political institutions, Madero favored the selection of a candidate and the preparation of a platform in a convention composed of delegates with represen-

[3] Madero to Manuel Pérez, Feb. 10, 1905, AdeM.

[4] In Viesca the authorities blocked these efforts by force.

[5] Lamicq, *El dolor mexicano,* p. 102.

tation proportional to the population in each district. The San Pedro club had scheduled such a convention for February 5, 1905. However, the Central Club of Torreón also was engaged in opposing the reelection of Governor Miguel Cárdenas. This group, operating independently of the Madero organization, represented the Corralista (supporting Vice-President Corral) element in the state and planned to advance Frumencio Fuentes as candidate. Realizing that any division would be fatal for the opposition, Madero's group agreed to postpone the convention until May in order that both groups might participate. However, after this delay had been conceded, the two clubs disagreed on the location of the assembly. The Corralistas, favoring Mexico City, argued that in Coahuila the state authorities they opposed would be able to dissolve the meeting. Madero, whose group preferred some point in Coahuila, disputed the selection of the nation's capital on the grounds that there the central government would be able to influence the choice of candidate and that anyway they ought not to be afraid to exercise their rights.[6] But, because of connections with the previous state administration of Garza Galán, the Torreón club enjoyed superior organization, and its convention site was selected.

At the convention, attended by over one hundred delegates, Madero and his followers supported the candidacy of Dr. Dionisio García Fuentes of Saltillo. Despite the good reputation of the candidate and the efforts of his supporters, the convention selected Frumencio Fuentes. Although Madero's group felt that the Corralistas had won by questionable devices,[7] they decided to accept the nomination of Fuentes rather than cause a division which could destroy the nascent democratic movement. The meeting approved a platform including extension of public instruction, guarantee of civil rights, and the principle of "No Reelection" for state and local

[6] Agrupación Pro-Madero, *Reseña de las ceremonias conmemorativas*, p. 142.

[7] The presiding officer of the convention, Praxedis de la Peña, represented a nonexistent club in Saltillo. Madero, "Mis memorias," p. 21.

officials. Frumencio Fuentes accepted the program, but he opposed publishing the "No Reelection" plank to avoid a slap at Porfirio Díaz from whom he hoped to receive support.

Although he had bowed to the will of the majority at the convention, Madero felt that the election of Frumencio Fuentes, the friend of Corral, could mean a worse despotism for the state than that suffered under Cárdenas. Therefore, he maneuvered in two directions. First, he tried to cause the central government to consider the independent party as hostile to it. Then, if their candidate triumphed, he would have to respect the popular will which had brought him to power. Secondly, Madero sought to obtain an independent legislative slate which, in its majority, would be in accord with him and his group. In this manner, should the independents win, there would be a legislative majority, devoted to the interests of the people, which would not hesitate to oppose the governor if necessary.[8]

In the meantime candidate Fuentes had obtained an interview with President Díaz. When the latter indicated his determination to support the incumbent Cárdenas, Frumencio Fuentes and his friends wired the independents in Coahuila to end the campaign. Madero hurried to Mexico City to try to salvage something from the situation. The telegram had demoralized the independents who now considered the fight lost. Madero tried to convince Fuentes that it was necessary to save the honor of the party by continuing the effort "even though we are headed for certain defeat," [9] but the candidate insisted that the campaign be stopped.

As a compromise it was agreed that a meeting be called in Torreón of the presidents of all of the independent clubs to

[8] Confident of the nominee from Viesca and certain that no independent would challenge him in Parras, Madero organized the club in Saltillo and assured, thereby, that the persons nominated from there were independents from the Maderista point of view. The legislature of Coahuila was composed of eleven deputies, including four from the district of Saltillo, three from the district of the Center, two from the district of the Frontier, and one each from the districts of Parras and Viesca.

[9] Madero, "Mis memorias," p. 24.

discuss the policy to be followed. Madero hoped, by this means, to force the candidate either to resign or to provide aggressive leadership. Neither objective was achieved. The delegates favored continuation of the campaign. Although Fuentes agreed, he instructed the independents to limit their action to protesting against illegally installed voting booths. Madero sadly observed that they "went to the polls only to save the honor of the party" without any hope of victory.[10]

On election day the independents found all of the polling places controlled by the government's representatives who were protected by the police. Nevertheless, the opposition still won in some communities, but these results were rejected by the boards of scrutiny. The electoral farce completed, the state authorities unleashed a wave of persecution against the opposition. An order of arrest against Madero was issued, but the central government directed that his person be respected. The arrest of the editors of *El Demócrata* and *El Mosco* was also ordered. Since these individuals could not be located in their homes, the authorities issued a search warrant for Madero's house, where, it was assumed, correctly, the fugitives were hiding. The searchers found their way blocked by Sara de Madero, who succeeded in delaying their entry until after six o'clock. Since the law prohibited execution of a warrant after that hour, she prevented the search for that day. Although the house was kept under surveillance, the wanted publicists managed to cross the wall to the next house and later to escape in one of three carts loaded with straw and headed for a hacienda belonging to Madero. When they found asylum in the United States, the incident was ended.

Madero was not discouraged by this initial defeat. He rejected the use of force, the traditional method of achieving power, "not because of fear, but because of principle." Said he, "We have faith in democracy." While recognizing that the triumphs obtained by democracy are slower, he felt that they

[10] Agrupación Pro-Madero, *Reseña de las ceremonias conmemorativas*, p. 145.

are "more secure and fruitful." [11] Accordingly, he proposed that the clubs organized for the campaign be made permanent and that the nation be invited to form a National Democratic party. He had learned the valuable lesson that efforts against the dictatorship in individual states inevitably would fail. However, friends convinced him that a prolonged political struggle would be difficult in Mexico, for the government would have time to annihilate the opposition before an election test ever occurred. Madero decided to await an opportunity more favorable to national political organization.

The next few years were busy ones for Francisco Madero. Independent journalists found him ready to provide funds and advice for those who were keeping alive the flame of opposition. Paulino Martínez, imprisoned in Mexico City, received two hundred and fifty pesos from Madero, who expressed the hope that he would be able to regain his freedom and continue the struggle. Madero also offered shrewd advice on the proper role of the opposition press. He recommended that the independent press confine itself to theoretical discussions and criticism of the government's conduct in general terms without specifying any subalterns who "are capable of committing the greatest infamies." He suggested that a full-scale effort should be postponed until the next presidential election. If at that time Díaz were to try to reelect himself, Madero was confident that there would be a strong anti-reelectionist movement throughout the country. "Then it will be opportune for us to try vigorously to recover our rights." The independent journalists were to defend their principles, arouse public spirit, and prepare the masses for that electoral campaign.[12]

After Paulino Martínez was released, Madero told him not to mention the money again. He wrote the journalist that, on the contrary, the latter had suffered too much for the cause. "It is just that . . . we should aid you in the expenses which you have incurred by your repeated and unjust imprison-

[11] Madero, *La sucesión presidencial,* p. 15.

[12] P. Martínez to Madero, July 31, 1905; Madero to Martínez, May 19, 1906, Nov. 8, 1907, and Sept. 17, 1908, AdeM.

ments." Madero realized that in the days ahead so many mutual services of diverse nature and difficult evaluation would be rendered that "it will never be possible to know on which side the balance lies." [13] Devotion to the cause and conviction of its greatness explain Madero's disdain for a mere material measurement of contribution. He was convinced that the efforts of the journalists would not be lost, that actually they were planting seeds. "We will gather that harvest inside of five years." [14]

Among the oppositionists who received aid from Madero were Ricardo and Enrique Flores Magón. These mestizo brothers had gradually become the leaders of the Mexican Liberal party which conducted a hit-and-run campaign against the Díaz regime. Persistent advocates of "lyrical" radicalism, they progressed from a simple spirit of rebellious opposition to a struggle for a visionary philosophical anarchism.

In 1892, Ricardo began his lifetime pattern of opposition with newspaper articles, participation in demonstrations against the reelection of Díaz, and the earliest of frequent imprisonments. In August of 1900 the first issue of his paper, *Regeneración,* appeared in Mexico. For about eighteen months the Flores Magón brothers repeated the cycle of opposition journalism interspersed with periodic interruptions in the prisons of the dictatorship. Released from Belem late in 1903,[15] Ricardo decided to seek refuge in the United States with the intention of organizing an attempt to overthrow the dictatorship from Texan soil.

For a half-dozen years after 1904 the Mexican exiles in the United States were subjected to relentless persecution by agents and officials of the Mexican government which endeavored, with some success, to enlist the agencies of the United States government in their behalf. This harassing caused the rebels to keep moving from San Antonio to St.

[13] Madero to Martínez, Nov. 16, 1907, AdeM.

[14] Madero to C. V. Márquez, Aug. 24, 1906, AdeM.

[15] By this date he was familiar with the writings of Kropotkin, Bakunin, Malatesta, and Gorki. *El Universal,* Jan. 17, 1933.

Louis, from St. Louis to Canada, and then back to Texas. In St. Louis, during September, 1905, the Junta of the Mexican Liberal party was established with the object of organizing a party and a struggle "using all means" against the dictatorship of Porfirio Díaz.

In July of the following year, under the slogan "Reform, Liberty, and Justice," the Junta published the platform of the party. This program was surprisingly comprehensive, including not merely political reforms but also sections on the economic and social order of the country. The exiles advocated stringent restrictions on the Catholic clergy to attract liberal elements and outlined the features of an incipient agrarian program. However, the authors of the document lacked political realism relative to the Mexican situation and exhibited the visionary thinking which increasingly characterized the movement.

The Mexican Liberal party attempted to circulate this program in an effort to awaken popular support. *Regeneración*, secretly distributed in Mexico, gradually achieved a circulation of twenty-eight thousand. The paper contributed to the growing consciousness among the textile workers of their estate. Party representatives were active in organizing industrial workers and in providing leadership for strikes, as in the case of that at Cananea. The journalistic propaganda and the organizing efforts of this group were part of the preparation for armed revolution.[16]

Francisco Madero loaned the liberals considerable sums of money to enable them to move to St. Louis from San Antonio and to continue the publication of *Regeneración* which he believed would contribute to the "regeneration of the Fatherland arousing Mexicans in noble indignation against their tyrants." [17] Ricardo credited Madero's assistance with saving

[16] Three times—in 1906, 1908, and 1910—the Liberals undertook armed movements against the government of Díaz. That Luis Cabrera termed the uprisings of Jiménez, Las Vacas, and Acayucán the "prodromes of the Revolution" and that Ricardo Flores Magón is considered a "precursor" of the social upheaval have some justification. *México Nuevo,* Nov. 22, 1932.

[17] Madero to R. Flores Magón, Jan. 17, 1905, AdeM.

the liberal cause.[18] However, by midsummer of 1906, Madero began to question and, then, to disapprove of the proceedings of the Liberal Junta. In August he wrote a supporter of Ricardo Flores Magón in Texas that he was uncertain of the goal pursued by that group. Madero felt that it was inopportune for them to begin a democratic campaign there which, in any event, ought to be conducted within Mexico. If revolution was their goal, he opposed it as unpatriotic. He also indicated his disapproval of the indiscriminate slander technique employed by the St. Louis group whereby they insulted recognized liberals. Madero concluded that such persons were not the appropriate ones to "direct the Liberal party along the path which it ought to follow." [19]

The Flores Magón group was headed for revolution. When Prisciliano G. Silva visited Madero in San Pedro in September, 1906, to invite him to support the planned uprising, Madero refused, stating that he considered it a crime to stain the country with blood in the interest of personal ambitions. [20] The Liberals attacked Jiménez, Coahuila, and Madero hastened to assure his grandfather that he was not associated with such disturbances and did not approve of them. Similarly, when attacks were made on Las Vacas and Viesca in 1908, he remained inflexible in opposing the revolutionary efforts of the Liberals. His analysis of these incidents constituted a studied effort to minimize and discredit the movement. Madero noted the small number involved, the cool reception accorded the revolutionists, and the failure of the effort. He concluded that these disturbances proved that the country did not want revolution. On the other hand, he emphasized the favorably receptive attitude of the public for a democratic campaign.[21]

Madero reacted to the incidents related to the strike at Orizaba in a very different manner. Earlier he had requested

[18] R. Flores Magón to F.Y. (*sic*) Madero, March 5, 1905, AdeV.

[19] Madero to C. V. Márquez, Aug. 17, 1906, AdeM.

[20] *Regeneración,* March 4, 1911.

[21] Taracena, *Madero: Vida,* pp. 53, 72-77; Madero to Dr. Espinosa, July 7, 1908, AdeM.

that Paulino Martínez keep him informed on the labor question "which interests me a great deal."[22] During the days of the trouble in the textile area Madero once again demonstrated his sympathetic interest in the workers. He was shocked by the government's role and by the brutal suppression of the strikers, and he believed that the incident would advance the democratic movement which he was trying to stimulate. While recognizing an inability to aid the workers, he hoped that "at least their beloved blood may water the tree of liberty, which is so withered in our country, in order to infuse it with new life and vigor so that it should serve to protect us with its beneficent shade in a not-too-distant period."[23] Madero sharply indicted the press which, because of fear, had not as yet assigned the responsibility to those to whom it belonged—the industrialists, who devised the lockout, and Porfirio Díaz.[24]

Francisco Madero was actively preparing the groundwork for a democratic movement. In addition to assisting and encouraging the independent journalists, he wrote many letters regarding political organization. For example, he urged Fernando Iglesias Calderón to assume leadership of the movement thereby bringing it the prestige of his name and the respectability of his reputation. Madero declared that a party of principles was needed in that age of personalism to attack the ruling despotism. Confident that victory was inevitable, he called on Iglesias Calderón to follow the example of his illustrious father by aiding the cause without hesitancy.[25]

Although Iglesias Calderón did not accept his invitation, Madero refused to be discouraged. Exalted by his ideal, he continued his search for men who were dissatisfied with the political situation. To Victoriano Agüeros, who persistently

[22] Taracena, *Madero, el héroe*, p. 50.

[23] Madero to F. de P. Sentíes, Jan. 19, 1907, AdeM.

[24] In this connection Madero wrote to Francisco de P. Sentíes that he should recommend to Sánchez Azcona, editor of *El Diario*, that the editor be sparing in his eulogies to Gen. Díaz to avoid embarrassment about his political past when the decision to begin the struggle came. Jan. 30, 1907, AdeM.

[25] Madero to F. Iglesias Calderón, Jan. 30, 1907, AdeM.

opposed the regime in his daily newspaper *El Tiempo,* Madero wrote that those who loved their country and were concerned for its future anxiously awaited the next electoral campaign. He warned of the danger that a desperate people might resort to revolution, a disastrous backward step. The alternative was a revitalization of republican practices through the formation of a national party with two primary objectives: the alternating of governing powers and the election of a congress truly representative of the will of the nation. The prerequisite for achieving these goals would be freedom of elections.[26] These objectives, more succinctly described, were to become the themes emblazoned on Madero's political and revolutionary banners: EFFECTIVE SUFFRAGE AND NO REELECTION.

From Agüeros's reply it is evident that he did not share Madero's optimism. Everywhere the editor found only "servilism, indifference and fear." A measure of the pessimism and resignation which filled many independents after years of Díaz control may be gathered from the journalist's sad conclusion: "I no longer have faith in our men nor in our country. I work without faith, without hope, only to fulfill an obligation." This gentleman, a Catholic, saw no remedy for the situation except by some act of Providence.[27]

Madero, unwaveringly optimistic, relentlessly persisted in his point of view. In 1908 he wrote Agüeros about the campaign in Coahuila and stated that he was convinced that a great deal could be done throughout Mexico along such lines. He reported that he was part of a nucleus of citizens who intended to form a national party of opposition.[28] And at this time the situation was more favorable for political organization on a national scale. The climate had changed because of the publication of an interview with Porfirio Díaz obtained by James Creelman, an American journalist.

[26] Madero to V. Agüeros, July 23, 1908, AdeM.
[27] V. Agüeros to Madero, July 29, 1908, AdeM.
[28] Madero to V. Agüeros, Aug. 5, 1908, AdeM.

IV. The Political Reawakening

FOR THE FIRST TIME IN YEARS there was a revival of serious political discussion in 1908. The stimulus was the interview granted that February by Díaz to James Creelman and published in *Pearson's Magazine.* After a brief description of the Mexican ruler in his seventy-eighth year and fullsome praise of his reign, Creelman reported the startling news that Díaz had affirmed that he was disposed to retire at the end of his current term and would not again accept reelection.

Don Porfirio recalled that he had tried to leave the presidency on several occasions, but that, under pressure, he had remained in power for the good of nation. However, he declared that he was now convinced that at last the Mexican people could elect a government without the danger of revolution. "I firmly believe that the principles of democracy have grown and will flourish in Mexico." Díaz indicated that he would view with pleasure the appearance of a party of opposition. "I will sustain it, I will counsel it, and I will forget myself in order to inaugurate with complete success a democratic government in the Republic." [1]

Past performance and subsequent events cast serious doubt on the sincerity of these declarations. Speculation on the intriguing question of the motivation for permitting the interview was and is inevitable. The fact that the interview was granted to an American for publication in an American periodical seems to support the view that the statements were

[1] *Pearson's Magazine,* XIX, No. 3, 241-77.

intended for foreign consumption, specifically, to mollify opinion in the northern republic.[2] Other commentators argue that, on the contrary, the message was really meant for domestic consumption to distract attention from a discouraging economic situation due to successive bad harvests and aggravated by repercussions of the financial depression occurring in the United States. Persecution of the opposition groups which responded to the invitation of Díaz is the basis for the charge by still others that the interview was motivated by a desire to bring his enemies into the open, the more effectively to deal with them. Lastly, there is the attempt to explain the statements to Creelman in terms of the extreme egotism of Don Porfirio which led him to expect, as had happened before, a demand from the sycophants that he remain in power for the rest of his life.[3]

In any event, trusting in the loyalty of the army and overly confident of the prestige and power of the government, Díaz committed a political imprudence in the Creelman interview. *El Imparcial* reprinted the interview beginning on March 3, 1908. The *Mexican Herald* and *El Tiempo* reproduced the important sections, and for weeks the leading papers both in the capital and in the states were commenting on the meaning of the dictator's declarations. It would be difficult to overestimate the effect of the Creelman report which "stimulated a feeling of great expectation in the whole nation." [4]

The reaction to the statements of Díaz to Creelman proved that the dictator had made a serious political miscalculation. A torrent of political literature and a flurry of political organization rapidly compromised the stability and equilibrium of the dictatorship. Regardless of opinion as to the sincerity of Díaz, the opposition proceeded on a literal, or pretended-literal, interpretation of his words. Within six to eight months

[2] Estrada, *La Revolución y . . . Madero,* pp. 37-40. Some authors charge, on circumstantial evidence, that the interview was the result of pressure from the United States. Rojas, *La culpa de Henry Lane Wilson,* I, 17-18; Molina Enríquez, *La revolución agraria,* IV, 159.

[3] López-Portillo y Rojas, *Porfirio Díaz,* pp. 376-77.

[4] Alessio Robles, *Historia política de la Revolución,* p. 10.

a series of folios emphasizing political questions had appeared to agitate the public mind. Francisco de P. Senties, in *El partido Democrático* (The Democratic Party), indicated the urgent necessity for forming political parties. Emilio Vázquez republished his folio of 1890 in opposition to *La reelección indefinida* (Indefinite Reelection). Raising the imperious question, *¿Hacia dónde vamos?* (Where Are We Going?), Querido Moheno endeavored to provide the information the people would need for political responsibility. Manuel Calero contributed a discussion of *Cuestiones electorales* (Electoral Questions), while Vázquez, Blas Urrea (the penname of Luis Cabrera),[5] and others penned equally challenging articles. The opposition newspapers echoed the political rumblings with articles discussing the folios.

More extensive publications were soon forthcoming. Andrés Molina Enríquez published his study of *Los grandes problemas nacionales* (The Great National Problems). Although it is doubtful that the work enjoyed a wide audience or was particularly influential at that time, this volume deservedly has been called "the most important single study of Mexican social problems."[6] The author presented an analysis of the complex land problem with a view to its solution. With meticulous care the matters which were agitating the Mexican people were sympathetically, yet thoughtfully, described. The ultimate direction which the revolution assumed, the important role of Molina Enríquez in formulating the agrarian legislation in later years, and the very paucity of intellectual leaders in that upheaval increased the significance of his contribution to prerevolutionary thought. A work of more modest title, *Algunos problemas nacionales* (Some National Problems), and of lesser importance was the contribution of the littérateur, Estebán Maqueo Castellanos. This writer was concerned about the danger inherent in a politically unstable Mexico confronted by the Yankee peril.

[5] Cabrera's earliest article appeared in *El Partido Democrático* on July 24, 1909.

[6] Tannenbaum, *Peace by Revolution*, p. 118.

Presuming on the utterances of the dictator, Madero and others urged the formation of political parties. From 1908 until the spring of 1910, Francisco Madero was concerned with the danger of a continuation of absolute power in Mexico. Notwithstanding the Creelman interview, he foresaw that Díaz would want to continue as president. However, he concluded that the statements by Díaz had provided the opposition with a powerful means of pressure. Madero hoped that the ruler, confronted by public opinion made articulate through an opposition political party, would hesitate to run or at least would concede the nomination of a more desirable vice-president. He expected, at the very least, to win a concession that would promise better political conditions for Mexico at the end of the Díaz regime.[7] The followers of General Bernardo Reyes intensified their political activities and organized nationally. A group in Mexico City established the Democratic party. Francisco Madero and his friends prompted the establishment of the Anti-Reelectionist party. The abortive Pure Liberal party and the Liberal party completed the growing list of "opposition parties."[8]

Obviously, Porfirio Díaz had stirred up the proverbial hornet's nest. When Filomeno Mata, the irrepressible editor of *El Diario del Hogar,* directed an open letter to Díaz asking him to confirm or deny the contents of the Creelman interview, the Mexican President refused to answer categorically, noting only that his statements were expressions of "personal desire."[9] The retreat was too late. Political discussion and organization had advanced too far, and in the future they would be pushed

[7] Madero to V. Agüeros, Aug. 5, 1908, AdeM.

[8] The Pure Liberal party was planned by persons who believed that the primary issue of the struggle was to be the question of the position of the Catholic Church. They mistakenly looked to Fernando Iglesias Calderón for leadership.

The Liberal party was supported by the Junta in Los Angeles, organized by Flores Magón. Ricardo Flores Magón, rapidly approaching anarcho-syndicalist beliefs, labeled the Democratic and Anti-Reelectionist parties "absolutely bourgeois." Flores Magón, *Tribuna roja,* p. 25.

[9] *El Diario del Hogar,* Oct. 27, 1908.

by a people grown restive through the stimulus of deep economic and social grievances.

Madero was encouraged by the excellent effect which had resulted from the folios and books published after the Creelman interview. In November of 1908 he predicted that there would be even further developments "after other books . . . are released."[10] Among the "other books" the book which Madero specifically had in mind was his own *La sucesión presidencial en 1910* (The Presidential Succession in 1910).

In his correspondence with Agüeros and Senties late in 1908 Madero from time to time would mention "confidentially" and in enthusiastic, but general, terms the volume he was preparing. He obviously intended to pique their curiosity and stimulate their interest. To their eager inquiries Madero replied that in his book he would deal boldly with the questions of the day and hoped the work would help to orient public opinion. He concluded each letter with a renewed request for complete reserve on the matter until the book was published.[11]

Shortly after the Creelman interview, probably in April, 1908, Francisco Madero began to write the volume which was to represent an important part of his contribution to the political excitement of the succeeding two years. His preparatory reading was heavily concentrated in the fields of romantic literature and history.[12] During the fall of 1908 the emphasis on historical material was even more evident. He added works by Tacitus, Sallust, Tertullian, Suetonius, and Lord Macauley to his collection.[13]

[10] Madero to F. de P. Senties, Nov. 4, 1908, AdeM.

[11] Madero de Agüeros and to Senties, cited in Taracena, *Madero: Vida*, pp. 111-13, 115-16; Madero to Senties, Dec. 3 and 19, 1908, AdeM.

[12] In August, 1907, Madero ordered the writings of Goethe, Lope de Vega, Lord Byron, Shakespeare, Victor Hugo, Napoleon Bonaparte, and Benito Pérez Galdós from B. de la Prida in Mexico City. Aug. 23, 1907, AdeM.

[13] Madero to B. de la Prida, Sept. 16, 1908, AdeM. At the same time Madero ordered the writings of Pedro de Alarcón and Alexander Dumas. His book orders late in 1908 reveal an increasing interest in economics and social theory, but these volumes arrived too late to have influenced the

In September, Madero suffered from eye trouble, undoubtedly resulting from the strain of concentrated reading. For a time he had to remain in a room with little light.[14] Neither this enforced inactivity nor a question of timing explain completely the delay in the publication of his volume. Although the prologue was dated October, 1908, *The Presidential Succession in 1910* was not released until January, 1909. Among the factors causing this delay was the author's desire, almost an obsession, to obtain the blessing and approval of his parents.

The attitude of the family toward the political activity of the eldest son went through several phases. While Gustavo and the sisters were consistently enthusiastic in their support, the parents and grandfather were convinced only gradually and only as political events unfolded. Grandfather Evaristo, who was an inspiration to his idealistic grandson, was the leader of the opposition. Practical and experienced, Evaristo recognized even more fully than Francisco where his path was leading him and the obstacles and dangers involved. Initially, his parents' attitude was marked by the same tolerance with which they had humored his other "fads." However, as the full scope of Francisco's activities was revealed, Francisco Madero the elder, fearful for his own interests, and his wife became alarmed. Beginning in November, 1908, the father resisted for several months Francisco's urgent and repeated requests for permission to launch his political career by releasing his book. The older man even tried to make his son give up the whole project. The letters from Francisco are those of a respectful son to whom the blessing of his parents is indispensable. He begged and cajoled; he resorted to every argument and overlooked no emotion as he deftly trod the narrow line between independence and obedience.

---

contents of his own book. Among the books ordered by Madero in Dec., 1908, were volumes by the following: Henry George, M. Gorki, Kropotkin, Proudhon, Herbert Spencer, and Manuel Ugarte. Works by lesser authors on collectivism, socialism, monopoly, dictatorship, and absolutism were also purchased. Madero to B. de la Prida, Dec. 11, 1908, AdeM.

[14] His trouble was diagnosed as an ophthalmia of the right eye. Madero to Sra. Mercedes G. de Madero, Sept. 8, 1908, AdeM.

In December, Francisco wrote his father a long letter in which he detailed his appeal. First, he played on anticipated parental concern for his interests. He noted the inconvenience of keeping copies of the book stored after some word of its contents had been divulged. The danger there lay in exaggerated rumors which might prejudice his situation. Madero warned his father that since events were occuring with great rapidity (the formation of the Democratic party nucleus in the capital and the demoralizing defeat of the independents in the municipal election in Saltillo), valuable time was being lost and that therefore it was impossible for him to defer publication or his participation in politics. The son foresaw dire consequences if he were not able to proceed with complete freedom. "If I enter the campaign with hesitation, . . . then failure will be certain not only for the cause but also for us. You know that from the fallen stick all the world makes kindling wood." [15]

Secondly, the idealistic Francisco appealed to his father's patriotism. His study had convinced him that if the nation did not make an effort in the next electoral campaign, Mexicans would be faced with the unpleasant alternatives of loss of nationality or a period of civil wars. Although he believed that it was "an obligatión of all Mexicans to make a vigorous effort to save our Fatherland," Madero emphasized that he was seeking permission rather than active support. "If you should decide not to fight, it is because it is not in your nature or your age to get involved in these matters. However, you are able to permit me to do it without any obstacle, and I know you will respect my right to do it." [16]

Lastly, Francisco had to contend with the practical basis of his father's objections. He expressed regret that "you judge that I have harmed you in your personal interests." Disdaining the material, Madero movingly stressed the transcendental nature of the struggle. "One ought not to consider personal

[15] Madero to Francisco Madero, Dec. 20, 1908, AdeM. *El Gráfico*, Aug. 21, 1930.
[16] *Ibid.*

losses . . . when he is treating . . . of the Fatherland for which it is necessary to be resolved to sacrifice even one's life."[17] Nevertheless, he proposed to withhold publication of the book until near the end of December in order to give his father an opportunity to arrange his affairs.

In that connection, Francisco recommended that perhaps his father should see Limantour to explain the situation. He suggested that the elder Madero tell the cabinet officer that the object of his son's political activity was to prevent the rise of a new despot after the death of Díaz. Specifically, Madero emphasized that he was anxious to neutralize the advance of the movement supporting General Reyes, an argument certain to appeal to the Minister of Finance. Francisco indicated that he had a great personal liking for Limantour, an old friend of the family, and that the cabinet officer would be his ideal candidate for the presidency or the vice-presidency. While he promised to work within the Democratic party to achieve that object, Madero reminded his father that "I am above all a convinced democrat, and I will work primarily for the triumph of democratic principles. These obligate me to support the candidate chosen by a democratic convention." He assured his father that in the book he primarily attacked the regime of absolute power and that, so far as prudence permitted, he spoke well of Limantour. "I did not want my sympathies for him to be too transparent because that could handicap . . . me later. People would say that I am not a sincere democrat which, in truth, I am."[18]

[17] *Ibid.*

[18] He pointed out to his father that "if we do tell Sr. Limantour something, he should not believe that I am an unconditional Limantourist, for above all I am a democrat." Since Madero was to be accused of Limantourism, a clarification of his attitude toward and relation with Limantour is needed. The sentiments expressed in this letter to his father were not merely words intended to impress the elder Madero or to throw the cabinet officer off guard. Unquestionably Madero was sincere because he had great confidence in Limantour as a financier and as a man of government. He wrote to Limantour as follows: "I know that you have democratic ideas, that within the cabinet you always have worked for a return to a constitutional regime, and that in all your acts you have followed the law." These words, together with the family's close ties with Limantour, help to

Francisco's filial conscience prompted him to add the following postcript:

You cannot imagine the effect on me of having to speak to you as I have done . . . I do not wish to cause you the slightest upset . . . I beg you to think calmly, aided by Providence, on all that I have said to you so that you should not give an unwarranted interpretation to my conduct.[19]

The same day, December 20, 1908, Madero wrote his grandfather announcing his plans. The letter, while obviously intended to flatter the older man, does reveal Madero's sense of mission and the inspirational role of Don Evaristo. "I have seen so clearly the hand of Providence protecting our family that I firmly believe that the protection has been given us not only to enjoy it, but to extend its benefits . . . I . . . wish to follow your example [of public service]." [20]

The practical-minded grandfather was not to be influenced so easily. He sarcastically observed that if Francisco had sent the book to others, then surely "already the whole world knows about it." Evaristo indicated his "great displeasure" that his grandson should continue endangering himself "trying to be a redeemer when you ought to know that redeemers end up crucified." Still worse was his apparent willingness to jeopardize his father's interests. Even if Francisco were to proceed without the consent of his grandfather and that of his father, Evaristo was certain that the authorities would not believe that the older Maderos had no part in the publication. The patriarch concluded his tirade with, "Each time I reflect on your conduct, I fear that you have lost your head since you do not consult the opinions of sensible persons." [21]

---

explain events in May, 1911. Between Francisco I. Madero and José Limantour there was no political arrangement, but rather a sympathy and respect which the former never concealed. Madero's supporters were aware of this attitude long before the military triumph in 1911. *La Opinión,* Feb. 18, 1934.

[19] Madero to Francisco Madero, Dec. 20, 1908, AdeM.

[20] Madero to his grandfather Evaristo Madero, Dec. 20, 1908, AdeM.

[21] *Ibid.*

Three days later Evaristo Madero, calmer and having read several chapters of the book, wrote another letter. He commented favorably on the volume, but again expressed his belief that publication would not be prudent because of the inevitable impression that it represented the aspirations of the father and grandfather. "I will tell you the truth that I do not consider you capable of writing such a book, and I wish to know who helped you to write it."[22] The grandson replied that "absolutely no one has helped me to write my book and few are the paragraphs which I have modified on the advice of some friend."[23] Francisco argued that General Díaz knew that his political ideas were "much more radical" than those of the older Maderos and would not misinterpret his conduct. He assured his grandfather that he would fight within the law and without fear of the consequences.

Despite this more moderate exchange, the attitude of the grandfather remained the same. Francisco, disappointed, peevishly attributed Evaristo's opposition to indifference toward him. The grandfather declared that, on the contrary, "because you are my beloved grandson... it displeases me that you should aspire to cover the sun with your hands." He expressed regret that Francisco should have undertaken "that campaign which makes you lose time and money... We know now that you do not pay attention to money or riches." After reiterating his belief that the grandson's first obligation was to aid his father, Evaristo concluded with a kindly word of caution: "I recommend that you be very careful and that you be not deluded, a weakness in youths who pretend everything is rose-colored."[24]

During the last days of December and the first three weeks

[22] Evaristo Madero to his grandson F. I. Madero, Jan. 5, 1909, AdeM.

[23] Evaristo was curious about the inclusion of data which he, as an older man, could not have had available. Francisco explained that his data was obtained from books (including the apocryphal memoirs of Sebastián Lerdo) and from conversations with persons (i.e., Gen. Treviño) who lived during the periods discussed. Madero to his grandfather Evaristo Madero, Jan. 7, 1909, AdeM.

[24] Evaristo Madero to his grandson F. I. Madero, June 21, 1909, AdeM; *La Opinión*, Feb. 25, 1934.

of January Francisco continued tirelessly to write letters in which he sought to convince his parents that they should authorize his projected political moves. His mother was pessimistic and expressed her concern that harm would come to the family and its interests. Madero attributed her fears mainly to the delicate state of her health which "makes her impressionable." He hastened to assure her that no harm would come to any of them and asked that she consider the elevated nature of the obligation with which he was about to comply. "I am meeting a highly patriotic obligation and even if I encounter danger, I believe that I ought not to hesitate a moment." Appealing to his mother's religious instincts, Francisco advised her to "have faith in God, for He always protects those who wish to work in accord with His designs and in harmony with His divine plan. A good action can never have bad consequences." [25]

Time passed without a reply, to say nothing of consent, from the father, and Francisco became impatient. He insisted that the danger which might arise must be ignored in a struggle for liberty undertaken so that "we may leave to our children a prosperous and great country." [26] Revealing clearly his deep sense of "calling," the son wrote in terms of spiritism which also had interested his father:

> You should know that among the spirits . . . there are some who concern themselves with the progress of humanity . . . Liberty is the most powerful means by which people may progress . . .
>
> Mexico is threatened by an immense danger. If we permit matters to continue, absolutism will perpetuate itself in our country . . .
>
> And I, who ought to play a role of importance in that struggle since I have been selected by Providence to fulfill the notable mission of writing that book, who recognize in my enthusiasm and faith aid from above, and who is acknowledged as the leader in this state by all who wish to fight—I feel that I am restrained, that a powerful force holds my arm and makes me useless for the struggle.

[25] Madero to Francisco Madero and Mercedes G. de Madero, Dec. 20, 1908; Madero to Mercedes G. de Madero, Dec. 22, 1908, AdeM.

[26] Madero to Francisco Madero, Dec. 26, 1908, and Jan. 8, 1909, AdeM.

I anxiously await your reply . . . In spite of my age, I do not wish to disobey you.[27]

On January 22, Madero received a telegram in which his father conceded the permission and the blessing of both parents. This was inevitable. The parents might regard Francisco's conduct as foolish and dangerous, but he was their son. Expressing his joy and appreciation, Francisco related how, that very morning, he had dreamed of seeing his father, who, with a tender expression on his face, had given his blessing. Madero reaffirmed his confidence that no harm would come to his parents or their interests and recommended that his father see Limantour again to explain the son's conduct. Promising that his actions would cause his parents the most legitimate pride and satisfaction, the son concluded: "Now I have not the slightest doubt that Providence guides my steps and protects me."[28]

Francisco Madero's book, *The Presidential Succession in 1910,* was released to the public late in January, 1909. Others, besides Don Evaristo, raised questions about the authorship and suggested that either Francisco's cousin Rafael Hernández, Francisco Sentíes, Juan Sánchez Azcona, or even Roque Estrada was the real author. Madero's correspondence with the first three individuals clearly eliminates them as possibilities, and he did not meet Estrada until after the book began to circulate. However, the most conclusive evidence of his authorship is the original manuscript copy in Madero's handwriting, located in his archive. This draft, with the exception of frequent spelling errors, does not differ, even in punctuation, from the first edition printed in San Pedro. Examination of the seventeen notebooks of the manuscript reveals that sometimes Madero would write up to seven or eight pages consecutively. He apparently wrote freely as thoughts came to him, moving rapidly from one subject to another. This, in part, would account for repetitions and the lack of order. Corrections and additions, in Madero's handwriting, are

27 Madero to Francisco Madero, Jan. 20, 1909, AdeM.
28 Madero to Francisco Madero, Jan. 23, 1909, AdeM.

numerous. In some instances whole pages are crossed out and substitute material placed in the margins or on loose sheets with indications as to place of insertion.[29]

The book is dedicated to the heroes of the country in whose example the author found inspiration for the task he was beginning, to the independent journalists who had sustained for thirty years the unequal struggle against dictatorial power, and to all good Mexicans who had not lost the ideal of the Fatherland and the concomitant concepts of liberty and sacrifice. Noting that he belonged to a privileged family with no cause for complaint against the administration, Madero declared that neither personal nor family hatred, but rather love of country guided him in the writing of the book. His purpose was to explain the current state of affairs in Mexico and to call on all Mexicans to establish a political party based on principles which would triumph sooner or later. His goal was to arouse his countrymen to an organized, powerful effort which would attempt to effect a change in the political destinies of the nation.[30]

The volume is divided into three parts. The first section, more than a quarter of the book, contains a brief summary of Mexican history, with emphasis on the problem of militarism. Madero believed that the seeds of the existing situation were to be found in the record of continuous revolutions and military dictatorships. Accordingly, after a brief but incisive indictment of the colonial period with its systematic exploitation of the area and the people, the author proceeded to describe the turbulence arising from the prolonged struggle for independence. Santa Anna appears as the prime example of a cynical, irresponsible, ambitious militarist. Madero solemnly concluded that "when a man, military or not, takes the tragic road of revolution to achieve power, we ought to be suspicious of all his acts and to distrust all his promises."[31]

With enthusiasm Madero recorded his impressions of the

[29] *La Opinión,* Oct. 8, 1933.
[30] Ferrer de M., *Vida . . . de Madero,* p. 45.
[31] Madero, *La sucesión presidencial,* p. 60.

Constituent Congress of 1857. This assembly was held up as proof of the aptitude of the Mexicans for democracy. However, he ignored the unreal, theoretical nature of Mexican constitutional problems and the fact that the application of such documents frequently served as justification or rationalization for revolt. Juárez received fullsome praise from Madero, while the revolutionary plans of Díaz were regarded as cloaks for his ambition and pretexts to justify his efforts to achieve power. Although some of his generalizations are debatable, Madero's summary of his country's past is comparable to an adequate brief school text. This section is concluded with an analysis of Díaz, his ambitions, his policies, and the means by which he had managed to maintain his power. Although Madero was complimentary to the President personally, he viewed him as a man constantly driven by a fixed idea: to achieve power and then to retain it by any and all means.

The second part of the study is concerned with absolute power which "corrupts those who exercise it and those who suffer it."[32] Madero began by analyzing absolutism theoretically and historically. His references to the history of other nations, of both antiquity and more recent times, are very superficial, and he selected only data which supported his ideas. With this material as a background Madero turned to a discussion of absolutism in Mexico. He attributed the rise of absolute power in his own nation to internal and foreign struggles. This section of the book ends with a balance sheet of the accomplishments and faults of the Díaz regime. Madero charged that under the rule of Don Porfirio Díaz grave offenses had been committed: the wars against the Indians, the treatment of labor, the neglect of education, subservience to the United States, and inadequate efforts to tighten the bonds with the sister republics to the south.

Madero regarded the final section of his book, containing his view of the immediate political situation, as the most important one. He was convinced that, despite the Creelman interview, Díaz desired to continue in the presidency and had

[32] Ferrer de M., *Vida . . . de Madero*, p. 48.

no intention of modifying his policy. If nothing was done, Díaz would select as his vice-president a person meeting *his* requirements rather than those of the nation. Madero regarded Vice-President Ramón Corral as the likely, almost inevitable, choice of Díaz. Either Corral or the other outstanding aspirant, General Bernardo Reyes, would mean, according to Madero, a continuation of absolutism without the moderation he credited to Díaz. Such a prolongation of the regime of absolute power "would be fatal for our institutions and dangerous for our independence." [33] Madero proposed to prevent this from happening by organizing the independents in a democratic political party for the next election.

The proposal raised two questions: Were the Mexicans ready for democracy? Would the government tolerate democratic action? Because Díaz had effected elimination of the divisions among the people and because of the growing appreciation of the idea that rule by law was desirable, Madero felt that his countrymen were ready for democracy, which he visualized in electoral terms. Conceding that thirty years of not practicing democracy had dulled somewhat the political organism, he argued that further delay would only mean more complete atrophy. Regarding the second question, Madero admitted that prevailing opinion held that the administration would not tolerate a political movement aimed at converting the personalist regime into a democratic one. Nevertheless, with characteristic optimism, he argued that the nation organized politically would win respect for its rights and that any concession or victory won for democratic processes would be lasting.[34]

Therefore, Madero issued a call for the formation of an Anti-Reelectionist party,[35] based on the principles of freedom

[33] Madero, *La sucesión presidencial*, pp. 279-80.

[34] Madero had no use for pessimists who "pretend that they do not enter the struggle because they will not be followed.... A handful of valiants is worth more than a legion of timid ones. The optimists, those who see in all others their own enthusiasm and resolution, will save the Fatherland." There can be no doubt as to which category Madero considered himself to belong and to which he did indeed belong. Madero, *La sucesión presidencial*, p. 392.

[35] National Democratic party was the name suggested by Madero in

of suffrage and no reelection. He believed that its candidate, who would be chosen in convention, should be a prominent member of the administration whose record indicated that he would respect the Constitution. Madero hoped that this proposal, intended to demonstrate that the independents were not guided by personal ambition,[36] would lead Díaz to agree to independent designation of his successor.

If no respected member of the administration were to accept this nomination, then, Madero recommended, a selection from among the independents and a full-scale electoral fight should be made. In the event that the government respected the law, the opposition, even though defeated, would have won freedom of suffrage and prepared the ground for further triumphs. If electoral freedom was not conceded, the nation would have been awakened and the independents would have acquired sufficient prestige to win concessions from Díaz's successor. Madero concluded with the following exhortation to the President, whose probable conduct he foresaw: "You are not able to find a successor more worthy of you . . . than the Law." [37]

Francisco Madero's book has been criticized for various reasons. One complaint—a complaint which has been directed against the author's whole career—is based on the neglect of economic and social factors. However, it must be remembered that the writer's purpose was immediate and political. He hoped that his book would contribute to the creation of a milieu conducive to the organization and successful operation

---

the first edition of his book. However, the organization of a Democratic party in Mexico City prompted a change in the second edition. In addition, as Dr. Howard Cline has emphasized, there is a shift in viewpoint and tone in the three editions of the book. These changes reflected the shifting of Madero's aims as, from an advocate of compromise aimed at ending dictatorship in time, he became, successively, a vice-presidential possibility and a presidential challenger of the aging dictator. Cline, *The United States and Mexico,* pp. 118-20.

36 While Madero undoubtedly had Limantour in mind, he probably also was trying to quiet any governmental concern which might lead to the liquidation of the movement.

37 Madero, *La sucesión presidencial,* p. 356.

of an independent party. While social and economic problems are treated briefly and superficially, they are not ignored. Facilities for education, which Madero regarded as the basis for all progress, are criticized as inadequate and unevenly distributed. The author lamented the precarious situation of the workers as well as the alliance between government and capital. He attacked the ill-considered concessions of mineral resources, water rights, and national lands. The failure of proprietors of large estates to cultivate their lands was condemned. And lastly, he criticized the alcohol industry, which transformed corn, the basic food of the people, into "one of the poisons most prejudicial to the progress of the Republic" and, incidentally, raised the price of the cereal.[38]

The most important consideration in evaluating this criticism is Madero's whole concept of the reform problem. Since he believed that the most urgent matter was the threat presented by continued absolutism, freedom of suffrage and no reelection became his immediate objectives. Madero did not overlook the need for other reforms. These, he believed, would come after study by the elected representatives of the people. With more justice it may be observed that Madero erred not so much in neglecting other reforms, but, rather, in considering political reform of first importance and immediately attainable.

A second criticism is based on the apparent contradiction in the author's attitude toward Díaz. On the one hand, Madero attacked the evils of a system of tyranny. On the other hand, he indicated his willingness to accept another term for Díaz whom he described as a prudent man and an absolute ruler exercising his power with moderation. The corrections on the original manuscript reveal Madero avoiding at times an exceptionally hard word against the government but also eliminating phrases which might be interpreted as too adulatory of the Mexican President. Some of the confusion is eliminated by the distinction Madero drew between the ruler and the system. The author's hope for compromise and concessions

[38] *Ibid.*, pp. 237-38.

must be considered. Then, too, it should be remembered that he was writing political propaganda in a dictatorial environment. Madero was attempting to describe the evils of the regime and the dangers of its continuance without antagonizing Díaz or placing himself in a position of direct challenge to the government. In sharp contrast are the opinions voiced in his correspondence when he felt free to express himself. As early as August, 1906, in a letter to his brother, Madero wrote that "if [we] should do something sometime, it would be against General Díaz, who has caused all the evils of the country." [39]

The political atmosphere alone does not explain Madero's opposition to revolution. He did not discriminate between a socio-economic upheaval and the more frequently occurring power grab. For him revolution meant sterile sacrifices with deadly consequences. He declared that a revolution could not give the people liberty, but would aggravate the internal situation. His attitude on this subject is too consistent to be explained solely in terms of external conditions. Madero was pacifistic, and, at the time, had a horror of revolution. Certainly it was the logical reaction for a person with his background who had decided that internal conflicts were the root of his nation's difficulties. He emphasized that he shrank from an appeal to arms not because of fear, but because he preferred the broad road of democracy to the tortuous path of civil war. Francisco Madero wrote as the "Apostle of Democracy," not as the chieftain of a prospective armed conflict.

The Presidential Succession in 1910 has scant literary merit, scholarly value, or social significance to recommend it. The volume suffers from repetitions, and the reader senses that the author had not digested his material sufficiently. However, Madero made no pretense to literary or scholarly achievement. "I am not the cool, calm and dispassionate historian who treats important events after many years have passed . . . and who judges the facts by the result." [40] On the contrary,

[39] Madero to his brother Evaristo E. Madero, Aug. 4, 1906, AdeM.
[40] Madero, *La sucesión presidencial,* pp. 28-29.

the book was a volume of political propaganda and political opportunism, and as such it must be judged.

Madero exhibited an excessive sentimentality in his study. The author, far from denying this characteristic, called attention to it explaining that if he had been guided by inflexible reason, the situation would have seemed frightful and insuperable. Therefore, he preferred to be guided by means variously called faith, intuition, inspiration, or sentiment which

> open a field where . . . reason is not able to enter. That faith has inspired the great sacrifices . . . but it is not blind faith which believes without . . . facts . . . [It is the faith] that knows how to discover the great destinies of nations and to perceive the mysterious hand of Providence which solicitously guides peoples.[41]

This very sentimentalism added to the simplicity and candidness which suggested the nobility of the author and made the study intelligible and appealing to its audience. Francisco Madero, seen through the pages of his book, was a humane person, deeply moved by the sufferings of others and by the evils and dangers threatening his country. Thus, patriotism is a dominant note throughout the volume and an element in its appeal to a relatively extensive audience. Within three months the initial edition of three thousand copies was exhausted, and a second edition was published in Mexico City. A toned-down third edition, issued in 1909, was intended to win the support of other groups developing in opposition to the regime.

Madero's book did come to grips with the political issues of the day and contributed greatly to the current political agitation and to the awakening of the public. It catapulted its author, then little known, into national prominence, making it possible for him to assume leadership of the opposition political movement which he was advocating.

[41] *Ibid.*, pp. 298-99.

V. The Reyes Boom

LATE IN 1908 the beginning of political organization occurred with the formation of the Organizing Center of the Democratic party by a group in Mexico City. The initial impetus appears to have come from a number of persons, including Manuel Calero, who were associated with the Díaz government, and the presence of these individuals created suspicions that the movement was officially inspired. However, the new organization also included some supporters of General Bernardo Reyes, like Rafael Zubarán Capmany, José León del Valle, and Heriberto Barrón, as well as some independents, like Francisco de P. Senties and Juan Sánchez Azcona. Because of the pressure from these elements the following two objectives of the Center gradually emerged: opposition to Ramón Corral as a candidate for reelection as vice-president and the formation of an active political party of principles.

Francisco Madero, in San Pedro, was considerably agitated by reports of the organization of the new group. For one who was anxious to see a national party formed he was singularly unenthusiastic. Cynics might attribute his reaction to personal ambition and egotism, but Madero gave substantial reasons. He felt that public opinion had not been aroused enough to support such a movement and that it would be unwise to begin with a failure.[1] In addition to regarding the movement as premature, he was disturbed by the participation of Heriberto Barrón, until recently a member of the National Porfirista

[1] Madero to Senties, Oct. 10 and Nov. 4, 1908, AdeM.

Circle (an organization formed by personal friends of Díaz in 1896 to "arrange" his reelections), a known supporter of General Reyes, and the perpetrator of an infamous attack on the liberal club in San Luis Potosí at the turn of the century. He expressed his fears that the new organization might be part of a plan to trap the independents.

The real danger that he envisioned was that the Reyists (supporters of General Reyes) would dominate the scene. Madero warned that "a party which begins with those inclinations will not go very far." Despite assurances from Sentíes that the independents had control of the group, reports persisted of increasing Reyist influence in the Democratic party. While advising his friends that "all the world considers you as Reyists," Madero still strove valiently to orient the Democratic party into the channels he considered desirable. He urged that the new group adopt the principles of "Freedom of Suffrage and No Reelection" and endeavor to attract outstanding independents in order to broaden its base. Lastly, in a move obviously aimed against General Reyes, Madero stated that the candidate of the party must be a civilian as evidence of its democratic tendencies.[2]

Despite Madero's warning the Democratic party did tend to favor Bernardo Reyes as the preferred alternative to Ramón Corral for the vice-presidential post. General Reyes had served long and meritoriously as a military and administrative official. He believed that official action should be reduced to a simple, direct regulatory function exercised with decision. An efficient, if stringent, governor, he had transformed Nuevo León into one of the most prosperous and progressive states in the nation. Monterrey, the state capital, with over eighty thousand inhabitants, was Mexico's chief industrial center. Enactment of the

[2] Madero to Sentíes, Dec. 19 and 27, 1908, and Jan. 8, 1909, AdeM. Denying a rumor that he was a candidate for governor of Coahuila, Madero frankly admitted the extent of his ambition at this time. "I myself have no pretensions to this post because I know that it would be absolutely impossible for me, with my radical ideas, to go along with the central government. What I do aspire to be is the active head of the political party." Madero to Sentíes, Jan. 24, 1909, AdeM.

first workmen's compensation law in Mexico attested to his enlightenment. General Reyes had prestige and enjoyed enormous popularity.

Notwithstanding evidence of brutality, as, for example, the violent suppression of the opposition in Monterrey on April 2, 1903, the northern commander, in contrast to Díaz, maintained some semblance of liberalism and was the outstanding personality who might be available to the opposition. That Reyes was a known enemy of the Científicos, the dominant government group who surrounded and supported Corral, was most significant for the organizers of the Democratic party. Considering all these factors and the presence of leading Reyists in the organizing group, it is not surprising that, as governmental elements withdrew, the Democratic party gravitated increasingly towards Reyes's candidacy.

The program of the Democratic party was formulated at a convention held in the Hidalgo Theater in Mexico City. The platform contained liberal ideals—revitalize municipal power by suppressing the *jefes políticos;* increased facilities for primary education; effective compliance with the Reform Laws; and respect for the life and liberty of the individual—but was rather indefinite on how to implement them. On the great economic issues of the day, the new party favored accident compensation for workers and "laws that would protect the liberty of the peasant and which, in a general manner, would improve his economic and moral condition." [3]

Program in hand and led by talented leaders, the Democratic party became the first national party to enter municipal elections and to campaign widely in Mexico. In Veracruz, Orizaba, and Tehuacán its spokesmen were greeted by cheering thousands. In Guadalajara, capital of General Reyes's native state, Democratic leaders called for the reelection of Díaz and the choice of a patriot, not a Científico, as vice-president. The crowd responded *Viva Reyes.*

Francisco Madero, actively engaged in his own political

[3] *"Programa político del partido Democrático,"* Jan. 20, 1909, cited in Cabrera, *Obras políticas,* pp. 391-94.

efforts, watched the progress of the Democratic party with interest. In an appendix to the second edition of *The Presidential Succession in 1910,* he evaluated the movement and its prospects. While conceding that the leaders seemed well-intentioned, Madero believed that their ties with the administration, their Reyist inclinations, and their obvious reluctance to face the presidential question would prevent any considerable achievement. Nevertheless, he recognized that the labors of the Democratic party would be useful in awakening the people.[4]

While General Reyes was increasingly the preferred choice of the Democratic party, he also had the complete support of the avowedly Reyist groups. The roots of the movement were in the Masonic lodges which the General, ambitious for the presidential succession, had fostered in the northern states and in the Second Reserve which he had sponsored while serving in Díaz's cabinet as Minister of War. The reappearance of political activity in 1908 was the signal for increased activity on the part of these Reyist groups. Their objective was to build up such pressure that General Díaz would accept Reyes as his running mate.

The Reyists organized clubs, started newspapers, and sent out speakers on propaganda trips.[5] Reyism found its support among the secondary bureaucrats and in the army. It also won

[4] He indicated the possibility of the Democratic party's serving as intermediary between Díaz and the independents in arranging a compromise. However, Madero predicted that if, as he expected, the electoral struggle was to be carried forward by a frankly Anti-Reelectionist, or at least completely independent, party, the Democratic party probably would split, with some following the government's standard and the majority supporting the independents. Madero, *La sucesión presidencial,* pp. 387-88.

[5] A Central Reyist club was formed in the capital in May, 1909. The following month the *Soberanía Popular* (Popular Sovereignty) club was founded by Dr. Espinosa de los Monteros, J. López-Portillo y Rojas, Dr. Francisco Vásquez Gómez, and Rafael Zubarán. Reyist newspapers included *El Voto, La República* (in Monterrey), and *La Opinión de Veracruz.* For a considerable time the columns of Sánchez Azcona's *México Nuevo* were sympathetic to the movement. R. Estrada called this paper the "thermometer of public opinion." As public sentiment became successively Reyist, Anti-Reelectionist, and revolutionary, *México Nuevo* changed too. Memorandum for José C. Valadés on activities of the Reyists, AdeV.

considerable following among the popular elements. However, all this activity was undertaken without public encouragement from the prospective candidate. Indeed, General Reyes had indicated in his comments on the Creelman interview that "the well-being of Mexico requires the continuance of General Díaz in the presidency" and that the vice-president ought to be designated with full regard for his wishes.[6] Reyes's followers continued their efforts in his behalf, confident that the northern commander would bow opportunely to public demand.

Tremendous success attended the efforts of the Reyists in the capital and in Jalisco. They also won considerable following in Veracruz and the northern tier of states. Reyism appeared uncontainable, for, as one adherent recalled, the "Reyist party traveled on the wings of prosperity."[7] This success inevitably produced a reaction in official quarters.

On February 9, 1909, the Reelectionist party was organized by a group dominated by José Limantour, Rosendo Pineda, the Macedo brothers, and other Científico leaders. This dominant element in the government had its origin in a group of young intellectuals gathered together by Romero Rubio, Díaz's father-in-law, and by Pineda almost twenty years earlier. In 1892 the arrangements for the reelection of General Díaz were entrusted to this group. The Rubio-Pineda followers not only presumed to present the dictator with a program, but advocated the development of a political party that would lead Mexico to a more democratic future. They insisted that the processes of government follow the principles of economic and political science and presented themselves as the scientists. Their repeated emphasis on science resulted in the group's being dubbed the Científicos.

Political idealism was soon forgotten. Most of the Científicos had studied in the National Preparatory School under Dr. Gabino Barreda, who had introduced the postivism of Auguste Comte into Mexican thinking. However, the Científicos accepted only the scientific side of the religion of humanity. To

[6] *La República,* Aug. 1, 1908.
[7] López-Portillo y Rojas, *Porfirio Díaz,* p. 422.

this they added a narrow derivative of the thought of Herbert Spencer and some racialist ideas. The result was an austere philosophy emphasizing material progress by and in behalf of those in the vanguard of civilization. The Científicos aspired to political and economic control of the nation.

These aspirants to a new creole oligarchy did not constitute a party. They remained always a clique without support from the people, the focus of opposition attack and popular hatred. José Limantour, Secretary of the Treasury, was the group's key man in the government and, after the death of Romero Rubio in 1895, its leader.[8] However, Limantour found his path and that of the Científicos opposed by General Reyes and blocked by Joaquín Baranda, old-time liberal and Minister of Justice and Public Instruction.

Porfirio Díaz was still in control and skillfully played one group against the other. The Científicos had to limit their efforts to blocking a new military dictator, specifically Reyes, and to insuring for their group constitutional inheritance of the power of the aging dictator. Baranda was forced out of the cabinet. In December, 1902, General Reyes resigned his portfolio and returned to Nuevo León as governor. The fall of Baranda and Reyes were victories for the Científicos and marked the turning point of their fortunes. In 1904 the post of vice-president was recreated at the insistence of Limantour and the Científicos who were concerned about the successor to the seventy-four-year-old Díaz. The President selected as his running mate Interior Minister Ramón Corral. The former Yaqui slave trader and governor of Sonora was acceptable to the ascendant Científicos who surrounded him.

The increasing debility of Don Porfirio permitted the Limantour clique to achieve mastery of the destinies of the nation. By 1909 the influence of the group in the government was represented by three cabinet secretaries, eight of the sub-

[8] In 1907, Madero wrote of the director of the Científicos: "Sr. Limantour, because of his antecedents, will be an excellent ruler, but not a chief of a militant party." He criticized the bureaucratic faction which "almost never concerns itself with public opinion." Madero to Manuel de León, May 8, 1907, AdeM.

secretaries, twelve governors, twenty-five senators, and one hundred and eighteen of the two hundred and thirty deputies. The Científicos were instrumental in accentuating the Díaz policy of encouraging foreign capitalist investment in Mexico by sacrificing national interests and in orienting that policy in favor of European (especially French and English) capital as opposed to that of North America. Advocates of the *status quo* and self-appointed heirs to Díaz's mantle, the Científicos rushed to the political defense of the regime by forming the Reelectionist party.

The convention of the Reelectionist party opened on March 25, 1909, with over seven hundred delegates present. A week later the convention had proclaimed the candidacies of Díaz and Corral. In a manifesto announcing the candidates the Reelectionists boasted confidently that "the triumph is assured beforehand" because "these men [Díaz en Corral] master all wills and calm all consciences." [9] The delegates approved resolutions calling for the organization of Corralista political clubs, the arrangement of propaganda trips, and the establishment of a biweekly political organ, *El Debate*. The National Porfirista Circle, the group composed of personal friends of the dictator, was the other pro-government party. This group, though unhappy about the Corral nomination, quietly followed, for the time being, the Reelectionist slate.

Reelectionist speakers were sent out on tour. However, in Morelia, Guanajuato, and Guadalajara they met with resounding failures. In the capital of Jalisco a public demonstration for Reyes interrupted the meeting and forced the speakers to abandon the platform. Later, a hostile crowd stoned the hotel in which the Reelectionists were quartered. State authorities retaliated by closing the Reyist clubs in Jalisco and by arresting outstanding Reyists. The full weight of the Díaz regime was thrown against the movement in behalf of General Reyes.

President Díaz moved to weaken the Democratic party by forcing government personnel to break with the organization.

[9] "Manifiesto de la convención del partido Reeleccionista," cited in Cabrera, *Obras políticas*, pp. 401-4.

Opposition campaign trips encountered innumerable obstacles. A virulent press attack, spearheaded by *El Debate,* referred to the unpatriotic tendencies of the Democratic party which "either deceives the people or is disloyal to General Díaz" and to "fiery military violence" which endangered the tranquility of the nation.[10] The Porfirian stick meted out punishment to Reyist sympathizers: a dozen army officers were banished to remote parts; Deputies Jesús Urueta and Lerdo de Tejada, Jr., were deprived of their seats in the Chamber; and Senator José López-Portillo y Rojas was ejected from the Senate and arrested.

Under this pressure the partisans of General Reyes began to demand that he accept openly the role of candidate and assume leadership of his party. The military commander hesitated. Late in July, General Reyes indicated that, as a supporter of General Díaz, he endorsed the candidacy of Corral and urged his followers to do the same.[11] Although this was a disheartening blow to the Reyists, they refused to accept the pronouncement as final and did not completely abandon their efforts.

President Díaz still considered Reyism a threat and moved with characteristic energy to neutralize the reluctant leader. Reyes was deprived of the command of the military forces in his state, and these troops were placed under the command of his personal enemy, General Gerónimo Treviño.[12] The Governor of Nuevo León regarded his position as one of weakness and danger. On August 20, 1909, he left Monterrey for his estate at Galeana. His political enemies, attributing his conduct to cowardice or to indecision, ridiculed Reyes as the "entrenched of Galeana." His partisans explain that reasons of health forced the General to leave Monterrey for the "pure air

[10] *El Debate,* June 5 and 9, 1909.

[11] *México Nuevo,* July 29, 1909.

[12] Gen. Treviño's function was to neutralize Gov. Reyes. The correspondence between the new military commander in Nuevo León and Ramón Corral from Sept. through Nov. 1909, clearly indicates their efforts to remove Reyes from the sphere of national politics. *La Opinión,* Oct. 10, 1937.

of the sierra." [13] His absence started rumors of rebellion which were stilled by his reappearance in the state capital in September.

Dr. Vázquez Gómez visited Reyes in Monterrey to urge him again to accept the candidacy. He showed the General a telegram from the Central Reyist Committee which stated that it was essential that he not refuse it. Reyes replied that he had already wired Díaz that he would not accept the candidacy in order not to be an obstacle to the development of the president's policy.[14] Early in November, after an interview with General Díaz, Reyes resigned his post as governor of Nuevo León and accepted a military study assignment in Europe which was, for all practical purposes, an official order of exile. Interviewed in New York, General Reyes declared that he was not an enemy of President Díaz, but rather his good friend. "I know that the public is anxious that he [Díaz] serve again as President, and he will be elected without contest." [15]

Bernardo Reyes rejected both political campaign and armed revolt. Neither the cowardice alleged by his enemies nor the patriotism praised by his friends adequately explains his conduct. Reyes, in addition to being a victim of his own political ineptitude, was too much a part of, too closely allied with, the Porfirian regime to break away and challenge it in any way. The political candidacy of General Reyes was dead by the end of 1909.

His withdrawal left the field clear for Francisco Madero. Madero's political organization grew as Reyism disintegrated. For the independents and for many Reyists, deserted by their selected leader, the Maderista movement was salvation. By closing the door on Reyes whom he feared, Porfirio Díaz opened the door for Madero whom he at first regarded with disdain.

The efforts of the Flores Magón group and of the Reyists stirred the Mexican people, but it was the persistent and

[13] López-Portillo y Rojas, *Porfirio Díaz,* p. 425.
[14] Vázquez Gómez, *Memorias políticas,* p. 17.
[15] New York *Herald,* Nov. 13, 1909.

courageous efforts of Francisco Madero in his correspondence, in campaign trips, and in his organizing activities which carried the political movement to its climax. Early in 1909 he noted in his memoirs his intention "to defend the cause of the people with all [my] energy . . . I do not pretend to be a great man, but I aspire to imitate one." [16]

During the first months of 1909 Madero expended his prodigious energy in setting the stage for the national political campaign. Through his book, which he distributed as widely as possible,[17] his newspaper *El Demócrata,* and personal contacts and letters, he sought to win followers for the movement. He corresponded frequently with Sánchez Azcona, Emilio Vázquez, and Toribio Esquivel Obregón. He flattered and praised them and, in some instances, insinuated a promising future for them. Madero emphasized the need for the opposition to organize and indicated that he and his friends probably would establish a completely independent party with "better selected elements" than those in the Democratic party.

Madero was very much interested in the state gubernatorial contests which preceded the national election. He had already learned the futility of fighting the regime merely on the state level, but he hoped that a similar lesson would lead current opponents of state governments to associate with his national movement. At the very least the local struggles would contribute to the awakening of the people. Therefore, he corresponded with state opposition leaders, encouraging their efforts. In Morelos, Sinaloa, Yucatán, and Coahuila considerable opposition to the official candidates developed.

In Morelos, despite obvious popular support for Patricio Leyva, the government candidate, General Pablo Escondón, was imposed on the state. The opposition in Sinaloa organized in support of José Ferrel against the official candidate, Interim Governor Diego Redo. Madero congratulated editor Heriberto

[16] Madero, "Mis memorias," pp. 7-8.

[17] Even Gen. Díaz received a copy as "proof of loyalty." Madero urged the President to prove the sincerity of his declarations to Creelman by deeds. Don Porfirio did not reply. Madero to Díaz, Feb. 21, 1909, AdeM.

Frías as the initiator of the local campaign which "has had repercussions throughout the Republic." In the event of defeat, which he anticipated, Madero hoped that the local independents would realize that they ought not to depend on Díaz's promises and that they must join with the national movement in order to fight against "this immense centralizing power personified by General Díaz."[18] Redo was victorious in the August election, and Madero was to find a sympathetic audience among the supporters of Ferrel.

In Yucatán the independents divided their support between Delio Moreno Cantón and José Pino Suárez. Madero wrote Pino Suárez that he believed that the independents had no reason to expect victory in the state elections and that, therefore, their logical objective would be preparation for the national election. He recommended that Pino Suárez offer to support Delio Moreno Cantón for governor in exchange "for the aid of all his elements for the [national] Anti-Reelectionist campaign of next year."[19] Although Madero believed that the long-range objective would be served best by the candidacy of Moreno Cantón, he revealed his respect for local wishes by withholding endorsement until after the state convention had been held. The government was not concerned about the preference of the people. Governor Enrique Muñoz Arístegui was reelected. Madero could then point to events in Morelos, Sinaloa, and Yucatán as proof that Díaz "would not promote a truly democratic movement by himself."[20]

Francisco Madero participated directly in the local contest in his own state of Coahuila. He organized clubs—the first Anti-Reelectionist club being formed in San Pedro in this connection—and began to publish his newspaper again. Venustiano Carranza, a senator with Reyist inclinations, had been appointed provisional governor to replace Miguel Cárdenas, who had fallen from official favor. When Díaz withdrew his promised support of Carranza's candidacy for constitutional

[18] Madero to H. Frías, July 27, 1909, AdeM.

[19] Madero to J. M. Pino Suárez, Aug. 15, 1909, AdeM.

[20] Madero, *La sucesión presidencial*, pp. 396-97.

governor, the latter chose to remain in the fight and to accept the endorsement offered by an independent convention held in Saltillo. Madero, assured by Carranza that he was in agreement with the independents' principles, approved the decision and prepared to campaign vigorously.[21]

When he heard the rumor that the official candidate would be a Corralista, Sr. Jesús del Valle, Madero felt that the independents would have a real opportunity to make an impressive fight supporting Carranza. "I am certain that we are headed for defeat, but the defeat must be noisy in order to add to the awakening of the Nation." [22] He recognized that only brute force could win against brute force and that, under the circumstances, the opposition might turn to violence from a sense of futility in the state campaign. Madero hastened to discourage any such temptation. He urged patience until the national campaign. By that time, he argued, their efforts would have created more favorable conditions for results by pacific means. "For no reason is it desirable for us to rebel against the Federation in any state in order to defend our sovereignty." [23]

Madero's plans for a vigorous campaign in Coahuila received a rude blow when the official candidate was revealed as the lawyer Peña, a friend of the Madero family and a relative of the family attorney rather than an unpopular Corralista. Apparently Madero's father and grandfather had exercised some influence in this change. They had visited General Treviño at Saltillo to counsel against the candidacy of Jesús del Valle. When Peña was selected to run, Don Evaristo and some friends of the family offered to support him. Francisco Madero lost his enthusiasm for a strenuous campaign. While conceding that the independents must continue to oppose the

[21] Madero also was influenced by the expectation that Carranza would contribute to the success of his efforts to attract the followers of Reyes. In an article written Aug. 4, 1909 (AdeV), he observed that "it is better for Coahuila to have a Reyist than a Corralista governor because . . . Reyes, with no possibility of coming to power, will not be able to exercise pressure on the local authorities." Madero to Emilio Vázquez, Aug. 15, 1909, CdeFFP.

[22] Madero to F. F. Palavicini, Aug. 15, 1909, CdeFFP.

[23] Madero to Pino Suárez, Aug. 15, 1909, AdeM.

government's candidate, he expressed the hope that the contest would not be very bitter. Madero did not hesitate to admit that if Carranza could be elected (which he again noted was impossible), he would be the best governor. He argued, however, that since Peña, a respected man, would make a better governor than Cárdenas had been, the nomination represented a compromise, a triumph for public opinion in Coahuila. Madero weakly excused his reversal on the grounds that he saw no reason for sacrificing independent elements in a futile electoral fight, particularly when they could expect a respectable administration. He preferred to have "our forces in tact for the presidential campaign next year." [24]

In Mexico City, Madero had conferred with various persons in order to initiate the national movement. However, the campaign in Coahuila prevented him from spending very much time in the capital during the early months of 1909. But in May he attended a series of meetings held in the Mexico City home of Alfredo Robles Domínguez. It previously had been agreed to sustain the principle of "No Reelection" and to take the name of Anti-Reelectionist Center. The group preferred the designation "Center" because it would have seemed pretentious, at this stage of organization, to claim to be a party. At the first official session Madero and host Robles Domínguez each presented a program. Neither insisted that his particular

[24] Madero to Palavicini, Aug. 31 and Sept. 7 and 15, 1909; Madero to Emilio Vázquez, Sept. 4, 1909, CdeFFP.

This early, minor example of family ties apparently handicapping Madero is especially interesting in the light of charges by his partisans against Carranza based on a letter allegedly written by the provisional governor to Gen. Díaz, March 25, 1909 (Bonilla, *Diez años de guerra,* chap. III). The letter contains a report of action taken to reduce Madero's influence on the syndicate concerned with the distribution of the waters of the Nazas River. Carranza indicated that this action would prevent Madero from gaining a new element in support of his campaign against the government. The Provisional Governor closed with a statement of his unconditional loyalty. Although the letter does prove Carranza's close association with the regime in power and his anxiety to obtain official endorsement, it cannot be taken as evidence of a betrayal of Madero and the independents whose endorsement of him was not defined until later that year.

recommendations be accepted. After a reading of both proposals, that submitted by Madero was approved for further study by the majority.

Three days later, on May 2, the Center was formally constituted with the designation of its directive board and the announcement of its program. The signers explained that they had united to fight for the democratic principles of effective suffrage and no reelection. To achieve the "gradual realization" of these principles, they planned: to encourage the people to exercise their rights; to promote conventions to discuss candidates and issues; to organize an Anti-Reelectionist party throughout the nation; and to urge all citizens to participate in the electoral campaign. The announcement concluded with a gesture of willingness to cooperate with other independent groups, obviously directed at the Reyist and Democratic organizations.[25]

The Anti-Reelectionist Center planned to wage a campaign based on Madero's book, aimed at awakening and organizing the Mexican people for political action. However, the movement began very slowly in an atmosphere permeated by Reyism. Another source of difficulty was an undercurrent of opposition to Emilio Vázquez, the presiding officer of the Center. A few months earlier he had proposed publicly that the candidates for the next election be Generals Díaz and Treviño. Discouragement and fear reduced attendance at meetings, some of which could not be held because there was not a quorum (thirty members) present. Those who sought to recruit new members found everywhere "a cool reception and a skeptical disposition." [26]

During June the Center began to display greater activity. The group initiated, on June 6, publication of the weekly *El Antireeleccionista,* under the direction of José Vasconcelos. Through this newspaper the Anti-Reelectionist Center endeavored to explain its principles, arouse the public, and attack Corral and Reyes. Madero, who supported the news-

[25] Martínez and Guerra, *Madero,* p. 9.
[26] Vasconcelos, *Ulises criollo,* p. 307.

paper financially, believed that *El Antireeleccionista* should serve as a "formidable battering ram against our enemies. If we win, it should remain as a severe voice of obligation that always reminds us of our pledges to the people." [27] However, as long as success smiled on Reyism and as long as the paper remained a weekly, its circulation was small and its influence insignificant. On June 15 the Center issued a manifesto in which the concepts of *The Presidential Succession in 1910* were summarized. Three days later Francisco Madero began his political tour of the southeastern section of the nation.

[27] Madero to E. Vázquez, Aug. 2, 1907, AdeM. Madero advocated that the tone of the paper be bold but that the boldness be tempered by prudence. He disapproved of general attacks on the Científicos, preferring as a target Vice-President Corral. He also opposed articles critical of Limantour. He undoubtedly was influenced not only by his admitted sympathy for Limantour, but also by his hope to use that connection to moderate the official persecution of his party. Madero to Palavicini, July 30, Aug. 16, and Sept. 7 and 9, 1909, CdeFFP.

VI. Apostle of Democracy

ON JUNE 18, 1909, Madero, accompanied by his wife, who feared for his safety, and Félix Palavicini took the Mexican Railway's daily train from Mexico City to Veracruz. Madero planned to develop the themes of his book, particularly Anti-Reelectionism as a means of combating absolutism, during the trip. In Orizaba they were greeted by some supporters, but at Veracruz they really received an enthusiastic welcome. Two thousand persons gathered to greet them, and the local independent paper exultantly noted that "few times have we witnessed so spontaneous a demonstration." [1]

On Sunday morning, June 20, a meeting was held in the Dehesa Theater. Madero, little experienced in public speaking and lacking in oratorical gifts, proved a disappointment to his listeners. Some persons attending the gathering even doubted that the speaker could possibly be the author of *The Presidential Succession in 1910.* A bit shaken, but undismayed, the travelers installed an Anti-Reelectionist club in the port city and then sailed on a Ward liner for Progreso. Only six persons, including Pino Suárez, met them at the dock.

This was the first meeting of Madero and José María Pino Suárez. Pino Suárez, a well-known lawyer of the Yucatán area, had undertaken a vigorous independent campaign in his state in 1905. The movement had been quashed, forcing him to flee to Tabasco, but changed conditions and the revival of political activity prompted his return to Yucatán. He began to publish

[1] *El Dictamen,* June 19, 1909.

a newspaper, *El Peninsular,* in which he attacked the local government. Then Madero's book converted him into a partisan of the author. He became the head of the Anti-Reelectionist movement in the peninsula and engaged in organizing independents and installing clubs in Tabasco, Campeche, and Yucatán.

It was in the Yucatán peninsula that the travelers achieved their greatest success. In contrast to the cool reception in the port of Progreso the greeting by three thousand persons at Mérida, the capital of Yucatán, was almost deliriously enthusiastic. The local chief of police requested that Madero make no address to the crowd since that would constitute a meeting which had not been authorized. Madero agreed with the proviso that permission for a public meeting be granted. This was the only official interference encountered during the trip to Yucatán. The Anti-Reelectionist movement was not taken seriously in official quarters at this time.

Madero and Palavicini published an invitation to the people of Mérida to join the vanguard of fighters for national regeneration in the Anti-Reelectionist party. "Victory is assured and the prospect is bright of hailing liberty at the completion of the centenary of our independence." [2] Thousands attended the two-hour, open-air meeting under a tropical sun and listened attentively to the speakers. The following day the travelers visited Campeche. Once a populous city, Campeche now had scarcely nine thousand inhabitants. Unable to gather sufficient supporters to establish a club, the capital delegates called a meeting that evening in an amphitheater. Many curious persons attended, but the reception for the visitors was marked by distrust and slight applause.

After returning to Mérida, Madero received an invitation to visit a henequen plantation to see for himself that the workers were happy. On July 3 he and his companions left for Progreso where a well-attended meeting was held and a club installed before they sailed for Tampico. On the boat Madero, noting that the plantation owners had permitted him to see

[2] Palavicini, *Mi vida revolucionaria,* p. 37.

only what they wished, remarked to Palavicini that "if there is a social revolution in Mexico, it will begin in Yucatán." [3]

Because of the obstacles created by the authorities and the fears of their local friends the travelers could accomplish little in Tampico. They continued to Monterrey where they received a warm reception. In the northern city at the time was a group of speakers representing the Democratic party. On Sunday, July 11, there were two meetings held in Monterrey, one by the Democrats in the morning, the other by the Madero group in the afternoon. At the latter session Madero, after discussing the danger inherent in a prolongation of absolutism, launched a direct attack on the candidacy of Reyes. "General Reyes is not able to be a democratic ruler . . . The nation should understand that he would be more despotic than General Díaz has been." [4] Three thousand persons in the audience applauded. The success of this meeting brought Madero the greatest satisfaction he was to enjoy during his first trip.

The day following the Monterrey meeting he returned to Parras. Rallies were held there and in Torreón on the next two Sundays. The meeting in Torreón coincided with efforts by the Corralistas and the Reyists in the same community. An overflow crowd at the Herrera Theater listened receptively as Madero attacked Reyes but distinguished between the leader and his followers. "We ought to consider the Reyists as friends, granted that, sooner or later, they will be our supporters." [5] Early in August, when there was growing disillusionment among the supporters of the General due to his indecision, Madero issued a manifesto directed at Reyists of "good faith" urging them to join the Anti-Reelectionist movement.

He expected that Reyism would disappear or lose its force within a few months. Anticipating that official pressure then would be turned against the Anti-Reelectionists, Madero urged that efforts be intensified to win adherents and perfect organization before that eventuality materialized. With the

[3] *Ibid.*, pp. 40-41.
[4] Taracena, *Madero: Vida,* pp. 179-80.
[5] Madero, *El partido Nacional Antireeleccionista,* p. 46.

decline of Reyism the Anti-Reelectionist movement made considerably more headway, particularly in the north and west. This was not the only encouraging sign that summer. Madero could note with satisfaction the unfriendly reception accorded the Reelectionists in Guadalajara. "It proves that the public is awakening and is resolved that its rights be respected. The public is not so cowardly as its detractors have pretended."[6]

In view of these developments Madero and his associates agreed that it was imperative for *El Antireeleccionista* to become a daily paper. The project was stymied by a shortage of funds. Madero's political activity had imposed a considerable financial outlay. He had expended four thousand pesos since the beginning of the campaign, and was supporting a newspaper in Torreón in addition to *El Demócrata* in Parras. Francisco turned to his family for assistance.

He wrote his grandfather of his successful trip and observed that "the utopias of yesterday are the realities of today." Apparently he believed that his grandfather had moderated his opposition and that reported success and reiterated assurance that the group did not oppose General Díaz would win the support of the elder Madero. Francisco told of the financial crisis which his party was experiencing and boldly asked his grandfather for five or ten thousand pesos. Evaristo's reply was temperate, but he refused his grandson's request. "Although the business with which you occupy yourself is good and useful for the Fatherland, it is first necessary to attend to one's own affairs."[7]

Undismayed, Francisco suggested that Gustavo go to see their grandfather. "I believe you can get a thousand pesos from him for it is not the same by letter as by word." In the same letter Madero expressed the hope that his uncles would

[6] Madero to Palavicini, July 29, 1909, CdeFFP.

[7] Madero to his grandfather, July 20, 1909, and the latter's reply, July 22, 1909, AdeM. Two months later, Evaristo, concerned about reports of revolutionary activity along the border, warned his grandson: "If, unfortunately, you should support a riotous crowd, . . . I, with my more than seventy-eight years, will be the first in the defense of the government." Sept. 29, 1909, AdeM.

contribute something, "for the affair affects all of us." He observed to Gustavo that their sisters had bonds, some of which could be sold in order to raise funds. His zeal for the cause and its need made him ready to commit the funds of his sisters as unconcernedly as he contributed his own.[8]

Gustavo, a member of the board of the club in Monterrey and an enthusiastic supporter of his brother's movement, personally contributed a thousand pesos and raised an additional twenty-five hundred for the party's paper. The sisters Mercedes and Angela volunteered financial support for the newspaper. By September sufficient funds were available to publish *El Antireeleccionista* as a daily, and Félix Palavicini was named director.

During the summer of 1909, Madero, in addition to attending meetings and organizing clubs in his own and neighboring states, sought to attract the support of outstanding personalities. He corresponded with independents in different parts of the country optimistically reviewing the situation, encouraging their efforts, and urging their adhesion to the Anti-Reelectionist movement. In August his activities were limited by illness. Still his efforts were astonishing. Madero's faith and determination to work regardless of circumstances constituted one of his most significant characteristics. Suffering from hepatic colic complicated by a high fever, he was forced to remain in bed for almost a month. A projected political trip to the western states had to be postponed, and after the middle of September, Madero left instead for Tehuacán to complete his convalescence with the aid of the medicinal baths of that resort.

He stopped, en route, at the capital and conferred with associates about taking steps to obtain the release of several supporters who had been arrested. As Madero had anticipated, the decline of Reyism and the strengthening of the Anti-Reelectionist movement resulted in the focusing of persecution on his followers. Local clubs were harassed and attacked. In Puebla, Anti-Reelectionist leaders were arrested. Late in Sep-

[8] Madero to Gustavo Madero, July 26, 1909, AdeM.

tember, using an article on the forthcoming Díaz-Taft interview and the Magdalena Bay concession as justification, the government ordered *El Antireeleccionista* closed and its directors arrested.[9]

Madero spent five weeks recovering his health at Tehuacán. The intensified opposition of the authorities prompted him to write a letter to Limantour. He called attention to the pressures and persecution which had been directed against his friends, specifically enumerating the closing of *El Antireeleccionista,* the arrest of Serdán in Puebla, and the events in the Yucatán election (Pino Suárez and Delio Moreno Cantón had been forced to go into hiding). "This discredits the administration... [and] separates the government from the people still further. The democratic movement is... so vigorous... that it would be madness to try to suppress it by force." Madero warned of unspecified consequences if the reign of terror persisted.

He reminded the cabinet officer of the purposes of the movement, emphasizing the opposition to Corral as successor to Díaz, and held out the possibility of a compromise arrangement. Madero urged him to use his influence to stop the persecution or, at least, to guarantee safety to the victims. Limantour, in a laconic reply, promised to try to do something for the individuals for humane reasons. However, he noted that the matter was judicial, not administrative. Nevertheless, Serdán and several others were released.[10]

This exchange between Madero and Limantour prompted

[9] Madero felt that Palavicini had erred in permitting the publication of an unsigned article without knowing the identity of the author (Lic. Leonardo Ballesteros). He also disapproved of the innuendo that Díaz would act unpatriotically. Madero to Manuel Urquidi, Oct. 5, 1909, cited in Casasola, *Historia gráfica de la Revolución,* I, 116.

The Taft-Díaz interview was arranged in June-July, 1909, as a conspicuous demonstration of cordial relations. Díaz was pleased by the opportunity to create the impression that he enjoyed American support and to distract public attention from the political agitation.

[10] Madero to Limantour, Nov. 18, 1909, and the latter's reply, Nov. 25, 1909, AdeM.

Grandfather Evaristo to write Francisco a letter in which he commented with acerbity on his conduct.

You are mistaken when you believe that you are speaking for the nation . . . Worst of all is that while we work to lift the stick which he [General Díaz] has above your father, you . . . persist in increasing his difficulties . . . I hope that you will not again direct a similar letter to any of the ministers or to the President for it would resemble the rivalry of a microbe with an elephant.[11]

A week later Madero's father wrote Francisco that his mother was ill and that it was his "sacred obligation" not to aggravate her condition by adding to her anxieties. The father asked the son to separate himself from politics "for an extended time" and to return to San Pedro where he was needed. He plaintively added that "the principal condition which I imposed in giving farms to my children was that they be attended personally." [12]

For Francisco Madero there was no turning back. Many of his companions, shaken by the pressure of the authorities, had to be encouraged; their confidence had to be restored. Madero wrote to Manuel Urquidi in Mexico City that he should not be concerned about the seeming disorganization of the party. He informed Urquidi that panic existed only in the capital while in the states the Anti-Reelectionists continued at their posts. He predicted that, as soon as the current difficulties were straightened out, they would reorganize perfectly.[13]

This situation was the background for an incident in which Madero clearly evidenced his quality as a prudent and effective leader. José Vasconcelos wrote him that if they were not preparing a rebellion, he was resigning because "I do not wish

[11] Evaristo Madero to his grandson F. I. Madero, Nov. 22, 1909, AdeM.

[12] Francisco Madero to Madero, Nov. 29, 1909, AdeM. The ranking members of the family looked askance on any attack on Díaz or any challenge of Limantour. In Feb., 1910, Ernesto Madero y Hnos., wine manufacturers, published an advertisement emphasizing their abstention from political activity and eulogizing Gen. Díaz. Insert, CdeM, I, Biblioteca Nacional.

[13] Madero to Urquidi, Oct. 5 and Nov. 22, 1909, cited in Casasola, *Historia gráfica de la Revolución,* I, 116, 125.

to be a victim of a democratic movement directed against ruffians." [14] Forced to flee the police, the young intellectual and journalist was disheartened by popular indifference to these attacks and discouraged about the prospects of the Anti-Reelectionist movement.

Madero was not surprised by Vasconcelos's attitude because an earlier letter had indicated that the journalist was demoralized. Unsuccessful in his efforts to speak with Vasconcelos in Mexico City, Madero wrote to him from Tehuacán. The Anti-Reelectionist leader neither denied the possibility of revolution nor committed himself to it, but rather defended the prospects of Anti-Reelectionism. He assured Vasconcelos that their sacrifices would not be in vain. While satisfied with the progress to date, Madero predicted imposing results from his forthcoming trip and the projected national convention.

These prospects, Madero suggested, offered unusual opportunities for a man of courage and consistency. "I do not speak... to flatter your vanity, but rather to appeal to your patriotism." He noted that if Vasconcelos remained decided to resign, the party would regret the loss of so valuable a member but that Vasconcelos "would be losing more." Madero warned him that, before deciding to continue with the group, he must realize that the road would not be an easy one. "Humanity has made no conquest without great efforts... Although our struggle is essentially democratic, there will be victims." [15] Vasconcelos reconsidered his decision.

A meeting in the capital's Tívoli Theater attended by fifteen hundred persons on December 19 inaugurated Madero's second political trip—this time to the west and north—postponed because of illness from September. The traveling party, including Madero, his wife, his stenographer, Elías de los Ríos, and Roque Estrada, left on the day train for Querétaro. There, despite the absence of official opposition, only a very small crowd attended the Anti-Reelectionist meeting. After installing a club, Madero and his companions departed

[14] Vasconcelos, *Ulises criollo,* p. 325.
[15] Madero to Vasconcelos, Nov. 13, 1909, AdeM.

for Guadalajara, capital of Jalisco, where they arrived on December 25.

Close to five thousand cheering persons greeted the travelers. From the balcony of the Hotel Francés, Madero announced a meeting to be held in a tavern the following afternoon. When a local authority, in the name of the governor, refused permission for the meeting, Madero and Estrada addressed the crowd from the hotel balcony. There was a very favorable popular reaction to this demonstration of Madero's courage.

In Colima the authorities forced the Anti-Reelectionists to hold their meeting on the outskirts of town near a dry stream bed and sent mounted police to discourage attendance. Nevertheless, a thousand persons gathered to hear the speakers, and a club was installed. On the last day of December, Madero's party took ship at Manzanillo for Mazatlán, where they arrived on January 2, 1910. A commission headed by journalist Heriberto Frías greeted the travelers, and five hundred people applauded as they disembarked.

In Mazatlán, Madero found the Ferrelista leaders disillusioned, but the general public excited. The local compaign against Redo had stirred the people. Two thousand persons attended a meeting which was held without difficulty, but even this response did not dispel the skepticism of the local opposition leaders. Continuing the trip in Sinaloa, Madero and his companions visited Culiacán where an enthusiastic crowd met them. Madero and Estrada addressed a gathering in the patio of a house where a workers' mutual society held its sessions. Madero praised his listeners' tenacity in attending the meeting. "It shows that you desire to hear our words because you know that we come to preach democracy." He talked of the two principles, "Effective Suffrage and No Reelection," which "incarnate the most profound and ardent aspirations of the Mexican people."[16]

Manuel Bonilla, who became director of the local club, recorded his impressions of the meeting. His keen observations penetratingly revealed the reasons for Madero's growing ef-

[16] Madero's speech at Culiacán, Jan. 4, 1910, AdeV.

fectiveness. He noted that Madero's speech did not provoke as much admiration as that of Estrada "because he did not use dazzling phrases. However, on hearing him speak so much truth... with that accent of profound conviction and manifesting that serene and tranquil valor which was his own, it was clear that in that man was embodied the true apostle." [17]

When the travelers entered Sonora, domain of Corral, General Torres and Governor Izábal, the pressure of the government increased greatly. In Navajoa a local official created difficulties, but finally permitted a meeting to be held in the central plaza. There were a few Yaquis in the audience when Madero spoke emotionally of the barbaric treatment accorded the native races by the government. The speaker revealed the depth of his emotion as tears welled up in his eyes, and he communicated his feelings to the audience. Estrada criticized Madero for the incoherency of his ideas, but felt compelled to admire the simplicity of his language and the evident sincerity of his words. "The depth of that apostolic harangue was a tremendous sincerity illumined by deeply felt faith in a cause." [18]

In Alamos official opposition forced the Anti-Reelectionists to resort to holding a political meeting under the guise of a dance-concert. The travelers then proceeded to Guaymas by rail. There José María Maytorena led the group which greeted them at the station. The local authorities conceded the right to hold a meeting but raised objections to every location proposed. As the hour for the meeting approached a crowd gathered near the visitors' hotel despite the efforts of the police. Madero finally decided to hold the meeting on the public beach, but the authorities refused to permit it. Without hesitation Madero addressed the crowd from a coach. Estrada was startled to see a new Madero, one he had not been aware existed. In that tense situation, Madero was decisive and forceful, and his words seemed to come forth more easily, his concepts more lucidly.

[17] Bonilla, Memorias (ms), pp. 63-64, AdeV.
[18] Estrada, *La Revolución y . . . Madero*, p. 155.

Official opposition was even more intense in Hermosillo, the capital of Sonora. No respectable hotel dared to admit the travelers. No printer would prepare an announcement for the meeting which, when held, was disturbed by a noisy, government-inspired claque. A local supporter invited the Maderos to spend the night at his home because he did not consider it proper or prudent for them to remain in a hotel of the lowest class. Estrada marveled at the striking energy and character of Madero's wife in this unpleasant situation. Sara Pérez de Madero revealed herself "calm, proud, and anxious to share the dangers." [19]

Because of reports that an attempt on Madero's life would be made in Cananea, the travelers decided not to visit that town and left Mexico by way of Nogales. After traveling through Arizona and Texas, they reentered Mexico at Ciudad Juárez where Abraham González met them and accompanied them to the city of Chihuahua. A very successful meeting was held in a theater in this state capital. Madero's last stop in the state of Chihuahua was at Parral. There, enthusiasm was so great that the town's merchants declared the day of the meeting a holiday. Madero then returned to San Pedro after speaking to a gathering at Torreón.

By this time the Anti-Reelectionist press campaign had been intensified: *El Antireeleccionista* was being published again; *El Constitucional* had been established in the capital; and *México Nuevo* was openly supporting the cause. Many clubs had been organized, and the results of Madero's travels could be gauged by the increased political excitement and by the augmented strength and prestige of the Anti-Reelectionist party. The local clubs of that party, encouraged by the Center in the capital, were discussing candidates for the promised convention. Although a number of persons were mentioned for both the presidential and vice-presidential nominations, Madero was clearly the popular choice to head the ticket. Opinion appeared divided between Toribio Esquivel Obregón and Francisco Vázquez Gómez for the second place.

[19] *Ibid.*, p. 163.

The distinction of being the first to sponsor Madero's candidacy belonged to the Benito Juárez Anti-Reelectionist Club of Chihuahua. Abraham González, president of the club, indicated that he would appreciate an indication of Madero's preference for a running mate.[20] It was on Madero's suggestion that the Chihuahua Anti-Reelectionists announced their support of Vázquez Gómez for the vice-presidential nomination.

Dr. Vázquez Gómez, a distinguished medical man with a lively interest in education, had served as head physician for Porfirio Díaz. His only direct political activity had been his participation in the Reyist movement in 1909. Early in 1910, Madero visited the doctor to urge his affiliation with the Anti-Reelectionist movement. He suggested that a person having prestige and friendly relations with the government, such as the doctor had, might, at the right moment, serve as intermediary between the government and the opposition. While the remote possibility of a compromise after the convention was not discarded, Madero had cooled to the idea of an arrangement with the government and was influenced by other considerations in his sponsorship of the doctor's candidacy. Vázquez Gómez's reputation would add to the respectability of the movement and would tend to reduce suspicions that its ultimate goal was revolution. Lastly, Madero anticipated that the doctor's candidacy would tend to attract Reyists to the Anti-Reelectionist standard.

Madero was anxious to crystallize popular sentiment and to attract independent (especially Reyist) adherence before the convention. In March, 1910, he published a booklet, *El partido nacional Antireeleccionista y la próxima lucha electoral* (The National Anti-Reelectionist Party and the Next Electoral Struggle), in which he described the program, labors, tendencies, and goals of his party. Once again Madero disclosed his plan: to definitively establish democratic practices so that the people would then have the means to make their desires known as well as the medium for effective remedial action. While he emphasized that the Anti-Reelectionist party aimed to popu-

[20] A. González to Madero, Jan. 21, 1910, AdeM.

larize democratic techniques and to demonstrate the necessity of establishing the principles of effective suffrage and no reelection, Madero pledged that his party would not be satisfied with these political objectives. They are "only the means which the Anti-Reelectionist party wishes to employ for the realization of much more transcendental objectives."

Madero assured his readers that the party members wished "to work for the happiness of the people and the aggrandizement of the Fatherland." To achieve these elevated, though general, objectives, he specified that

> the law should be complied with and should protect all citizens; ... the government should be concerned with the improvement of the situation of the workers ...; and national lands, instead of passing into the hands of a few favorites of the government who do not exploit them properly or ... who dispose of them to foreign companies, should be divided among small proprietors. This would augment the well-being of many citizens as well as ... of the Republic ... The only way to make a people strong is to educate it and to elevate its material, intellectual, and moral level.[21]

While the social and economic objectives listed were lacking in detail and development, this folder constituted additional evidence that Madero's thinking was not exclusively political.

During the second half of March, with the opening of the convention less than a month away, Madero renewed his second political trip by journeying through the mining regions of Durango, Zacatecas, San Luis Potosí, and Guanajuato. He was accompanied by his wife, Estrada, and a stenographer. At the meeting in Durango, Madero, realizing the probability of his candidacy, considered it necessary and important that he outline his ideas on the future program of the government.

[21] Madero, *El partido Nacional Antireeleccionista*, p. 49. Madero's proposal regarding the agrarian question did not reveal an appreciation of the dimensions or urgency of the problem. It was not, however, merely a preconvention political maneuver. In the fall of 1909 he had written to Toribio Esquivel Obregón as follows: "I am very much in agreement that the division of property will contribute greatly to the development of agriculture and the national wealth. I believe more. I believe that the division of property will be one of the strongest bases of democracy." Taracena, *Madero: Vida*, pp. 203-6.

He indicated, among other things, his belief that all Mexicans were in agreement with the religious conciliation policy of General Díaz. The statement was greeted by hisses from the audience. It was obvious that his listeners disapproved of his position on the Reform Laws. However, the reaction was, in part, also due to the fact that because of a too rapid transition in Madero's speech, the audience incorrectly assumed that he was approving the existing political situation in its entirety.

Madero's ideas on the clerical question should not have surprised his supporters. In his book he had judged the frequently criticized policy of conciliation as "one of the most legitimate achievements of General Díaz." [22] Madero believed that the object of the Laws of the Reform had been to combat the Conservative party. He argued that, for all practical purposes, that party no longer existed, that liberal doctrines were generally accepted, and that no one was trying to use religious power in a political sense. Therefore, any further application of such laws constituted an attack on public liberties, the enjoyment of which Madero felt should be absolute. Although some of his premises are open to serious challenge in the light of known facts and later developments and although he misgauged popular reaction to the institutional role of the church, Madero's statement was forthright and consistent with the viewpoint expressed in his book.

The travelers were unable to do anything in Zacatecas because of the governor's opposition, but in Aguascalientes over four thousand persons greeted them at the station and almost twice that number attended a political meeting. In the states of San Luis Potosí and Guanajuato the Anti-Reelectionists encountered increased opposition from the authorities. In the capital of the former state Dr. Rafael Cepeda had been arrested for circulating cards inviting the public to greet the travelers at the railroad station. Although his release was obtained the next day, only five hundred persons attended the meeting held on the boulevard in front of the penitentiary. In León (Guanajuato), Madero and Estrada conferred with Esquivel

[22] Madero, *La sucesión presidencial*, pp. 80-81.

Obregón, who, considering the situation in the state unfavorable, was not disposed to aid the visitors. After many difficulties, Madero managed to hold a meeting in the Cock Plaza with about a thousand persons in attendance.

Madero and his companions arrived at the city of Guanajuato on April 2. An enthusiastic crowd awaited them at the station, and some three thousand persons attended the meeting there. The visit to Guanajuato marked the completion of the latter part of Madero's second trip. His political travels, intended to bring the gospel of democracy to the Mexican people, would be resumed after the Anti-Reelectionist convention.

VII. Candidate of the People

MADERO WAS ANXIOUS that the convocation for the convention be issued as early as possible in order to permit the press to discuss candidates and the local clubs to decide on them. Consistent with his democratic sentiment he was determined to avoid dictation of the nominees by the Anti-Reelectionist Center. He felt that the setting of the convention date would prove heartening, after a wave of persecutions, to the disillusioned and the disheartened. Public attention would be focused on the movement, making it more difficult for the government to try to prevent the holding of the convention. Accordingly, the call for the Anti-Reelectionist convention to be held April 15, 1910, was issued on the fifteenth of the preceding December.

When this call was issued Madero already had modified his thinking on a compromise and on opposition to Porfirio Díaz. The pointed evidence that the administration would not make concessions led him to conclude that "we will not compromise before the convention, nor do I believe that we will do so after it."[1] He wrote Vasconcelos that "we will not chose General Díaz, Corral or any of the members of the government as candidate."[2] Madero was convinced that the people wanted a true opposition party. He warned Emilio Vázquez, head of the Anti-Reelectionist Center, that they had to follow public

[1] Madero to Emilio Vázquez, Aug. 2, 1909, AdeM.
[2] Madero to J. Vasconcelos, Sept. 16, 1909, CdeFFP.

opinion or "others would take the banner... It is important that the people know... our intentions." [3]

Madero wished to form a bloc of all independent parties in order to give the convention as broad a base as possible. He worked energetically to win the cooperation of the Democratic party, its subsidiary, the Independent party of Jalisco, and the Nationalist Democratic party. The last named, a Reyist group, continued in the field as an independent organization after General Reyes's withdrawal. Friends of Madero within these groups—Alfredo Robles Domínguez in the Nationalist Democratic party and Juan Sánchez Azcona in the Democratic party—supported his efforts. All three organizations were invited to participate in the convention, but only the Nationalist Democratic party accepted.

Delegates to the convention began to arrive in Mexico City on April 13, though some delegates were detained in their home communities and some were arrested en route. When it became apparent that the convention would proceed as scheduled, the government decided to create legal obstacles to Madero's candidacy in a theatrical move timed for the opening of the opposition convention.

The administration resorted to an old technique, that of converting a civil action into a criminal proceeding. For some months the Científicos had been bringing economic and legal pressure to bear on the Maderos in connection with a property dispute in Coahuila. Early in April, with the civil suit pending in Parras, an accusation of robbery against Madero was entered in a Saltillo court under the same case. An arrest order was issued by the judge in Saltillo on April 14, the same day that the court in Parras decided the civil suit in Madero's favor. Madero, warned of the warrant for his arrest, hid in the house of Federico González Garza located near the convention site. Because of the incongruity of pressing a criminal suit after Madero had won the civil action and because the property was found to be in his father's name, the government cancelled

[3] Madero to E. Vázquez, Sept. 4, 1909, CdeFFP.

the warrant on April 15, the very day that the capital press carried the report of Madero's impending arrest.[4]

[4] In 1904, Francisco I. Madero purchased a ranch, Australia, in Coahuila in order to raise cattle. He soon discovered that the property contained a great quantity of guayule, a shrubby herb native to northern Mexico and southern Texas. The plant yields a type of rubber which occurs in solid particles in the form of a colloidal suspension in the cell sap. Madero and his father organized a corporation, Cía. Ganadera de la Merced, S.A., to exploit the property, though before entering politics Madero liquidated his holdings to obtain capital for his campaign, and Australia then became the exclusive property of his father.

Madero surveyed the property and obtained an approval of title from the district judge of Parras in March, 1905 (Madero to Agent of Minister of Fomento, May 26, 1906, AdeV). However, in the western section of the property his title overlapped with that of the Filipinos Co., owner of the neighboring property. Actually, by possession and prior deed he had every right to exploit the section.

This disputed section became the subject of extended legal controversy aimed at embarrassing the Maderos and bringing economic pressure to bear on them. When the Filipinos Co. cut a line indicating that their property included the disputed section (which produced guayule valued at not less than two hundred thousand pesos monthly), Francisco the elder had the family lawyer, Adrián Aguirre Benavides, bring civil suit in Parras. The Filipinos, counting on the aid of Corral, instituted criminal proceedings in Saltillo, charging Francisco I. Madero with stealing guayule from their property.

Governor Peña advised Lic. Aguirre, his nephew, that Corral had ordered him to push the case and recommended that Aguirre get young Madero to abandon politics. It was then that the elder Francisco wrote his son along those lines mentioning the mother's illness and the increased complication of the property litigation (Nov. 29, 1909, AdeM). On Feb. 4, 1910, the father asked Limantour to intervene in the matter. The Minister, while protesting his friendship, regretted his inability to intervene in court matters.

With the approach of the Anti-Reelectionist convention, the Corralistas decided to press matters. On April 13, 1910, they requested that the Saltillo court order the arrest of F. I. Madero. Félix Díaz, nephew of the President, was Inspector of Police in the Federal District. A friend of Gen. Reyes, he was an enemy of Corral. Félix Díaz not only warned Madero, but also refused to comply with the order of arrest on the technical grounds that it had been issued by the governor of Coahuila and not by the governor of the District. The delay permitted Madero to go into hiding. (Interview with Lic. Adrián Aguirre Benavides, Aug., 1947).

A few months later the American Ambassador, Henry Lane Wilson, mentioned this incident in a dispatch to the State Dept. The report provides an early gauge of the diplomat's accuracy. He reported, on the basis of an interview with Díaz, that the "indictment of the court in Coahuila was based on the fact that Madero forcibly entered the lands of an

That morning one hundred and twenty delegates attended the opening of the National Independent convention in the main salon of the Tívoli de Eliseo. At the first session the delegates named a directive board, agreed on rules of procedure, heard read a letter from Madero, in which he requested that all delegates who had instructions to vote for him proceed freely as their conscience and the situation dictated, and appointed a committee to formulate a general statement of program.

The committee met at the home of González Garza because of its nearness to the convention hall and because Madero was hiding there. With his assistence the committee drew up a statement of principles which included: reestablishment of the rule of the Constitution; reform of the Constitution establishing no reelection; passage of laws to better the conditions of the workers and to combat monopolies, alcoholism, and gambling; improvement of public education; promotion of irrigation and credit institutions to benefit agriculture, industry, and commerce; reform of the electoral law to achieve effective suffrage; revitalization of the power of the municipalities by abolishing the political prefectures; and encouragement of good relations with foreign countries, especially with Latin-American nations.

This program was presented and approved at the afternoon session after the delegates had discussed candidates and voted for a presidential nominee. Francisco Madero won the nomination by a wide margin over Fernando Iglesias Calderón and Toribio Esquivel Obregón. The last-named attended the convention, apparently motivated by personal ambition to receive a nomination. When his hopes were disappointed, he retired

---

American company [*sic*] . . . and aided by some of his servants stole something like 150,000 pesos of guayule." Wilson added that the President had told him that he had urged the interested parties to wait until after the election so that the controversy would not appear to be political. However, Madero's "political agitation [was] so bold and menacing to the welfare of the country, severe action was needed." (Wilson to Secretary of State, June 27, 1910, SDF, 812.00/332).

from active participation in the movement. Madero's victory was acclaimed by the delegates, and a commission was designated to offer him the candidacy.

At the morning session held the following day candidates for the vice-presidential nomination were discussed. Madero considered the choice of his running mate an urgent and vital matter. "I wish the convention ability in the designation of a candidate for the vice-presidency so that I may count on a loyal, active, and patriotic collaborator . . . who could substitute for me. Everything leads me to believe that I will lose my liberty very soon." [5]

That afternoon Dr. Francisco Vázquez Gómez won the second place on the ticket with a clear majority over three opponents. A delegate from Veracruz, Manuel Alonso, stated that he did not feel that the winning candidates met the demands of the people and that he was leaving the convention and the party. Gabriel Gavira hastened to assure the delegates that Alonso did not speak for the entire delegation from his state.[6]

Late in the afternoon of the sixteenth a very important event occurred. Through the efforts of Governor Teodoro Dehesa of Veracruz an interview was arranged between Madero and Porfirio Díaz. Since Dehesa merely introduced the principals and then withdrew, no direct third-person account was possible. However, from Madero's correspondence and from second-hand accounts of his associates and of other commentators, some of the details, Madero's purposes, and his impressions may be deduced.

[5] Madero to Pino Suárez, April 16, 1910, AdeM. He explained that he was hiding because "I do not want my arrest to cause an interruption of the work of the convention . . . As a candidate it seems to me indecorous to remain hidden longer than is strictly necessary to comply with so important an obligation. I never will commit the cowardice of fleeing to foreign soil to avoid the blows of my political adversaries."

[6] Gavira had lead a liberal element out of the local organization headed by Alonso. Both factions were represented at the convention. Gavira charged that Alonso, who was friendly toward Gov. Dehesa, had come to promote the nominations of Díaz and Dehesa. Gavira, *Su actuación*, pp. 13-17.

Dehesa, motivated by his opposition to the Científicos, arranged the interview because he was anxious to promote a compromise. He was aware of his own eligibility as a compromise choice and was not averse to the idea. Díaz received Madero at his residence for the interview which lasted almost an hour. Madero had agreed to the meeting with the intention of discovering if compromise was possible. Were Díaz to agree to some arrangement that assured democratic procedures and a constitutional regime, Madero was prepared to withdraw his candidacy. In any event, he hoped that the interview would clear the air and serve "to establish friendly and fruitful relations between both parties." [7]

Madero discussed with Díaz the general political situation, and, befitting his role as the head of an opposition party, refused to be intimidated by any contemptuous or authoritarian remarks made by the President. Díaz, underestimating his opponent, showed no inclination to modify his position. Madero was struck by the decrepitude of the dictator and his lack of information about the Anti-Reelectionist movement. The interview marked the second great change in his attitude. Madero hoped that he had impressed upon Díaz that there were persons who were not afraid to oppose him, since he no longer believed that a compromise solution was possible. Indeed, convinced that the Porfirian regime was determined to perpetuate itself by any and all means, he concluded that only by revolution would the people achieve political liberty. After returning to his place of refuge, he stated his changed attitude: "Porfirio is not an imposing chief. Nevertheless, it will be necessary to start a revolution to overthrow him. But who will crush it afterwards?" [8]

On April 17, Madero and Vázquez Gómez addressed the convention accepting their designations as candidates. Madero's speech was vibrant, impassioned, and stirring. He

[7] Madero to Pino Suárez, April 16, 1910, AdeM.

[8] Ferrer de M., *Vida . . . de Madero,* p. 68; Madero to Adrián Aguirre Benavides, April 20, 1910; Madero to Carolina V. de Madero, April 17, 1910, AdeM.

warned the administration that no attempt against the sovereignty of the people would be tolerated. "I will vigorously defend the right of the people . . . resolved now to make its sovereignty respected and anxious to be governed by the Law." [9] For the good of the nation Francisco Madero was ready to go wherever circumstances led him. The speech of the vice-presidential candidate was calm, and he emphasized the necessity for avoiding reprehensible means. "We ought to fight in the press, in the court, in the meeting, and in the polling places . . . Victors or conquered, we will have the satisfaction of not having done anything bad and of having met our obligations with nobility and dignity." [10] Although sharp differences on ultimate means were foreshadowed in these two speeches, the candidates seemed to complement each other. Before adjourning, the convention appointed a committee to prepare a public announcement of the results of their labors and designated an Executive Electoral Committee to prepare, organize, and direct the campaign throughout the nation.

The convention served as a clarion call. National enthusiasm increased and was channelized. A source of personal satisfaction for Madero was the changing attitude of his family. Angela wrote him that "you have the blessings of Mama and Papa and the prayers of your brothers and sisters." [11] She was accurately reporting the attitude of the parents. Madero's father, the litigation in Coahuila concluded favorably, became enthusiastic and proud after the convention. He wrote his son that "we are astonished by the success of the convention." However, he attributed the fact that they had not been molested to the influence of General Díaz who "truly wishes to see the awakening of the public spirit." [12] The father's naïve

[9] *Madero y su obra,* p. 18.

[10] Vázquez Gómez, *Memorias políticas,* pp. 35-38.

The candidates published a "Program of Government" late in April. The directness of style and the emphasis on education indicate that this was largely the work of the vice-presidential candidate.

[11] Angela Madero to Madero, April 14, 1910, AdeM.

[12] Francisco Madero to Madero, May 9, 1910, AdeM.

confidence in Díaz and certain counselors in high places persisted a few weeks longer.

The favorable popular reaction to the convention prompted an intensified campaign by the government-sponsored press. While the directors of the opposition party were anxious to take advantage of public excitement, the question arose of whether it was wise for the candidates to undertake a campaign trip in view of the threatening attitude of the administration. After a long and bitter discussion, a majority of the Electoral Committee agreed that Madero would campaign while Dr. Vázquez Gómez remained in the capital.

The committee arranged a demonstration in honor of the candidates on May 5. Seven thousand persons gathered at the Madero house on Berlín Street. Madero's itinerary was arranged to permit a second visit to Guadalajara, to be followed by a tour of the populous manufacturing regions in the states of Puebla, Tlaxcala, and Veracruz.

In Guadalajara ten thousand persons greeted the candidate with cheers and applause. On the fourteenth of May the traveling party of seven departed from the capital of Jalisco for Puebla. The tremendous reception there left the visitors with the impression that they were engaged in a triumphal march. Twenty-five thousand delirious supporters met the train, and an uninterrupted rain of flowers descended from the balconies overlooking the route they followed through the city. In response to popular demand, Madero spoke many times in Puebla. He remained there through the sixteenth. Enthusiasm also characterized the reception in Jalapa, where a meeting was held in the main plaza. But in Veracruz, in contrast, the reception was small and the response moderate.

Brief station stops were arranged at Atoyac, Córdoba, and Fortín. At the last-named, the "City of Flowers," the local club had decorated the station with gardenias. The train arrived in Orizaba at 10 A.M. on the twentieth of May. Twenty thousand Anti-Reelectionists roared a welcome for their candidate. From the balcony of the Hotel de France, Madero addressed a crowd of about fifteen thousand persons. In this speech he once again revealed his faith in political reforms, not to the neglect of other problems, but as a means to their solution. The significant passage, often reproduced incompletely to prove that Madero offered only political freedom, was the following:

> Increases of wages or decreases of working hours do not depend on the government. We do not offer such a thing because that is not what you want. You want liberty and your rights to be respected. You want to be permitted to form powerful associations so that, united, you will be able to defend your rights. You want freedom of thought so that those . . . who sympathize with your sufferings should be able to show you the road to happiness . . . You do not wish bread. You only want freedom because it will serve you to win bread.[13]

The response to the Anti-Reelectionists' efforts was gratifying, but the repercussions in the form of persecution were disturbing. After his return to the capital, Madero wrote Díaz a letter in which he complained that while his political rights had been respected, those of his followers were being violated. He advised the dictator that he had directed his supporters to work within the law and to limit their protests against violations of their rights to legal channels. However, he warned that if the persecution continued, he would not be able to restrain his followers. In that case the responsibility would rest solely with the authorities who provoked such reactions.[14]

If the government needed any added evidence of the rapid progress of the opposition movement, the demonstration organized by the independent press in Mexico City in honor of the candidates provided it. Beginning at eleven in the morning a compact column of partisans carrying the standards of clubs and newspapers paraded past cheering crowds in front of the

[13] Madero's speech at Orizaba, May 22, 1910, AdeV.

The candidate's father, in a letter dated May 23, 1910, noted with pleasure the success reported in his son's telegrams. He felt that the results proved that the people were desirous of a change due to the *oppression of local authorities!* "Would that General Díaz would be convinced of that." He rejoiced that the President had tolerated the meetings. "That is proof that he was sincere." AdeM.

[14] Madero to Díaz, May 26, 1910, AdeM.

National Palace and down the main avenues of the city. On Balderas Street over thirty thousand persons demonstrated in orderly fashion their support of the independent candidates.

Francisco Madero's political travels won for him the title of "Apostle of Democracy." With a messianic sense of mission he preached the new life of liberty and democracy. In an extensive country, handicapped by inadequate transportation facilities, a presidential candidate is unable to have widespread personal contact with the people. Given that limitation, however, no election campaign in Mexican history was more far-reaching and active than that of Madero, although he concentrated on major population centers. He visited twenty-two of the twenty-seven states and made major stops in eighteen in addition to the Federal District.

Madero's campaign was a dynamic effort requiring energy, decision, courage, and perseverance. His assets included these qualities and also: his family name and its association with persons known as practical and successful businessmen; personal funds to underwrite the costly effort; and an atmosphere characterized by desire for change prompted by conditions created by Madero's predecessors. Not imposing physically nor a polished orator, the opposition candidate, nevertheless, demonstrated personal valor through his conduct, and his words so evidenced his sincerity and good faith that they made a deep impression.

Madero provided, or seemed to provide, in himself a leader and a symbol for the people he had helped to awaken. His democratic crusade had the great virtue of preparing the Mexican people to follow at first him and then others in what became a social revolution. An observer, often critical of Madero, eulogized this phase of his career: "Madero the apostle is simply magnificent, enormous, indisputable and sublime. Guide of the popular conscience which he awakened from the lethargy of thirty years, he deserves gratitude." [15]

On the evening of June 3 some friends gathered in the National Railway Station to see Madero, his wife, his secretary,

[15] Magaña, *Emiliano Zapata*, II, 318.

and Roque Estrada depart on the fourth and last campaign trip. In the car behind Madero's pullman on the northbound train was Juan R. Orcí, a henchman of Corral, who was assigned to follow the travelers.

The candidate was greeted with enthusiasm in each station where the train stopped. At San Luis Potosí he addressed the crowd from the train. In Saltillo a thousand persons cheered Madero at the station, and it seemed as if they were joined by all the rest of the city's population on the trip to the Hotel Coahuila. Here, Madero decided to address the crowd from the hotel terrace, but a police inspector ordered him to desist. A violent argument ensued while mounted police restrained the crowd. A note of comedy was interjected into the charged atmosphere when Madero and Estrada alternated with one another in delivering speeches and engaging the police official in argument.

The travelers arrived in Monterrey on the fifteenth of June. Despite the efforts of the authorities, the reception for Madero and his party was impressive. The police used threats and rough tactics to keep supporters from gathering along the route followed by Madero's car from the station to his father's home. About fifteen hundred, of an estimated ten thousand, managed to break through the police blockade and to gather near the house. They heard Madero sharply attack the conduct of the police. Estrada also spoke critically of the situation although ordered by a police official not to continue.

About 8:30 the following evening when Madero and Estrada entered an automobile which was to take them to the station, a group of men in civilian clothes stopped the car and demanded that Estrada be surrendered. Madero, refusing to submit to men without uniforms, argued with them while his companion escaped back into the house. The candidate proceeded to the station where he boarded a train for Ciudad Victoria. The train was delayed while officers searched for Estrada. When the search proved unsuccessful, Madero was detained for protecting a fugitive.

Sara Madero insisted on accompanying her husband to the

state penitentiary. The following morning Estrada surrendered to the authorities, expecting thus to obtain the release of the opposition leader. However, the "aiding a fugitive" charge against Madero was only a pretext. That morning he was accused of fomenting a rebellion and insulting authorities, including the President, in San Luis Potosí and in Monterrey. Estrada was charged with sedition and insulting authorities in both cities. Juan Orcí appeared as the principal witness to the crimes allegedly committed in San Luis Potosí.

American Ambassador Henry Lane Wilson reported to the State Department that Madero "has never, so far as I have been able to ascertain, sought to incite the people to armed uprising. I have been reliably informed that Madero's arrest was directly inspired by the central government." [16] Consul General Philip Hanna in Monterrey noted that "many people believe that the only offense Mr. Francisco Madero ever committed was that of being a candidate for office. His arrest has caused considerable excitement throughout this part of the country." [17] The arrest of Madero was a political blunder, inopportune and stupid. He became the object of sympathy and enjoyed even greater popularity. Madero had expected some action against him by the authorities, and he regarded his imprisonment and the reaction it precipitated with satisfaction.

Madero's family responded nobly, demonstrating their loyalty. The Electoral Committee of the Independent Parties published a "solemn protest before the Nation and the civilized world." Dr. Vázquez Gómez published a manifesto protesting against the "violent and unexpected imprisonment" of his fellow candidate.[18] Other groups and individuals joined the chorus of protest. Madero himself, capitalizing on the situation, issued a broadside directed to the Mexican people in which he explained in detail the circumstances of his arrest. He charged that his imprisonment and that of his partisans in various parts

[16] June 9, 1910, SDF, 812.00/323.
[17] June 8, 1910, SDF, 812.00/322.
[18] *El Constitucional*, June 11, 1910.

of the republic were intended to intimidate the independent voters and urged the people to exercise their constitutional rights.

The following day, June 15, Madero published an open letter to Porfirio Díaz. He charged that while his followers had observed the law, the supporters of Díaz in public posts had violated it. The evidence confirmed the public belief that "you are the one responsible for the acts of your followers." The opposition leader asserted that the nation "is tired of *continuismo* and demands that it be governed constitutionally and not . . . 'paternally' as you say that you are trying to govern it." He warned that if Díaz and Corral insisted on reelection in violation of the national will and that, as a result, the peace was broken, "you [Díaz] will be the only one responsible before the Nation, before the civilized world and before History."[19]

Madero was merely the outstanding victim of governmental persecution. Several members of the Electoral Committee were arrested. Because of members in jail and in hiding and because of defections, only eight of the original fifteen-man committee were still active on election day (June 21). The directors of a women's club, Daughters of Cuauhtémoc, were arrested for protesting Madero's arrest and the closing of the independent press. The opposition newspapers had been suppressed a week before the primary elections. Throughout the country, especially in the states of Puebla, Veracruz, San Luis Potosí, Coahuila, Sonora, Sinaloa, and Jalisco, many members of the Anti-Reelectionist party were imprisoned. At least five thousand of Madero's supporters were in jail on election day.[20]

In this oppressive environment the first sparks of violence occurred. Though some of the incidents were local in origin, all reflected the general unrest. On June 4 a group of fifteen hundred rose in rebellion against the state government of Yucatán and seized the town of Valladolid. The federal government mobilized troops who recaptured the plaza after bloody

[19] Madero to Díaz, June 15, 1910, AdeV.

[20] Taracena estimated that there were 60,000 prisoners at the time of the secondary elections in July. *Mi vida en . . . la Revolución*, p. 92.

fighting in which the rebels were annihilated. Some of the leaders were captured and, after a summary trial, executed. In Sinaloa, Gabriel Leyva rebelled against the government on June 8. An active Ferrelista and a local Anti-Reelectionist leader, Leyva was persecuted until he felt compelled to fight back. Wounded and captured in an encounter with federal troops, he was brought back to Culiacán where the authorities applied the *ley fuga.* There were several other outbreaks in June, 1910. Among them was that led by "Santanón" (Santa Ana Rodríguez), who unfurled in Veracruz the banner of the Liberal party, then plotting its third assault on the regime.

During Madero's imprisonment serious difficulties developed between him and the Vázquez Gómez brothers. On June 15, Dr. Vázquez Gómez wrote Madero to advise him that an official of the National Porforista Circle had visited him to propose a compromise arrangement involving Díaz and Teodoro Dehesa. The doctor liked the anti-Científico aspect of the proposal and the possibility of avoiding a revolution, which, he wrote, "we ought to avoid at all costs." He recommended that Madero accept the compromise.[21]

Madero did not reject the idea of compromise completely, but indicated that the only possible arrangement would be for a member of their party, preferably the doctor, to be chosen for vice-president. He probably was catering to the known antirevolutionary sentiments of his colleague. Madero's reply gave new proof of the sense of dignity which characterized his conduct. "It seems to me unbecoming and undesirable to enter into arrangements while I am a prisoner." [22]

On June 21 the primary elections were held. That evening Madero and Estrada, since the alleged offenses were regarded as continuous, were transferred to the prison in San Luis Potosí where the "crimes" had been initiated. The day following the primary elections the National Porfirista Circle openly announced its support of the Díaz-Dehesa formula. This move undoubtedly was intended as a new balance against the Cien-

[21] Vázquez Gómez, *Memorias políticas*, pp. 48-50.
[22] *Ibid.*, pp. 50-51.

tíficos. It also was aimed at dividing the opposition. The fading Democratic party accepted the Díaz-Dehesa formula. Dr. Vázquez Gómez believed that if Dehesa should triumph, the opposition ought to accept the situation.

Madero, on the other hand, was discussing plans for armed rebellion with his associates, particularly with his brother Gustavo and with Dr. Rafael Cepeda. Projects for rebellion were planned and discarded. After the secondary elections, on July 8, had reaffirmed the triumph of the Reelectionists, Madero planned an uprising for the fourteenth of that month. However, the lack of organization, deficiencies in the needed elements, and the fact that the recognized leader was in prison confronted the plotters as insuperable obstacles. This plan too was discarded.

Madero's friends and family labored assiduously to secure his release. Early in July, Minister Limantour passed through San Luis Potosí on his way to Europe. Francisco the elder conferred with him at the station on behalf of the prisoners. Limantour advised Madero's father that the prisoners should request their release on bail and implied that the petition would be favorably received. On July 19, under bailbonds provided by Dr. Cepeda, Madero and Estrada were granted conditional releases requiring them to maintain residence in the city.[23]

Partisans visited Madero to confer and to receive instructions on future procedures and plans. While Madero was discussing plans for protesting the election, for escape, and for revolution, the differences with the Vázquez Gómez brothers continued to grow. Emilio used the Anti-Reelectionist organ *El Constitucional* to praise the proposed Díaz-Dehesa formula. Madero immediately published a statement to the effect that Emilio's opinion was a personal one which did not represent the position of the party or its candidate.

[23] Msgr. Ignacio Montes de Oca, Bishop of San Luis Potosí, undoubtedly deserved credit, together with Limantour, for effecting Madero's release. The prelate made a special trip to Mexico City where he conferred with Sra. Carmen de Díaz and the Papal Legate Ridolfi.

He explained that before the election he would have considered a compromise arrangement, subject to approval by a new Anti-Reelectionist party convention. "Now the situation is changed. The people have been cheated." Charging that the election of the president was as illegal as that of the vice-president, Madero declared that neither could be accepted. "Our conduct is not in doubt. We ought to prefer a complete defeat to an arrangement which would involve a betrayal of the people." [24]

Dr. Vázquez Gómez did not believe that the party should assume a position which might prevent a pacific settlement. He was opposed to having recourse to other means than those conceded by law. "If our campaign began inside the law, so it ought to end next month in order to give proof of our capacity as a party of government." [25] Emilio Vázquez echoed his brother expressing his opposition to Madero's idea of revolution. "It would be a useless, sterile sacrifice." [26]

The last legal avenue which was open to the Anti-Reelectionists consisted of protesting the election before the federal Congress and seeking its nullity. The Electoral Committee instructed the party's local units to assemble evidence on election irregularities.[27] On the basis of the data submitted, the committee prepared a memorial petitioning the Chamber of Deputies to declare the elections, held in June and July, legally invalid. Madero not only approved this action but also insisted that the petition apply to all elections including that

[24] *El Diario del Hogar,* Aug. 15, 1910.

[25] F. Vázquez Gómez to Madero, Aug. 24, 1910, AdeM.

[26] Emilio Vázquez to Madero, Sept. 26, 1910, AdeM.

[27] Although many electoral frauds were committed, with the noteworthy exception of the capital, Ambassador Wilson reported that "the Mexican electorate have been given a fair chance to express their opinion." The diplomat blamed the "reprehensible" campaign methods of the opposition for the arrests. Contradicting his earlier dispatch, he wrote that "for more than two years [Madero] has been arraigning the government by a series of abusive pamphlets and by making seditious speeches." The explanation of this reversal perhaps is to be found in Mr. Wilson's report that "all important interests" will cooperate with the government in its "peaceful, prudent and progressive policy." June 27, 1910, SDF, 812.00/332.

of the president. On September 1 the petition, exceeding six hundred sheets and consisting of one hundred and ninety documents, was filed. The material was turned over to the Great Commission of the Chamber for study and decision. Supplementary petitions were submitted on September 8 and 23.

The outcome already had been foreshadowed by September 23. A public demonstration in the capital in support of the petitions was broken up by the police. On the sixteenth of September, General Díaz addressed the Congress and brazenly declared that the elections had been held with "regularity" all over the country. Eight days later the Chamber of Deputies, assembled as the Electoral College, approved the decision of the Great Commission in rejecting the memorials requesting that the elections be set aside. On October 4, Díaz and Corral were declared to have been reelected. The cynicism of the administration was demonstrated further when the Chamber rejected the credentials of the only Anti-Reelectionist deputy declared victorious by a local election board. When these Congressional decisions were announced, Aquiles Serdán, opposition leader in Puebla, was reported to have exclaimed: "Do not intone the hosanna of victory, Señores Porforistas and Corralistas, for we Anti-Reelectionists have not yet fired the last cartridge." [28]

The month of September was set aside as a holiday to celebrate the centenary of the nation's independence. The distinguished guests, the flood of oratory, the flow of champagne, and the glow of electric lights brightened the façade of the Porfirian regime and detracted attention from the holocaust which was developing in the shadows. Despite increasing pressure on his family intended to weaken and discourage the opposition movement and its leader, Madero decided against any movement during the national holiday.

However, a plan for his escape, the necessary prelude to the revolution, went forward. Details were worked out with Dr. Cepeda who made the necessary arrangements. As part of the

[28] Amaya, *Madero y . . . revolucionarios*, p. 82.

preparations for his flight, Madero took almost daily walks into the outskirts of the city. On these hikes he gradually walked further and nearer to the railroad line, and the hour of his return became progressively later. When rumors from Mexico City indicated that orders for his rearrest had been issued, the plan was placed in operation.

Madero spent the night of October 5 in the quarters of his manservant, Julio Peña. The next day Madero appeared disguised as a railroad mechanic in an outfit of pepper-and-salt cloth, with a red handkerchief around his neck and covering his beard and a broad-brimmed straw sombrero on his head. He and Peña set out at dawn for the railroad station of Peñasco, thirteen kilometers north of San Luis Potosí. By 8 A.M. the agent on a northbound train had hidden them in the baggage car.

At Monterrey the fugitives transferred to a third-class coach. Safely at the border, Madero crossed the international bridge to Laredo early on October 7. He was delighted by his successful escape and by the surprise of his friends who accidentally met him at the railroad station in San Antonio. To a journalist's suggestion that he had been "released," Madero quickly replied, "Oh, but I was not released. I escaped; I escaped." [29]

[29] San Antonio *Express,* Oct. 8, 1910. Estrada and Dr. Cepeda escaped by the same route.

VIII. Revolution

AFTER A BRIEF RESIDENCE in the home of a sympathizer, attorney Ernesto Fernández Arteaga, Madero moved for security and convenience to the Hutchins, a small hotel frequented by his family. Prior to the outbreak of the revolution he and his followers in exile enjoyed relative freedom in the city. Madero was received enthusiastically by the Mexicans living along the border, and his presence was expected to provide a stimulus to antigovernmental activity in the area. The newspapers published by Mexican exiles devoted considerable space to "the candidate of the Mexican people for the presidency of the Republic."

On all sides Madero's flight was interpreted, logically, as the first step toward revolution. For the protection of those who remained in Mexico and to avoid an open challenge to the neutrality laws of the United States, Madero hastened to deny any intention of organizing a revolution. Peaceful propaganda, on the other hand, he considered "within the requirements of right and justice." His pronouncements reveal his saturation with the ideas of political democracy, which provides at least a partial explanation for the popular sympathy and support which his movement was to attract in the United States. "I am here because citizens of the United States are free and their liberties are guaranteed by the Constitution and maintained unmolested. In Mexico it is different." He charged that Mexico, though a republic, was free in name only, since "everything is subservient to the will of President Díaz." Nevertheless,

Madero declared that he was not seeking aid, but only the boon of hospitality.[1]

Despite these judicious public avowals, he was in reality preparing the financial, military, and ideological foundation of an armed rebellion. The Plan of San Luis Potosí was formulated to serve as the ideological banner of the revolution. In October, Madero commissioned Federico González Garza, Roque Estrada, Juan Sánchez Azcona, and Enrique Bordes Mangel to discuss and edit a rough draft of the Plan which he had prepared after his arrival in Texas. The commission made some additions and modifications, but preserved the style and intention of the author. Although the Plan was prepared and published in San Antonio, it was dated, for reasons of convenience, dignity, and neutrality, as in San Luis Potosí, the fifth of October, the last day Madero was in that city.

This revolutionary plan is presented in an unaffected but convincing manner. It is not weakened by repetitions or purely demagogic touches. The Plan of San Luis begins with a political analysis intended to justify the armed movement. "Peoples, in their constant effort to obtain liberty and justice, find themselves forced in certain historic moments to make the greatest sacrifices." Mexico, it was asserted, had reached one of those moments because a "tyranny oppresses us in such a manner that it has become intolerable." Peace is offered in exchange for that tyranny, but "it is a shameful peace . . . because it has force not right as a base and because its goal is to enrich a small group."

There followed a description of the most recent political events arising from the effort of Díaz to impose as his successor Ramón Corral. Madero related how the Anti-Reelectionist party was organized and how it proclaimed the principles of "Effective Suffrage and No Reelection" as "the only ones capable of saving the Republic from the imminent danger with which the prolongation of a dictatorship each day more onerous, more despotic and more immoral threatened it." He claimed that from the beginning of the campaign he knew

[1] San Antonio *Light and Gazette,* Oct. 8 and 10, 1910.

that General Díaz would not bow to the will of the nation, but that the electoral struggle was necessary to prove that the Mexican people had aptitude for democracy and desired liberty and that the present authorities were not responsive to those aspirations.

Having reviewed his party's efforts in the elections and the subsequent exhaustion of all legal recourses to protest the result, Madero declared that "this violent and illegal situation must not be permitted to continue." He announced that he was assuming the provisional presidency until "the people should choose its government according to law." Madero defended his action as meeting a patriotic obligation:

> If the people designated me as their candidate, it was not because they had the opportunity to discover in me the talents of a statesman. Rather they saw in me the vigor of a patriot who is determined, if necessary, to sacrifice himself in order to . . . aid the people to free themselves from the odious tyranny which oppresses them . . .
>
> It would be weakness on my part and a betrayal of those who have trusted me not to lead my fellow citizens who, from all parts of the nation, call on me to oblige General Díaz by arms to respect the national will.[2]

In addition to declaring the recent elections null, assuming the provisional presidency, and proclaiming the principle of "No Reelection," Madero pledged respect for all governmental obligations contracted prior to the revolution. The Provisional President was committed to convoke general elections as soon as the capital and more than half of the states were in hands of the revolutionary forces and to name provisional governors for each state occupied. These officials would hold state elections as soon as that was judged possible by the Provisional President. Regarding finances, Madero pledged scrupulous accountability of public funds employed. Additional monies were to be obtained through loans, voluntary or forced, but were only to be contracted with Mexican citizens or national in-

[2] González Garza, *La Revolución mexicana*, pp. 203-11.

stitutions with receipts issued for postrevolutionary restitution.

Madero, designating Sunday, November 20, for the start of the revolution, appealed to his fellow citizens to take up arms against the government of General Díaz. "Throw the usurpers from power, recover your rights as free men and remember that our ancestors left us a heritage of glory which we are not able to stain. Be as they were: invincible in war, magnanimous in victory."[3] This was the Plan under which Madero summoned the Mexican nation. Once more he revealed his preoccupation with political democracy. Once again he proclaimed the immediate, urgent goal of the overthrow of the administration. That his ideal, the panacea that would provide the machinery to meet all problems, was attainable must be seriously doubted. That the Plan did not correspond to the needs of Mexico in 1910 must be frankly admitted.

The twenty-five-hundred-word program contained but one paragraph on the agrarian problem—the critical question in the country, soon to become the pivotal issue of the revolution—and not a single word on the labor problem. Madero merely proposed the restitution of lands to proprietors who had been despoiled of their holdings through abuses of the Law of *Terrenos baldíos* (empty lands). Though this proposal was of a limited nature and did not plumb the depths of the problem, it does provide additional evidence that Madero's program was not purely political. Paragraph Three appeared as a ray of hope for those suffering from land hunger. It won for Madero the support of many agrarian groups. There was no pledge of expropriation and no commitment to divide the land. Some intentionally and consciously misinterpreted. Many others blindly, hopefully, subconsciously presumed a more extensive change than had been promised.

Francisco Madero did not create the revolution. The Mexican Revolution already had a foundation and would have

[3] Other clauses in the Plan provided: respect for foreigners and their interests; military rank for insurgent leaders; maintenance of discipline and punishment for sacking and killing prisoners; and respect for the rules of warfare contingent on reciprocal conduct by the forces of Díaz. *Ibid.*

erupted with or without a program. Indeed, its true and complete program evolved gradually, pragmatically. Madero helped to prepare public opinion and popular support for the movement; he provided the revolution with a banner to rally around and a leader to follow; and he became a symbol for the discontented. He came to symbolize the deep desire for a change—a social and economic, as well as a political, change. That he did not appreciate fully the depth, the breadth, and, most important, the urgency of the problem may be explained in part by the fact that the desire for fundamental changes was ill-defined, often unconscious.[4] Considering the difficulties that would have to be overcome and the developments which would have to transpire before the demands of the revolution became conscious, expressed, and defined, not to mention placed in a legal framework and applied, Madero's limitations as a revolutionary may be condoned.

One factor contributing to these difficulties was the dearth of intellectuals in the revolutionary camp. The vast majority of the recognized Mexican intellectuals in 1910 were committed to the established regime. Although Madero came to count on some young intellectuals, who matured as children of the revolution, this first phase of the Mexican social upheaval lacked, as did many of the phases which followed, intellectual leadership. This circumstance, combined with the hesitation of certain outstanding personalities—the Vázquez Gómez brothers and Venustiano Carranza, for example—forced Madero to lean heavily on his family.

The revolutionary leader, ever the dutiful son, found that he needed the financial and personal assistance of his parents, his brothers and sisters, his uncles and cousins. These, in turn, for reasons of personal interest and patriotism and because Francisco was a Madero, interested themselves actively in the undertaking. The whole family was suspect in the eyes of the government, and measures were instituted to break the financial power of the Maderos. In October many members of the family joined Francisco in San Antonio. His father explained

[4] Tannenbaum, *Struggle for Peace and Bread*, p. 51.

thus to reporters the official pressure on the family: "I am not a politician and have never mixed in politics. If my family is persecuted it is because my son . . . so stirred up the common people of Mexico that they are demanding their rights." [5]

The outstanding instance of official action against the family was the arrest of Gustavo. General Meliton Hurtado declared that Francisco's brother had sought to induce him and other military leaders to revolt. Together with two other persons, known friends of Madero, Gustavo was arrested and placed in Belem. Francisco felt certain that the move was intended to hinder his own efforts and doubted that any harm would come to his brother. Under no circumstance would he hesitate to carry out his plans. "My obligation is to consider the interests of the Fatherland higher than the interests of family and higher than my affections." [6]

A fortuitous group of influences resulted in Gustavo's release. Since he was interested in a number of companies in which the majority of the stockholders were French, the government of France protested his arrest. The protest proved effective because at that time Limantour was in Paris seeking a loan on behalf of his country. General Hurtado conveniently declared that his charges were the result of a mind distorted by an overdose of opiate taken to relieve paralytic pain. Gustavo Madero's substantial contribution to the Anti-Reelectionist campaign in time, money, and energy earned for him a leading role in the revolutionary movement. Two months before the armed rebellion began Gustavo raised considerable funds in Paris for the building of a railroad, and these monies he diverted to the cause. He was also the logical choice for financial agent of the revolution in the United States. Gustavo's strenuous efforts earned for him the nickname "Muscle of the Revolution."

Critics have acidly charged that Francisco Madero and his relatives treated even the most serious questions as "family matters." The circumstances of the early months of the rev-

[5] San Antonio *Light and Gazette,* Oct. 23, 1910.
[6] Madero to Dr. Vázquez Gómez, Oct. 17, 1910, AdeM.

olution, filial loyalty, and the very real contributions of the Maderos to the cause explain Francisco's great dependence on members of his family and their influence on him. He himself was concerned about this situation which eventually proved so deleterious for him and for the true course of the revolution.

One of the most bitter commentators on the influence of Madero's family was Dr. Francisco Vázquez Gómez. However, it was the delay of this individual and others in joining Madero which forced or permitted the leader to rely on his relatives. Writing from the Hutchins, Madero advised the doctor of his plan to initiate the armed struggle on November 20 and urged that he and his brother come to the United States. "You should decide to join us in the revolution in a determined manner. You would share, as is just, all the glory of this great national event." The leader warned that in any event Vázquez Gómez would have to share "the persecution in the unfortunate, and very remote, possibility of a defeat."[7] Madero planned to name the doctor Provisional Vice-President and Minister of Foreign Relations and to commission him to obtain recognition from the United States government.

Five days later the doctor answered Madero in a handwritten letter signed "Catón" and couched in very obscure language. He advised that neither he nor his brother would be able to make the trip. Madero wrote again insisting on the desirability of the doctor's joining him. However, he warned that, if Vázquez Gómez were to remain in Mexico City, it was "absolutely necessary that you should not make any statements in opposition [to the revolution], for that would harm you greatly." Despite this urgent request and admonition, the doctor replied that he was determined to remain in the capital, that he hoped his name would not figure in any plans Madero might have, and that, if something serious developed, he would make categorical statements of opposition to protect himself.[8]

The realization that they would suffer persecutions even

[7] *Ibid.*

[8] "Catón" to Madero, Oct. 22, 1910; Madero to "Catón," Oct. 30,

though not associated with the revolution prompted the Vázquez Gómez brothers to leave Mexico in November. Madero met them at the San Antonio railroad station the night of November 3. In a conference held shortly thereafter Madero outlined his plans for the military uprising. The doctor considered the planning deficient and the expectation that the federal army would join the revolution illusory. Having taken no part in this preparation, which he regarded as inadequate, Dr. Vázquez Gómez refused to enter the ranks of the revolution at that time. He proceeded to Washington to continue his medical studies. His brother, Emilio, maintained in San Antonio an existence apart from the revolutionary exiles. It was not until February 6, 1911, that the doctor joined the revolution, accepting the post of Confidential Agent in Washington.[9]

From San Antonio copies of the revolutionary plan were dispatched to Mexico. Some money, munitions, and supplies were sent into the country. Agents were dispatched to confer with local leaders some of whom were designated provisional governors or chiefs of the revolutionary forces in their respective areas. Madero was counting on uprisings by Serdán in Puebla, Cosío Robelo in the capital, Robles Domínguez in Guerrero, Ramón Rosales in Hidalgo, and Abraham González and José de la Luz Soto in Chihuahua. Madero himself planned to cross the Bravo on the night of November 19 to join his Uncle Catarino with "three hundred armed, mounted men" for an assault on Ciudad Porfirio Díaz (now Piedras Negras). Unjustifiably, he was confident that the federal army could be won over. He addressed a manifesto to the officers and men of the Mexican army inviting them to join the revolution. Madero declared that victory was inevitable, but that the

---

1910; and "Catón" to Madero, n.d.: all published in *La Prensa*, Sept. 22, 1935.

[9] Federico González Garza charged that the doctor again refused to be designated as successor to Madero when the latter was about to enter Mexican territory. Included in González Garza's valuable archive is the original document in which Madero named Abraham González as his successor, apparently in consequence of the doctor's second refusal.

rapidity with which it would be won depended upon the action of the government's forces. "Remember that the mission of the army is to defend institutions and not to be the unconscious support of the tyranny." [10] The leader was confident of a speedy triumph. If, as he anticipated, the federal army deserted Díaz, complete victory could be expected, Madero thought, within a month!

Day after day supporters of the cause and opponents of the Díaz regime arrived in San Antonio, conferred with Madero and received instructions to be followed upon their return to Mexico. The movements planned in the capital and in Puebla proved abortive. In Mexico City the government, provided with information, uncovered in mid-November the bold, but imprudent, purchases of arms by Francisco Cosío Robelo, Alfredo Robles Domínguez, and Abel Serratos. On the seventeenth of November the capital press announced that a plot against the government had been discovered and that almost all the conspirators were in the penitentiary.

Not only did the capital conspirators fall into the hands of the authorities, but the latter also captured correspondence outlining the movement and listing persons involved in various localities. In many communities, particularly Puebla, Tlaxcala, Michoacán, Guerrero, Hidalgo, and Veracruz, hundreds of suspects were arrested and transferred to the Federal District to answer sedition charges. Ambassador Wilson reported to the State Department that "the conspiracy appears to be widespread, but lacking in coherency and character and it will be easily suppressed by the government which is vigilant and well-informed." [11] These developments prompted the premature and tragic events which occurred in Puebla.

Aquiles Serdán, a shoemaker, had read Madero's book in 1909 and was attracted by the author's democratic ideas. He began to correspond with the rising political leader, and, at Madero's suggestion, organized the Anti-Reelectionist Club, Light and Progress, with a membership drawn largely from

[10] Taracena, *Madero: Vida,* pp. 342-45.
[11] Nov. 18, 1910, SDF, 812.00/388.

the textile workers. Continuously persecuted by the chief of police and the *jefe político,* Serdán spent the last three months of 1909 in prison. After participating in the campaign, he emigrated to the United States. A party to Madero's plans for armed rebellion, Serdán agreed to return to Puebla to instigate an uprising there. For this trip a disguise consisting of a black dress, wig, and heavy veil was procured. Before leaving, Aquiles, with ominous prescience, told Sra. Madero that "I am wearing the outfit for my widow." [12]

As the date for the rebellion approached, the conspirators still lacked adequate arms. Carmen Serdán, Aquiles's sister, went to San Antonio where she obtained twenty thousand pesos to be divided between the capital and the Puebla movements. His brother Máximo bought arms and munitions in Mexico City, and Aquiles armed over five hundred persons for the struggle against Puebla's garrison which he estimated at one thousand. Actually the city was so well garrisoned that the rebels had no chance for success. The whole plot had an aura of romanticism and unreality about it.

The Serdán house on Santa Clara Street was practically in the center of the city. In one of the three apartments in the house dwelled a colonel who was an unconditional supporter of the state government. The uprising was planned for November 20, but fear of discovery prompted a change in plans. Expecting an attack on his home on November 18, Serdán arranged for this to serve as the signal for those of his supporters with carbines to attack the barracks and those with pistols to seize the towers of the churches of Santa Clara and Santa Teresa. The house was to be defended by eleven men, including the Serdán brothers, and three women, Aquiles's sister, wife, and mother.

At seven o'clock on the morning of the eighteenth, Miguel Cabrera, chief of police, with a platoon of men, came to search the house. Aquiles shot the notorious police officer, and the uneven fight was under way. Within an hour the defenders were joined by five men and a boy. However,

[12] Estrada, *La Revolución y . . . Madero,* p. 333.

rurales joined the besiegers surrounding the house. Aquiles, thinking the other parts of his plan were in operation, continued the bitter struggle. He was deceived. The rest of Puebla was peaceful. The barracks were not attacked. The government forces, not rebels, occupied the strategic church towers. From roof and window the defenders maintained a glorious, fruitless defense. By midday all the male defenders had been killed, except Aquiles, who, with his sister, continued firing from the windows. The federals having occupied the roof, the fight was lost; his wife and mother persuaded him to give up the fight and to hide in a minute cellar where the arms were stored. Late that night Aquiles, his cramped hiding place revealed by a coughing spell, was shot by a guard left to watch the house. The battle on Santa Clara Street had cost the government one hundred and fifty-eight men.

The Serdán brothers and their followers had by their action given the Madero revolution its first martyrs. Madero, near the Bravo, heard, with tears in his eyes, of the tragedy in Puebla from Federico González Garza. Choked with emotion, he said, "It does not matter. They have shown us how to die." [13]

These premature debacles and the inadequate organization of the movement resulted in a very unimpressive showing around November 20. The rebellion was not simultaneous or general as promised. In many localities the prospective revolutionary leaders had been arrested. In other communities fear and uncertainty encouraged the cautious policy of awaiting news of the first revolutionary triumph. Nevertheless, the prediction of Guillermo de Landa y Escandón, governor of the Federal District, that the twentieth of November would "pass as calm as the preceding day" [14] proved to be merely the first of many official statements attempting to minimize the disturbance, particularly in the eyes of the United States.

The Federal District and Puebla, scenes of the earlier incidents, remained quiet on the day designated for the revo-

[13] Fernández Güell, *Episodios de la Revolución*, p. 51.

[14] Ortiz Rubio, "Medio Siglo," in Franco, *Tres años . . . del ejército*, p. 155.

lution. In Jalisco only a small, easily suppressed effort at Etzatlán broke the calm. Also suppressed were disorders in the states of Mexico and Guerrero. In half a dozen states armed movements began between the nineteenth and twenty-second of November. In Veracruz, Cándido Aguilar and Rosendo Garnica declared against the government in the outskirts of Paso del Macho, while in Río Blanco, Gabriel Gavira and Rafael Tapia led some workers in rebellion. The former were dispersed after a few skirmishes. The Río Blanco group dissolved at its first contact with the rurales. The Anti-Reelectionist club in Tlaxcala rose in rebellion and was easily suppressed. In San Luis Potosí the forces of Dr. Rafael Cepeda had to resort to guerrilla tactics. To the northwest José María Maytorena, in Nogales, Arizona, called for rebellion in Sonora, while in Sinaloa Juan Banderas and Ramón Iturbe led an unsuccessful assault on Culiacán. Defeated, the rebels retreated to the mountains of Sinaloa and Durango.

The most widespread disorders occurred in the northern states of Durango, Chihuahua, and Coahuila. Even in this region the early blows were sporadic and unsuccessful, but it was here that the revolution maintained the continuity which proved a powerful determinant in its ultimate success. On November 20, in the Laguna District of Durango and Coahuila, Jesús Agustín Castro, Orestes Pereyra, and some sixty rebels captured the community of Gómez Palacio. However, the triumph was shortlived, for when a federal force from Ciudad Lerdo attacked, the revolutionists were dislodged. That same day Guillermo Baca attacked Hidalgo del Parral in Chihuahua with four hundred men, but the defenders repelled them.

Chihuahua was the scene of a number of declarations against the government: Toribio Ortega with eighteen men in Cuchillo Parado near Ojinaga; José de la Luz Blanco near Temosáchic; Ceferino Pérez and Francisco Villa, under the orders of Castulo Herrera, in the vicinity of San Andrés; and Pascual Orozco, Jr. with twenty-five men in San Isidro. Aside from minor skirmishes and the fact that Orozco's men were besieging Ciudad Guerrero, it was a week before the first serious encounter occurred between the revolutionists and federal troops. On November 27, General Navarro, enjoying the advantage of a slight numerical superiority, defeated the forces of Pérez and Villa at El Fresno.

Although the rebellion in the north appeared better organized and the forces remained intact despite initial setbacks, the results were nonetheless discouraging. Psychologically, the most disturbing failure was that which involved Madero himself. The revolutionary leader planned to lead an assault on the border town of Ciudad Porfirio Díaz. Madero, with a small group, was to go to the border where his uncle Catarino Benavides was to meet them with a force expected to number three to four hundred men recruited in Coahuila. Roque González Garza was to be within the border town to coordinate an internal uprising with the external attack. Arms and ammunition were purchased in San Antonio and shipped to Eagle Pass for the operation.

On the eve of Madero's departure word was received of the discovery of the conspiracy in Mexico City. Despite this formidable blow, the revolutionary leader's optimism was hardly diminished. Accompanied by his brothers Julio and Raúl and two servants, Madero left San Antonio on the evening of November 18. The following day a report from Carrizo Springs, Texas, told of a party of Mexicans who had purchased horses. The night of the nineteenth was dark and intensely cold. The small party lost their way and wandered for hours in the semidesert area. Finally, at one o'clock in the morning, near El Indio ranch, about forty-five miles from Eagle Pass, the wanderers encountered five colleagues led by Rafael Aguilar, who had come from Eagle Pass where they had been arranging for the expedition. They proceeded together to the northern bank of the Bravo River where they arrived at 8 A.M. on the twentieth of November.

They established a camp facing one of the islets which dot the river at the point appropriately designated Las Islas (The Islands). Of the promised contingent from Coahuila there was no sign. Absolute calm reigned on the Mexican side of the border stream. The only movement across the river that the anxious observers could discern was that of a few oxen which from time to time went down to the water to satisfy their thirst. A smoke signal was built, but there was no response. Fatigued by the ordeal of the preceding night, Madero slept briefly. One of the company set forth to seek food, for none had eaten since the previous night. Finally, at four-thirty in the afternoon, Uncle Catarino arrived accompanied by ten mounted men. Four were armed with carbines, the rest only carried pistols, and all were short of ammunition. It was agreed that the expedition would be foolhardy, and the group decided to disperse.

In San Antonio, unaware of the fiasco on the banks of the Bravo, Francisco's father was interviewed at the Hutchins. With the leader's mother standing at the top of the stairs weeping, the elder Madero spoke of his son's plans. "If my son has crossed the border, Mexico is in the throes of a real revolution . . . When my son departed, he told me that he was going to change the government of Mexico or die in the attempt." The father's concept of the revolution was clearly evidenced in his emphasizing that people of "quality" were supporting the movement. He declared that "twenty-six Mexican senators . . . are waiting for my son to cross the border . . . This is no small revolt, but a revolution in which the monied interests of Mexico are taking an active part." After repeating that millionaires were supporting the undertaking, he concluded that "today my son is fighting the battle of the exile and the forgotten man." [15]

At the moment Francisco was in hiding at El Indio. There he learned of the tragedy at Puebla and of the dearth of favorable news. For over two hours Madero and a few associates nervously discussed the situation. All evidence pointed to the fact that what had been intended as a revolution had become a disorganized, unsuccessful series of disorders with the semblance of a political riot. It was agreed to go to Eagle

[15] San Antonio *Light and Gazette,* Nov. 20, 1910.

Pass to await further developments. After two days of futile waiting, Madero, greatly discouraged, decided to abandon the projected entry into Mexico and to return to San Antonio.

Certainly the reports of the first week were hardly calculated to raise the spirits of the rebels. After an initial burst of enthusiasm and glowing reports, the San Antonio press, with startling suddenness, went to the opposite extreme, publishing the most discouraging reports. With some reason the Díaz government issued optimistic communiques. The Secretary of Foreign Affairs, Enrique Creel, wired Ambassador to the United States de la Barra that complete order reigned in the republic except in the district of Guerrero in the state of Chihuahua, and Ambassador de la Barra assured Secretary Knox that President Díaz would quash the revolt in three days.

Observers, accustomed to the forceful effectiveness of Díaz, awaited the vigorous elimination of the rebels. The government ordered the Madero lands and goods confiscated. The bishops of Linares and Sonora warned the people against the disturbers of order and counseled respect and obedience to constituted authority. Lord Cowdray, favored English oil promoter, told the London *Times* representative that "this affair will be forgotten within a month." [16] Henry Lane Wilson, the American Ambassador, reported that the movement had failed, but warned that the uprising, "while apparently unorganized and without responsible leadership, was ramified throughout the republic and was remarkable for its intensity and bitterness showing the deep-seated antipathy and antagonism to the government." [17]

However, to Madero and his family it seemed that the people had not responded. The early defeats depressed Madero, and the enthusiasm of his family abated considerably. Indeed, the family decided to accept the defeat as final and urged Francisco to flee to Europe. Madero, discouraged and surrounded by relatives on whom he was increasingly depen-

[16] Beals, *Porfirio Díaz,* p. 423.
[17] Nov. 26, 1910, SDF, 812.00/517.

dent as his own resources dwindled, wavered in his determination to continue the struggle.

Roque Estrada pointed up these factors when he related the nature of two meetings he had with Madero in the house occupied by Alfonso Madero in San Antonio. Francisco and members of his family were eating at the time of the first meeting. The atmosphere was one of gloom, and the conversation directed to Madero centered on the failure and the necessity of leaving for Europe. Francisco, desperately looking for an alternative, asked Estrada for his opinion. The reply that it was still too early to judge what was happening and that the spark had been lighted in Chihuahua was exactly the support Madero anxiously desired. However, Estrada noted that Madero alone received this encouraging opinion with satisfaction.

The following day Madero, again dispirited, confided to Estrada that he had exhausted his financial resources. He told his follower that "the revolution has failed. The people accepts resignedly or servilely the government of General Díaz." [18] Once again Estrada insisted that the revolution had not failed and that the spark was burning in Chihuahua. After this second interview, Estrada concluded that Madero's family, controlling the finances and possessing influence over the leader, had decided that the insurrection should be halted.

When Madero distributed twenty dollars to each of his officers to enable them to live while looking for work, it seemed that he had agreed to end the rebellion. However, there are indications that his submission was even then not so complete. Madero indicated to Rafael Aguilar that he "was thinking of going to Havana in order to enter Mexico at the first opportunity if some serious movement occurred" [19] in Veracruz along the Gulf coast. He instructed Aguilar to keep in touch with his wife in case he might be needed. The illusory hopes that significant outbreaks would occur along the Gulf coast, the need for greater security from probable perse-

[18] Estrada, *La Revolución y . . . Madero,* p. 350.
[19] Aguilar, *Madero sin máscara,* p. 24.

cutions by American authorities, and the pressure of family counsellors prompted Madero's secret trip to New Orleans. His actions and correspondence while there do not support the charge that he was preparing to flee and that only the improving situation prompted his return to Texas.

Accompanied by his brother Raúl and by Roque González Garza, Madero traveled incognito to New Orleans. The trio remained in the Gulf port during most of the month of December. The difficult economic straits in which they found themselves may be judged by the fact that Madero found it necessary to darn his own socks and to repair his own shoes. The expedition to the coast of Veracruz did not materialize, but the leader refused to accept defeat. In this connection Raúl Madero told of an incident that revealed the single-mindedness of Francisco. The two brothers took a walk down St. Charles Street to the park. While Raúl sat smoking cigarette after cigarette, Francisco, full of nervous energy, walked around the park. Suddenly he stopped in front of his brother and announced blandly, "I have decided on my cabinet!"[20] Raúl, in reply, could only make appropriate explanations about the desperateness of their situation.

Francisco Madero's correspondence from New Orleans reveals his devotion to the cause and his determination to continue the struggle. He grasped at any rumor favorable to the cause.[21] He wrote Estrada his agreement that the revolution would triumph and granted permission for Estrada to enter Mexico when he deemed it appropriate to do so. To Venustiano Carranza, who was delaying taking an active part in the armed rebellion, Madero wrote several letters urging him to join the movement.[22] Despite the advice of his companions to

[20] Gen. Raúl Madero told the author that in New Orleans his brother conceded that he should be careful during the first phase of the upheaval because "the revolution without a visible head is lost." However, he expected to lose his life afterwards no matter what "because the fruitful revolution must be bathed with blood."

[21] F. (Madero) to Sr. J. MacCarthy (González Garza), Dec. 26, 1910, AdeGG.

[22] The whole history of the relations between Madero and Carranza

formulate sensible plans, Francisco Madero spoke repeatedly of his determination to enter Mexican territory with or without an army.

---

has been clouded by partisanship and animosities arising from Carranza's subsequent role as a revolutionary leader and chief of state. There is no doubt that his conduct in the early months of the revolution was very circumspect. Caution and a sense of loyalty and obligation to Gen. Reyes help to explain his reluctance to act decisively.

IX. The Spark in Chihuahua

DURING THE LAST MONTH of the year favorable reports from Chihuahua brought a reawakening of the spirits of the exiles, a renewal of the willingness of the Madero family to subsidize the revolutionary cause, and the decision of Francisco Madero to return to Texas in order to enter Mexico from the north. It was in Chihuahua that the revolutionary fighters had kept their forces intact by employing guerrilla tactics and avoiding major engagements.

December opened with the capture of besieged Ciudad Guerrero by the revolutionists under Orozco. General Navarro promptly led a strong federal force from the city of Chihuahua toward Ciudad Guerrero. The government could not afford either physically or psychologically to allow the situation to go unchallenged. On the other hand, it was equally important for Orozco to try to block the federal advance. On December 11, at Cerro Prieto, a point on the Mexican Northwestern Railroad, eight hundred to a thousand rebels attacked the twelve hundred federals. For some five hours the revolutionists assaulted the government troops entrenched in the cemetery area. The attackers revealed order and discipline, but had to withdraw into the hills after failing to dislodge the numerically superior enemy.

The federals under Navarro burned the houses of rebel sympathizers in Cerro Prieto and executed some twenty persons. During the early months of the revolution the authorities were ruthless toward captured revolutionists, and executed rebels were frequently exhibited publicly to intimidate the people.

The insurgents reciprocated in kind. At Ciudad Guerrero a revolutionary tribunal had ordered death sentences for the local judge, the *jefe político*, and several others.

With regrouped forces Orozco continued to harass the Navarro column. When the revolutionary commander learned of reinforcements coming to join Navarro, he moved quickly, by forced marches, to cut off the new opponents. In the Canyon of Mal Paso the federal train-convoy was caught in a crossfire from Orozco's men who commanded the heights on both sides. The federals were forced to retreat after suffering heavy losses. This triumph, though of small military significance, redounded to the glory of Orozco and stimulated revolutionary spirit, as did political events, especially the appointment of a member of the unpopular Terrazas family as governor.

After strong forces did succeed in reinforcing General Navarro, Orozco modified his tactics. He decided to sacrifice Ciudad Guerrero in favor of a move to the northeast, in the direction of Ciudad Juárez. This action would bring his unit closer to the American frontier and the source of needed supplies and munitions. It would also serve in the campaign of attrition against Navarro by forcing him to make countermoves. Lastly, the presence of Orozco's band near the border would encourage and facilitate Madero's entry into the national territory.

Francisco Madero returned to San Antonio on December 29 greatly encouraged by the fire which had flamed from the spark in Chihuahua. Since the middle of the month his associates in the Texas city had been discussing projects for his entry into Mexico to assume leadership of the revolutionary forces. After several plans failed to materialize, an expedition was organized to cross the Bravo near Las Vacas in Coahuila. The rebel force crossed the river, but was dispersed after a skirmish with a group of rurales. Madero was preparing to join this expedition when word of its failure was received. Since it was considered dangerous for him to remain in San Antonio, he decided to proceed to Dallas to await another opportunity to fulfill his obligation as the leader of the revolution.

In Dallas he continued to participate in the revolutionary planning through the frustrating medium of the mails. Madero realized the necessity of establishing himself in Mexican territory. It was vital to his personal prestige, to the unity and discipline of the insurgents, and to the legal basis of a revolutionary government. He recognized the problem and was impatient to comply with his obligation. Complaining to González Garza of being "condemned to relative inactivity," he noted that "I am playing a sad role, hidden instead of being in the place of operations. My prestige and authority have been undermined to a considerable degree." As soon as an opportunity presented itself, he planned to join the principal group of revolutionary forces in Chihuahua and, from there, direct elements operating elsewhere. "I see very clearly that as long as there is no unity of command . . . we will never obtain decisive triumphs nor will we be able to gather the fruits of our victories." [1]

Despite Madero's resolution members of his family and some advisors recommended delaying such action. The revolutionary leader rejected this counsel with firmness and dignity.

> We must have discipline in our party. Since I am its natural chief, I wish to be recognized and treated as such. Titles and honors mean little to me, but I believe that there must be unity of action in our party. If I abdicate my rights and allow myself to be ruled by everyone who surrounds me, anarchy will descend upon our party. I would have dishonored the post which I have assumed and would have demonstrated that I am not worthy to occupy it.

Madero showed himself determined to assume his post as leader of the revolution, revealing at the same time a sense of his personal mission in the future. He felt that any other course would reveal that "I have neither the talents to rescue the Fatherland from the difficult situation through which it presently passes or to govern it afterwards. Weak men never serve for anything in such circumstances." [2]

[1] F. Mercier (Madero) to W. Olliphant (González Garza), Jan. 30, 1911, AdeGG.

[2] *Ibid.*

After a week in Dallas, Madero went to El Paso from which point he now planned to join the forces of Orozco. Various of his associates were sent to the Chihuahua rebels to prepare the way for the leader. Events in January and early February fed the flames of the revolution. There were new uprisings in Coahuila, Zacatecas, Durango and Veracruz. From Guerrero and Veracruz emissaries arrived in Texas to obtain funds. Pino Suárez requested aid for a movement in Yucatán. Naturally, there were setbacks as well as victories for the insurgents, but time was on their side. As long as they could maintain their principal forces intact and avoid a crushing defeat, the rebel forces would grow, and their prospects of victory would be enhanced. This was particularly true of the main rebel movement in Chihuahua. Pascual Orozco had marched northward until his army reached the railroad running from Chihuahua City to Ciudad Juárez, which was his objective. Using captured railroad equipment, Orozco's men traveled to the environs of the frontier town.

The Díaz government, recognizing that the heart of the rebellion was in Chihuahua, concentrated its efforts in that state. Since a formal, full-scale campaign was beyond the police-type rurales, regular army troops in the area were reinforced. Federal forces in the zone exceeded five thousand by early February, but the reinforcement program was badly managed. Instead of bringing the full power of the government's resources to bear simultaneously, the new personnel were assembled sporadically by companies or fragments of batallions. The federal army lacked cohesion and unity of command and, as time went on, suffered increasingly from long-range direction from Mexico City. The fabulous military machine, commanded by superannuated generals, had lost much of its efficiency and discipline and was debilitated by graft.[3]

[3] Ambassador Wilson, reversing his earlier estimate—i.e., "failure"—of the uprising and increasingly critical of the government, reported the rising tide of rebellion and the inability of the federal army to cope with the situation. Feb. 6 and 8, 1911, SDF, 812.00/739 and 796.

Though the government also resorted to political measures in an effort to eliminate Orozco, these too were ineffectual. Convinced that the rebel commander had revolted primarily against Terrazas rule, Díaz substituted Miguel Ahumada, former governor of Jalisco, for young Alberto Terrazas as governor of Chihuahua. That move came on the last day of January and was much too late.

Madero, in El Paso, was prepared to join the forces of Orozco. A major problem had been resolved when Dr. Vázquez Gómez, after several conferences with the revolutionary leader, had agreed to return to Washington as the Confidential Agent of the movement. However, the military situation became complicated. Several unfavorable events occurred affecting Orozco's position. A shipment of munitions from El Paso intended for the revolutionaries was seized by Mexican authorities. To complicate matters it was learned that a force under Colonel Rábago was proceeding by the Northwestern Railroad to the aid of the garrison at Ciudad Juárez. Orozco met this threat at Bauche, a short distance south of the frontier town. Despite a sustained skirmish lasting all day, the federal reinforcements managed to enter Ciudad Juárez under cover of darkness. Unable to attack the reinforced town, short on munitions and supplies, and with some of his men deserting across the American border, Orozco decided to retreat.

These developments near the frontier prompted Madero to name José de la Luz Soto to assume command in Chihuahua. This impolitic appointment, resented by Orozco, had to be withdrawn. The need for Madero to provide the revolutionists with his personal leadership was imperative. Nevertheless, some of his advisors counseled further delay. Then word was received that Madero's hiding place had been discovered and that American authorities had ordered his arrest on the charges that he was preparing a military expedition against a friendly nation and had sent arms and munitions to Mexico in violation of the neutrality laws. Accompanied by one hundred and thirty men, including about fifty American volunteers, Madero hurriedly crossed the frontier early on the morning of February 14 at La Isleta, about sixteen miles to the east of Ciudad Juárez. They were met by a force under José de la Luz Blanco.

The circumstance of an American order of arrest combining with Mexican military developments to hasten Madero's entry into Mexico raises the much debated question of the role of the United States in the Madero revolution. No revolution against the Mexican government could have succeeded so long as the United States government maintained a policy of positive support of the existing regime. At the very least an attitude of "neutrality" would be necessary if a revolutionary group was to be able to organize, operate, and supply its forces from American soil. The attitude of the United States government, which for over twenty years had supported the Díaz regime and dealt summarily with trouble-making exiles, appeared to have changed by December, 1909. During that month Henry Lane Wilson took charge of the American Embassy and shortly delivered a speech in which he implied his government's dissatisfaction with the continuing of the dictatorship of Díaz.

A number of factors affecting American national and individual interests explain this change of attitude toward General Díaz and his government. Much of the irritation arose from the tendency of the Mexican President, with Científico influence and support, to favor European as opposed to American interests. The American government was not indifferent to the fate of its citizens' interests or to the political implications of the Mexican policy. American petroleum companies were being subordinated to the English firm of S. Pearson (Lord Cowdray) and Son, Ltd. in the matter of oil concessions. Limantour was seeking French capital for the National Bank. Edward H. Harriman's scheme for consolidating the Mexican railroads was first rejected and then appropriated by the Finance Minister who carried out the project retaining control for the Mexican government. Limantour also irritated the influential Guggenheim family when he sold the rich silver mine at Real del Monte to other interests.

Several actions of President Díaz were interpreted as unfriendly toward the United States. The Mexican ruler stalled on the request for a renewal of the treaty granting the United States naval rights in Magdalena Bay. In Central America also he appeared to be opposing the conduct of the northern neighbor. For example, in 1907 he provided a Mexican warship for the flight from Nicaragua of Zelaya whose rule had been condemned and opposed by the United States, and afforded him asylum in Mexico. Lastly, the United States was concerned about the presidential succession for which, it was felt, the aging dictator was not making adequate provision. The changing attitude of the American government and the antipathy of certain American interests toward the Díaz government were reflected in the reports of Ambassador Wilson.

Complicating the relations between the two governments was an outbreak of anti-American sentiment in Mexico during the month of November. Ostensibly, these riots and demonstrations were provoked by the lynching of Antonio Rodríguez, allegedly a Mexican citizen, by a mob in Rock Springs, Texas. Violent and inflammatory articles appeared in the press. Ambassador Wilson protested on behalf of his government. General Díaz charged that the anti-American riots were the work of the revolutionists endeavoring to stir up trouble and discredit his government. He promised his cooperation in modifying the tone of the press and in suppressing the outbreaks.

Mr. Wilson believed that the demonstrations and articles were inspired by certain government officials to divert public attention from the growing discontent and to discredit the revolutionary leaders.[4] Available evidence seems to substantiate this suspicion. The effort to stigmatize the Madero movement as anti-American was without justification. Although the Mexican Revolution later developed a strong antiforeign strain, there was none in the early stages. Madero, an admirer of American institutions, wanted cordial relations with the United States, and in his first formal communication to the American Secretary of State he pledged recognition of all international treaties existing prior to November 20, 1910, and the assumption of responsibility by the provisional government, once

[4] Wilson, *Diplomatic Episodes*, p. 191.

recognized, for damages and injuries to citizens of the recognizing nation.[5]

Against this background of dissatisfaction with the Díaz government and of assurances from the Madero group the United States followed a seemingly tolerant policy toward the rebels. Little molested were the revolutionary agencies in San Antonio, El Paso, and Washington. There is no question that American policy toward Madero and his group lacked the ruthless aggressiveness previously employed against rebellious Mexican exiles. In 1911 the United States demonstrated a meticulous concern for legal detail. The frontier between the two nations is a long one, and contraband, in the small amounts that were shipped in 1911, was difficult to apprehend, particularly in view of the large numbers of border residents who were sympathetic to the rebels. It was estimated that three quarters of the large Mexican population of San Antonio approved of the movement.[6] Besides, the insurgent cause, with Madero's emphasis on democracy and liberty and his flattering observations on American political institutions, attracted the support of American public opinion and a sizeable portion of the American press. Because of the prestige which Madero enjoyed from his candidacy he seemed to fall into a different category from the earlier Mexican exiles.

The Mexican government recognized its unfavorable position and took steps to correct the situation. Dr. Fortunato Hernández was commissioned to undertake a vigorous journalistic campaign in the United States. Late in January, Joaquín Casasús was sent to Washington as special envoy to thank President Taft for American participation in the centenary celebration. This trip was more than a polite diplomatic visit, for Casasús also visited the governor of Texas to request cooperation in enforcing the neutrality laws. The Mexican government maintained a substantial number of spies and hired American detectives not only to harass the exiles, but

[5] Wilson to State Dept., March 27, 1911, SDF, 812.00/1194.
[6] San Antonio *Light and Gazette,* Nov. 19, 1910.

also to gather evidence on their movements for submission to American authorities.

Officials in Washington were deluged with rumors and reports from the Mexican Ambassador, the Mexican Foreign Office, and even American consuls in border towns about the whereabouts and intentions of Francisco Madero. The Mexican government, submitting captured documents and reports of Madero's provisional appointments and appeal to the federal army, complained that the opposition leader was attempting "to subvert the government of a friendly nation" and requested that he be prosecuted as a violator of the neutrality laws.[7] There were other complaints about recruiting in border towns, arms purchases and shipments, and reported movements of rebels across the border. American officials were asked to take appropriate action.

As time passed and the military situation worsened, the notes directed to the State Department revealed, despite diplomatic language, growing Mexican irritation and dissatisfaction. The American Ambassador reported early in April that Mexican authorities had complained "that the rebels continue to receive large supplies of food and ammunition from across the Texas border" and had declared that "military operations could be brought to an end in one month if the source [of supplies] were rendered unavailable."[8]

The conduct of the United States government was scrupulously correct in form. American officials chose to insist that the strictest legal conditions be fulfilled before action was instituted. Complaints were courteously acknowledged and referred to the War and Justice Departments for study and any warranted action. The State Department assured the Díaz government that the United States was disposed to enforce strictly the rules of international law governing neutrality as well as the penal code sections of its own law governing the

[7] Wilson to State Dept., Nov. 18, 1910, SDF, 812.00/388; Ambassador F. L. de la Barra to Secretary Knox, Dec. 10, 1910, SDF, 812.00/559.

[8] Wilson to Secretary of State, April 6, 1911, SDF, 812.00/1234.

subject. Agents of the Justice Department were directed to "prosecute vigorously any violators of the law." [9]

From the beginning the American government emphasized that prosecution would require evidence and could not be based on mere rumor. Subsequent replies to Mexican complaints tended to detail the limitations of the laws including conduct not considered in violation of the statutes. The Mexican government was advised that neither mere revolutionary propaganda nor the passing of men from the United States into Mexico, unless constituting an expedition, could be considered a violation.[10] American officials argued also that "mere shipment of arms" from the United States to persons in Mexico was "not in itself a violation." Secretary Knox advised that even in a state of war, which did not exist, trade in contraband articles "is considered legal and subject to no penalty save loss of goods captured in the trade." [11]

Despite this legalistic attitude, the Mexican complaints did result in some action by the United States. Specific charges were investigated; several shipments of guns and munitions were seized; and a number of armed expeditions were stopped. On two occasions warrants for the arrest of Francisco Madero were issued, but the first order was withdrawn for lack of evidence and the second forced him across the border. Sánchez Azcona, Secretary of the Washington Agency of the revolution, was arrested. However, he was released after a court refused to accede to the extradition request of the Mexican government. Cavalry troops were ordered to the border towns to assist the civilian authorities in enforcing the neutrality laws. In at least one instance the Mexican government obtained positive cooperation from the United States. When General Luque was beseiged in Ojinaga on the northern

[9] Acting Secretary of State Adee to Wilson, Nov. 9, 1910, SDF, 812.00/427.

[10] Secretary Knox to Mexican Ambassador, Jan. 24, 1911, SDF, 812.00/654; Secretary Knox to Mexican Chargé d'Affaires, April 18, 1911, SDF, 812.00/1284.

[11] Attorney General to Secretary of State, March 8, 1911, SDF, 812.00/911; Secretary Knox to Wilson, Dec. 14, 1910, SDF, 812.00/447.

border of Chihuahua, the Department of State granted permission for the Mexican commander to obtain provisions and fodder from American territory.

The most startling and significant action by the American government in connection with the disturbed conditions in Mexico was the mobilization of twenty thousand troops on the Texas-Mexican frontier in March, 1911. In addition, American warships were ordered to proceed to Mexican ports on the Pacific and Gulf coasts. A tremendous uproar followed this action, and both the Mexican government and the rebels hastened to proclaim their irrevocable opposition to intervention. President Taft ordered that the vessels only call for coal and then leave promptly, and assured the Mexican government that the mobilization was intended to facilitate enforcement of the neutrality laws and was not a hostile move. President Díaz accepted the American explanation and even declared that he believed that it "would strengthen the hand of the Mexican government." [12] However, the American troop movement had a most unfavorable effect for the Díaz government because public opinion blamed General Díaz for seeking intervention.

American interests in Mexico, led by influential members of the American colony close to Ambassador Wilson, opposed any intervention by the United States in the revolution. American business interests, apparently convinced that Díaz was through, preferred a hands-off policy. This attitude raised the question of whether there was American financial support for the Madero movement. Rumors were current both during and after the Madero revolution to the effect that Standard Oil had provided financial assistance. While there is good reason to believe that many of the rumors were started by Pearson Company,[13] Standard Oil's English rival, there seems to be little doubt that some members of the Madero family

[12] Acting Secretary of State Adee to Mexican Ambassador, March 13, 1911, SDF, 812.00/922; Wilson to Secretary of State, March 21, 1911, SDF, 812.00/1033.

[13] Consul Clarence Miller to State Dept., Feb. 15 and May 8, 1911, SDF, 812.000/846 and 1781.

would have been willing to enter into such arrangements.

Francisco Madero the elder and his son Alfonso conferred during April in an El Paso hotel with three men purportedly serving as intermediaries of an alleged representative of Standard Oil. According to an informant the Maderos were willing to meet with the oil company representative to discuss a loan in return for oil concessions.[14] The United States government was disturbed by these rumors. Secretary Knox wrote John D. Archbold, Vice-President of Standard Oil, about the charges. He declared that the attitude of the United States was one of "absolute impartiality" and bluntly told the oil executive that his government "cannot be compromised in its position of impartiality by any such improper negotiation." Mr. Archbold replied that the charges were without foundation.[15]

Francisco I. Madero was opposed to accepting money tied to concessions. The revolutionary leader believed that "each concession constitutes a precedent and many precedents constitute a right." In San Antonio several loans were offered by private persons, but were not accepted because the terms were considered burdensome for Mexico. After the fighting ended, Madero was visited by several American capitalists who proposed to pay all expenses for his forthcoming presidential campaign as well as those which had been incurred by the revolutionary movement in return for certain privileges. Madero's published reply was as follows:

> I represent the party in Mexico which fights against trusts and monopolies. Are you able to suppose that I would accede to your demands and impose new yokes . . . on my country? As for the money which you offer me, I am not able to accept nor do I need it.[16]

[14] There is no evidence that C. R. Troxel, the "representative," was an authorized agent of the company. He never arrived in El Paso for the meeting scheduled for April 26. It is conceivable that the whole idea originated with the intermediaries who anticipated receiving a commission from Standard Oil and concessions from the rebels. Attorney General to Secretary of State, May 2, 1911, SDF, 812.00/1593.

[15] Secretary Knox to J. D. Archbold and reply, May 10 and 15, 1911, SDF, 812.00/1593 and 1796.

[16] Dispatch, Agencia Regagnon (A.R.), Ciudad Juárez, May 26, 1911,

Madero did appoint a commission to obtain a million-dollar loan in exchange for bonds or notes to be issued by the provisional government and payable one year after the revolutionary group had come to power. The arrangements were never completed, and the bonds were not even printed. Aside from small individual contributions, it appears that the Maderos, especially Gustavo, financed the revolution from their own funds and under their own credit without compromising the national interests. Nor does there appear to be any foundation for extravagant assertions that the White House made common cause with the revolutionists of 1910. The United States stood as a neutral regarding the contending forces rather than as a positive supporter of the existing government or as a conspiratorial cohort of the revolutionists. This neutral position, however, did strengthen the Madero movement morally and materially.

After crossing the frontier on February 14, Madero and his escort proceeded slowly southward. On February 22 they reached Villa Ahumada. Shortly thereafter, at Guadalupe (Chihuahua) the revolutionary leader undertook his first official acts on Mexican soil. He directed his first note to the American government; in it he enumerated the justifications for the revolution and offered assurances of responsible government. He also appointed a commission to arrange the bond issue. Madero was anxious to have outstanding individuals, other than his family, handle the delicate question of the proposed negotiation of the loan. Aware from past experience of the dangers and difficulties involved in permitting his family to assume preponderant influence, he felt there would be more discipline and order with outsiders. "I intend to make a clear division between questions of family and of policy... In the latter I will gladly accept the aid of [members of my family], but I do not intend that they should replace my natural coun-

---

cited in Rojas, *La culpa de Henry Lane Wilson*, I, 312*n*.

The absence of concessions during his administration and the dissatisfaction of American interests with his regime are the best evidences that Madero abided by his own principle.

sellors whom I ought to select from among the men of greatest merit in our party." [17]

A more immediate and serious problem confronting Madero on his southward march was that of military discipline. Mexican revolutionary forces often have been refractory in regard to subordination to a commander. Loyalty to a revolutionary superior regularly lasted as long as it was convenient, but sooner or later proved to be nominal. Madero recognized this danger and insisted on discipline and recognition of his position as commander and provisional president. Such a stand prompted charges of egotism, but the matter was critical, particularly as the revolution mushroomed all over the republic with only nominal centralized control.

On February 28 several officers protested against Guisseppi Garibaldi, whom Madero had entrusted with a responsible post, as a foreigner and an incompetent. The revolutionary leader met this challenge to his authority and judgment. He refused to deprive the cause of the services of Garibaldi merely because he was an Italian. Madero declared that "the deed is sanctioned by history. Every time a people has fought for its liberty, numerous foreigners have fought in the ranks of the liberators." Reminding his men that the grandfather and father of Garibaldi "always have placed their sword at the service of the oppressed," Madero asserted that he was the proper person to judge the aptitudes of Garibaldi. With devastating sarcasm he noted that "Señor Garibaldi has given proofs of modesty and subordination which I have not found in all those who surround me." [18]

Two other incidents were related to the question of discipline. José Flores Alatorre, who was accused of having ordered a federal prisoner shot, was tried and dismissed from the revolutionary army. More significant was the arrest of Liberal leader Prisciliano G. Silva. Although charges of banditry were

[17] F. Mercier (Madero) to W. Olliphant (González Garza), Jan. 25, 1911, AdeGG.

[18] Communication of the Provisional President, Field of San Lorenzo, Feb. 28, 1911, cited in Taracena, *Madero: Vida*, pp. 351-54.

raised by the Maderistas, the main issue was Silva's refusal to recognize Madero's position and authority. This incident provided the excuse for the inevitable schism between the Liberals and Madero.

Ideologically and politically the two opposition groups had been drifting apart. The Liberals under Flores Magón were moving toward belief in a form of anarchism. Ricardo Flores Magón raised the cry of "land and freedom" and asserted that political liberty could not bring happiness to the people. The contrast with the ideas of bourgeois, political-minded Madero was apparent. At the very time that Madero was organizing his revolutionary movement the Liberal Junta in Los Angeles was preparing its third assault on the Díaz regime. Liberal supporters were advised that there was no connection between their movement and the Madero uprising, but that they should be prepared to capitalize on the situation by coordinating their rebellion with any disturbance created by the Maderistas.

By January the Liberals had small bands operating in Lower California, Sonora, Chihuahua, Veracruz, and several other states. The following month occurred the incident involving Prisciliano Silva. Afterwards Ricardo Flores Magón attacked Madero as a "traitor to the cause of liberty." Some of the Liberals—Gutiérrez de Lara, Antonio I. Villarreal, and José María Leyva—went over to the Madero forces, but the majority remained vitriolic critics of Madero and his work. Indeed, the revolutionary leader was subjected to as bitter attacks by this radical group as by members of the old regime: the Liberal Junta proclaimed that it was not fighting to "overthrow the dictator Porfirio Díaz in order to put in his place a new tyrant"; Ricardo Flores Magón bitterly described Madero as "the stunted politicaste and the vulgar ambitious who wishes to elevate himself on the shoulders of the poor people to collect for supposed services." [19] However, the Liberal uprising revealed a sustained effort only in Lower California. There the movement rapidly developed a separatist character with the chimerical goal of a socialist state and constituted a

[19] *Regeneración,* Feb. 25 and April 3, 1911.

serious problem in pacification after the Madero rebellion had ended.

The split with the Liberals out in the open, Madero proceeded to the town of San Buenaventura where the women, dressed in white, greeted him with flowers. It was now the beginning of March, and the prospects of the revolution began to appear more promising. The movement was gaining in Sonora and spreading to Sinaloa. In the southern part of the country it was beginning to assume threatening proportions. The federal commanders were disturbed because the type of campaign being waged in the north required the splitting of the main bodies of their troops.

Madero learned that Casas Grandes to the northwest was lightly garrisoned. He was unwilling to wait for Orozco's forces which he had ordered to meet him at Galeana. Therefore, he directed José de la Luz Soto, in Asunción to the northeast of Casas Grandes, to make contact with him for a joint attack on that center. Coincidentally, General Navarro sent the cavalry forces under Colonel García Cuéllar to retake Asunción. When the Colonel learned that Asunción had been abandoned, he too headed for Casas Grandes.

Madero and his men arrived in the vicinity of Casas Grandes on March 5. The revolutionists, as was their custom, advanced in close-order double file with twenty-one carts of equipment included in the rear guard. The approach to the town was across an exposed plain, and the defenders were able to observe the insurgents' movements through field glasses. At 4:30 in the afternoon the Maderistas crossed the River of Casas Grandes, and Madero, Eduardo Hay, Raúl Madero, and Garibaldi advanced with a small group to a ridge overlooking the town to reconnoiter defense positions. At five o'clock the rebels established their camp at the Anchondo Ranch, about two miles south of Casas Grandes. That evening Madero ordered the heights known as Moctezuma to be occupied as a prelude to an attack the following day.

It was a bright, starlit night, and the slight chill in the air seemed to add to the tingle of excitement which ran through the encampment. At 1 A.M. Madero addressed the soldiers urging them to conduct themselves as they had before. The force of five hundred, which enjoyed a moderate superiority over the defenders, was divided into three columns. At 3:30 A.M. the main body of the troops marched on the town while Madero and an escort remained at the Moctezuma position from which they would be able to fire down on the defenders. Practically every man was committed to the action. The insurgents were so confident of victory that no provision was made for a reserve force or for retreat.

At five o'clock, before the curtain of night had lifted, the firing began. The battle was joined by 7 A.M. and lasted until five in the afternoon. The first rebel assault was repulsed. The tide of battle swung first one way and then the other. At last it appeared that the outnumbered defenders would have to withdraw. At this juncture the cavalry force of García Cuéllar appeared, giving the federals the advantage of surprise as well as turning the numerical balance in their favor. The rebel force, panic-struck by the unexpected cavalry attack, was forced to retreat.

About seventy-five or one hundred rebels joined Madero at the Moctezuma position which was under heavy artillery fire. The disorderly mass was an ideal target, and the fire on the position was intensified. Despite Madero's efforts to prevent it, a wild retreat followed. The leader finally withdrew too, but only after the bulk of his soldiers had deserted him. Slightly wounded in the right forearm, Madero proceeded on foot to the Anchondo Ranch where he obtained a horse. At Casas Grandes the revolutionary leader, indifferent to his personal safety, demonstrated great personal valor.

The insurgents had suffered heavy losses in the battle. Fifty-eight of their number lay dead on the battlefield, and forty-one others, including Eduardo Hay, had been captured. Eight carts of supplies had fallen into federal hands, and an equal number were destroyed. The federals suffered only twenty-five killed and thirty-eight wounded. The leader of the revolution was in great danger of being captured, but the fleeing rebels were not pursued. García Cuéllar, severely wounded, was unable to lead the pursuit and refused to delegate authority to his subordinate. Despite the fact that the revolutionists spent the night only a short distance from Casas Grandes, the federals failed to follow up and complete their victory either that night or the following day.[20]

Francisco Madero was not disheartened by the unexpected setback. He remarked that "revolutions are not lost by a mishap."[21] Paradoxically, the defeat at Casas Grandes appeared to favor the revolutionary cause. *El Imparcial* could scoff at "General" Madero, as it had laughed previously at the idea that Madero would cross the frontier, but his personal valor attracted supporters. His leadership had proclaimed to Mexico and to the world that the scattered bands of the insurrection now had in the field a center of responsibility and direction.

Madero, joined by Orozco and Villa, began to regroup and reorganize the rebel forces at Bustillos Ranch about sixty miles from Chihuahua City. The headquarters was well located: to the west the protecting Sierra Madre; to the south the Northwestern Railroad, held from La Junta to Madera by the rebels; to the north some advance posts, guarded against the hardly probable attack from Casas Grandes; and to the east the Central Railroad line, which connected the state capital with Ciudad Juárez. Madero's general plan of campaign involved threatening Chihuahua City to force a concentration of federal forces and then cutting the Central Railroad north of Chihuahua City and between that city and Torreón to neutralize the enemy there. This second phase would also be marked by a rapid rebel movement against Ciudad Juárez on the frontier. Madero was correct on his fundamental strategy though he often erred on secondary details through lack of military experience. His plan of campaign would permit vic-

[20] "Report of Col. A. Valdés," in Secretaría de Guerra y Marina, *Campaña de 1910 a 1911*, pp. 186-205; Aguilar, *Madero sin máscara*, pp. 63-74; Goríbar, *El Maderismo en cueros, passim.*

[21] Fernández Güell, *El moderno Juárez*, p. 10.

tory with a minimum of effort and loss of life. The result would be due to effect on morale and the revelation of the military weakness and insufficiency of the federals, rather than by direct military action. Despite the recent setback at Casas Grandes, Madero was confident of victory and ignored the possibility of defeat.

The revolutionary leader spent the remainder of March at Bustillos. During this month the cause of the insurgents advanced noticeably. General Díaz, in an interview the day after the battle at Casas Grandes, had declared that the situation was improved and that the revolt would soon end. However, the appraisal of the situation by Ambassador Wilson, who returned to his post on March 17, differed sharply. He reported that the revolutionary forces were growing in numbers and extending their activities. Reports of consuls in Tampico, Durango, Saltillo, Hermosillo, and Progreso tended to confirm his opinion. Armed rebellion was spreading in Sonora, Durango, Sinaloa, Coahuila, Zacatecas, Aguascalientes, and part of Jalisco. It had broken out or reappeared in Guerrero, Morelos, Puebla, Tlaxcala, Veracruz, Tabasco, and Yucatán. The inability of the government to smother the revolutionary fire in its early stages suggested that the regime had come to lack the strength and solidity which had been taken for granted.

X. *Compromise at Ciudad Juárez*

THE FEDERAL COMMANDERS were disturbed by the rebel concentrations near Chihuahua City and by reports that Orozco was preparing to attack that state capital. To meet this danger there was a scurry of federal activity during the first days of April. The 18th Infantry Battalion and a cavalry unit at Casas Grandes were ordered to the threatened city. These reinforcements were joined by General Rábago, who proceeded from Ciudad Juárez with a sizeable column. A battery of cannon was shipped from Mexico City, and General Laura Villar, new chief of the zone, arrived in Chihuahua City on April 8.

The government believed that these arrangements would meet the demands of the situation. Actually, a double error was committed. On the one hand, Ciudad Juárez was deprived of possible assistance. The forces that had been at Jiménez, Casas Grandes, and Ojinaga would have been able to render prompt and probably sufficient support to Ciudad Juárez. But the bulk of these forces were ordered southward, and General Navarro had less than seven hundred men, of the over six thousand in the zone, with which to defend the frontier town. On the other hand, large armed forces were being enclosed in the state capital and thus were in danger of being isolated when the railroad lines to Torreón and to the north were interrupted.

The federal action had placed the bulk of the government forces in an unfavorable situation while leaving virtually the whole northern part of the state to the rebels. Near the end

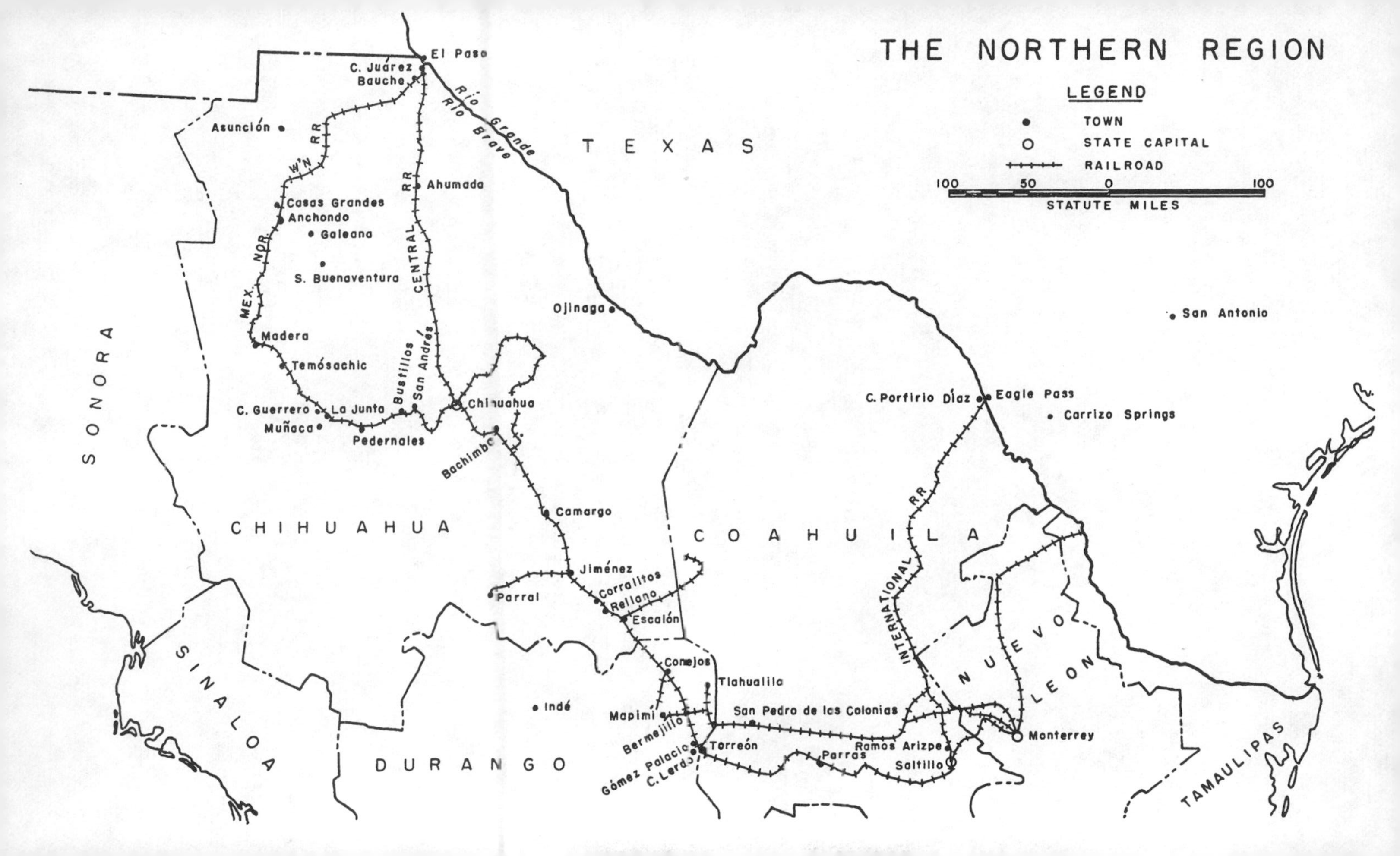
THE NORTHERN REGION
LEGEND
TOWN
STATE CAPITAL
RAILROAD
100 50 0 100
STATUTE MILES
TEXAS
SONORA
CHIHUAHUA
COAHUILA
NUEVO LEON
DURANGO
SINALOA
TAMAULIPAS
Rio Grande
Rio Bravo
MEX. NOR. W'N RR
CENTRAL RR
INTERNATIONAL RR
El Paso
C. Juárez
Bauche
Asunción
Ahumada
Casas Grandes
Anchondo
Galeana
S. Buenaventura
Madera
Temósachic
C. Guerrero
La Junta
Muñaca
Pedernales
Bustillos
San Andrés
Chihuahua
Bachimba
Camargo
Ojinaga
Jiménez
Parral
Corralitos
Rellano
Escalón
Conejos
Tlahualila
Mapimí
Bermejillo
Torreón
Gómez Palacio
C. Lerdo
Indé
San Pedro de las Colonias
Parras
Ramos Arizpe
Saltillo
Monterrey
C. Porfirio Díaz
Eagle Pass
Carrizo Springs
San Antonio

of March, Madero and Orozco broke camp at Bustillos and began to move toward Ciudad Juárez. Madero was determined to capture the frontier town because it would provide a sure point for the introduction of arms and supplies and, in addition, a basis for American recognition of the revolutionists as belligerents. In addition, the revolutionary leader, always an admirer of Juárez, wanted to emulate that great Mexican by making Ciudad Juárez (called Paso del Norte in the days of Juárez) his provisional capital.

The rebel army traveled by rail to Madera, Chihuahua, without meeting any obstacles. From that point they proceeded toward Ciudad Juárez, passing through Casas Grandes, now abandoned by the federals. On April 14 the revolutionists arrived at the station of Bauche, a scant ten miles short of their objective. A skirmish occurred between advance units on the following day, and General Navarro had to use virtually his entire garrison to rescue the small force he had sent toward Bauche. The federals retired within Ciudad Juárez, and the rebels surrounded the town on all sides except the north (United States territory). Madero established his camp a little south of Bauche. The government now recognized its error. On April 19 the President ordered the zone commander to send a relief train to the besieged community.

Mexico was aflame with revolution. With the federals concentrated in Chihuahua City, the revolutionists were taking towns in that state at will. The rebels were also making progress in Coahuila, while in Sonora their forces captured Agua Prieta, a frontier town opposite Douglas, Arizona. However, during that encounter two persons were killed and a number wounded in Douglas, prompting a strenuous protest by the American government to both sides. Federal troops recaptured Agua Prieta within a week, but the dangers of diplomatic controversy with the United States as a result of frontier fighting remained a part of the rebels' thinking, acting as a deterrent to further military operations close to the international boundary. After unsuccessfully attacking Mazatlán, the Sonora insurgents besieged Culiacán.

Armed rebellion was not limited to the northern tier of states. On April 8, Indé (Durango) fell to the rebels. Luis Moya, ranging over Durango and neighboring Zacatecas, captured Mapimí (Durango) and assaulted the capital of Zacatecas. In San Luis Potosí, Ciudad Valles was attacked. The southwestern part of Michoacán was controlled by the Maderistas. The insurgents in southern Mexico also extended their activities. Emiliano Zapata captured Chiautla, Matamoros Izúcar, and Acatlán in Puebla and briefly held several towns in the state of Mexico. Figueroa's forces, operating mainly in Guerrero, threatened Cuautla, Morelos. In the southeastern part of the country rebel activity increased, but was not uniformly successful. General Gavira threatened Jalapa in Veracruz without effect, but San Andrés Tuxtla in that state fell to the Maderistas. There were clashes in Tabasco, Yucatán, and Chiapas.

The government did not know where to turn first. The vaunted federal army, reported to exceed thirty thousand, was able to place only about fourteen thousand men in the field. All the governors were calling for help, but there was not enough man power or munitions despite heavy past and current expenditures. Miserably small, inadequate detachments of fifty, one hundred, or two hundred men were dispatched. The government tried to form volunteer battalions with the inducement of good pay, but few found the offer tempting. In contrast, the rebels were short of money, arms, and munitions, but they had some man power. With each day that passed more and more men joined the ranks of the revolution, yet even in this respect the revolution was far from impressive. The number of fighting effectives of the Maderista movement probably never exceeded twenty thousand, and at least sixty percent of these were concentrated in the northern tier of states.

The direction of the government campaign revealed startling inadequacies. The report of the Secretary of War and Marine reviewing this campaign noted that orders were given without apparent motive in some cases and because of lack of news of the enemy in others. There were shortages of supplies and of cavalry. These conditions prevailed despite the fact that the government was spending, above normal expenses, one hundred and seventy thousand pesos daily for the campaign during April and May. Federal military measures would continue to be handicapped by the initial underestimate of the true force of the rebellion, by the supposition that the campaign would be fought in terrain favorable to the government, and by direction from the capital limiting the initiative of commanders in the field.

The Díaz government also resorted to a whole series of other measures in its efforts to defeat the revolution. Toward the middle of March it submitted a request to the Chamber of Deputies for the suspension of individual guarantees contained in the Constitution. On March 17 the Congress approved the proposed law which provided for trial by military tribunal for those accused of banditry or the destruction of railroad or telegraph lines and the death penalty for those convicted. Madero declared that the measure was unconstitutional, and Luis Cabrera predicted that it would prove "the least effective [device] to suppress the revolution."[1]

With military and juridical devices proving ineffective, Porfirio Díaz resorted to political means. In critical states he replaced unpopular governors, but the sacrifice of Terrazas in Chihuahua, Mucio Martínez in Puebla, and Muñoz Arístegui in Yucatán did not bring the desired results. There followed a new series of headline moves designed to indicate a change of system and of men with the object of depriving the revolution of its thunder and thus bringing it to an end. Limantour's return from Europe was much publicized and hailed as the beginning of the change and the salvation of the government.

The first major development was a sweeping change in the cabinet. Six members of President Díaz's cabinet resigned on March 24. Limantour resumed his post as Minister of Hacienda (Treasury), and General González Cosío remained as

[1] *Diario del Hogar*, March 29 and 30, 1911.

Minister of War in the new cabinet formed four days later. The new ministers, Norberto Domínguez (Communications), Manuel Marroquín (Development), Jorge Vera Estañol (Public Instruction), Demeterio Sodi (Justice), and Francisco de la Barra (recalled from the Washington Embassy to take charge of Foreign Relations), were men of character and ability. Apparently it was intended that General Reyes, who had conferred with Limantour in Europe and had made declarations in support of the government, would join the cabinet as Minister of War or Government.

It was generally considered that the new cabinet reflected the will of Limantour, but there were signs that General Díaz was reluctant to surrender his authority.[2] Madero, in an interview, expressed his opposition to General Reyes as a cabinet member and called the revamped cabinet a "concession to public opinion, but too late and insufficient."[3] Roque Estrada interpreted the change as evidence of the "vacillations, weakness, and decrepitude" of the regime. He reminded the revolutionists that changes of personnel were not guarantees of reform or even promises of reform.[4]

On April 1, General Díaz addressed the opening meeting of the 2d session of the 25th Congress. After reviewing the outbreak of the revolution and measures which had been taken to halt it, he described a series of planned reforms. A startled Congress broke into applause as the President proposed the prohibition of reelection, division of large rural properties, judicial reform, and local autonomy as government policy. Francisco Madero claimed credit for the revolution for any reforms obtained, but charged that the proposals were intend-

[2] Gen. Díaz retained control of two of the three agencies (War and Justice) affecting internal administration. If Reyes had been able to serve in the ministry of Gobernación, the dictator's internal control would have been complete. In addition, Díaz appointed his son, Col. Díaz, as head of his private secretariat and personal guard and his nephew, Félix Díaz, as director of police in the Federal District. Limantour complained that the President was "averse to delegating his powers." Wilson to Secretary of State, March 27 and 29, 1911, SDF, 812.00/1037 and 1210.

[3] Consul Letcher to State Dept., April 3, 1911, SDF, 812.00/1279.

[4] *México Nuevo,* March 29, 30, and 31, 1911.

ed to disarm the rebellion. He declared that mere promises, which the government had made frequently, were not enough. The revolutionary leader demanded that the past election be declared void and new elections be held with full guarantees.[5]

The last of the political palliatives offered by the Díaz government was the request for a leave of absence for unpopular Vice-President Corral on the grounds of failing health. On April 8, Congress granted Corral leave for eight months, and the Vice-President departed for Europe. Luis Cabrera wrote that the changes and promises were not enough, that General Díaz ought to retire to private life.[6]

The final strategem of the government consisted of trying to defeat the revolution through a series of "peace negotiations." Using several members of Madero's family and other persons, the administration sought to achieve by guile what it was unable to accomplish by arms and by political means. This proved to be the means, aided by certain conditions, which enabled the old regime to salvage a partial victory from a complete defeat.

Toward the end of February a commission, composed of Ernesto Madero, Evaristo Madero, and Rafael Hernández (all related to the revolutionary leader) and the Spaniard Iñigo Noriega, arrived at Corpus Christi (Texas). Noriega reportedly had means of contacting President Díaz. Madero's father and his brother Alfonso hurried to confer with this commission. They indicated their willingness to recommend to the revolutionary leaders that they end hostilities and seek a general amnesty. Alfonso Madero wired Dr. Vázquez Gómez in Washington requesting that he join the conference. The doctor, although not opposed to a compromise, quite properly refused to participate unless: the government's representative brought authorization (implying recognition of belligerency), the conferences were public and formal, and there were facilities to consult with Francisco I. Madero (preferably through the occupation of a frontier town by the revolution). He was

[5] Letcher to State Dept., April 3, 1911, SDF, 812.00/1279.
[6] *La Opinión* (Veracruz), April 5, 1911.

also concerned that the Corpus Christi meeting was a "family affair." The refusal of the revolution's Confidential Agent to attend the conference brought the first, premature, negotiation to an unsuccessful close.[7]

Another series of conferences took place in New York upon the arrival of Limantour. Considering the strong political and personal ties of members of Madero's family with Limantour and the anxiety of Madero's father to reach some agreement, the New York meetings augured well for the objectives of the shrewd cabinet member. Gustavo Madero called Dr. Vázquez Gómez to New York for the series of talks held on Sunday and Monday, March 11 and 12. At the first meeting of Francisco Madero, Sr., Gustavo, the doctor, and Limantour on Sunday morning in the Astor Hotel, where the Maderos were staying, there was a general exchange of ideas. At the next two sessions the discussion progressed to general bases for a settlement.

Limantour appeared cooperative at these meetings, but at the final session on Monday afternoon his attitude was noticeably changed. Perhaps the receipt of encouraging news from Mexico was the explanation. Nevertheless, a set of proposals for possible negotiation was drawn up to be carried by Limantour to Mexico and to be submitted to Francisco I. Madero. The proposals included: announcement of the peace negotiations; honorable amnesty for the revolutionists; suspension of hostilities; resignation of Corral; establishment of the principle of "No Reelection"; and retirement of four ministers and ten governors and their replacement by Anti-Reelectionists not engaged in the fighting. The absence of any mention of the resignation of General Díaz is notable, but it must be pointed

[7] Ernesto Madero, in a letter to a newspaper editor in Monterrey, gave the following explanation of the origin of the meeting: "It is not, then, the government of Mexico which has sent commissioners to Corpus Christi to treat of peace. We, who form part of the Madero family, have committed that pretension because we are not in accord . . . that Mexican blood should continue to be spilled without cause . . . . We are the first to recognize the legality of the authorities." Ernesto Madero to J. A. Robertson, March 11, 1911, cited in Amaya, *Madero y . . . revolucionarios*, pp. 149-50; Vázquez Gómez, *Memorias políticas*, pp. 79-84.

out that these propositions represented only bases for discussion and involved no commitment by either side.

Dr. Vázquez Gómez wrote Madero a letter in which he recommended to him that he enter into negotiations. However, the negotiations were once again premature, and none of the participants was authorized to conclude the arrangements. In private conversations Limantour complained that the obstinacy of Madero himself, who would concede nothing at this time, was the major obstacle to a settlement.[8]

Toward the end of March, Rafael Hernández and Salvador Madero, who claimed to represent Limantour, arrived in San Antonio. On the afternoon of March 31 a conference was attended by Hernández, Sánchez Azcona, Pino Suárez, Alfonso Madero, Roque Estrada, and Gustavo Madero. Points of view were exchanged, and Hernández urged agreement in the face of the threat of American intervention. Several of the revolutionists denied that there was any such danger and opposed the secrecy which enveloped the negotiations. Pino Suárez had no faith in the conference and expressed his belief that a compromise arrangement ran the risk of being disavowed by the men in the field.

It was agreed that a commission composed of Madero's father, Hernández, Alfonso Madero, and Roque Estrada should go to Chihuahua to explore the sentiments of Madero and the other chiefs of the revolution. The heavy Madero family representation caused the revolutionists some concern. However, the failure of the government to provide promised safe-conduct and the indefiniteness of Madero's whereabouts frustrated this effort. Once again the negotiations lacked official character. A few days later Madero told Associated Press Correspondent Thomas Steep that he had not authorized

[8] Article by Manuel Amieva cited in Vázquez Gómez, *Memorias políticas,* p. 206.

Gustavo wrote his brother that he never had any intention that the New York talks should reach a conclusion. He hoped that news of the talks would favor the rebel cause. "I believed and believe still that the old tyrant never has complied with his offers and never will." April 18, 1911, AdeM.

any negotiation, but considered it natural for his father and friends to take advantage of any opportunity to consider the matter. "I approve of their efforts because I consider them patriots." He revealed a willingness to compromise and to make personal sacrifices. However, he declared that such action could only be based on the retirement of General Díaz.[9]

By April 18 the twenty-five-hundred-man revolutionary force had taken up positions around Ciudad Juárez. Madero set up his headquarters in an adobe hut at Rancho de Flores near the international boundary to the west of Ciudad Juárez. A force was left at Bauche as a rear guard and to cover the line of retreat. The revolutionary leader had an ultimatum delivered to General Navarro in the city demanding its surrender. The federal commander replied that he was not authorized to take such action.

Dr. Vázquez Gómez, with the Agua Prieta-Douglas incident fresh in his mind and concerned about international complications, urged postponement of the attack. He wired de la Barra that Madero was preparing to attack Ciudad Juárez with three thousand men, an excusable exaggeration, and urged evacuation of the town as a basis for peace negotiations. To Madero he recommended an armistice, first, on the grounds that an attack on Ciudad Juárez, just across the river from El Paso, would result in American intervention, and, second, in order to immobilize government reinforcements which either were on their way or might be sent to the besieged garrison. Gustavo Madero opposed suspension of hostilities because he anticipated that the most favorable situation would result from a vigorous, rapid, and successful attack. Francisco Madero was reluctant to agree with the doctor because he believed that he had sufficient man power and artillery to take the town and because he regarded an armistice as highly disadvantageous to the revolutionists' position. "It is preferable to continue the war and only to cease the hostilities when some arrangement has been reached."[10]

[9] Letcher to State Dept., April 7, 1911, SDF, 812.00/1243.

[10] Madero to González Garza, April 19, 1911, AdeGG; Gustavo Madero

The revolutionary leader felt that any cease-fire should be conditioned on the retirement of General Díaz and the surrender of Ciudad Juárez. However, the repeated warnings of Vázquez Gómez that an attack on Ciudad Juárez would lead to American intervention prompted Madero to accept a five-day armistice, beginning April 24, without prior conditions. The armistice was to apply in the limited quadrilateral area formed by the territory between Ciudad Juárez, Chihuahua, Muñaca, and Casas Grandes. The cease-fire and the accompanying negotiations paralyzed operations and facilitated the compromise abbreviation of the Madero revolution. This prompted Luis Cabrera to label the armistice as the "abortion of the revolutionary triumph."[11]

Another influence, in addition to the urgent suggestion of Dr. Vázquez Gómez, explains Madero's acceptance of an armistice. On April 19, Oscar Braniff and Toribio Esquivel Obregón arrived in El Paso to arrange for peace as emissaries of Limantour. At their first interview with Madero, surrounded by his revolutionary chiefs, they urged an armistice to permit negotiations. The revolutionary leader replied that an armistice would serve no purpose unless it was based on the condition of Díaz's resignation "within a reasonable time." Madero did agree to a twenty-four hour postponement of the attack on Ciudad Juárez to give the commissioners an opportunity to communicate with the government. Dr. Vázquez Gómez attributed Madero's categorical stand to the presence of the other insurgent commanders, but the revolutionary leader's attitude was perfectly consistent with his conduct up to this point.[12]

The next meeting, on April 22, presented a strikingly different situation. Braniff and Esquivel Obregón, assured in advance by Madero's father that his son's disposition was more favorable and that peace would result, found the revolutionary

---

to Madero, April 18, 1911, AdeM.

[11] Cabrera, *Obras políticas*, p. 144.

[12] Vázquez Gómez, *Memorias políticas*, p. 235; Esquivel Obregón, *Democracia y personalismo*, pp. 35ff.

leader more docile. With satisfaction they reported that Madero agreed to the following terms: establishment of the principle of "No Reelection and Effective Suffrage"; nomination by the revolution of fourteen governors and four cabinet ministers; evacuation of Sonora, Chihuahua, and Coahuila by federal forces and restoration and preservation of order in the area by revolutionary troops; and the resignation of Corral.[13] Although followers of Madero have argued that the resignation of Díaz was implicit, that this requirement was not specified glaringly revealed the influence of the Madero family. Madero, torn between the revolutionists' insistence on the retirement of Díaz and his family's anxiety to end the struggle, was vacillating. He endeavored to justify the negotiations on the grounds that he hoped to obtain such conditions as to make it impossible for Díaz to continue in power. "What is going to happen is that we will give General Díaz an honorable way of retiring." [14]

Madero invited various partisans who would be affected by the negotiations—including the provisional governors of Yucatán, Coahuila, and Zacatecas—to participate in the discussions. Sánchez Azcona, concerned about Madero's willingness, under family pressure, to accept only the resignation of Corral, telegraphed Dr. Vázquez Gómez to attend the negotiations. On April 27 the armistice was extended for an additional five days to permit the attendance of a government commissioner with authority. Limantour designated Francisco Carbajal, Magistrate of the Supreme Court, as the official representative of the government with permission to utilize the services of Braniff and Esquivel Obregón.

In the adobe hut which served as headquarters for Madero the insurgent leaders held preliminary negotiations. The building consisted of a kitchen and a meeting room, and was only large enough to house Madero, his wife, a secretary, and a homeopathic physician who attended the revolutionary leader. Later the house was jocularly referred to as the "Grey House,"

[13] *Ibid.*, pp. 37-38.
[14] Madero to Emilio Vázquez, April 25, 1911, AdeM.

residence of the Provisional President. For two long days the other insurgents, led by Dr. Vázquez Gómez, argued the absolute necessity of demanding the resignation of Díaz. At first, Madero objected to that demand because he was "compromised with Limantour," apparently a reference to the agreement of April 22. Finally, the revolutionary leader agreed to the requirement that Díaz resign "in a short time" and to the doctor's recommendation of de la Barra, Minister of Foreign Affairs, for interim provisional president.[15]

Carbajal arrived on May 3, and due to the formal character of the forthcoming talks the armistice was extended for seventy-two hours and was to cover the additional territory between Ciudad Juárez and Ojinaga. The first meeting between Madero and Carbajal took place late that afternoon at a point midway between Ciudad Juárez and the rebel camp. Seated in an automobile the two men talked for over an hour arranging the details for the first conference to be held the following day. Carbajal rejoined his fellow negotiators in an optimistic mood because Madero had not insisted "on presenting the proposition that Díaz should retire."[16]

The government commissioner may have misjudged Madero's attitude, for in the instructions, dated May 4, which the revolutionary leader prepared for the peace negotiators, Vázquez Gómez, Pino Suárez, and Francisco Madero, Sr., there was provision for the resignations of Díaz, Corral, and Madero (as provisional president) and for de la Barra to assume charge of the government. About ten o'clock on the fourth Carbajal and the three revolutionary commissioners met near the little grove of trees which had been selected as the conference point. Credentials were exchanged, and, after some preliminary remarks, the meeting was adjourned until four that afternoon.

A half hour before the appointed time Madero provided his commission with the aforementioned instructions. His father refused to attend the meeting because of the resignation

[15] Vázquez Gómez, *Memorias políticas*, pp. 135-43.
[16] Esquivel Obregón, *Democracia y personalismo*, p. 49.

clause. At the official conference, with only three delegates in attendance, Dr. Vázquez Gómez presented the condition relative to the resignation of Díaz. Carbajal, expressing his surprise and indignation, declared that since he lacked instructions to negotiate on that basis, the conference was ended. On May 6, with the armistice time running out, Carbajal notified the revolutionists that he was unable to continue under the conditions proposed because of political and patriotic considerations.

That last day of the armistice Braniff, Esquivel Obregón, and Rafael Hernández requested a conference with the revolutionary leaders. Madero acceded to this petition, and the meeting was held in the conference room of the adobe hut. The room was crowded with the military and civilian leaders of the revolution. Madero, simply dressed in a Norfolk jacket, casual shirt, and trousers thrust into tan riding boots, frequently left the room to issue orders or to attend to some detail. Several spokesmen presented the views of their respective sides. Esquivel Obregón spoke on the desirability of ending hostilities, and Braniff warned of the foreign intervention which would undoubtedly follow an attack on Ciudad Juárez. Madero, his foot on a chair and supporting himself on its back, rejected this argument as specious. Pino Suárez and Federico González Garza spoke for the revolutionary cause.

Rafael Hernández, sensing that the negotiations were headed for failure, vehemently interjected:

> What do you wish, revolutionary gentlemen? Are you perhaps not satisfied? Do you wish still more blood? Has not enough been spilled? Are you not satisfied to see a distinguished and strong government treating with rebels who are not yet in possession of a single important city? [17]

The negotiations were thereupon renewed with a discussion of resignations and a mixed government. It was at this juncture that Venustiano Carranza pronounced his prophetic

[17] *Ibid.*, p. 55.

warning that a "revolution that compromises, is a revolution lost . . . The revolution that compromises, commits suicide." [18] Madero ended the meeting stating that the Mexican nation could not tolerate this opprobrium and that, therefore, the revolution must go forward until the tyrant should fall.

The following day, May 7, Madero executed two significant actions. He addressed his troops advising them of the failure of the negotiations because of the refusal of Díaz to surrender his position. He informed the insurgents that to avoid international complications he was ordering, over the protests of some of his officers who desired to attack Ciudad Juárez, a withdrawal to the south. He promised that conditions shortly would permit a march on the national capital and complete victory.[19] In the light of the decision to withdraw, the revolutionary leader appointed a permanent peace commission, composed of Dr. Vázquez Gómez, the elder Francisco Madero, and Pino Suárez, which was to remain in El Paso prepared to consider any new peace proposals.

That same Sunday evening General Díaz issued a manifesto to the nation in which he summarized the efforts of the government to deal with the revolt. The President charged that despite the good will of the government, the peace negotiations had failed because of the exorbitant demands of the revolutionists. He indicated that he would retire "when his conscience told him that on retiring he would not be surrendering the country to anarchy." [20] The public reaction was the opposite of that which apparently had been anticipated. The manifesto was taken as a confession that the government lacked elements sufficient to cope with the rebellion, and the pledge of retirement was considered vague. Military developments frustrated any hope of renewed negotiations on the basis of the Díaz statement.

On May 8 there occurred an unexpected attack on Ciudad Juárez. The customs town, with about eight thousand inhabi-

[18] Fernández Güell, *Episodios de la Revolución*, pp. 70-71.
[19] CdeM, III, No. 1282, Biblioteca Nacional.
[20] Cabrera, *Obras políticas*, pp. 448-50.

tants, was a brutish community contrasted with El Paso across the river. The defense force of General Navarro numbered less than seven hundred effectives among federal soldiers and auxiliaries, and the much talked-about fortifications constructed by Colonel Tamborrel consisted of rough trenches and some barbed wire. The revolutionists were breaking camp and beginning the southward march ordered by Madero at 10:30 A.M. when shots were heard. A part of the rear guard under Orozco, located in the small valleys formed by some arroyos which opened into the Bravo, had exchanged fire with the federals entrenched near the river.

Although there are many accounts of how the attack started, there is good reason to suppose that the one attributing its initiation to revolutionary chiefs who opposed the withdrawal is correct. Madero quickly gave a ceasefire order and advised Navarro that the attack was unauthorized. He told the federal commander that he had ordered the suspension of fire and requested that Navarro do the same. However, Madero's order was not obeyed. The insurgent leader attributed this situation to the fact that with the opening of hostilities sympathizers within the city (estimated at four hundred) and volunteers from El Paso, elements refractory to discipline, entered the fray. Madero persisted in his efforts to end the fighting by sending an envoy carrying a white flag with orders to cease fire. The messenger was fired on and had to return to camp.

By three in the afternoon the revolutionists had captured the front line of trenches, and the federals had fallen back. An hour later Madero finally alerted his troops to prepare for a general attack. Some of his men acted immediately, but the revolutionary leader again ordered suspension because he did not want to initiate action without advising Navarro. Francisco Madero had accepted the elemental logic of the situation which he had not been able to control.

The general plan had Garibaldi and Orozco advancing along the right bank of the river from the west, Villa attacking from the south, and José de la Luz Blanco attacking from the east. By eleven that night the federals had withdrawn from all the outlying trenches, and the rebels had captured four blocks in the northern part of the city and were advancing toward the south. All night the fighting continued. The insurgents neutralized the street trenches of the defenders by boring their way through the rows of adobe houses with bars of iron and sticks of dynamite. At midnight a three-man commission was sent to demand the surrender of the plaza, but Navarro refused.

The following morning the revolutionists began to take positions for the final assault. The water pipes and electric lines supplying the defenders were cut. That afternoon the firing was intensified. By 5 P.M. the federal positions were reduced to a handful of fortified points in the southwest part of the town: the jail, the church, the barracks, the bull ring, and the park. A sharp attack on the left forced the defenders, also under blistering fire from the roof tops, to withdraw from the bull ring and the park. Colonel Tamborrel died in this fighting. The post office was set on fire to drive the federals out of the nearby church. On the right flank another force endeavored unsuccessfully to cut communications between the various positions and the barracks. However, the rebels did succeed in so surrounding these points that the enemy could only retreat to the barracks where Navarro was located.

Because of these developments and to avoid the destruction of his forces bit by bit, the federal commander ordered all his troops to concentrate in the barracks. This position was the main munitions depository, and there was a blocked well near by which Navarro hoped, in vain, would yield some water. By 9 A.M. on the tenth of May, with the barracks position virtually surrounded, the defenders, outnumbered and exhausted by weariness, hunger, and thirst, realized the futility of continued resistance. Early that afternoon Navarro surrendered "to avoid the useless sacrifice" of his men.[21]

It is an oversimplification to assert that the surrender of

[21] "Report of Gen. Juan Navarro to Secretary of War and Marine, June 8, 1911," in Secretaría de Guerra y Marina, *Campaña de 1910 a 1911*, p. 288ff.

Navarro and some four hundred soldiers and the fall of the frontier town more than a thousand miles from the capital caused the fall of the Díaz government. The victory at Ciudad Juárez was the drop that overflowed the bucket, the *coup de grâce* for the Díaz regime. The revolutionary flame had spread like a prairie fire throughout the republic. Public opinion had been awakened creating an atmosphere that was inimical to the dictatorship. Only five of the thirty-one territorial entities were untouched by the revolution, and in most of the others the insurgents dominated the major portions. In many states effective federal control was limited to the capital and a few principal cities which, in most instances, were besieged by the rebels. Ambassador Wilson reported that by the time the definitive treaty of peace was signed the revolutionists controlled two thirds of the country and the "remaining one third was rapidly tending to the same direction." [22]

The success of the revolution, as the government's power to resist disintegrated during the second and third weeks in May, was remarkable. There was a mad rush of those sarcastically labeled "revolutionaries of the last moment" to scramble aboard the successful revolutionary band wagon. A seemingly unending stream of rebel successes were reported. In the north Saltillo, Torreón, Hermosillo, and Durango City were captured. On the west coast the port of Mazatlán and the capital of Colima fell to the insurgents. In the center of the nation the revolutionary forces captured Pachuca, capital of Hidalgo, while Morelia remained the only government foothold in Michoacán. To the east Tehuacán in Puebla and the capital of Tlaxcala were captured. The forces of Zapata and Figueroa in the south gobbled up Iguala, Chilpancingo, Cuautla, and Cuernavaca, and appeared as a threat to Mexico City.

Considering the dispersion and disorder with which the revolutionary bands were created and multiplied, the victory was exceedingly rapid. Indeed, the triumph was too easy and too rapid. Five months were inadequate for the situation to become clarified, for a sharp line to be draw between the old

[22] Wilson to Secretary Knox, May 23, 1911, SDF, 812.00/1981.

and the new, between reaction and revolution, for a cohesive revolutionary party to be organized, and for a common philosophy to be evolved and diffused for that party. There was not even time to create the channels of relations or the discipline of organization for the scattered revolutionary elements. There had not been evolved larger commands, let alone a single, over-all command. Madero remained, at best, a symbol rather than a chief of the revolution which he had initiated.[23]

The revolutionary chieftain entered Ciudad Juárez in triumph late in the afternoon of May 10. He established his headquarters in the customs-house and proceeded to name his Council of State: Dr. Vázquez Gómez (Foreign Relations); Gustavo Madero (Treasury); Pino Suárez (Justice); Federico González Garza (Government); Manuel Bonilla (Communications); and Carranza (War). This "cabinet" met daily in the salon of the customs-house to discuss the affairs of the provisional government.

General Navarro and his staff were being held in a room of the Jefatura Política (prefecture). Some of Orozco's men were demanding the life of the federal commander who, it was remembered, was associated with the killings at Cerro Prieto. Madero was determined to protect Navarro, and in this resolve he was inflexible to the point of heroism. At considerable risk he personally conducted the federal commander in an automobile to the bank of the Bravo where he permitted him to cross to safety on the American side as a prisoner under his word of honor. Madero was a civilized, not a sanguinary, person who was anxious to avoid needless spilling of blood. His conduct was admirable, but incongruous in the Mexican milieu.

The revolutionary leader was prompted to take steps to insure the safety of his prisoner by an instance of insubordination which occurred on May 13. That morning Madero was meeting with his counselors when Pascual Orozco entered and declared the Provisional President a prisoner. Outside was

[23] Molina Enríquez, *La revolución agraria,* V, 64-65; Tannenbaum, *Peace by Revolution,* p. 151.

Villa and one hundred and fifty soldiers. The troops apparently had been brought there unaware of the role they were to play. Shouting that he would die first and that Orozco was dismissed, Madero dashed outside where, avoiding efforts to seize him, he succeeded in addressing the soldiers. These ended by cheering the Provisional President. Madero and Orozco exchanged further words, but through the efforts of others present, a reconciliation was effected and embraces exchanged. Once again the revolutionary leader had displayed extraordinary presence of mind and courage.

The cause of the incident has been much discussed. Sympathizers of Orozco have argued that the military commander was moved by the plight of his men to complain of the lack of provisions. Unquestionably, he did complain to Madero of supply problems, but this condition probably was only the pretext for the incident. The protection afforded Navarro had caused dissatisfaction among the military. In addition, some of the officers were unhappy about the cabinet which Madero had named. Orozco particularly objected to the designation of Carranza to hold the war portfolio. The revolutionary leader told his military commander, quite properly, that he was not the person to tell him whom to appoint. Lastly, it was suggested that Orozco fell victim to the machinations of Esquivel Obregón and Braniff who desired to divide the insurgents. Although these gentlemen denied the allegation, some circumstantial evidence tended to confirm this suspicion, for it was known that Orozco had taken the two government representatives as his counselors and had conferred with them both in the revolutionary camp and at the Hotel Sheldon in El Paso.[24]

Naturally Orozco's act of insubordination created consider-

[24] Taracena, *Madero: Vida*, pp. 417-19; Amaya, *Madero y . . . revolucionarios*, pp. 194-99. Madero wrote to Esquivel Obregón that he did not believe that the government's representative was responsible for the incident. However, he charged that Esquivel Obregón's attacks against Vázquez Gómez and Carranza and his flattery of Orozco had influenced the commander powerfully. Accordingly, Madero informed Esquivel Obregón that he was *persona non grata* to the provisional government. May 16, 1911, AdeM.

able stir. Dr. Vázquez Gómez hastened to assure the world that the affair had no importance, and Madero and Orozco exchanged public letters in an effort to prove their solidarity. Madero assailed rumors of disunity and exaggeration of the incident and assured his general that he never had doubted his loyalty to the Provisional Government nor his personal friendship. Orozco proclaimed their indestructible union and assured Madero of his respect, loyalty, and constancy. He pledged that he would continue faithful to the revolution.[25] Villa was separated, with some extra compensation, from the revolutionary army, and Orozco, having effected his public reconciliation, withdrew to Casas Grandes. An unfortunate incident was closed.

The day after the surrender of Ciudad Juárez peace negotiations were renewed. Madero conferred with Carbajal on May 15 and 16. The discussion proceeded on the basis of the resignation of Díaz and the designation of de la Barra as interim president. De la Barra was to name a cabinet and fourteen provisional governors approved by the revolutionists.

Madero was inclined to accept the continuance of Limantour in the cabinet. The influence of Madero's family and the high estimate the revolutionary leader held of the minister's talents rather than any agreement explain this attitude. However, Dr. Vázquez Gómez successfully maneuvered privately and without authorization to eliminate Limantour. This action by the doctor was one more factor leading to division between him and Madero. Nevertheless, on May 17 the revolutionary leader, over his father's objections, accepted the *fait accompli* and signed the wire to Díaz stating the following conditions for peace: resignation of the President and the Vice-President; complete renovation of the cabinet; and detention of General Reyes, who was returning to Mexico at the government's request, at Havana.[26] A subsequent message that day listed

[25] *Dos Cartas Interesantes . . .*, May 15, 1911, CdeM, Biblioteca Nacional.

[26] Madero to Díaz, May 17, 1911, CdeM, I, No. 513, Biblioteca Nacional.

the persons recommended for cabinet and gubernatorial posts.

After these conditions had been accepted, a new five-day armistice embracing the whole country was arranged. On Sunday morning, May 21, in the customs-house, Dr. Vázquez Gómez dictated while Sánchez Azcona wrote the draft of the peace treaty. That night Madero's father, the doctor, and Carbajal met in the lobby of the Hotel Sheldon in El Paso. Pino Suárez could not be located, and he did not sign the treaty until the following day.

The trio drove by car to the customs-house in Ciudad Juárez followed by another car filled with newspapermen. They found the customs-house closed and dark. Therefore, by the light of the car's headlights the celebrated Treaty of Ciudad Juárez was signed. The pact provided that the resignations of Díaz and Corral should take place by the end of the month, that de la Barra would serve as interim president and call for general elections, that hostilities should cease with the understanding that the revolutionary forces were to be discharged, and that the interim government was to study popular desires with a view to satisfying them and to arrange for the indemnification for damages directly due to the revolution.[27]

The Treaty of Ciudad Juárez and what it signified was sharply criticized. The agreement was a transaction and not a triumph. Madero's acceptance of this arrangement was the result of his ideas and nature as well as of the influence of his family. Madero, with a horror of war, was anxious to end the bloodshed. He also was motivated by the fear that continued civil war would eventually result in the revival of the militarism which he blamed for much of Mexico's troubles since independence. A believer in democracy, he was anxious to prove his devotion to legal practices and constitutional procedures. He dreamed of leading his country with a policy of cooperation which would include all Mexicans, conciliate all interests, and return the nation to peace. Ingenuously he believed that the resignation of Díaz and the inception of

[27] Treaty of Ciudad Juárez, CdeM, III, No. 1290, Biblioteca Nacional.

political democracy would lead to needed reforms and the realization of his ideals.

These concepts meant compromise government. Unfortunately, Mexico was not ready for political democracy, and the existing institutional system had proved and was to prove inadequate for the revolutionary changes needed. Madero was warned that compromise did not answer the exigencies of the revolution and would have tragic consequences. Luis Cabrera, in an open letter to the revolutionary leader, observed that Madero's position was analogous to that of the surgeon who "ought to think very seriously before opening the wound," but that, "however, once the wound was opened, he must not heal it without having disinfected it completely."[28] And Carranza reportedly told Madero that he was "delivering to the reactionaries a dead revolution which will have to be fought over again."[29]

On May 24 crowds gathered in Mexico City shouting adherence to the revolution and demanding the resignation of Díaz. A large group gathered near the building of the Chamber anxious to learn the text of the rumored resignation. However, the sending of the message was delayed, and the crowd roared in protest interspersing cheers for Madero and the revolution with the ominous *Muera a Díaz* (Death to Díaz). Many proceeded to the private house of the President on Calle de Cadena to demand his resignation, but the presence of federal troops reduced the crowd to shouting.

Elsewhere in the city there were bloody clashes between police and the citizens. In the main plaza a tremendous mass of people gathered near the National Palace. Four times mounted police tried to disperse the crowd, supported the last time by riflemen in the towers of the Cathedral and machine gunners on the roof of the Palace. There were many casualties of this final, futile flaying by the Porfirian stick. The carnage might have been worse, but a pouring rain helped scatter the aroused crowd.[30]

[28] Cabrera, *Obras políticas,* pp. 204-13, 222.
[29] Fornaro, *Carranza and Mexico,* pp. 15-16.
[30] An alleged telegram from Madero relating to the alarming situation

The following day a vast, apparently peaceful, throng gathered near the doors of the Chamber of Deputies. They sang the national anthem and cheered Madero. Occasionally a shout for de la Barra was heard. That afternoon Porfirio Díaz reluctantly submitted his resignation. He explained that he was surrendering his post "respecting, as I have always respected, the will of the people" and avoiding "the continued spilling of blood, the destruction of the credit of the nation, and the [danger] of international conflict which would be necessary to retain it." [31]

De la Barra, on assuming the interim presidency, pledged free elections and declared that under no circumstances would he accept candidacy in the next electoral campaign. "The happiest day of my public life will be that on which, inside the shortest time which the electoral law and the situation in the country permits, I shall be able to transmit the power I have received today to the citizen whom the Republic elects." [32]

Francisco Madero, too, on May 26, issued a manifesto to the people. The revolutionary leader resigned the provisional presidency and asserted that the principles of the revolution had triumphed. Madero admitted that all the aspirations aroused by Article 3 of the Plan of San Luis Potosí (regarding land) would not be satisfied in full. However, he considered the sacrifice worth while to avoid prolonging the war and promised that constitutional means would satisfy legitimate rights under that article.

The insurgent leader called on all to recognize the interim government as the legitimate authority. He felt that the cabinet, "with ample" revolutionary representation, the provision-

---

in the capital was published in *El Heraldo*. The message to Robles Domínguez included the phrases "order the public" and "repress disorders with all energy." Madero was criticized, particularly for his choice of language. However, Manuel Amieva later admitted that he wrote the telegram, that Robles Domínguez signed Madero's name to it, and that de la Barra approved it and even added a sentence. Vázquez Gómez, *Memorias políticas*, p. 228.

[31] Cabrera, *Obras políticas*, p. 454.

[32] *Ibid.*, pp. 457-58.

al governors, and the honor of the Interim President should allay any fear among his followers. "Sr. de la Barra does not have any other support than public opinion, which unanimously proclaims the principles of the revolution. Therefore, we are able to say that the President of the Republic is entirely with us." As leader of the revolutionary party, Madero pledged his cooperation with the government. "I realize that, since I prompted the revolution, I am the chief of its party, and I have a sacred obligation to contribute to the reestablishment of order and public peace." [33]

Cooperation was the theme spoken on all sides, but at Veracruz on the last day of May an old man sailed into exile convinced that his way was the only way to govern Mexico.

[33] *Ibid.*, p. 459ff.

XI. An Anomalous Situation

ON THE FIRST DAY of June, Madero was ready to depart for the capital. Since the Central Railroad was disrupted north of Torreón, he found it necessary to proceed from Ciudad Juárez to Ciudad Porfirio Díaz across American territory. On leaving the United States the revolutionary leader restated his friendly attitude toward the country and its people. Escorted by one hundred men Madero boarded a train of the International Railroad. At the principal stations he was greeted by officials and applauded by the people. The reception which probably meant most to Madero occurred in San Pedro de las Colonias. Nine thousand persons gathered at the station, and a chorus of little girls sang the national anthem. After a brilliant reception and banquet at the Casino, Madero told his friends and neighbors that he was more proud "of the victories which I have obtained in the field of democracy than of those obtained in the field of war." [1]

At Torreón, Madero, his escort more than doubled, transferred to a special train of the Central Railroad for the journey to Mexico City by way of Zacatecas, Aguascalientes, and San Luis Potosí. At every station huge crowds gathered to see and hear the victorious leader of the revolution. By horse and foot the people of Mexico came to line the right of way for a glimpse of Madero. Slowly the train moved across the gently rising terrain of central Mexico in an unprecedented triumphal journey. Madero was scheduled to arrive at the Colonia Station

[1] CdeM, III, No. 1287, Biblioteca Nacional.

in the capital at 10 A.M. on June 7. That morning, about dawn, Mexico City was shaken by an earthquake. Perhaps it was an omen, but, if so, what did it augur? Proof that popular enthusiasm was not to be dampened was the following couplet:

Cuando Madero llegó
hasta la tierra tembló.

When Madero arrived
Even the earth trembled.[2]

The natural phenomenon filled the streets of the city with people, and they remained, a noisy, jubilant throng, to await a glimpse of the apostle. The station and the streets between it and the National Palace were jammed with people. Every vantage point along the route, including roofs and the statues on the Paseo, were occupied by the swarming mass of humanity. Finally, shortly after midday, Madero's train pulled into the station. The bells of the Cathedral and of ninety other churches pealed the joyous message. Factory sirens shrieked, and the whistles of locomotives in the various stations shrilly joined in the din. It seemed as though the pent-up feelings of an entire people had been released in a momentous explosion of emotion.

It required more than an hour for Madero to accept the initial greetings and to work his way through the crowded station. A group of workers presented him with a tricolor band which he placed over his right shoulder. A large carriage, drawn by a superb team of four horses mounted by grooms and led by stableboys in red dresscoats, was provided for the ride along the Paseo to the Palace. As Madero passed, there were shouts of *vivas,* tramping of feet, clapping of hands, and blowing of horns. Many threw flowers and green branches as the carriage passed. An estimated hundred thousand persons cheered deliriously for Francisco I. Madero, leader of the revolution and symbol of change.

Madero was deeply moved by the unprecedented reception. Edith O'Shaughnessy noted his "pleasant, ready smile" and

[2] Fernández Güell, *Episodios de la Revolución,* p. 88.

reported that "there is something about him of youth, of hopefulness and personal goodness." The same observer noted that Sra. Madero, riding beside her husband, "might be a dark type of New England woman with a hint of banked fires in her eyes. There is a sort of determination in the cut of her face, which is rather worn, but with an expression of dignity." [3]

Amid the cheers for Madero were interspersed some shouts of *viva democracia* (hurrah for democracy). It was reported that a peasant inquiring of another about the nature of *democracia* was told that it was probably the lady with Sr. Madero.[4] The story may be apocryphal, but it is suggestive of the tremendous task facing Madero, the advocate of political democracy as the key to the solution of Mexico's problems. An opposition newspaper, making a startlingly speedy appearance, commented ironically that the "delirious, insensate, and slavish popularity" which was showered on Madero "we have seen only for the celebrated bullfighter Rodolfo Gaona." [5] The pessimism of the opposition paper was shared by the American Ambassador. Although he withheld final judgment on Madero, Wilson reported that "by the country at large [!] and by a portion of his own family he is regarded as a dreamer of uncertain tendencies and a vendor of political nostrums unsuited to these peoples and these times." He warned the State Department that Mexico undoubtedly was entering upon a "long period of turbulence and political unrest." [6]

The triumphal procession proceeded to the National Palace where the revolutionary leader and his party were received by Interim President de la Barra. After a brief conversation, Madero and de la Barra went out on the central balcony of the building to be acclaimed by the people in the plaza below. Madero, exhausted physically from the journey and emotionally from the reception, went to his father's house to rest. The keen observer must have been conscious of an anomalous

[3] O'Shaughnessy, *A Diplomat's Wife in Mexico*, pp. 74-75.
[4] Gruening, *Mexico and Its Heritage*, pp. 96-97.
[5] *El Manaña*, June 18, 1911.
[6] May 23, 1911, SDF, 812.00/1981.

situation that June day. The people cheered wildly for Madero, victorious leader of the revolution, while another man occupied the National Palace.

Unfortunately, the anomaly did not end there. The interim period proved to be a grave political error. What was necessary for the re-establishment of peace was a strong government animated by a desire to satisfy the aspirations of the people. Instead, the interim period was one of ambiguity and confusion with the government simply drifting through its allotted span of existence. Madero, superbly confident, regarded the de la Barra government as a sort of antechamber of his own and erroneously believed that the Interim President, dependent on the revolution which had placed him in power, was incapable of a will of his own.

De la Barra complained increasingly that his government was being handicapped by the interference of Madero. On the one hand, the presence of Madero with his prestige as the successful revolutionary leader vitiated the effectiveness of de la Barra. On the other hand, the interim government, transitory though it was, proved most damaging to the revolutionary cause. This period tended to deprive Madero of his individuality and force. During these few months deep and dangerous divisions developed among the revolutionary chiefs. Worst of all, the interim government, instead of giving legal character to the revolution, appeared to restore the situation as it existed under the old regime. The victorious revolution was represented by a minority in the government on practically all levels.

Francisco León de la Barra, lawyer and diplomat, had served the Díaz government. The distinguished-appearing, ceremonious, somewhat affected Interim President had no tie with Madero or with the revolution. Although he recognized that he owed his position to the revolution and that he had to lean on Madero for support, he did not consider himself bound to either. De la Barra retained the portfolio of foreign affairs in a cabinet with only three persons truly representing the revolution. Manuel Calero (Development) and General Rascón

(War), like the Interim President, had been associated with the old regime. The ministries of Treasury and Justice were headed by Madero's uncle Ernesto Madero and his cousin Rafael Hernández. Despite the relationship both cabinet officers represented conservative thinking and action.

Minority representation of the revolution in the cabinet was provided by Dr. Vázquez Gómez (Public Instruction), Emilio Vázquez (Government), and Manuel Bonilla (Communications). Below the heads of the executive departments the old Porfirian bureaucracy remained in their posts and directed public affairs, though a number of revolutionaries were offered posts in the executive departments. Some refused for personal reasons or as a matter of principle; others were prevented from participating by the machinations of de la Barra.[7] The practice of utilizing experienced persons regardless of affiliation with the dictatorship was the inevitable consequence of the compromise of Ciudad Juárez and the policy of conciliation.

The personnel of the Supreme Court remained unchanged, and the 25th Legislature, the last of the Díaz period, remained as the legislative organ throughout the interim period. Although Madero expected the Chambers to accept the implications of the revolution's victory, the members of the Congress, composed overwhelmingly of supporters of the old regime, proved increasingly refractory. As though suddenly aware of their new freedom the legislators criticized the disturbances of the public order, the slowness and ineffectiveness of the discharge of the revolutionary forces, and the reimbursement of Gustavo Madero for revolutionary expenses. They even found cause to criticize the conduct of the antirevolutionary interim executive.

The position of the revolution was the same in the state and local governments. As a result of the victory of the revolution, provisional governors recommended by Madero and his associates were named. To the credit of the revolutionary leader most of those designated were well received by the people of

[7] Chargé d'Affaires Dearing to Secretary of State, Sept. 1, 1911, SDF, 812.00/2334.

the respective states, all were civilians, and all but two, in contrast to those of the Díaz regime, were natives of the states they were named to head. However, the old, conservative state legislatures remained, and conflict was the order of the day between the two branches of the provincial governments. In Coahuila, Carranza almost lost his freedom of action due to legislative opposition. In Veracruz the legislature sought to designate Emilio Leycegui as provisional governor rather than León Aillaud, who had been selected by the revolutionists. In Sinaloa and Jalisco the provisional governors found it necessary to dissolve the refractory legislatures.

This situation was made more difficult by Madero's insistence that the provisional governors preserve a neutral, impartial legal position in the state elections. He wrote Pino Suárez in Yucatán that he recognized the importance of victory in the state elections, but that nothing should be done which "may serve as a pretext for our adversaries to say that there has been the slightest pressure." When Governor Banderas of Sinaloa was reported to be exercising pressure on the legislature in the matter of the gubernatorial election, Madero angrily promised to hold him responsible for his conduct. He declared that he was determined to collaborate with de la Barra "in guaranteeing that the will of the people would be respected."[8] This insistence on neutral conduct, admirable and idealistic as it may appear, meant dependence on federal forces, loss of popular support, and increasingly conservative governors.

The conservative newspapers were the most numerous and included the most influential organs. *El Imparcial* lauded and supported de la Barra and other conservatives against Madero and the revolution. *El País,* a Catholic paper which had opposed the Díaz government, was joined by *La Nación,* organ of the National Catholic party, in an anti-Madero campaign. *El Demócrata Mexicano* and *El Progreso Latino,* revolutionary papers, became supporters of Reyism, a position endorsed by

[8] Madero to Pino Suárez, June 30, 1911, and to Gov. Juan M. Banderas, Sept. 20, 1911, AdeM.

a whole group of periodicals. *El Diario, El Mañana, La Tribuna,* and *El Heraldo Mexicano* were other publications devoted to opposing the Maderistas whose principal organ was *Nueva Era.*

Perhaps the most disturbing condition in the eyes of the revolutionists was the maintenance of the federal army intact while the discharge of the revolutionary troops proceeded. De la Barra consciously availed himself of every opportunity to fortify the military forces of the old regime. One of his first acts was to award Military Merit Crosses to General Porfirio Díaz, Colonel Reynaldo Díaz, and other prominent military figures of the old regime. Madero, in the interests of conciliation, also tended, unaware of the consequences, to fortify the federal army. The revolutionary leader repeatedly pointed out that the dictatorship and not the federal army had been defeated. He praised the heroism and abnegation of the federal soldiers and described them as the defenders of republican institutions. As proof of his desire for order and lawfulness and in the name of conciliation Madero endorsed and supported the rapid discharge of the revolutionary forces. The insurgents, distressed and fearful, viewed these developments with a jaundiced eye, and conflicts between the forces were inevitable and frequent.

Outstanding revolutionists were disturbed by the conditions described, and wrote their leader of their fears and disapproval. From Guadalajara, Roque Estrada warned Madero that he was being accused of "weakness and complacency with the enemies" of the revolution.[9] Luis Cabrera advised that the government should eliminate and replace all the old elements, but, actually, he doubted very much that de la Barra would take such action. González Garza warned against the discharge of revolutionary forces beyond those who had been guilty of disturbing the peace.

Madero's replies affirmed his confidence in a glorious future for the revolution. His attitude was based on optimism, a generous interpretation of events, and a faith in the democratic

[9] June 26, 1911, AdeM.

potentialities of the people. He could not understand the wave of pessimism which made the situation appear so grave. Regarding his declining prestige, Madero argued that it was only an apparent, relative, easily explained loss. The defeated, he felt, recovered from the initial shock and finding themselves at liberty, were logically assuming the opposition. The reversal of previously friendly newspapers he attributed to thoughtless reactions to the false impressions of the moment. In any event, Madero declared that he was not alarmed by the attitude of the press because "the people have an admirable instinct and are not easily deceived." In conclusion, he praised the patriotism of de la Barra, who "has given proofs of perfectly understanding his patriotic mission." [10]

Although some of this confidence was only for public consumption, it nevertheless serves to illustrate the excessive optimism of the revolutionary leader and his wholehearted determination to adhere to the compromise solution and the conciliatory policy. Understandable, even though predicated on false premises, were Madero's various conciliatory gestures: his insistence on the discharge of his revolutionary followers; his obsequiousness toward federal Colonel Aureliano Blanquet after a bloody clash in Puebla between federals and insurgents; and his attendance at a banquet in the Borda Gardens with representatives of the conservative clique of Morelos. To the majority of revolutionists, who had not accepted the compromise solution, this conduct was reprehensible, and Madero found himself criticized and attacked by elements of the revolution.

Particularly distressing to those persons who were devoted to order was the continuation of disorders after the termination of the revolutionary conflicts. The rural security enjoyed under the dictatorship seemed to have disintegrated. Brigandage and the lack of discipline of some revolutionary leaders and troops were only a partial explanation of conditions. In Chihuahua, Durango, Jalisco, and Hidalgo, but particularly in Puebla and Morelos, rural properties were invaded and seized by groups

[10] Madero to Cabrera and to González Garza, July 30, 1911, AdeM.

of peasants. These were outcroppings of the rural discontent and warnings of the urgent need for agrarian reform. There were encounters and disturbances in other areas, and American Ambassador Wilson reported that conditions close to anarchy existed in seven states.[11] Labor too manifested its discontent over unsolved problems by strikes which were facilitated by new-found freedom and the relative tolerance of the authorities. In the capital transportation was hobbled by a strike of the electric transit workers which was accompanied by violence. A few days later the city's bakers went on strike.

The conservative and foreign elements complained bitterly about the violence and the failure to deal with it energetically. The impatience and disgust of these elements found expression in the press and on the floor of Congress. Much of this criticism was directed against Madero and the revolution. Henry Lane Wilson advised the United States State Department, in a report that now appears disturbingly prophetic, that if the disorders were allowed to continue, a formidable opposition to Madero might develop "backed by the army, the Catholic Church, and the foreign and commercial elements."[12] Madero was beginning to find himself between two fires which were to harass him to the very end: the revolutionists, angry and disappointed with the compromise and demanding change; and the conservatives, critical of disorders, cynical regarding Madero's political ideas, and fearfully opposed to any change.

De la Barra's government had to deal with three major problems: the pacification of the country and the restoration of order; the repayment of revolutionary expenses and the discharge of revolutionary forces; and the arrangement of presidential elections. The Interim President regarded the pacification of the country as his most difficult and immediate task. In this Madero cooperated wholeheartedly from the first. Immediately after signing the Treaty of Ciudad Juárez he dispatched scores of telegrams to his civil and military leaders advising them that he had signed the agreement and ordering

[11] Wilson to Secretary Knox, July 11, 1911, SDF, 812.00/2219.
[12] June 23, 1911, SDF, 812.00/2181.

them to honor the cessation of hostilities and to assist in the restoration of normal conditions.

One telegram carried instructions to the revolutionary leader in Cananea, Sonora, to assure the Yaqui Indians that those of their tribe outside the state would be repatriated and that their lands would be returned quickly to them. The Yaquis, long victims of the oppressive dictatorship, had risen in support of the Madero revolution. Madero recognized the urgent need for action in this case in the interests of justice, pledges, and pacification. Just before leaving Ciudad Juárez he had issued a statement thanking the Yaquis for their services and reiterating the promises of repatriation and of return of lands for cultivation. He asked them to have faith and to return to their homes.[13]

On the first of September, Madero, representing the government, signed a treaty with eleven representatives of the Yaquis. By this agreement the government ceded to the tribes national territory in the various *ejidal* regions to be cultivated on the government's account at a stated daily salary. When all the land had been irrigated and opened to cultivation and when the first successful harvest had been gathered, the lands were to be divided among the inhabitants. If additional lands were needed, the government would acquire them in adjacent areas. The lands so distributed were to be inalienable for thirty years. The government also committed itself to furnishing provisions until the first harvest, schools, a pair of mules for each family receiving between five and ten hectares, and tax exemption for thirty years.[14] This agreement was a major factor in the reestablishment of peace in Sonora.

In Lower California the followers of the Liberal Junta, associated with American filibusters, continued their campaign. By early May the Liberals were virtual masters of the northern district of that area. They refused to accept the agreement of

[13] Madero to Eugenio H. Gayou, May 26, 1911, CdeM, II, No. 774; Manifesto to Yaqui Chiefs and Soldiers, June 1, 1911, CdeM, III, No. 1296, Biblioteca Nacional.

[14] *El País*, Sept. 2, 1911.

Ciudad Juárez, and Ricardo Flores Magón called on the Maderistas to "turn your rifles . . . against your chiefs the same as against the federals." [15] Despite the apparently irreconcilable differences, Madero hoped to achieve a peaceful solution. He arranged for the release of Juan Sarabia from prison and commissioned him to negotiate with the Liberals. Jesús Flores Magón, a brother of the Liberal leaders, accompanied Sarabia to Los Angeles early in June. They urged the Liberals to suspend hostilities and promised that under the new government there would be liberty in politics, press, and speech. The mission failed, and Madero endorsed and supported more energetic measures by the government.

The rebels in Lower California met increasing resistance from the inhabitants and from federal troops reinforced by Maderista revolutionaries in that area. Madero prepared to order General Viljoen with a thousand revolutionaries to assist in the pacification, and he facilitated the transfer of federal troops from Chihuahua. On June 18 a federal-Maderista force captured Mexicali, and four days later filibuster General Mosby surrendered Tijuana. Little aid was forthcoming from Los Angeles where American authorities arrested the Flores Magón brothers and others for violations of the neutrality laws. The major subsequent efforts of the Liberals were in the field of propaganda. Ricardo Flores Magón attacked Madero, charging him with betrayal of his promises and of the revolution.[16]

Elsewhere in the country unrest continued. By mid-July chaotic conditions persisted in half a dozen states. In the others, where federal authorities were nominally in control, sporadic outbreaks continued to occur. De la Barra blamed the disturbances on the continuance of revolutionary forces in arms. He indicated that he would push for the discharge of the insurgents and, abandoning his policy of toleration, take drastic action to meet the disturbances.

To provide for the indemnification and discharge of the

[15] *Regeneración,* May 27, 1911.

[16] The Liberal Manifesto of Sept. 23, 1911, which replaced the program of July 1, 1906, revealed that the Junta had moved far along the path

revolutionary forces the de la Barra government requested the authorization of six million pesos. During the discussion of this matter the Secretary of Development, Manuel Calero, informed Congress that the expenses of the revolution approximated six hundred thousand pesos, that Francisco Madero did not seek any reimbursement for his personal expenditures, and that there had been no foreign debt contracted. During June, Gustavo Madero, Financial Agent of the Revolution, requested of the Secretary of Government payment of some three hundred and nineteen thousand dollars for revolutionary expenses. The Secretary, Emilio Vázquez, recommended payment. The cabinet approved the reimbursement from the funds allocated by Congress on the basis of the clause in the Treaty of Ciudad Juárez which provided for indemnification of damages caused directly by the revolution.

Actually, of course, Gustavo was being reimbursed for the funds of French investors which he had diverted to the cause of the revolution. However, neither this circumstance nor the fact that the matter was handled publicly stayed the chorus of criticism. Arguing that the payment was based on a strained interpretation of the peace treaty and resorting to innuendo, conservatives in Congress and in the press lashed out at Gustavo and Francisco Madero despite the exemplary conduct of the latter. Defenders of the action indulged in sophistry when they argued the relative cheapness of this revolution.

The major portion of the funds appropriated by Congress on May 31 were to be used in the discharge of the revolutionary forces. If the compromise agreement of Ciudad Juárez was the first major error committed by Madero, the discharge of the revolutionary army provided in that agreement was his second great mistake. It deprived Madero and the revolution of independent support and placed the fate of his government in the hands of the federal army. The Interim President justified the move on the ground that the insurgents constituted

leading to an anarchist philosophy. This program spoke of the abolition of political, social, and economic institutions as well as of private property. Flores Magón, *Semilla libertaria,* II, 36-45.

a threat to order and a heavy drain on the federal treasury. The conservatives, who predominated in the interim administration, demanded the immediate disbandment of the revolutionists.

The lack of discipline among some of the revolutionary forces, particularly those who had joined the movement at the last hour, was notorious. While the revolutionary army consisted of some forty thousand men before the treaty, this force had grown to sixty thousand afterwards. These new supporters, many of whom had joined for economic reasons, evidenced the greatest lack of discipline. The conduct of these troops and their efforts to obtain discharge funds provided the opposition with an opportunity to attack and ridicule the revolution. Such conditions and the conservative clamor for discharge inclined Madero, committed to conciliation and anxious to reestablish order, toward discharge of the troops, particularly those recruited last.

The revolutionists, from Secretary of Government Emilio Vázquez down, instinctively opposed and consciously resisted the discharge policy. Numerous followers indicated to Madero the dangers involved. Insurgents in the field resisted the execution of the policy. The discharge program encountered such difficulties that on June 19, President de la Barra issued a sensational decree proclaiming that all revolutionaries who had not accepted discharge by July 1 would be considered as bandits to be pursued and annihilated. No such deadline for the discharge had been set in the Ciudad Juárez agreement.

A further complication was the fact that the insurgents, especially those in the south, viewed the federal army with hatred and fear. Conflicts between revolutionary and federal forces were numerous after the peace had been signed. Disturbances occurred in Hidalgo, Toluca, Pachuca, and Torreón. A bloody clash broke out in the city of Puebla. The fight, on the eve of a visit by Madero to the city, ended with a slaughter of insurgents quartered in the bull ring by troops of Colonel Blanquet. The next morning Madero tried to calm the situation by ordering the revolutionists, to whom he attributed a lack of discipline, to retire to the outskirts of the city. Apparently with much the same purpose he proceeded to follow his arranged social schedule. The insurgents, many of them considering that their forces had been provoked, felt neglected and betrayed. Madero's efforts to support the compromise and re-establish peace were costing him his defense and his supporters.

The discharge of the revolutionary forces proved to be a difficult and costly project. At the close of the interim period de la Barra reported that the cost of pacification of the country had exceeded five million pesos.[17] Ultimately, the most serious situation arising out of the discharge policy and the friction between the revolutionaries and the federals was that involving the forces of Emiliano Zapata, centered in the state of Morelos.

[17] This figure included the payment to Gustavo, "the only direct debt which has been paid for the account of the said revolutionary government." De la Barra, *"Informe . . . el 16 de septiembre de 1911,"* in *Diario Oficial,* 66, No. 14, 209-18.

XII. "The White President"

CONSERVATIVE ELEMENTS lauded the conduct of de la Barra whom they designated "The White" or "Pure President". The revolutionaries questioned that description in the light of the Interim President's overall performance and, most particularly, his policy in Morelos. A combination of factors produced an explosive situation in Morelos. Practically all of the state enjoys a temperate climate, and virtually from the conquest, large estates devoted to the growing of cane and the fabrication of sugar dominated the economy. The hacendados enjoyed a position of political and economic supremacy which they tenaciously refused to surrender. The landless population mass was mute testimony to the need for change.

The Madero revolution was supported instinctively as a means to rapid, fundamental change. When Madero arrived in Mexico City early in June, he was greeted by Emiliano Zapata and several members of his staff. The following day, after lunch, the revolutionary leader conferred with the thirty-eight-year-old general on the situation and problems in his state. Zapata, tall, dark, and with large mustaches, spoke of the immediate return of lands to the communities. Madero promised that it would be done, but only after careful study and in proper order within the law. Agreement existed on the principle, but the two men differed on the time and form for action. Zapata invited Madero to visit Morelos to see for himself the needs of the people.

In response to this invitation and to arrange for the discharge of the forces in the south Madero undertook a trip through Morelos and Guerrero, beginning on June 12. For the revolutionary leader, who was accompanied by his wife and several members of his staff, the trip was another triumphal tour marked by popular enthusiasm, cordial words, and reviews of revolutionary forces in Cuernavaca, Iguala, Chilpancingo, and Cuautla. In Cuernavaca the troops of Zapata escorted Madero to the Palace of Cortés where the revolutionary leader stated that he was proud to visit the land which bore the name of the famous Morelos and where the democratic struggle had been started by the people opposing the official gubernatorial candidate. During this visit Madero arranged for the discharge of the revolutionary troops. The discharge and disarming began with Gabriel Robles Domínguez representing Madero who returned to Mexico City on June 16.

According to the Zapatistas the discharge was proceeding on schedule, but the conservative elements charged that it was neither rapid nor effective and that disorders continued in the state. The press took up the cry. *El Imparcial* labeled Zapata the "Modern Atila." [1] There was even a rumor that the Morelos commander had rebelled against the government. Belying this charge was the presence of Zapata in the capital on June 24 to confer with Madero. Once again the man from Morelos spoke on the land problem, and once again Madero indicated that it was a difficult question that must be resolved within the law. Zapata reaffirmed his willingness to complete the discharge of his forces, and Madero agreed to a change of governors in the state.

However, during the next month reports continued that Zapata was resisting the discharge of his army. Madero's brother Raúl reported from Morelos his fears that Zapata was considering an uprising. Therefore, when a Zapatista commission came to the capital to confer with him, Madero suggested that Zapata come personally as his guest. Expressing fear of a plot against his life, the Morelos leader politely side-stepped the invitation at the same time reassuring Madero of his faith-

[1] *El Imparcial*, June 18, 1911.

fulness to Madero personally and to the principles which he sustained.

As an alternative Madero suggested that Zapata meet him at Tehuacán where he was planning to spend several weeks for medical treatment. Zapata again excused himself, this time on the grounds of illness, and sent his brother Eufemio to confer with Madero. The handwritten message delivered to the revolutionary leader assured him that Zapata's refusal was not "an act of disloyalty . . . I always will be the most faithful of your subordinates." [2] Eufemio Zapata told Madero that the disarming of the forces was eighty percent complete, but that there were reports of machinations by the landowners with the support of the Interim President to block the election of deputies. Madero expressed his confidence in de la Barra and urged completion of the discharge. Three days later he repeated his invitation to Zapata, pointing out the magnificent curative effects of the waters of Tehuacán.[3]

While Madero was trying to pacify Morelos and yet please the Zapatistas as much as possible, a significant change occurred in the cabinet of President de la Barra. On August 3, Alberto García Granados took charge of the Ministry of Government replacing Emilio Vázquez. The change, which Madero publicly sanctioned in another instance of cooperation with de la Barra, was regarded as a victory for de la Barra and the conservative elements. The entrance of García Granados into the cabinet coincided with an increase in the intrigue relating to Morelos.

President de la Barra decided to discharge the Zapatistas without awaiting the results of Madero's efforts, and García Granados ordered the demobilization in August. Zapata, displeased by these developments, telegraphed Madero, requesting that he interpose his influence to prevent the execution of the order. Not satisfied with Madero's reply, Zapata sent a

[2] Zapata to Madero, Aug. 4, 1911, AdeM.

[3] Madero to Zapata, Aug. 7, 1911. Taracena doubts the authenticity of this letter because it was dated in Mexico City. *Madero: Vida,* pp. 447-49.

second message asking for a "frank and sincere reply" if it was not possible to do as he had suggested in the earlier message.[4] Alarmed at the tone of this communication, Madero resolved to go to Morelos.

Madero left the capital hurriedly with the intention of conferring with Zapata at Cuautla. That evening he received a message from de la Barra advising him that the Interim President felt the government's prestige would suffer from prolonged negotiations which would "give no more result than to augment the effective forces of Zapata."[5] He told Madero that General Huerta had been directed to proceed to military operations if the immediate disarmament of the Zapatistas could not be arranged. However, if the disarming was accomplished, de la Barra promised to withdraw the federal forces and replace them with Maderistas.

Huerta's column arrived at Cuernavaca on August 10, causing profound distrust among the insurgents. Forces of Zapata committed various acts of rebellion, including the capture of Jojutla and Yautepec, as a reaction to the federal invasion. President de la Barra used this defiance as justification for sending Colonel Blanquet with reinforcements. Disruption of traffic by the Zapatistas prevented Madero from reaching Cuautla, and he returned to the capital.

Upon his return Madero received a message from Zapata blaming the bloody events on the federal intrusion and requesting that Madero use his influence to get the federals to leave Morelos. Emiliano told Madero's representative, Robles

[4] Zapata to Madero, Aug. 9, 1911, AdeM.

That same day Madero allegedly wrote Ambrosio Figueroa at Iguala offering him the post of governor and military commander in Morelos. Although it is conceivable that Madero, exasperated with Zapata, took this step, his subsequent conduct toward Zapata was at variance with this appointment which Figueroa declined.

Taracena, emphasizing the fact that the bearer of the letter was an envoy of García Granados (!), questioned the authenticity of the letter. Gen. Magaña implicitly discounted Madero's action by attributing it to the influence of de la Barra. Taracena, *Madero: Vida*, p. 448; Magaña, *Emiliano Zapata*, I, 265-69.

[5] De la Barra to Madero, Aug. 9, 1911, AdeM.

Domínguez, that he would not disarm his people until the lands had been restored to the *ejidos* (semi-collective land-holding villages). Thus was stated briefly the two principal demands of Zapata: evacuation of federal troops and land for the peasants. Madero notified Zapata that he would try again to reach Cuautla through Cuernavaca.

Despite the efforts of various persons to dissuade him and the rumors of dangers to his person, Madero departed for Cuernavaca with some members of his family and some of his staff on August 13. By telephone Madero conferred with Zapata. At the former's request the Morelos commander provided the following summary of his demands: the sovereignty of the state should be respected; a new provisional governor, but not Ramón Oliveros, should be appointed; the new government must conduct itself in accordance with the aspirations of the people; and federal troops should not be the ones responsible for the public safety. Zapata indicated his disposition to discharge his troops, but asked that some of them be chosen to preserve order in the state. Lastly, he stated that he was inclined to retire to private life.[6]

Madero reported this telephonic interview with Zapata to de la Barra. He indicated that the Morelos commander was well disposed and expressed his belief that an arrangement was merely a matter of settling details. Madero advised the Interim President that he had established "good relations" with General Huerta. De la Barra expressed his pleasure on receiving the favorable report. The following day Madero telegraphed his general impressions of the situation. He stated that the sending of federal troops was the worst possible measure if the discharge of the Zapatistas was desired. He argued cogently for a peaceful solution. He assured de la Barra that the imposition of a provisional governor would have to be accomplished by force and should not be attempted.

De la Barra replied affirming his desire to attain a peaceful solution, but he declared the necessity for "saving the principle of authority and the decorum of the government," "protecting

[6] Zapata, Aug. 14, 1911, at Cuautla, AdeM.

lives and property," and "assuring that the peace will be permanent." He suggested Ramón Oliveros, to whom Zapata had already objected, for governor![7]

Madero departed for Cuautla on August 17, arriving there about noon on the following day. In the central garden of the city he delivered an impressive speech, which, when reported in summary form in the capital, caused a sensation. Before Zapata and his principal generals the revolutionary leader presented his analysis of the situation. He spoke of the terrible struggle still fresh in everyone's memory and of his wish to be magnanimous with the conquered. Intrigues were to be expected, he said, but "we will show that we have sufficient judgment, prudence, and intelligence in order to confuse our enemies and make their intrigues fail." He stated that the trouble in Morelos had been the intrigue of "our enemies" who "do not resign themselves to the defeat they have suffered."

The revolutionary leader spoke bitterly of the calumnies of the opposition, which alleged that anarchy existed in Morelos, that the liberating army did not keep order, that he did not have authority with his followers, and that "your valiant General Zapata" is an assassin. He related how he had come to Morelos to quiet criticism and to arrange the discharge because "I know very well that even though you should be discharged, each one of you . . . always would be ready for our first call to take up arms in defense of our liberties."

[7] Madero to de la Barra, Aug. 14 and 15, 1911, and replies, Aug. 14 and 15, 1911, AdeM.

On August 15, Madero advised de la Barra that he was returning to the capital the following day for a conference and that Huerta and he had agreed that "if, unfortunately, hostilities were to break out, it would be preferable that all . . . [the Zapatistas] be united in order to deal them a decisive blow." Col. Magaña Cerda interprets this telegram as evidence of Madero's perfidy. A less severe judgment is more logical on the basis of Madero's consistent efforts to achieve a peaceful solution. Madero to de la Barra, Aug. 15, 1911, CdelaB.

Madero conferred at length with de la Barra on the sixteenth and supported most of Zapata's demands. Before departing for Cuautla Madero telegraphed Zapata that he believed the conflict would be resolved on a basis acceptable to the insurgent leader. "The essential condition is that you should continue having faith in me as I have in you." Madero to Zapata, Aug. 17, 1911, AdeZ.

Affirming his determination to avoid bloodshed, Madero concluded that

I have come here to bring calm and traquillity, and I will not leave your state . . . until you have security that your rights will be respected in every sense. Have faith in me, as I have in you, and we will continue marching without any obstacle along the new path of Democracy and Liberty.[8]

After this discourse Madero conferred with Zapata in a local hotel. Agreement was achieved, and Madero advised de la Barra that the Zapatistas had accepted the government's conditions. He reported that they would acquiesce to Eduardo Hay for governor, though preferring Professor Miguel Salinas, and would subscribe to Raúl Madero as area chief of arms. The discharge would begin the next day, but Madero urged that the federal troops be reconcentrated in Cuernavaca and withdrawn from Morelos "as soon as possible," because "it is very difficult otherwise to overcome the distrust [of the Zapatistas]." However, President de la Barra, disturbed by alarming reports from Governor Juan Carreón, ordered General Huerta to be ready to take whatever measures might be necessary to counter depredations.[9]

While Madero continued his pacific efforts, General Huerta, apparently on governmental orders, made suspicious moves which aroused the distrust and fears of the Morelos insurgents. On August 19, Madero reported that the discharge had begun, but to facilitate it he again urged that Huerta be ordered back to Cuernavaca. He advised that Huerta and Blanquet "are hated in the region," and that it seemed as if the former desired to provoke a conflict. He noted that the agrarian question was the principal one agitating the Morelos leaders and that he had told Hay that, if he became governor, "he ought to organize immediately a local agrarian commission . . . to study the problem here and to solve it as soon as possible."[10]

Madero's concern about Huerta was justified that very day

[8] Speech of Madero at Cuautla, Aug. 18, 1911, AdeM.

[9] Madero to de la Barra and reply, Aug. 18, 1911, AdeM.

[10] Madero to de la Barra, Aug. 19, 1911, AdeM.

when the federal commander mobilized his forces and marched threateningly toward Yautepec not far from Cuautla. Madero quickly protested to de la Barra that the move had interrupted the discharge and that unless the troops were withdrawn the situation would worsen. "I consider commanders like Huerta and Blanquet the least appropriate for the mission of peace particularly in these states." The revolutionary leader also wired the Chief of the Federal Forces advancing on Yautepec warning against an attack.[11]

However, de la Barra was more impressed by other counsels and by reports of disorders from other sources. Gustavo Madero informed his brother that Governor Carreón was alarming the President and that Secretary García Granados was making imprudent statements to the effect that Zapata ought to surrender unconditionally and submit to trial![12] The Interim President telegraphed Madero that he was receiving disturbing reports from Morelos of Zapatista depredations and that he did not believe the insurgents would complete the discharge. He concluded that the "present situation . . . requires energetic action which I have decided to administer . . . I am giving orders to General Huerta to impose order in accord with earlier instructions."[13]

Madero felt that, as the observer on the scene, he was better able to judge the situation. He knew that the reports of depredations were exaggerated and that while federal forces remained in Morelos there would be neither pacification nor discharge. Therefore, he quickly replied to de la Barra, differing with the Interim President's decision and the bases on which it had been made. He declared that

> I am better able to appreciate the circumstances and the mode of realizing the government's desire in a dignified, decorous, and bloodless manner. I know what they are saying about Zapata in Mexico City, and it is not correct . . . The hacienda owners hate

[11] Madero believed that Huerta was working in agreement with General Reyes who had reentered the political picture. Madero to de la Barra and to Commander of Federal Forces, Aug. 19, 1911, AdeM.

[12] Gustavo Madero to Madero, Aug. 19, 1911, AdeM.

[13] De la Barra to Madero, Aug. 19, 1911, AdeM.

him because he is an obstacle to the continuation of their abuses and a threat to their undeserved privileges.[14]

The next day Madero tenaciously continued his efforts to obtain a peaceful settlement. Before leaving for Yautepec to try personally to avoid an armed clash he wrote de la Barra reminding him that the Zapatistas had agreed to the government's conditions, seeking only that the withdrawal of the federals should coincide with the discharge. "You gave your approval to these arrangements, and the fact that there has been one or another disorder in the rest of the state does not justify an attack on the towns of Yautepec and Cuautla where all has been quiet." [15]

In the face of Madero's urgent telegrams and an imposing popular protest demonstration in the capital, de la Barra and his cabinet ordered Huerta to suspend all movement until Yautepec was evacuated by the Zapatistas who were to concentrate at Cuautla for discharge. That the government remained unrelenting and unreasonable was confirmed by the ultimatum that if Zapata resisted the discharge or did not do it within forty-eight hours, "all elements will be concentrated against him." [16] Madero advised from Yautepec that the Zapatistas had agreed to evacuate that town and to proceed to Cuautla for discharge. He recommended that rurales or other acceptable forces occupy Yautepec. He told de la Barra that "I consider the conflict solved for which I congratulate you cordially." [17]

Indeed, it appeared that the difficult situation had been resolved. Yautepec was garrisoned by forces of Almazán while Huerta encamped a short distance away. Zapata's forces were formed at Cuautla, and the discharge was begun, for the third time, on August 21. Congratulations poured in for mediator Madero. De la Barra assured Madero that "I am sincerely pleased and I congratulate you for your effective and spon-

[14] Madero to de la Barra, Aug. 19, 1911, AdeM.
[15] Madero to de la Barra, Aug. 20, 1911, AdeM.
[16] De la Barra to Madero, Aug. 20, 1911, AdeM.
[17] Madero to de la Barra, Aug. 20, 1911, AdeM.

taneous intervention in that matter." However, that very day de la Barra confided to the American Chargé d'Affaires that "Madero's interference is most embarrassing." [18]

The President at times appeared to go along with Madero's efforts because the government could not afford to reject openly the activities of the popular revolutionary leader. However, de la Barra and his advisors really preferred others' evaluations of the situation. That the Interim President had not accepted unconditionally Madero's reported success in Morelos was indicated by his message late on the twenty-first informing the latter of the alarming reports from Governor Carreón that Eufemio Zapata was about to attack Cuernavaca. The revolutionary leader squelched that false charge with his reply informing the President that Zapata's brother, "submissive and obedient," was with him in Cuautla.[19]

Meanwhile, Madero's friends in the capital began to regard President de la Barra with marked distrust. The discontent of the Maderistas burst into the open in an editorial signed by Sánchez Azcona and published in *Nueva Era.* The journalist charged that "either the government of Sr. de la Barra has deceived Sr. Madero or General Huerta has disobeyed or has flouted the government." [20] De la Barra, extremely annoyed, protested the editorial which "places in doubt the correctness of my procedure and the veracity of my statements." [21]

In the interests of conciliation and to avoid the repercussions of a break between the revolutionaries and the government Madero telegraphed a public declaration to the director of *Nueva Era.* He stated that from the beginning de la Barra had favored "a firm, honorable, and conciliatory policy," and that though the Minister of Government (García Granados) had advocated an intransigent policy, the opinion of de la Barra had triumphed. Regarding Huerta, Madero charged that he had advanced not according to orders, but because he had

[18] De la Barra to Madero, Aug. 21, 1911, AdeM; Dearing to State Dept., Aug. 21, 1911, SDF, 812.00/2299.

[19] De la Barra to Madero and reply, Aug. 21, 1911, AdeM.

[20] *Nueva Era,* Aug. 22, 1911.

[21] De la Barra to Madero, Aug. 22, 1911, AdeM.

interpreted badly some of his instructions through not understanding or not wanting to understand the wishes of the government.[22]

The revolutionary leader returned to Mexico City on August 24, outwardly satisfied, but fully convinced that his efforts at pacific settlement had failed. The preceding day General Huerta had seized Yautepec and had begun to advance on Cuautla. Madero's protest to de la Barra fell on deaf ears. The Interim President excused himself on the grounds of a cabinet meeting. On August 25, Minister of Government García Granados declared that since the disarmament of the Zapatistas "has been a farce," the government took steps intended to "guarantee lives and haciendas in that state which has suffered too much."[23]

Under these circumstances Madero wrote a long letter to de la Barra in which, without ambiguities, the revolutionary leader challenged the conduct of the Interim President. This letter marks the formal break between the two men. Madero reminded de la Barra that he had come to power through the revolutionary power and cited examples of its support and cooperation. Madero then noted, however, that on the preceding day

> you told me that you wished to be left with more liberty, giving me to understand that you do not want me to mix any more in the affairs of government. Since I am guided by no personal ambition and am not impatient, . . . I am disposed to respect your wishes. I assure you that I will not again disturb you with my visits.

The revolutionary leader advised the President that while he would continue to support the government loyally, he would not be able to prevent his partisans and friends from attacking the president and the ministers for criticizable acts.

Madero counseled de la Barra against discharging any more insurgent troops. "Although you may believe in the loyalty of

[22] Madero to Sánchez Azcona, Aug. 22, 1911, AdeM.

[23] Reported in a telegram from Raúl Madero to Robles Domínguez, Aug. 25, 1911, AdeM.

the federal army, I do not have confidence in it as long as the changes in leaders, which I have indicated to you so many times and which you offered to make, have not been made." Regarding Morelos, Madero pointed out that he had intervened, at the risk of his life, to avoid a serious conflict. He noted that if what he "offered in your [de la Barra] name, with the approval of the Council of Ministers, is not complied with," he would be open to ridicule. Worse yet, the Zapatistas would believe that he "went there to betray them." Madero warned that in that case he would be forced to make public declarations justifying his conduct.[24]

The revolutionary leader's reaction against the conduct of the government may also be judged by his notes the next day to Zapata and to the other southern insurgent chiefs. He promised them all compensation for their services and assured Zapata that he did not credit the attacks directed against the Morelos revolutionary by his enemies.[25] The de la Barra government cynically attributed Madero's activities in Morelos to political motives. The administration apparently was determined to follow an aggressive policy. Huerta continued his threatening moves, and on August 29 the Cabinet approved orders to prosecute the war and to arrest Zapata. García Granados explained the policy with the following expression: "The government does not treat with bandits."[26]

Hostilities broke out that very day with a clash between federal forces and Zapatistas in Chinameca. Madero, on hearing the report of the clash, reportedly commented: "If they would have attended the suggestion which I made from Cuautla, Zapata would not have rebelled."[27] Although he made additional efforts to achieve peace through his brother Raúl, Madero, perhaps feeling that he had done all that was possible, departed on a political trip to Yucatán. From Campeche he wrote de la Barra that García Granados' "blindness

[24] Madero to de la Barra, Aug. 25, 1911, AdeM.
[25] AdeM.
[26] Ferrer de M., *Vida . . . de Madero,* p. 116.
[27] Magaña, *Emiliano Zapata,* I, 328.

is incomprehensible. It seems that his principal desire is to resolve every question by means of arms." [28]

During September the federal forces pressed the attack, and Ambrosio Figueroa, personal enemy of Zapata, was named governor of the troubled state. This martial political policy helped to strengthen the Zapatista movement. By the end of the month the rebels decided to take the offensive. The Zapatista rebellion spread through Morelos, and its forces advanced on Milpa Alta. On October 24 this town, on the border between Morelos and the Federal District, was assaulted by 3,000 rebels.

The government's defeats in Morelos and this threat to the capital, only kilometers away from it, caused a veritable panic in Mexico City. The conservatives turned their ire on Francisco I. Madero. The Chamber of Deputies held a tumultuous session. Deputy José María Lozano labeled Emiliano Zapata "the bandit of the Villa de Ayala," noted Madero's noble but fruitless effort, and complained of the failure to suppress Zapata after two months of trying to do so. He observed that with each passing day his admiration for Porfirio Díaz grew. Francisco M. de Olaguíbel, a lawyer, lashed out viciously at Madero. What the revolutionary leader had done, he charged, was "to postpone and hinder the action of the federal forces for fifteen days and to stop the advance of General Huerta." The legislator declared that de la Barra, "the immaculate first functionary of the Republic, is not to blame . . . The culpable are Sr. Madero and Sr. González Salas [Subsecretary of War]." [29]

The conservative legislative body declared itself in permanent session and called on the government to explain its inability to cope with the rebellion. Specifically, the Secretary of Government and the Subsecretary of War were called to appear before the Chamber. Subsecretary of War González Salas, hostilely received by the legislators, explained that the Zapatistas enjoyed the sympathy of many people, not only in Morelos but also in neighboring states. García Granados had

[28] Madero to de la Barra, Sept. 17, 1911, AdeM.
[29] *El Imparcial*, Oct. 26, 1911.

another explanation of the difficulties encountered in suppressing the revolt. He charged that "a powerful influence exists which prevents compliance with the orders of the government." [30]

The repercussions of the uprising in Morelos and the legislative uproar included a ministerial crisis. Resignations were submitted by García Granados, González Salas, and Francisco Vázquez Gómez. That very day, October 26, Madero issued some statements on the Morelos difficulties. Reviewing his efforts to find a peaceful solution, the revolutionary leader charged that the government's failure to comply with its offer of Eduardo Hay as governor and the advance of Huerta caused Zapata to rebel. Madero declared that he had had no further contact with Zapata because the government had opposed his idea to send an emissary to offer Zapata safe-conduct out of the country. Since General Huerta had "followed a truly incxplicable conduct," he had recommended, without avail, the substitution of another commander. Lastly, Madero indicated his confidence that as soon as he entered the presidency, Zapata would lay down his arms because "he knows that I will carry out the earlier propositions of the government which I believe are the only means of pacifying the state of Morelos." [31]

General Huerta, indignant because of Madero's public attack on him, demanded that the revolutionary leader specify his misconduct. The General wrote that he had remained in Morelos "with the unconditional approval of the President" and had done no more than "to fight the rebels victoriously." Madero replied detailing Huerta's misconduct. He charged the federal commander with deception when he claimed that he was not advancing on Yautepec, but rather engaging in military maneuvers. "It seems to me only just to tell the truth so that it may be known who provoked the war and who is to blame that it has not been possible to end it." [32] To counter any ill feeling created by the exchange with Huerta, Madero

[30] Ponce de León, *El interinato presidencial,* p. 217.
[31] Magaña, *Emiliano Zapata,* II, 49-53.
[32] *Ibid.,* II, 55-59.

wrote a letter reaffirming his esteem for the federal army for publication in *Nueva Era.* [33]

President de la Barra publicly defended his course of action asserting that he had "the profound conviction ... that the Executive had proceeded ... with complete consciousness of its obligations." [34] This statement did not explain the intrigue which surrounded events in Morelos. Nor did the rationalization of a de la Barra partisan that the military moves did not hurt negotiations which were "destined to fail" justify the policy of the government.[35] If Zapata's basic demands had been met, it is reasonably certain that the Morelos insurgent would have submitted to the government.

[33] Madero to Sánchez Azcona, Oct. 31, 1911, AdeM.
[34] Magaña, *Emiliano Zapata,* II, 53.
[35] Ponce de León, *El interinato presidencial,* p. 223.

XIII. A Democratic Election

DURING THE INTERIM PERIOD a break occurred between Madero and the Vázquez Gómez brothers. Although the brothers had moved slowly, almost reluctantly, toward seconding the revolutionary movement, they emerged not only as its defenders in the de la Barra cabinet but as opponents of compromise. Emilio Vázquez's conduct as Secretary of Government was the essence of radicalism. He tried to eliminate persons associated with the old regime from political authority and to substitute revolutionaries. This brought him into conflict with the Interim President and with the conservative majority in the cabinet.

Emilio Vázquez's proposals and actions relative to the insurgent army also were in sharp contrast to those of the dominant element in the administration. He pushed the idea of employing revolutionary troops for irrigation work and agricultural improvement projects. Unquestionably, he tenaciously opposed and endeavored to block the policy of discharge of the revolutionary forces. Whether from devotion to revolutionary ideals or to win personal adherents, he encouraged insurgent chieftains to delay and to disobey the government's disarmament and discharge program. Granted the premise on which the interim government had been established this situation was contrary to necessary concord and harmonious government.

De la Barra had never been enthusiastic about having Emilio Vázquez in his cabinet. The conduct of the minister gave the President additional reasons for suggesting to Madero the desirability of Vázquez's retirement. Madero, through weakness or, more likely, due to his conciliatory spirit, agreed to the move. Dr. Vázquez Gómez charged that the elimination of his brother was part of a plan, attributed to Gustavo Madero especially, to eliminate him as vice-presidential candidate. The matter came to a head as the result of a cabinet meeting held on July 12. In view of what he regarded as an alarming and grave political situation Vázquez proposed that de la Barra resign and Madero assume the presidency. The issue between the minister and the President could no longer be dissimulated. The elimination of Emilio Vázquez from the cabinet was now inevitable.

Dr. Vázquez Gómez wrote to Madero in Tehuacán protesting the proposal to separate his brother from the ministry as impolitic because the revolution was not adequately represented in the cabinet and because it would divide the revolutionary party. He urged that Emilio be permitted to remain until the elections approached when he could resign with a good excuse (his brother's candidacy!) and without disrupting the party. Madero denied that Gustavo was working against the doctor and that there was any danger in the removal of Emilio from the cabinet. "We agreed that your brother would retire at the end of this month. There has been no circumstance that would indicate the need for a change of decision." [1]

The doctor sent Madero the report of conferences held with de la Barra by a group of revolutionary chiefs on July 18 and 21 during which they had sought compliance with the Plan of San Luis Potosí and the retention of Emilio Vázquez in the cabinet. Madero telegraphed Gustavo to tell the insurgent chiefs involved that he disapproved of their conduct and that they had no right to address de la Barra to stop a change in ministers or to form a group with political ends. The revolutionary leader also wired the Interim President to assure him that "I am entirely with you." [2] On July 27, Madero in-

[1] Vázquez Gómez to Madero and reply, July 22, 1911, AdeM.

[2] Madero to Gustavo Madero and to de la Barra, July 25, 1911, AdeM.

dicated his acceptance of García Granados as Vázquez's replacement. The unfortunate nature of this choice was clearly shown in the Morelos incident.

Dr. Vázquez Gómez wrote again to Madero painting a dark picture of the situation and urging that Emilio's separation be "as late as possible." Madero was adamant. He wrote the doctor that "we ought to please Sr. de la Barra. Since he has conducted himself loyally from the beginning, it is our obligation to facilitate his task." He concluded that it was useless for the doctor to try to convince him regarding the separation of Emilio from the government "since my opinion . . . has been formed for quite some time." [3]

De la Barra requested Emilio Vázquez's resignation, which was submitted on August 2. However, the Secretary couched his resignation in terms which cast full responsibility on the Interim President. He charged that after various difficulties arising from the fact that de la Barra represented the conservatism of the old regime while he represented the radicalism of the revolution, "the President has had to order me to present my resignation." [4] Madero advised Dr. Vázquez Gómez that the terms of the resignation were "undesirable" and that he, Madero, would have to publish a statement to the effect that the President was working in agreement with him and was correct in discharging Emilio.

In his public statement Madero denied the accuracy of Emilio's declaration. He asserted that Emilio Vázquez was removed from his post "for his lack of tact in handling delicate questions" and that the President, to avoid trouble with the revolutionary party, had consulted with him on the matter. The expediency of the political conciliation policy was a major element in Madero's conduct in this matter. Later that month, in a letter to de la Barra, Madero emphasized as evidence of his disinterested cooperation the fact that he had not hesitated to break with Emilio Vázquez, "one of my most faithful and

[3] Madero to Vázquez Gómez, July 29 and Aug. 2, 1911, AdeM.
[4] Vázquez Gómez, *Memorias políticas,* pp. 389-90.

constant collaborators who had been considered as one of the most conspicuous members of our Party." [5]

The dismissal of Emilio created considerable excitement. *El Demócrata* stated that the incident was the "suicide of the revolution." [6] A group of insurgent chiefs protested publicly, hinting at the withdrawal of their support from Madero. The revolutionary leader was not to be intimidated. He instructed Dr. Vázquez Gómez to "make known to the dissident insurgent chiefs that they do not frighten me with their threats and that if they do not change their attitude, I will move energetically against them." [7]

With the resignation of Emilio Vázquez there remained no doubt that a break was coming between Madero and Dr. Vázquez Gómez. The two men differed in background, and their views had clashed concerning a compromise while Madero was in prison, the desirability of revolution, the elimination of Limantour, and the developments of the interim period. Certainly the attitude and conduct in the cabinet of the Vázquez Gómez brothers made the Madero–Vázquez Gómez election slate illogical if not impossible. This was clearly the view of Gustavo Madero and a group of associates to whose manipulations the doctor attributed his elimination. They feared that if the doctor were elected with Madero, he would follow a personal policy within the new government dangerous to its stability and leading to an inevitable split in the revolutionary party. Sánchez Azcona contended later that Madero, considering himself morally bound to the doctor, resisted the modification of the election ticket.[8]

The first step toward erasing the Madero–Vázquez Gómez formula was Madero's manifesto on July 9, 1911, in which he declared the Anti-Reelectionist party ended and announced steps for the formation of a new organization designated the Progressive Constitutional party. He endeavored to justify this

[5] Madero to de la Barra, Aug. 2 and 25, 1911, AdeM.
[6] *El Demócrata,* Aug. 2 and 9, 1911.
[7] Madero to Vázquez Gómez, Aug. 2, 1911, AdeM.
[8] *El Gráfico,* Nov. 29, 1930.

action on the grounds that the revolution had altered the continuity of the Anti-Reelectionist party. Pledging the new organization to the constitutional fulfillment of the program of San Luis Potosí, Madero designated a twenty-two man committee to organize the new party.

This maneuver by the revolutionary leader was considered, with some justice, an arrogation of faculties which he did not possess. Dr. Vázquez Gómez protested that it would mean the division of the revolution. Madero wrote the doctor that his vice-presidential candidacy had been discussed with the members of the committee and that they had accepted it. Claiming that he had been unable to avoid a new convention, Madero assured the doctor that he had advised the committee that neither he nor Vázquez Gómez would be able "to accept the result [of the new convention] if other candidates were designated"[9] in place of themselves. Either the revolutionary leader was deceived by his associates who were influencing him in this matter, or he was misleading the doctor to avoid a premature break. The committee, composed largely of Madero adherents, issued a convocation for a convention to be held August 27.

The announcement of the new party prompted a reaction by a group of revolutionary chiefs already concerned about what they regarded as Madero's excessive complacency towards de la Barra. They announced their intention to do everything in their power to see that the Plan of San Luis Potosí was complied with in "all its parts." The Anti-Reelectionist Center of Mexico City, strongly influenced by Emilio Vázquez, sent a commission to Tehuacán to interrogate Madero. The revolutionary leader told the commissioners that if they came to threaten or intimidate him, the interview was ended, but that, however, if they came as comrades, he would answer their questions. To their queries he reaffirmed his views on the separation of Emilio Vázquez and the organization of a new party. Madero reportedly asserted that the

[9] Madero to Vázquez Gómez, July 26 and 31, 1911, AdeM.

party change was made in spite of him and over his objections.[10]

As anticipated, the visitors were not satisfied and submitted a very unfriendly report to the Center. This body issued a manifesto on August 11, withdrawing support from Madero and proclaiming Dr. Vázquez Gómez as the chief of the Anti-Reelectionist party. Emilio Vázquez undertook a secret campaign to win adherents to the Center's stand. Letters were written to the heads of the various regional committees of the new party telling how some revolutionary chiefs would disown Madero, as the Center had done, for aligning himself with the Científicos. Madero found it necessary to warn his supporters to guard against this maneuver.

On August 27 some fifteen hundred delegates assembled in the Hidalgo Theater for the convention of the Progressive Constitutional party. There was only minor disagreement on the question of program. Essentially, the old Anti-Reelectionist program was accepted with the following additions: reform of the federal judicial system for greater efficiency; reform of judicial proceedings to provide greater guarantees for the individual; reestablishment of the injunction in civil proceedings; passage of laws favorable to the creation of the small agricultural holding; establishment of equitable taxation; abolition of the death penalty; and introduction of direct elections. Madero was nominated by acclamation, and a commission was sent to notify him of this action.

Madero addressed the convention on August 31 indicating acceptance of the nomination and of the program. However, he expressed the belief that the delegates were entitled to know how he would interpret and execute the program. He spoke of the need to guarantee the press freedom to fulfill its mission and of the need to establish the principle of "No Reelection" in the Constitution. He promised that public education was going to be a matter of utmost concern, "for on it depends the future of the new generation which will form the citizens of tomorrow. The school must reach the last ham-

[10] *El Demócrata*, Aug. 6, 1911.

let, hacienda, and smallest ranch so that every Mexican will receive the benefit of instruction."[11]

The candidate felt that encouragement of the small agricultural property, "the firmest base of democracy," was another necessity. However, this development must come by progressive steps with study to assure the principle of property. Once again Madero recognized the faulty property distribution and the need for revision. Consistent though his stand for a gradual solution was, it foreshadowed difficulties in the face of the urgent need and the incessant demand for agrarian reform. He was also consistent in his remarks on the Reform Laws. Madero considered the establishment of freedom of conscience through the separation of Church and State as a glorious achievement. He believed that those laws were generally accepted. "Now that the triumph has been obtained, it is necessary to treat all Mexicans as brothers and to work to bury the old hatreds completely."[12]

The lack of serious open differences ended when discussion of a vice-presidential candidate began. Four men were nominated: Fernando Iglesias Calderón (choice of the newly organized anti-Reyist Liberals who were not affiliated with the Los Angeles organization); Dr. Vázquez Gómez (choice of the Anti-Reelectionist Center); Pino Suárez (choice of the Madero group); and Robles Domínguez (choice of the Democratic faction). The discussion was loud and acrimonious. The initial vote narrowed the choice to Vázquez Gómez and Pino Suárez, and the bitter debate was renewed.

Madero was called before the convention and questioned as to whether he would refuse to collaborate with the doctor. The presidential candidate, with typical candor, spoke of his differences with the doctor and of his preference for Pino Suárez, but assured the delegates that he would accept the decision of the convention which was free to choose its candidate. Pino Suárez, forty-year-old revolutionist from the Yucatán peninsula, was selected as Madero's running mate.

[11] *Madero y su obra,* pp. 6-13.
[12] *Ibid.*

To Pino Suárez this development was a surprise. He had not engaged in intrigue to obtain the nomination. In fact, for almost two months he had rejected suggestions in that direction on the grounds that he was affiliated with the Anti-Reelectionist party whose candidate was Dr. Vázquez Gómez. However, pressure of friends and the action of the convention made refusal "impossible." So he wrote the doctor offering "sincere adhesion" and asking him "to calmly place your heart and conscience at the service of the Fatherland." [13]

It would have been well had that advice been followed. If Madero contributed to division of the revolutionaries by organizing a new party, the Vazquistas did likewise by refusing to bow to the will of the convention. Although the losers charged irregularities in the seating of delegations, the presence of a sizeable opposition and of independent groups speaks well for the gathering which an official American observer called the "first untrammeled political convention, really free and open, ever held in this country." [14]

Instead of accepting defeat gracefully, the Vazquistas raised the cry of imposition. Vicious comparisons were made with Díaz's imposition of Corral. If there had been imposition, it was on a party and not on the nation. The fact that Madero conducted himself legally and was entitled to a partner who would not be in opposition to his views made no difference. The dissident insurgents took up the cry, and the conservatives gleefully echoed it. The temper of the times was such that the accusation found wide acceptance. Madero bent all his efforts to counter this development. Through letters, interviews, and speeches he reviewed his difficulties with the doctor and sought to obtain support for the Madero–Pino Suárez formula. This was essential to prevent the division in the revolutionary ranks from deepening.

When he renewed his campaign travels, Madero found it necessary to defend the new formula. He encountered varying degrees of opposition which he met with commendable deci-

[13] *La Opinión,* March 18, 1934.

[14] Dearing to State Dept., Sept. 4, 1911, SDF, 812.00/2345.

siveness and courage. In Veracruz he told his audience that the doctor always had been with him in times of prosperity and never in adversity. After touring the southeastern section of the country, Madero visited Querétaro and Jalisco before turning northward. He was accorded the coolest receptions in Guadalajara and Chihuahua. When he spoke of Pino Suárez in the northern city, he was greeted by the shrill cry, "Pino no, Pino no." Madero asked them to whistle at him too. When the crowd shouted "No! No!", the candidate told them then to listen. The crowd, thus silenced, heard Madero tell them of the virtues of Pino Suárez. He declared that if they would not vote for his running mate, they were not to vote for him.[15] Despite these valiant efforts, the division existed and the Vazquistas entered the lists with the doctor as their vice-presidential candidate.

Another unfortunate development of this election involved General Bernardo Reyes. The military commander had been permitted, with Madero's approval, to return to Mexico early in June. Shortly after his arrival he conferred with Madero and de la Barra at Chapultepec Castle. It was agreed that Reyes would decline any proferred candidacy and would urge his followers to support Madero, who, if elected, would name the General to head the War Department. Reyes explained his action as being a patriotic gesture to avoid the commotion that might accompany an electoral struggle in view of the overwhelming popularity of Madero.[16]

The immediate reaction to the arrangement was favorable. However, *El Mañana* expressed regret that the General had decided to decline candidacy.[17] Moreover, many revolutionists did not take kindly to the arrangement which was for Madero another opportunity for cooperation. To their protests and suggestions of alternatives for the cabinet post, Madero replied, "I cannot change my decision without being disloyal. Besides, I congratulate myself on the decision of General

[15] Figueroa Domenech, *Veinte meses de anarquía,* p. 40.
[16] *La Opinión,* March 25, 1934.
[17] *El Mañana,* June 18, 1911.

Reyes to collaborate with me."[18] Madero reminded the fearful that Reyes had always been loyal to the constituted government. "In my decisions I consider the general interests of the Nation and not those of a small group of persons who have intransigent and radical ideas ... I can be wrong because I am not infallible, but I will always work in conformity with my conscience."[19]

Among those expressing concern regarding Reyes was González Garza. Madero's reply to him revealed the candidate's good faith, confidence, political shrewdness, and democratic conviction. He reiterated his faith in Reyes's sincerity. If the General were not sincere, Madero pointed out, his only alternatives would be to become either a candidate or a rebel. In the former case he would have to explain his change of mind even though Madero had written him that he was not bound in this respect. If, despite his public declaration, Reyes were to become a candidate and that candidacy were to prosper, Madero declared that he

> would not see any threat in it since the Mexican people are capable of electing the governors they prefer. I would be the first to respect the vote of the majority of my fellow citizens ... It always has been my deep conviction that the people never ought to show their pleasure to citizens who serve them by awarding [them] public posts which ought to be reserved for the most capable.[20]

The candidate rejected the idea that Reyes, the man of discipline and military honor, would elect the alternative of rebellion. It must be added that Madero recommended publication of this letter!

The candidate soon began to regret his arrangement with Reyes. The protests of his followers had started to tell. In addition, it was apparent that Reyes did not now retain, as had been assumed, the strength which he once possessed. Reyes too, under the impulse of ambition and the encouragement of friends, regretted his act of abnegation. Taking advantage

[18] Madero to Anti-Reelectionist Electoral Center, July 1, 1911, AdeM.
[19] *La Opinión,* March 25, 1934.
[20] Madero to F. González Garza, July 30, 1911, AdeM.

of an opening provided by a letter written by Madero on July 16, Reyes visited him at Tehuacán on August 7 to advise him that he had decided to accept candidacy for the presidency.

Madero telegraphed de la Barra the results of the conference. He had assured General Reyes that he was under no obligation regarding the election. The military commander indicated his decision to become a candidate and expressed the wish that the electoral struggle should be a democratic one. Madero agreed that "we ought to set an example for the world by waging a purely democratic campaign." He warned that recourse to arms would be dangerous and that the government would proceed energetically against anyone who disturbed the peace. As proof of his agreement Reyes signed the message to the Interim President.[21]

The Reyists began campaigning, and Madero received accusations that they were conspiring. On September 3 the supporters of the General organized a demonstration in the capital. A mob, allegedly organized or encouraged by some of Madero's associates, threatened and practically engulfed the Reyists. When Reyes arrived at San Francisco Street (today Francisco Madero Avenue) and attempted to calm the crowd, he was stoned. Despite efforts of conciliatory elements in both parties, who held meetings to try to stop the agitation, and despite assurances from Madero and de la Barra that Reyes would have all necessary guarantees, the General, in the face of attacks and criticisms by the extreme revolutionists, decided he could not prosecute his campaign and preferred to exile himself.

On September 22, General Reyes instructed his followers to stay away from the polls. Six days later he departed quietly from Veracruz. In a farewell message Reyes urged his followers to remain active "in order to obtain the guarantees which today they lack." [22] Although the Reyes candidacy had attracted little support, the turmoil and the break with Ma-

[21] Madero to de la Barra, Aug. 2, 1911, AdeM.
[22] *La Opinión,* March 25, 1934.

dero added to the confusion of the moment. With the exception of the brief period of their agreement, Madero consistently showed in his speeches and writings an aversion for Reyes. The General, in turn, did not neglect any opportunity to scoff at the revolutionary leader. The triumph of Madero aggravated this antagonism, and some of the Reyists were so opposed to Madero that they even cooperated with their old rivals, those formerly associated with the Científicos.

The withdrawal of General Reyes did not leave any dearth of candidates. A Catholic party was organized and realistically accepted Madero as the presidential choice. This action was taken "because to oppose then the triumph of [Madero] was to assure failure, since the immense majority of Mexicans had become fanatical supporters of the [revolutionary] chief." [23] Therefore, the members of the Catholic party decided to concentrate on winning the vice-presidency for de la Barra. *El Mañana,* challenging the endorsement of Madero, questioned whether "an apostolic Roman Catholic is able to make common cause with a mason." This violently anti-Madero newspaper wanted to know how the "Catholic party could support . . . a freethinker, atheist, and spiritualist."[24] Although the Interim President did not accept the nomination of the Catholic party, neither did he insist on its withdrawal.

A group calling themselves the Liberal Radical party went even further by naming de la Barra as its candidate for the presidency. Luis Cabrera warned de la Barra that those postulating his candidacy were "indubitably . . . all the elements opposed to the revolution." He also warned that such a candidacy would be regarded as a betrayal since the Interim President had been placed in office by the revolution.[25] And there were other parties and candidates. Jorge Vera Estañol announced the formation of the Popular Evolutionist party. His

[23] Ponce de León, *El interinato presidencial,* p. 99.

[24] *El Mañana,* Aug. 17 and 25, 1911. Despite the moral endorsement implicit in the solemn mass celebrated in the cathedral on the occasion of the opening of the Catholic party's convention, a careful distinction was maintained between the Church and the party.

[25] Cabrera, *Obras políticas,* pp. 289-94.

principal argument was that needed reforms ought to be accomplished through evolutionary means inside the law. He repeatedly attacked Madero for nepotism and Caesarism and the revolution for militarism and anarchy, but his program attracted only a few intellectuals. The Anti-Reelectionist Center postulated the candidacy of Emilio Vázquez while the Liberal party backed Iglesias Calderón.

Madero, realizing the danger of prolonging the period of transition, had urged the setting of the election dates as early as legally possible. Thus the elections were scheduled for October 1 and 15. However, the Reyists petitioned the Chamber to postpone the elections. The Liberal Radicals, the Popular Evolutionists, and the Vazquistas seconded this request. The opposition press, led by *El Imparcial,* enthusiastically supported the idea. When Madero, campaigning in the southeast, learned of the proposal, he excitedly protested to the Chamber. Emphasizing that the election date had been set by Congress and accepted by the revolutionary party, the candidate warned that any postponement would cause the people to believe themselves betrayed. Yet, if the deputies were to take such action, he promised to "do everything possible to calm the people." However, he cautioned that he could not be responsible "for what might happen." [26]

Manuel Calero and Ernesto Madero telegraphed the candidate that his message had been regarded as an implied threat and had produced an unfavorable reaction. Madero hastened to send a clarifying message assuring the legislators that no threat was intended and that he only was endeavoring to advise of a danger that would arise from popular misunderstanding in case of postponement. He assured the Chamber that "my purpose is to aid the present government." [27] Dominant opinion was frankly averse to postponement, and the Chamber rejected the petitions.

The elections were held on schedule, and unquestionably they were among the cleanest, most enthusiastic, and most

[26] Madero to President of Chamber of Deputies, Sept. 11, 1911, AdeM.
[27] Madero to President of Chamber of Deputies, Sept. 13, 1911, AdeM.

democratic elections in Mexican history. The people's wishes were well known, and the returns undoubtedly accurately represented them. Ambassador Wilson reported that "order prevailed everywhere." *El Mañana* admitted that the elections had been "free and spontaneous." [28] The people voted in the primary elections for electors—one for each five hundred inhabitants—who, in turn, voted for president and vice-president in the secondary elections. The electoral colleges reported the following results:[29]

For President	
Madero	19,997
de la Barra	87
Emilio Vázquez	16
Others	45

For Vice-President	
Pino Suárez	10,245
de la Barra	5,564
F. Vázquez Gómez	3,373
Iglesias Calderón	173
Others	51

Despite the absolute majority obtained by Francisco Madero and José María Pino Suárez, the Reyists and Vazquistas criticized the results through newspapers and public conferences. These groups asked the Congress to nullify the elections. Recognizing that the irregularities complained of were of little importance, almost all the deputies voted to uphold the legality of the elections. On November 2, Madero and Pino Suárez were declared elected.

The interim government of Francisco León de la Barra had lasted five months and ten days. In the interests of cooperation and legality Madero had committed a grave political blunder. Instead of assuming power as a revolutionary leader in his moment of victory unanimously supported by his followers, Madero was entering office with diminished popularity and prestige, with his partisans divided, and with disorders continuing in the country. The interim period had emboldened the conservative elements and provided the circumstances for the breaks between Madero and the Vázquez Gómez brothers, Reyes, and de la Barra.

[28] Wilson to Secretary of State, Oct. 2, 1911, SDF, 812.00/2393; *El Mañana,* Nov. 4, 1911.

[29] Ponce de León, *El interinato presidencial,* pp. 195-97.

The role of the Interim President was the subject of acrimonious debate. Conservatives proudly proclaimed the success of the man they called *El Presidente Blanco* ("The White President"). Luis Cabrera summarized the verdict of the revolutionaries when he called de la Barra "a hypocrite, capable of betraying Madero and the revolution." [30] Although placed in power by the revolution with the purpose of "legalizing" it, the Interim President, whether from deceit or conviction, refused to follow the role designated for him. His policy in Morelos had succeeded only in creating conditions for further revolution and turmoil in that area. All his actions tended to strengthen the old and to weaken the new. Less than two weeks before Madero assumed the presidency, de la Barra confidentially expressed to Ambassador Wilson "his serious apprehension concerning the prospects of the Madero government." He also saw danger in "Madero's lack of fitness for executive work and questioned his adherence to sound principles of government." [31] De la Barra was the "multicolor" president for the revolutionists.

[30] Cabrera, *Obras políticas,* p. xx.
[31] Wilson, *Diplomatic Episodes,* pp. 219-20.

XIV. President of the Republic

AMID CHEERING THRONGS Francisco I. Madero came to the Chamber of Deputies on November 6 to be sworn into office as President of Mexico. Characteristically, Madero indicated that he did not want a military guard at the entrance to the legislative hall. The result was a state of confusion which irritated some diplomats but which did not seem to disturb the enthusiastic crowd. After the traditional ceremony, the new President proceeded to the National Palace to receive congratulations from officials, diplomats, and friends.

Madero's ascension to the presidency was acclaimed in an unprecedented manner. Unquestionably, the almost frantic adulation was for Madero the symbol: symbol of the revolution, which he was, and symbol of change, which he was thought to be. It has been asserted frequently that Madero was a poor administrator, an inadequate president. The disturbing aspect of this indictment is that it was reached in some quarters before Madero took office! He did lack the emotional make-up desirable for political position involving great responsibility, but the conditions and circumstances of the fifteen months he spent in office make difficult a just evaluation of his government.

Two great forces in the country continued to cajole, attack, and threaten to engulf the new executive. On the one hand, there were the advocates of the old regime—landed, bureaucratic, clerical, and foreign interests. They were entrenched, and the interim period had enabled them to re-form their ranks. They were dominant in the legislature, the judiciary, the civil service, the press, and the army. With the exception of some revolutionaries converted into federally supported rurales, Madero had to depend on the old federal army.

These advocates of the old were able to count on the conservative inclinations of Madero's own family. The conservative elements feared and opposed change. They hailed challenger after challenger against the government in an effort to destroy it. Madero had to dedicate his energies and the resources of his government to defeating the successive blows of Reyes, Orozco, and Félix Díaz.

On the other hand, there were the demanding elements of the revolution. With aspirations instilled and awake the people were expecting and demanding far-reaching social and economic changes. The rebellion of Zapata, originally fomented by the action of conservative elements, was a product of those demands and constituted another threat to the stability and a drain on the resources of the Madero government. Strikes in the cities, disorders in the rural areas, and a number of local rebellions contributed to the difficult conditions facing Madero in power.

Between these two forces, conservative and revolutionary, Madero appeared to oscillate. Even Molina Enríquez, who was often critical of Madero, admitted, however, that the President "leaned more to the side of the revolution,"[1] but Madero did not recognize the urgency of meeting the demands of the revolution. He regarded his election as the triumph of a political movement, as the victory of democratic principles. Other changes, he expected, would be accomplished in time and within the law by the duly elected representatives of the people.

Madero was preoccupied with giving the people democratic conditions under which they, through their representatives, could devise the needed laws. He still hoped to create a government that would represent and unite all Mexicans. Even his own partisans distrusted this policy with its consequent

[1] Molina Enríquez, *La revolución agraria,* IV, 100.

delay in meeting the demands for change. Ineffective as Madero's well-intentioned ideas proved to be, there was a notable consistency between his words and promises and his efforts and deeds. Unfortunately, the adherents of the revolution felt that he had promised more or that he ought to do more.

Francisco Madero faced this difficult and trying period with a smile that expressed his confidence. By philosophy and nature optimistic, he found that his electoral victory fortified and exalted his confidence in himself, his destiny, and the democratic future of Mexico. This consciousness of the legality of his government and the conviction that he had won with the support of the people, which he would continue to enjoy, explain Madero's complacency in the face of press attacks, conspiracies, rebellions, and uprisings.

There is something appealing, if unreal, about Madero's profoundly trusting that all men were as well-intentioned as he, and about his believing in the possibility of an easy transition from the old to the new with all Mexicans working together devoted to the "restoration" of never-enjoyed liberties. He was confident that this mere presence in office would have a quieting effect. Madero reportedly remarked to one of the diplomats on his inauguration day: "Now I am going to be able to arrange it all."[2] These hopes and dreams help to explain Madero's forgiveness of men who deserted, disobeyed, or even rebelled against him, his trust in the federal army, and his willingness to retain men of the old regime in the government.[3]

Madero's cabinet was composed of a mixture of conservatives and revolutionaries with the former predominant. From the de la Barra cabinet was retained a conservative core com-

[2] Lara Pardo, *Madero,* p. 167.

[3] Félix Palavicini, who left the cause when Madero led it to revolution, was welcomed back with open arms. Juan A. Almazán, who disobeyed orders by organizing forces to attack and pursue Zapata, also won Madero's forgiveness. The President felt that the triumph of the revolution had caused many to forget that "liberty must be within the law to be fruitful." Concluding that Almazán had reflected on his acts, Madero ordered his release. Madero to Palavicini, July 31, 1911, CdeFFP; Madero to Almazán, June 22, 1912, AdeGG.

posed of Manuel Calero (Foreign Relations), Rafael Hernández (Development), and Ernesto Madero (Finance). This group was reinforced by the appointment of Manuel Vázquez Tagle as head of the Justice Department. The conservatives could count on the support and the influence of Madero's father. These members of the cabinet impeded any changes in policy and obstructed any moves toward needed reforms. Vázquez Tagle used his position to fight the revolutionaries and, therefore, became the principal target of their attacks on the conservative element in the cabinet.

Members of the cabinet who were revolutionaries or personal adherents of Madero included González Salas (War), Manuel Bonilla (Communications), Abraham González (Government), and Miguel Díaz Lombardo (Public Instruction). These men were the targets for the conservative press. Indeed, the complaints against his ministers were so numerous that Madero reportedly exclaimed, "If I wanted to please everybody, I would remain without a cabinet." [4]

The first major change in the cabinet was the product of the Orozco rebellion in the north. Abraham González found it necessary to return to Chihuahua and had to resign his portfolio. Jesús Flores Magón was promoted from Undersecretary of Justice to the post of Secretary of Government to succeed González. A few days later Minister of War González Salas, under fire because of the spread of the Orozco uprising, requested a field assignment against the rebels. He was replaced by General Angel García Peña. One other change at this time was due to the desire of Madero, influenced by brother Gustavo, to make a place in his cabinet for the Vice-President, Pino Suárez. Díaz Lombardo resigned to permit Pino Suárez to take the post of Public Instruction.

Gustavo Madero and the Vice-President maneuvered to eliminate Calero from the cabinet. Early in April the Foreign Minister was designated Ambassador to Washington, a move which Madero felt provided an honorable withdrawal from the cabinet and, at the same time, one which would permit

[4] Figueroa Domenech, *Veinte meses de anarquía*, p. 96.

continued use of his undeniable talents. Calero was replaced by Pedro Lascuráin, who, Ambassador Wilson reported with satisfaction, was "a prominent, wealthy, and excellent man of an old Mexican family." [5]

Calero, though talented, was a vain man, convinced of his own superiority; he broke with Madero in December. Returning to Mexico, he joined the opposition in the Senate. In an interview the former Ambassador explained that he had resigned because "I was not in agreement with the policy of the government" and because he felt that "the Republic is approaching an abyss of misery and desolation." [6] In the Senate, Calero made a sensational speech in which he charged that during his mission he could do nothing but lie in trying to make the government to which he was accredited believe that the Mexican situation was improving. Manuel Calero certainly contributed to the confusion, uncertainty, and distrust of the early months of 1913.

The new cabinet revealed as deep divisions as the old. In November, Madero, at the instigation of Pino Suárez, agreed to remove Jesús Flores Magón from the Government post. There was then a suggestion that Luis Cabrera be invited to join the cabinet. However, since the assignment to him of the portfolio of the principal agency for internal administration would signify a change of policy and the abandonment of political conciliation, it was thought better to name him instead to the Secretariat of Development where he could use his energies to resolve the agrarian problem. The influence of Ernesto Madero, Francisco Madero, Hernández, and Lascuráin discouraged the President from making the appointment. Instead, Hernández became Secretary of Government, Manuel Bonilla was transferred to the Development post, and Jaime Gurza, Subsecretary of the Treasury, was promoted to Minister of Communications.

Madero's cabinet of all factions did not work. The squabbles,

[5] Wilson to Secretary of State, March 23 and April 9, 1912, SDF, 812.00/3352 and 812.002/22.

[6] *El País,* Jan. 13, 1913.

of the members tended to discredit the government, and the President failed to moderate or silence the controversies. At the very top policy-making level of the administration were some persons who did not sympathize with the revolution and others who opposed it. And this was not the only charge leveled against Madero's cabinet and government. The presence of his relatives in the affairs of state made the cry of nepotism inevitable.

Holding portfolios were the President's uncle (Ernesto Madero), a first cousin (Rafael Hernández), and a man related to the Madero family by marriage (González Salas). Madero justified these appointments on the ground that he knew they would be honest. Five relatives in Congress, one a member of the Supreme Court, two in the postal service, and one a subsecretary in the cabinet hardly justified the assertion that many members of the President's family "were distributed through all the governmental spheres."[7] Certainly this so-called nepotism was trivial compared to the nepotism which characterized the Díaz regime.

The necessity for having friendly, dependable persons in key places, so neglected by Madero and so crucial in the Mexican political pattern, was not overlooked by some of those associated with the government. Deputy Gustavo Madero, who loyally had followed and supported his brother, was a devotee of the practical methods of earlier Mexican politics. He recognized the danger from the right and the need for a revolutionary cabinet. He worked toward this end with little success. Gustavo undertook to be the political boss of his brother's government and of the Progressive Constitutional party. He interfered in congressional and state elections and endeavored to organize and manage the government's supporters in Congress.

Gustavo formed a strong-arm committee to direct mobs for the political purpose of terrorizing opponents. The group arranged demonstrations against the Interim President, was charged with the assault on the Reyist supporters, and alleg-

[7] Lara Pardo, *Madero,* p. 190.

edly inspired the mob which attempted, with little success, to burn the offices of several opposition papers. Sánchez Santos, editor of *El País,* labeled the group the Porra ("Stick"), the name of a notorious band in Madrid. Although the Progressive Constitutional party publicly dissociated itself from the group, the editor scornfully wrote that the government party was not a party, but the *partida* (factious band) of the Porra.[8]

There was a marked contrast between the policy and conduct of the President and the technique of the group, and the group was not capable of effectively dealing with the situation which confronted the government. Gustavo became the focus of opposition attacks, and the activities of the Porra did much to discredit the government and the President. To save Madero's brother from the constant criticism and to relieve the government of what was rapidly becoming a serious disability it was arranged that Gustavo be sent as Special Ambassador to thank the Japanese government for participating in the Mexican centenary celebration.

Francisco Madero was determined to permit independent functioning and the application of democratic procedures in the other branches and levels of government. The judicial system continued to be dominated by the old regime. Indeed, during Madero's term the Supreme Court elected Francisco Carbajal, who had represented the Díaz government in the negotiations at Ciudad Juárez, to serve as its president. Nevertheless, Madero insisted on the independence of the judiciary. During his brief administration the judicial power, so debased under Díaz, recovered its independence. There is no record of any executive orders to justices or of any intervention in judicial proceedings. Dr. Lara Pardo conceded that of all the Mexican presidents Madero was "the most respectful of judicial liberty."[9] Since the judiciary was not reformed, the improved conditions were due to the character of the President and lasted as long as he did. No one was able to gainsay

[8] Vasconcelos, *Ulises criollo,* p. 379; Hernández Chávez and López Ituarte, *La angustia nacional,* p. 32.

[9] *Madero y su obra,* p. 186.

Madero's statement that the federal executive "has respected the law . . . even [in connection with] the rights of its enemies." [10]

While Madero was overly sanguine about the possibility of democratic government, there were a few signs that under the stimulus of the unaccustomed political activity and of the President's example democracy made some, progress. A Women's League made its appearance. In Monterrey a local election was contested by six candidates who received, respectively, 1,563, 1,418, 1,076, 1,062, 562, and 337 votes. It was not a very convincing triumph for the winner, but obviously it had been a very real election.[11]

Although the President had experienced considerable difficulty with the Porfirian Congress, he insisted on democratic procedures in the election of the 26th Congress, which was chosen during his administration. In an interview early in 1912, he said:

> Those gentlemen who miss the methods of the dictatorship should be assured that I have avoided those methods not through lack of energy, but because I am determined to do everything possible to implant democracy in Mexico. And I will do it in spite of them.

Admitting that "in moments of crisis those [dictatorial] methods can be indispensable," Madero declared that "it would be a disillusion for me to have recourse to them in order to govern the country." [12]

Early in 1912 the electoral campaign for the new congress began. Late in April it was announced that the majority of the state legislatures had approved the reform of the Constitution providing that thereafter elections of the president, vice-president, senators, and deputies were to be by direct vote. It was hoped that the change would make it more difficult, particulary for the governors, to control elections. Madero recommended to all authorities that effective suffrage be respected.

[10] Madero, "Informe . . . el 16 de septiembre de 1912," in *Diario Oficial,* 122, No. 13, 137-49.

[11] Callcott, *Liberalism in Mexico,* p. 219.

[12] *Nueva Era,* Feb. 11, 1912.

Although there were a number of parties and factions contending, the main struggle in the congressional election developed between the Progressive Constitutional and the National Catholic parties. Madero's conciliatory policy did not win for him the support of the Church or of the Catholic party, whose spokesmen and newspapers attacked the President bitterly, opposing his policies, censuring his alleged weaknesses, and impugning his motives. While Madero directed the Progressive Constitutional party to undertake an active electoral campaign to try to obtain, through legal means, a healthy, disciplined majority for the government, Gustavo Madero and others in the government sought to impose certain candidates. Lack of experience in the exercise of suffrage and the military operations in the north probably explain the fact that less than twenty percent in the Federal District and not over eight percent in the states voted in this congressional election which was held without incident.[13]

Opponents of the President were in the majority in the Senate. In the Chamber the government party and affiliated groups won a majority. The Catholic party won twenty-three and the opposition independents nineteen of the two hundred and thirty-three seats. This achievement of forty-two seats by the opposition is an exceptional situation in modern Mexican politics. Despite the charges and proven cases of imposition, this congressional election was the freest Mexico ever had enjoyed. Francisco Madero hailed "a Congress freely elected" and the fulfillment of the "principal promise of the revolution—the free exercise of the vote," but the activities of the Porra tended to discredit the government's victory.[14]

Unfortunately, the government's majority in the lower chamber was not effective, coherent, or well directed. Actually, the

[13] The people had rushed to the polls the preceding fall to participate in the presidential election. However, as one author noted, "That was not an election, it was an acclamation." Figueroa Domenech, *Veinte meses de anarquía*, p. 156.

[14] Lamicq, *El dolor mexicano*, p. 100.

The Catholic party charged that it had been deprived arbitrarily of seventy-seven other seats which it claimed to have won.

supporters of the administration had to depend on the cooperation of deputies of all shades of opinion who had no exact affiliation with the government and were not subject to party discipline. In each case a majority had to be formed through the bloc device with the inevitable danger of defections and defeat. Included among the government's supporters was a group of thoroughgoing revolutionists, the Renovators, who did not sympathize with Madero's policy of conciliation and cooperation.

The opposition, hoping to capitalize on the dissatisfaction of the Renovators with some members of the cabinet, proposed a vote of censure of the cabinet. However, the Renovators supported the President on this test. Gustavo Madero endeavored to organize and direct the governmental group in Congress. However, he and his associates were inexperienced. The government's party lacked men of great oratorical skill and of sufficient prestige to be capable of leading opinion in any given case.

If the majority was confused and ineffective, the opposition proved influential beyond its small numbers. Although the opponents of the government could defeat the administration only occasionally with the support of dissident liberal deputies, they attacked, criticized, delayed, and hampered legislative action. Francisco M. de Olaguíbel, José María Lozano, Nemesio García Naranjo, and Querido Moheno, the famed "quadrilateral" of the opposition, had prestige, experience, and oratorical skill. A claque in the gallery applauded and encouraged their efforts. They attacked the government for weakness in the face of disorders and opposed the granting of power and resources to meet the situation. They filled the air with charges and innuendos. When the government requested authorization to contract certain loans, the opposition attacks left the impression of rascality in high places.

In October an opposition deputy suggested that a commission be appointed to check whether the nation's reserve had been properly reported by the Finance Minister. The proposal was rejected, but the public, already upset by rumors of revolution, anarchy, and governmental inadequacy, received the added scare of national bankruptcy. The old, unsubstantiated charges of American aid to the revolution were revived, and the disarming of the port of Salina Cruz was attributed to a shameful agreement with the United States. Actually, the dismantling of the fortifications had been initiated during the de la Barra period after a technical commission had recommended the action describing the defense works as useless and ridiculous. The activity of this congressional group contributed to the ineffectiveness of the government, to the confusion, and to the diminution of the prestige of the administration.

Regarding the states, Madero apparently tried to give his democratic ideas a chance to work. The provisional governors were all civilians and all but two were natives of the states which they were appointed to head. Traditionally, Mexican executives tend to control gubernatorial elections to insure success for their friends and to avoid local anarchy. Madero was torn between this tradition, the importunities of his revolutionary friends for support, and his own principles. His action was neither consistent nor decisive, and in eleven states he had gubernatorial troubles.

In the state elections held during Madero's incumbency candidates of the Catholic party triumphed in Jalisco, Mexico, Querétaro, and Zacatecas. The Catholic group charged that official intervention prevented their candidates from achieving the top state posts in Guanajuato, Michoacán, and Puebla. In Michoacán, for example, the Catholic party nominated the interim governor P. Ortiz, while the revolutionaries supported Dr. Manuel Silva. When the conservative legislature began to declare many votes for Silva void, the local revolutionary leaders protested to Madero. After the President indicated that he would not support the legislative chamber's action, Dr. Silva was conceded the election. In other states the opposition charged pressure by Gustavo Madero and others close to the government.

In several states Madero hesitated to indicate whom he supported among a number of candidates. The consequences of his indecision were soon apparent. In Tlaxcala the retiring governor refused to surrender his post to his elected successor. The new governor seized the state palace, was besieged, and appealed for federal help. The local revolutionary forces aided the old governor, and the new official was not installed until federal army forces had intervened. In Veracruz, after a bitter electoral struggle over the filling of a short (ten-month) term, there was a wild competition for the full-term governorship. There were five active candidates, and Madero at first favored his old Chief of Staff, Hilario Rodríguez Malpica. When this candidate proved to be unpopular, Madero hesitated to indicate a preference among the remaining four: Manuel Alegre, journalist, who had served as interim governor during the short-term period; Guillermo Pous, former editor of *El Debate;* Tomás Braniff, millionaire; and Antonio Pérez Rivera, a little-known conservative from Jalapa.

Braniff charged that the President had broken pledges made to him. Madero accused the candidate of treating elections as a "question of money," and an unseemly public controversy was joined. Because of a rumored financial deal involving the governor, Francisco Lagos Cházaro, in a plan to elect either Braniff or Pous, Madero ordered the legislature to designate as interim official Manuel Levi to supervise the full-term election. Pérez Rivera, endorsed by the followers of the local revolutionary leader Gabriel Gavira as the "least bad" of the candidates, was elected for the full-term governorship.[15]

The gubernatorial elections held during Madero's term obviously were not all irreproachable, but his over-all policy represented a step forward in the direction of democracy. The revolution did not completely dominate the highest state posts. There were four governors from the Catholic party who were opposed to the President. Others were of conservative inclinations, and their cooperation with the central government was unpredictable. In January, 1913, nineteen of the governors were between thirty and fifty years of age, seven were between fifty and sixty, and one was sixty-two years old. The

[15] Gavira, *Su actuación,* pp. 52-67.

majority proved to be men of fitness and probity. At least in respect to age and character the revolution resulted in wholesome changes in the persons directing the states.

Although the relations of the central government with the local governments were harmonious enough, there were a number of local disturbances and conditions which required federal action. In Tamaulipas, General Rómulo Cuéllar assumed an attitude contrary to the government. In Sinaloa, General Juan Banderas continued to be a storm center. Finally, he was ordered to the capital to answer numerous charges. He was imprisoned, but there were complaints because Madero did not order the liquidation of the prisoner. In the same state Justo Tirado, a revolutionary chief, rebelled against the governor who was forced to flee when his capital fell to the rebels. Federal action was necessary to restore order to Sinaloa. In Oaxaca the partisans of Félix Díaz, nephew of Porfirio, dissatisfied with the victory of Miguel Bolaños Cacho over their candidate in the special gubernatorial election, rose in arms led by "Chuché Viejo." This revolt, which extended to the Isthmus of Tehuantepec and included an attack on the state capital, was suppressed by federal troops who captured and liquidated the rebel leader.

In the same state Madero, on taking office, had to handle the difficult situation created by the local rebellion in the Juchitán district. The popular governor, Benito Juárez Maza, stirred up trouble in the district when he sought to replace José F. (Ché) Gómez as *jefe político*. Gómez revolted, proclaiming the separation of the isthmus from Oaxaca and the establishment of a territory (including the districts of Juchitán and Tehuantepec). Hundreds were killed, and the governor sent frantic requests for assistance. Madero sent Cándido Aguilar and Gabriel Gavira to negotiate directly with the rebel leader. The envoys proposed the laying down of arms, a compromise appointment as *jefe político*, and safe-conduct for Ché to the capital. The governor then protested this "invasion" of his state and sounded the cry of state sovereignty. The state legislature disavowed the central government. Ché and members of the town council of Juchitán, on their way to Mexico City, were arrested on the governor's orders and executed.

With some of the revolutionary governors Madero had difficulties relating to the support and control of irregular forces. The central government regarded it as awkward to sustain forces which remained under the control of the governors. Finally, it was decided, in view of the heavy financial demands on the government, to discontinue federal disbursements for this purpose. For almost a year Governor Carranza of Coahuila sustained a controversy with President Madero with regard to this problem. At last, in December, 1912, he visited the President to protest in vain the government's decision on the matter.[16]

Regarding the lower levels of government, very little was accomplished during Madero's ephemeral administration. He did appoint a commission to study the question of local government. The President expressed the hope that as a result of this commission's studies he would be able "to initiate the necessary reforms to restore the personality of the municipal governments."[17]

The press constituted one of the major obstacles which confronted the Madero administration. The new President maintained freedom of the press to a superlative degree, but the opposition journalists, taking advantage of this situation, twisted freedom into license. Press attacks and opposition began during the interim period. Madero refused to become concerned about this development which he regarded as the natural reaction to newfound freedom. Papers of the old regime, *El Imparcial* and *El Diario,* led the opposition. The American-controlled *El Heraldo Mexicano,* ostensibly neutral,

[16] Friends of Carranza attribute his conduct to concern about the drift of events and to his desire to retain loyal forces capable of defending the interests of the revolution. Critics of the Governor charge that at the very least he wanted command of a personal force financed by the National Treasury, if he was not actually contemplating rebellion.

[17] F. I. Madero, "Informe . . . el 1 de abril de 1912," in *Diario Oficial,* 119, No. 27, 405-13.

actually engaged actively in discrediting the Madero government. The Catholic press, which in the closing years of Díaz's rule had opposed the dictatorship and had lauded the revolution, joined the opposition to Madero. Its principal organs were *El País* and *La Nación.*

A host of new journals appeared to join the calculated campaign against the government, including the following: *El Mañana,* intelligently, if poisonously, directed by Jesús M. Rábago; *La Tribuna,* an afternoon daily, directed by a former editor of *El Debate,* Nemesio García Naranjo, who enjoyed constitutional immunity as a deputy; and *El Noticioso Mexicano.* On a lower level were *Frivolidades* and *Multicolor.* Still lower were the usually anonymous little sheets filled with obscene caricatures and licentious writing. They ridiculed the personal life of the President without consideration or respect for the man, his wife, or his family. One example of these foul personal-political attacks was entitled *El sarape de Madero* (The Blanket of Madero), a wordplay on Madero's wife's name, Sara P. de Madero.[18]

The opposition was cruel and relentless in its efforts against Madero. Many of the attacks were vicious personal diatribes. Madero was ridiculed as a spiritist, homeopathist, and vegetarian. He was chided for shedding tears in public. Madero had appointed, despite criticism by revolutionists, the distinguished educator of the old regime Justo Sierra as Minister to Madrid. When Sierra died at his post, the President attended the memorial services held at the University and cried when Jesús Urueta delivered an address of tribute. Madero was even criticized for having taken a flight in an airplane. Doubt was cast on his mental stability.

Similar personal attack was leveled against others in the government, particularly against Gustavo Madero and Manuel Bonilla. Sánchez Santos applied the cruel nickname "Ojo Parado" (Closed Eye) to the President's brother, alluding to his artificial eye.[19] The opposition journals were guilty of con-

[18] Cabrera, *Obras políticas,* p. 355.
[19] Bonilla, Memorias (MS), AdeV.

duct other than calumny. Prostituting their sacred trust, they exaggerated, distorted, and engaged in sheer fantasy. Revolts were enthusiastically reported, and disorders were magnified. The old rumors of foreign influence in the revolution were revived. The government was attacked both for not solving the agrarian problem and for intending to solve it!

Implicitly and explicitly, day after day, the journalists sought to show the inadequacy of the government and the incompetence of the executive. *El Mañana,* surveying the year following the departure of Díaz, asked rhetorically: "What remains for us of the order, peace, and prosperity internally and the credit, respect and prestige abroad which Mexico enjoyed under the government of General Díaz?" [20] As early as February, 1912, this paper was demanding that the President resign. The activities of the opposition newspapers contributed to the confusion, uncertainty, and distrust of the period. Some praised, encouraged, and even incited rebellion. They played a major role in creating an environment hostile to Madero and his government.

Two incidents occurred early in 1912 which reflected very favorably on Madero's attitude toward freedom of expression. Early in January the cabinet decided to expel three Spanish journalists under Article 33 of the Constitution which empowered the government to expel pernicious foreigners. Mario Victoria, director of *Multicolor,* and two fellow countrymen were charged with mixing in the internal affairs of the nation. The Association of Metropolitan Journalists protested the decision to President Madero. The President pointed out that he had never complained about the attacks of the national press which he was determined should be free. He expressed his belief that the foreign journalists had abused the freedom of the press and had violated the law. Nevertheless, he honored the protest and revoked the expulsion order.

In February the Argentinian poet Manuel Ugarte arrived in Mexico. He was engaged in an energetic campaign for a Latin American union in the face of American imperialism. Journal-

[20] *El Mañana,* May 28, 1912.

ists, students, and intellectuals of the old regime welcomed him enthusiastically. Manuel Calero, Minister of Foreign Affairs, opposed Ugarte's projected talk entitled "We and They" as inappropriate and inopportune. Undoubtedly, the cabinet official desired to avoid increasing the American Ambassador's aversion to the government. José Vasconcelos, head of the Ateneo, also opposed the appearance of the visitor and attacked the students who supported him. A group of demonstrators marched to the National Palace where Madero invited a committee to visit his office. He expressed his regrets that Vasconcelos had taken the stand he did and assured the protestants that Ugarte could speak when he pleased. On February 3, Ugarte delivered his talk in the Virginia Fábregas Theater.

Madero's friends and associates urged that some effort be made to regulate the press. The President resisted efforts to muzzle the newspapers. "I prefer to sink with the law than to sustain myself without it." [21] Nevertheless, cabinet ministers Hernández and Díaz Lombardo discussed suspension of Article 7 of the Constitution (relating to freedom of the press) with the Permanent Commission of the Congress. Word of this meeting "leaked out," and Madero was charged immediately in the press and on the floor of Congress with tyranny and suppression of free speech despite the fact that he had promised that "he would not place any obstacle to the freedom of the press as long as its acts were guided by truth and honor." [22] A restraining law submitted to Congress created such a furor that it was withdrawn, and the uncontrolled press attacks continued.

Gustavo Madero fought back with *Nueva Era* and with organized demonstrations against the opposition press. Despite his brother's opposition to a subsidized press, Gustavo arranged for control of several other papers in the capital. However, these efforts were heavy-handed and proved ineffective in the face of the flood of opposition journalism. *El*

[21] Lamicq, *El dolor mexicano,* p. 94*n.*
[22] Cabrera, *Obras políticas,* p. 355.

Imparcial, supposedly controlled by Ernesto Madero, remained in the hands of the old publishers and did not make itself felt as a government organ.

On the anniversary of the revolution in 1912, Madero addressed the members of the other branches of the government. He protested against the libertinage of the press: "In no other country of the world . . . is there freedom of the press as excessive as that which Mexico has." The President assured his listeners that it was not a personal question with him but one of authority which must be respected to be strong. Therefore, he asked for a law, "a liberal law that would honor you and the Republic," to put an end to these abuses.[23] The congressional session ended without action being taken on this request. Madero remained at the mercy of the press, a press "without pity and without moderation." [24]

[23] *Ibid.*, pp. 497-502.
[24] Lara Pardo, *Madero,* p. 230.

XV. Progress despite Difficulties

In addition to an entrenched reaction, a demanding revolution, an obstreperous Congress, and a virulent press, Madero had to contend with the activities of American Ambassador Henry Lane Wilson. Despite the antiforeign, and particularly anti-American, sentiment which was part of the Mexican upheaval, Madero, admirer of American institutions, continued to proclaim his friendship for the United States. The American government indicated, at least by its conduct in the early months of the Madero regime, its desire to contribute to the stability of the new administration.

Henry Lane Wilson, who had become Ambassador to Mexico in the waning days of the Díaz period, was not unhappy about the change of government. Although he was concerned lest the revolution increase disrespect for authority and was not enthusiastic about the elevation of a reformer to the presidency, his early reports were not unfavorable to Madero. In July the American diplomat reported that he had met Madero on several occasions and had endeavored to form some opinion of his character.

> He is insignificant in appearance, of diffident manners and hesitating speech, and seems to be highly nervous and uncertain as to his course in regard to many important public questions. He has, however, one redeeming feature—a pair of excellent eyes, which indicate to me earnestness, truthfulness, and loyalty, and, it may be, reserves of strength and force of character which time may more fully reveal.[1]

[1] Wilson to Secretary of State, July 11, 1911, SDF, 812.00/2219.

Wilson, though repelled by the confusion and "anarchy" which attended the inauguration, nevertheless reported that

> my observation up to the present time leads me to think that Mr. Madero is an honest and patriotic man, dealing with a most difficult situation and embarrassed by the difficulty of reconciling his peculiar creed [!] and the program of the revolution with the prevalent condition and the stern necessities of the hour . . . Mr. Madero must change his ideas of government or the people [will] . . . hang him. I am now of the opinion that Mr. Madero will change his ideas of government and that as time passes he will be compelled by the forces of circumstances to revert more and more to the system implanted by General Díaz.

The Ambassador expressed his belief that the new President would protect foreigners and that he and his cabinet would "do justice to American interests." [2]

Within a few months Wilson had become the severest critic, censor, and, ultimately, fanatical enemy of the government to which he was accredited. The reasons for this change were inherent in the personalities, backgrounds, and objectives of the two men involved. There was a very real personality conflict between the realistic, practical American diplomat and the idealistic, emotional Mexican president. Wilson was disappointed that Madero did not recognize his experience and consult with him. The background of the two men included the economic rivalry between the Madero family and the Guggenheim interests with which friends and relatives of the Ambassador were associated. As soon as it was evident that the new government did not propose to grant favors to American capital and, in Wilson's opinion, could not be trusted to maintain order and to protect American property interests, the Ambassador became an active opponent of Madero.

Now Wilson was the perfect representative of the foreign colony in Mexico City which was antagonistic to the new government. The American Ambassador surrounded himself with a small clique, which came to be known as 'The Society

[2] Wilson to Secretary of State, Nov. 30, 1911, SDF, 812.00/2601.

of Friends of the American Ambassador', and it was their interests which he came to represent and their views that he reflected. By circumstance or intention the American diplomat was isolated from the Mexican people and representative public opinion.

Wilson's attitude found expression in his complaints to the Mexican government and in his reports to the State Department. The Ambassador protested disorders and demanded protection for American life and property. He harassed the Mexican government with real and imaginary grievances and insisted on immediate settlement of claims, including compensation for the deaths of from forty to over one hundred Americans reported murdered. Under careful investigation the number diminished to seventeen, of which only a handful merited consideration. Not content with representing American interests, Wilson pressed the claims of German, Spanish, Belgian, French, and Chinese nationals. He complained, for example, of action against the violently antigovernment *Mexican Herald;* of the "discriminatory and confiscatory" oil tax, which was scarcely exorbitant (three *centavos* per barrel) and which applied to all producers; and of the proposal of the Madero government to enforce the Spanish language requirement, which had fallen into disuse under Díaz, for railroad workers.[3]

In his reports to the American government Wilson repeated all the stock criticisms of the Madero government, noted optimistically the prospects and usually wrote flatteringly of the leaders of the revolutionary movements against the Madero administration, and painted a gloomy picture of conditions in Mexico. His dispatches, too often based on rumors and inflammatory newspaper accounts, clearly show his relentless efforts to discredit the Madero government. Wilson's news of certain districts was, on occasion, at variance with the dispatches of consular agents in the locality. In March, Wilson felt compelled to submit as evidence that the Embassy dispatches were "written in a most conservative spirit and

[3] Gruening, *Mexico,* p. 563.

with close adherence to established facts" clippings from the *Mexican Herald*![4]

Personnel at the State Department by early 1913 were entertaining serious doubts about the reliability of Wilson's reports. Attached to the Ambassador's telegram of January 20 was the following note by Dearing of the Division of Latin American Affairs:

> Please keep this newspaper [a copy of the *Mexican Herald*] attached to this telegram . . . It bears the same date as the Embassy telegram and was probably delivered to the Embassy early in the morning. It would seem likely that the Embassy's telegram had been made up solely on the newspaper accounts of various happenings; that no effort was made on the part of the Embassy to verify the news transmitted to the Department; that the newspaper's information is uncertain and vague at best and apt to be played up in a more or less sensational way. It may be observed in this connection that almost all of the pessimistic reports of the Embassy during the immediate past seem to have been made up in the same way, i.e., wholly from a cursory reading of this one newspaper printed in Mexico City.[5]

Secretary Knox felt compelled to write to Wilson about his "uniformly discouraging reports" since his return to Mexico. The cabinet officer, noting the more pessimistic nature of Wilson's reports compared with those of the Chargé d'Affaires, tactfully suggested that perhaps it was due to a difference of viewpoint. He concluded that

> the Department welcomes, of course, and expects at all times from its officers in the field the frankest expression of opinion and would be glad at the present delicate moment to have the state of affairs so represented, without either over or understatement, that it will not err in its judgment.[6]

The aggrieved Mr. Wilson replied that the Embassy's reports "are plain narratives of facts . . . I will gladly report all favorable indications, events or tendencies, where such exist."[7]

[4] Wilson to State Dept., March 22, 1912, SDF, 812.00/3422.

[5] SDF, 812.00/5904.

[6] Knox to Wilson, Jan. 21, 1913, SDF, 812.00/5913A.

[7] Wilson to State Dept., SDF, 812.00/5916.

The Madero government regarded the Ambassador's conduct as intolerable, but the election of Woodrow Wilson as President of the United States encouraged Madero to anticipate a change in the American Embassy. He told Vasconcelos that the President-Elect was his friend and that "the first favor I am going to ask him is that he should change the representative for me." [8] Madero wrote Lascuráin, new Mexican Ambassador to Washington, that he should confer with Woodrow Wilson and advise him that Henry Lane Wilson was *persona non grata* to the Mexican government. Lascuráin apparently made little or no effort in this direction. However, Ambassador Wilson learned of this letter, and his distaste for the Madero government reached a new peak. He explained Madero's hostility as "due solely to my vigorous and uncompromising attitude on American matters." [9] The Mexican President looked forward hopefully to March 4, Inauguration Day for Woodrow Wilson. To Ambassador Wilson that day loomed as a deadline for his activities.

The most critical problem facing the Madero administration was the agrarian question. Once more the President's policy of conciliation was caught in the cross fire of conservatives opposed to change and revolutionaries demanding reform. Conditions in rural Mexico had created an insistent demand for change, and the milieu created by the revolution encouraged the expectation of immediate fulfillment of pledges broadly interpreted.

Agrarian discontent was manifested in local disturbances and outbreaks in the northern and central states. In Durango and San Luis Potosí peasants were attacking haciendas and seizing land. The rebellion of Zapata centered in the state of Morelos, but it also affected the neighboring states of Puebla, Tlaxcala, Guerrero, and Mexico. By mid-1912 disturbances rooted in agrarian conditions had extended into Yucatán, Tabasco, and Campeche. These disorders complicated the situ-

[8] Vasconcelos, *Ulises criollo,* p. 413.
[9] Wilson, *Diplomatic Episodes,* pp. 234-36.

ation for the government and provided grist for the reactionary propaganda mill.

Madero's efforts to deal with the agrarian problem were circumscribed by his desire for a democratic, legal solution and by his policy of political conciliation. He denied that extensive commitments had been made by the revolution. Careful review of the Plan of San Luis Potosí and of his speeches and programs of government, he asserted, would prove that the only promises made were those relative to the restitution of lands to those despoiled of them illegally and to the encouragement of the development of the small property unit. The latter pledge was not interpreted to mean expropriation. "I always have advocated the creation of the small property, but that does not mean that any landowner should be despoiled of his properties." [10] Unfortunately for Madero many persons insisted upon regarding him as the instrument for far-reaching, immediate changes.

Despite the Mexican President's emphasis on the limited commitments of the revolution, he did recognize that the agrarian problem was important. He conceived as his principal mission the "reestablishment" of democratic political practices. He expected that the representatives of the people would devote time and study to the other problems of the day. In an interview in February, 1912, he emphasized that "one of the greatest national necessities is . . . to divide the great properties and to encourage small agriculture." However, Madero felt that the agrarian question "is the most difficult to resolve in a short time." [11] At a dinner in Xochimilco he told the assembled legislators that the social and agrarian questions were among the most important problems. "The people continue in misery and in ignorance. One of the greatest obligations of all Mexicans is to work for the people's aggrandizement." [12] He urged the legislators to work together to produce an equitable solution of the agrarian question.

[10] *El Imparcial,* June 27, 1912.
[11] *Nueva Era,* Feb. 11, 1912.
[12] *El Diario,* Sept. 24, 1912.

The planning of the agrarian program of the Madero administration was entrusted to the first National Agrarian Commission, presided over by Rafael Hernández, Minister of Development. The commission was composed of distinguished agriculturalists, lawyers, engineers, and bankers, but all the members were of conservative orientation. Early in February, 1912, the commission presented what Madero described as a "luminous project" for the solution of the agrarian question.[13]

The report submitted by Lic. Hernández was an academic document complete with good intentions and attractive promises. The commissioners wrote of conservation of the forests, of improvement of communication, transportation, and agricultural credit, and of advances in stock breeding, intensification of cultivation, and better utilization of water resources. Regarding the land question, the commission recommended the restitution of the lands of the *ejidos* and the allocation of national lands and the purchase of private lands for division and sale. An Agrarian Executive Committee, composed of three members, was to be designated to carry out the program. The government was already authorized to proceed under powers obtained through the agricultural relief law of December 18, 1911.

The program provided for the purchase of private estates and the division of the land for cash or credit sale, on easy mortgage terms, to farmers, to Mexican *émigrés* who desired to be repatriated, and to immigrant colonists. The government planned to reorganize and extend the activities of the Caja de Préstamos de Irrigación y Fomento de Agricultura (Department of Loans for Irrigation and Development of Agriculture). This corporation had been established three years earlier by Limantour to finance large agricultural improvement projects. Despite belated directives in behalf of small proprietors, the Caja had operated primarily for the larger interests. The Madero government planned to utilize this corporation to provide discountable mortgages for the new small proprietors. These operations were to be guaranteed by the government

[13] *Nueva Era,* Feb. 11, 1912.

by means of a bond issue of one hundred and fifty thousand pesos. In addition, the Caja was authorized to assist hacendados in the preparation of the land in order to insure against failure by the new owners.

Rafael Hernández reported that "the offerings of the landowners have been numerous." [14] Indeed, the Executive Committee, which began functioning in April, 1912, reported that owners dreamed of selling to the government at fancy prices lands which were a burden to them. As soon as the government's intentions were known, speculators became active, and unproductive lands tripled in value. The committee, concluding that the cost would prove prohibitive for the government, recommended that the system be discarded for financial and ethical reasons. The alternative policy recommended was to concentrate on the restitution of the *ejidos.*

A modest beginning in that direction already had been made. On January 8 and February 13, Minister Hernández, on the instruction of President Madero, issued two circulars. The first indicated that municipal councils would be authorized to proceed to the survey and occupation of the village lands. The second circular directed the governors to cooperate in this recovery of communal lands and to protect those lands from encroachments by neighboring proprietors. By September, Madero reported that one hundred and thirty-seven town councils had applied for the restitution of lands and that many of these cases had been settled.[15] However, this policy barely scratched the surface and covered only those communities which could prove they had been victims of despoliation. Furthermore, Hernández, confirmed his conservative reputation when he arranged that *his department* would settle *administratively* differences which arose between hacendados and villages.

The third prong of the Madero attack on the land problem involved the use of national lands. A circular of February 24

[14] Molina Enríquez, *La revolución agraria,* V, 107.

[15] F. I. Madero, "Informe . . . el 16 de septiembre de 1912," in *Diario Oficial,* 122, No. 13, 141-42.

directed the National Agrarian Commission to survey and recover illegally alienated national lands which were to be transferred or rented to Mexican nationals. The division into small lots of one hundred and thirty-two thousand hectares (approximately three hundred and thirty-three thousand acres) of national domain in Chiapas, San Luis Potosí, Tabasco, Veracruz, and Lower California was to start immediately. The commission dispatched representatives to Guerrero, Michoacán, San Luis Potosí, and Baja California to establish survey offices. By September the government had twenty-one million hectares (about fifty million acres) of public land at its disposal, and this amount was constantly being increased as the government recovered lands fraudulently granted and those on which the grantees had failed to comply with concession stipulations. In the Mayo and Yaqui Rivers area an even more detailed and constructive plan was undertaken.[16]

The Madero administration also established seven agricultural experiment stations at selected points throughout the country, as well as three model farms in Nuevo León to facilitate the study of cultivation under very dry conditions. Irrigation projects initiated under Díaz were continued, and the construction of a large dam in Hidalgo was begun. Lastly, the government contracted with the Caja for a loan of almost four million pesos to be used for the improvement of the lands of Lake Texcoco. Summarizing these efforts in his report to Congress, Madero declared that the evidence "shows that the Executive is deeply concerned with the agricultural problem upon the solution of which .... depends the economic future of the Republic."[17] However, popular demand remained unsatisfied by these moderate, gradual measures. Madero excused the delay in undertaking more extensive action in terms of the disorders which plagued the country.[18]

During the closing months of the Madero regime there were indications that more radical determinations regarding the

[16] *Ibid.*, pp. 143-44.
[17] *Ibid.*, pp. 144-45.
[18] Speech, Nov. 20, 1912, cited in Cabrera, *Obras políticas,* p. 503.

agrarian question might be in the making. The November cabinet changes placed the Fomento portfolio in the hands of Manuel Bonilla who pushed the study of the land question seeking an integral solution. The Agrarian Executive Committee had recommended that it would be desirable to "add means that would tend to reconstruct the *ejidos* of the towns . . . and that reconstruction ought to be under the form of [inalienable] communal property." [19] Hernández had not followed up this recommendation. Luis Cabrera, providing the Renovators in the legislature with leadership, gave these doctrines spectacular form in a speech in the Chamber of Deputies on December 3, 1912.

Cabrera attacked the policy of peace first and economic reforms second. Reconstruction of *ejidos*, he said, was essential to peace. He criticized what he called "ingenuous means" to resolve the agrarian problem: to buy lands to sell them was impractical as the government had discovered; to divide national lands was not the answer because these did not include the best lands and were not appropriately located where the need existed; and to recover ejidal lands illegally held would be difficult since ninety percent of the current holders had some sort of title. In words that recalled his earlier famous phrase, "The Revolution is the Revolution," Cabrera lamented the failure to resolve the problem quickly. "Sociologically, when one is in the moment of revolution, it is necessary to hasten to resolve questions." [20]

This had not been done, and the speaker recommended that the Executive be given the power to expropriate private lands to be used to reconstruct the *ejidos* of villages which had lost them and to give them to communities which needed them. The Renovators began publishing a paper, *El Reformador*, in January, 1913. In the January seventeenth issue it was claimed that the government was swinging to the revolutionary cause and that thorough-going land reforms would be started. Conservatives were alarmed. Madero's political ideas had seemed

[19] Molina Enríquez, *La revolución agraria*, V, 115.
[20] Magaña, *Emiliano Zapata*, II, 325-52.

to them peculiar, unreal, and unsatisfactory, but any effort at reform seemed dangerous. The conservative opposition intensified and accelerated its moves against the administration.

The emphasis on legality, the difficulties encountered, and the paucity of results tend to blind many to the agrarian efforts of the short-lived Madero regime. Andrés Molina Enríquez, a penetrating analyst and a persistent advocate of agrarian reform, looking back over twenty years since the 1910 movement, wrote that the attempt of Madero's administration to resolve the agrarian question placed Madero and those in the government who supported his ideas in the camp of the reformers.

> The Madero government, despite his personal repugnance and only through his respect for the free action of his collaborators, in accordance with his democratic creed, ought to be considered as the most *agrarista* government which we have had. It lasted a year, and if it had lasted the four [years] of his term, the agrarian question probably would have been solved. The great mass of the Nation always has believed that. Therefore, it has cried on the tomb of Madero.[21]

There was hardly a branch of governmental activity in which Madero's regime did not demonstrate some activity. From almost the beginning of his term the labor question was studied. Four points were emphasized in the investigation: reduction of hours; strikes; protection of women and children in industry; and workingmen's accident compensation. In December, 1911, the Subsecretary of Government began to collect data on the labor question. In January, 1912, Lic. Antonio Ramos Pedrueza was appointed to organize a National Labor Office which was to carry out the needed studies and to intervene in industrial disputes. Inside of eight months this office had contributed to the settlement of seventy strikes.

Under the auspices of the National Labor Office a convention of employers and employees in the cotton fabrics and yarn industry was held. Owners of one hundred and fifty factories reached an accord with the one hundred and four-

[21] Molina Enríquez, *La revolución agraria,* V, 111, 122-23.

teen delegates of the Central Workers' Committee establishing minimum wages, the ten-hour working day (formerly twelve to thirteen hours), and workmen's compensation. In December, 1912, the Congress gave this Labor Department legal status and placed it under the jurisdiction of the Ministry of Fomento.

Although the tangible and lasting gains of labor during the brief Madero administration were few, for the first time an environment propitious for labor existed. Workers were able to meet, to talk, to organize, and to strike. It was during this period that the Casa del Obrero Mundial, later to play an important part in the Mexican labor movement and in the revolution, was organized as a sort of meeting place and propaganda center for a group of young, radical leaders.

In another area vital to the Mexican Revolution—education—the Madero government made a worthy effort. The federal appropriation for this purpose, never over eight million pesos under Díaz, was increased to twelve million pesos. The whole educational system had been disrupted by the revolution and by the subsequent disturbances. It was the Madero administration which established the first rural schools sustained by the central government. This action had been authorized during the interim period, and three hundred thousand pesos were appropriated for this purpose. However, in September, 1912, Madero admitted that only slightly over half of this amount had been expended. With these monies fifty schools had been opened.[22]

Because of the difficulties involved and the slow progress being made elsewhere, it was to be expected that the President, in his reports, would emphasize the accomplishments within the Federal District. He announced the inauguration of the following: several special evening schools; two Sunday schools, one for men and one for women; two high schools; and two industrial schools. It was during Madero's term that the later famous student dining rooms were initiated. Twenty-

[22] F. I. Madero, "Informe . . . el 16 de septiembre de 1912," in *Diario Oficial*, 122, No. 13, 140.

nine such food establishments, sixteen in the capital and thirteen more in the Federal District, were opened, and approved pupils could obtain breakfast and light lunch. Pupils who were able paid two *centavos* for a meal, the money being used to improve the food, but the majority were fed gratis. Almost fifty-eight hundred children were fed daily under this program. In addition, the government distributed over twenty thousand suits of clothes and twelve thousand pairs of shoes to the needy children of the District.[23] The administration's activities in the field of education included the establishment of a museum at Apatzingán, meeting place of the first Mexican Congress, the convocation of a national congress on primary education, and a full investigation of educational conditions by Alberto J. Pani, Subsecretary of Public Instruction, in which he emphasized the problem of Indian education.

Public works projects also were initiated by the Madero government, but the emphasis was necessarily on reconstruction rather than on new projects. Almost all the damaged railroad mileage was repaired and over three hundred kilometers of new railroad were constructed. To remedy the damaged and neglected road system Madero created an inspector's office for roads, wagon roads, and bridges. This office surveyed road conditions and began work on the roads connecting Puebla, Toluca, Pachuca, and Veracruz with the capital, as well as on the road between Iguala and Chilpancingo.[24] Port improvement works initiated during the Díaz administration were continued, and the important project at Frontera, Tabasco, was inaugurated.

The state of Tabasco was experiencing a difficult economic situation because of the failure to dredge the port of Frontera. The mouth of the Grijalva River was so badly blocked that boats with a draught exceeding eight feet were unable to approach close enough to load and unload. Madero visited Frontera in September, 1911, as candidate for the presidency

[23] *Ibid.*

[24] F. I. Madero, "Informe . . . el 1 de abril de 1912," in *Diario Oficial*, 119, No. 27, 405-19.

and promised to provide the needed public works.[25] In December a contract was approved under which the government advanced the funds and the North American Dredging Company undertook to dissolve and canalize the sandbar at Frontera to permit the entry of ships with a draught up to twenty feet. Two other noteworthy undertakings were projected. The first company to provide Mexico City with gas was organized, and the electrification of the central plateau was planned. The fall of Madero prevented completion of these projects.

Another abortive project of the Madero regime related to the reform of the army. Madero created a Superior War Council to study reorganization of the military system. The only effort made in this direction was the presidential project for compulsory military service. Madero argued that this measure would make the nation strong because "an army formed from all the social classes has to reflect the national sentiment." He foresaw immense advantages for the reestablishment and assurance of peace, the reduction of illiteracy, and the unification of the national spirit. "I believe that the most opportune moment to establish compulsory military service is at present. The [recent] terrific commotion has shown clearly the necessity that all citizens should serve the Fatherland."[26] The legislature never acted on this proposal.

It has been charged that Madero failed to carry out his promises, but José Vasconcelos refers to "all that which we [the Mexicans] did not permit him to realize."[27] As Madero began to formulate an economic and social program, he galvanized into action the opposition of conservative interests. Considering the conditions, obstacles, and the opposition encountered by the short-lived Madero regime, its efforts at constructive activity were notable and its accomplishments really not completely insignificant.

[25] Sept. 21, 1911, AdeV.

[26] Speech by Madero, Oct. 16, 1912, cited in Lamicq, *El dolor mexicano,* pp. 109-15.

[27] Taracena, *Madero: Vida,* p. xiv.

XVI. Rebels and Rebellions

MADERO'S ADMINISTRATION was challenged by a series of rebellions. These movements, in a sense, represented the traditional Mexican practice of probing the power of the new executive. In fifteen months the President had to deal with two major uprisings involving vast sections of the nation, the conspiracy and abortive effort of Bernardo Reyes, and the *cuartelazo* of Félix Díaz in Veracruz. These developments disrupted the economic life of the nation, consumed the time, energy, and resources of the government, and provided ammunition for the opposition press which, while the rebellions lasted, attacked Madero for not dominating them.

The earliest major attack on the Madero regime came from the revolutionary side, and it persisted the longest. The problem of Zapatismo was inherited from the interim period. If at that time Madero's advice had been followed, the insurgents of Morelos might not have been so distrustful, bitter, and impatient. The forces of Zapata remained under arms, and their demands for immediate reform were more insistent than before. The situation conflicted with the President's policy of conciliation, with his willingness to discharge the revolutionary forces, and with his belief that the solution of the agrarian question would require time and study.

One of the first acts of Madero's cabinet was to agree to dispatch Gabriel Robles Domínguez to try to negotiate peace in Morelos. This emissary conferred with Zapata at the village of Ayala where the Morelos commander had concentrated his forces after suspending hostilities. Zapata presented his conditions on November 11: withdrawal of federal forces within forty-five days; five hundred Zapatistas to remain as rurales under an acceptable chief, preferably Raúl Madero or Eufemio Zapata; replacement of the governor; and promulgation of an agrarian law. Robles Domínguez returned to the capital to confer with the President.

Zapata's conditions were not acceptable to the government. Madero handed the negotiator a letter in which he asked him to advise the Morelos insurgent that he and his men should yield unconditionally. "Then I will pardon his soldiers for the crime of rebellion." He instructed the emissary to tell Zapata that "his attitude of rebellion is damaging my government a great deal and that I am not able to tolerate its continuation for any reason." [1] Robles Domínguez was encouraged that the President instructed him to transmit orders to the Secretary of War to suspend hostilities while a peaceful arrangement was being concluded. The negotiator returned to Morelos, but his efforts were doomed to failure.

Conflict reappeared, and the Zapatistas were in full rebellion against Madero just as they had been against Díaz and de la Barra and just as they would be against subsequent governments for a half a dozen more years. Always from Morelos came the same insistent, urgent demand for land and for the withdrawal of federal troops. Zapata was convinced very soon, too soon to constitute a fair trial for the new government, that Madero would not provide the action demanded. The Morelos insurgent reportedly remarked, "Be it known to Sr. Madero and with him the rest of the world that we will not lay down our arms until we are given possession of our village lands." [2] On November 28, less than a month after Madero assumed the presidency, the Plan of Ayala was launched.

This revolutionary proclamation was drawn up by the

[1] Madero to Robles Domínguez, Nov. 12, 1911, printed in *El Mañana*, June 28, 1912.

[2] Melgarejo, *Crímenes del Zapatismo*, p. 140.

schoolteacher Otilio Montaño and signed by Zapata and his officers. The Zapatistas disavowed the leadership of Madero, who "did not carry to a happy end the Revolution so gloriously initiated," and called for his resignation. The Plan was essentially agrarian and local in its ideas of reform. The peasants were to occupy immediately the lands of which they had been despoiled. In addition, one third of the land in private estates was to be expropriated, with indemnification, to provide lands for the *ejidos* and for individuals. Nationalization of the remaining two thirds of the property of those who opposed the Plan was promised. The Zapatistas voiced the lamentation, frequently repeated during the Mexican Revolution, that "the Nation is tired of false and traitorous men who make promises as liberators but who on reaching power forget them and become tyrants." [3] The Plan of Ayala was published, with Madero's permission, in Mexico City in December, 1911.[4] The President had demonstrated again that the press was to be free.

During the remaining days of 1911 the struggle was active, bitter, and bloody. The Zapatistas were very aggressive, attacking federal concentrations with lightning thrusts followed by rapid withdrawals. The *agrarista* revolt extended rapidly into the neighboring states of Puebla, Guerrero, Tlaxcala, and Mexico. As railroad and communication facilities were interrupted, as pillaging and violence increased, and as pacific settlement became more remote, the government resorted to other measures beside armed force. The administration requested permission from Congress to suspend constitutional guarantees in the affected areas. On January 19 martial law was declared for four months in Morelos, Guerrero, and Tlaxcala and in districts of Puebla and Mexico. The decree revealed that three whole states and a considerable part of two others, in addition to the Federal District, were affected by the movement.[5]

[3] Magaña, *Emiliano Zapata,* II, 128.

[4] *El Diario del Hogar,* Dec. 15, 1912.

[5] The rebellion had echoes in parts of Michoacán and Oaxaca. Other

Madero vacillated in his policy toward the insurrection. He alternated severe with moderate commanders, orders to fight with orders to negotiate. To all, Zapata remained unyielding, uncompromising. General Juvencio Robles, named military commander late in January, was to initiate one of the bitterest phases of the struggle. Undoubtedly Madero was influenced by the challenge to his government, by the conservative members of the administration, and by the persistent attacks by the opposition press alleging the ineffectiveness of his regime. *El Imparcial* warned that "either the Government destroys 'Zapatism' in a very short time or 'Zapatism' will destroy the government in the long run." [6]

During February the Zapatistas attacked trains and various towns and spread terror through the area. Cuernavaca was threatened, and rebels appeared at several points in Hidalgo. In the second half of the month General Robles won several victories, but that did not quiet the concern in the capital. Ambassador Wilson, reflecting conservative criticism, reported that "public opinion is disposed to regard the situation as hopeless." [7]

Robles remained in command for six months. The campaign was one of persecution and cruelty by the government's forces and pillaging and violence by the Zapatistas. In March the rebels sacked Jojutla, and Eufemio Zapata with two thousand men seized Cholula briefly and threatened the city of Puebla. Cuernavaca was besieged and communication with the nation's capital was broken. The rebel forces, using guerrilla tactics that fitted their organization and means, appeared suddenly, attacked unexpectedly, and retired abruptly.

In April twenty-five hundred new troops were sent to reinforce the government's army, but until the middle of 1912 the Zapatistas had the better of the fighting. The rain, the climate,

---

agrarian outbreaks occurred in Chihuahua, in the Yucatán peninsula, and in San Luis Potosí, where the Cedillo brothers seconded the Plan of Ayala in Nov., 1912.

[6] *El Imparcial,* Feb. 5, 1912.

[7] Wilson to State Dept., Feb. 11, 1912, SDF, 812.00/2768.

and the tactics of the opposition were blamed. Beginning in June, General Robles, employing a ruthless technique, began to exterminate some of the rebel groups. In the process many towns were razed and many persons shot. Late in July the federal commander returned to Mexico City and stated that the war in Morelos was similar to the Yaqui conflict during the Díaz regime! He advocated a war without quarter, a war of extermination.[8]

That very month an unofficial negotiator visited Zapata, and in August, General Felipe Angeles, Director of the Military College, was sent to Morelos to assume the federal command. General Angeles conducted a much more benign campaign after studying the situation in Morelos. Despite his efforts and Madero's report in September that the main rebel groups were disbanded and the situation almost settled,[9] the Zapatistas remained in opposition to the government. During the closing months of 1912 their forces displayed renewed activity, attacking federal detachments and defending positions, and as late as February 4, 1913, less than a week before the final conservative blow against the government, the forces of Zapata attacked a passenger train from Toluca.

Oddly enough, it was not the action of Zapata but the attitude of General Reyes which caused the most concern for the Madero government during its first weeks in power. Late in September, 1911, the General had left Mexico precipitously, charging that he knew that the elections would not be conducted fairly. After stopping in Havana, General Reyes sailed for New Orleans. From there he proceeded to Texas with the intention of heading an armed movement being organized by his partisans.

In mid-November a revolutionary plan was prepared at a border ranch in Tamaulipas, where Reyes was supposed to cross the frontier. The Mexican government, with news of the plot, ordered troops to Saltillo, Monterrey, and points along the border. The Mexican Embassy called the situation to the

[8] Magaña, *Emiliano Zapata*, II, 200.

attention of the United States government and requested that immediate steps be taken to block Reyes's revolutionary designs.[9] On November 17, General Reyes was arrested in Laredo on a charge of violating the neutrality laws. When, two days later, he was released on a five-thousand-dollar bond, the Mexican government increased its forces on the frontier.

The Reyists accelerated their preparations. The General, who had been unable to bring himself to oppose the Díaz regime, prepared for a theatrical blow which he hoped would duplicate Madero's feat earlier that year. He later admitted, "I believed that I was the called and I tried to rebel against the state of things in the Nation."[10] Reyes thought that he still enjoyed his former prestige as a soldier and governor, and he was confident that he could count on thousands of armed men once he entered Mexico. With the threat of prosecution by American authorities hanging over his head the General precipitately entered Mexico at the head of a small armed band during the night of December 13. A group of his partisans attacked Ramos Arizpe in Coahuila, and there were minor declarations of support in Teapa (Tabasco) and Ameca (Jalisco). Federal forces were soon pursuing the little band led by General Reyes. His partisans, who had misled him about the prospects and preparations, blamed the hostility of the United States for his premature entry into Mexican territory. The main reason for the failure was the fact that neither the people nor the army responded.

On the night of December 25, Reyes surrendered to a startled rurales barracks commander in Linares (Nuevo León). The prisoner received permission to send the following telegram to General Treviño, Chief of the Third Zone: "I called the army and the people, but not a single man came to my support . . . Declaring the impossibility of waging war, I . . . place myself at your disposition."[11] General Treviño ordered that the prisoner be freed in Linares under word of honor.

[9] Nov. 10, 1911, SDF, 812.00/2483.
[10] B. Reyes, *Defensa*, p. 28.
[11] *Ibid.*, p. 40.

The following day the cabinet decided that General Reyes should be brought to Mexico City for safekeeping. He was interned in the military prison of Santiago Tlaltelolco, accused of the crime of rebellion. Ambassador Wilson disgustedly reported that the Reyes rebellion, "to the relief of all factions," had run its course and had come to a "most ignominious, undignified, and grotesque end." The Ambassador hastened to add that the General's failure was not due to "any universal satisfaction with the Madero government." [12]

Also in the northern part of the Republic another, more serious, rebellion broke out. This movement began as a reformist drive inspired by Emilio Vázquez, but evolved as the rebellion of Pascual Orozco, Jr., with strong indications of conservative machinations. The situation in Chihuahua was complicated by revolutionary discontent, local dissatisfaction with absentee rule due to the leave granted Governor Abraham González to serve in Madero's cabinet, and conservative reaction against the government and threatened reforms. In Texas, Emilio Vázquez, who actively had sought and won adherents while serving in de la Barra's cabinet, continued to appeal to revolutionary discontent. In a letter circulated to sympathizers in Mexico, dated December 15, 1911, in San Antonio, before the debacle of General Reyes's movement was known, he wrote that

> the fall of Sr. Madero is going to be realized with astounding rapidity. No one, absolutely no one, is able to avoid it.
>
> The question now is not Madero. Madero falls alone. The question is Reyes. Either we [the Revolution] turn the situation over to Reyes or we take it ourselves.[13]

Late in January there were disturbances in Ciudad Juárez and in Chihuahua City. In the border town the garrison rose in rebellion and took charge of the community. The incident probably was prompted by Vázquez's propaganda coinciding with the news that General Pascual Orozco had submitted his

[12] Wilson to Secretary Knox, Jan. 23, 1912, SDF, 812.00/2710.
[13] *El Gráfico,* Nov. 28, 1930.

resignation. A few days later, February 2, there was an uprising in Chihuahua City which resulted in the release of Antonio Rojas who had headed a rebellion in the name of Emilio Vázquez. Unexpectedly, Orozco did not openly encourage these movements. In fact, he telegraphed the revolters at Ciudad Juárez that "the hour has arrived when all true patriots ought to work for the reestablishment of order."[14] Through personal negotiations he did succeed in reestablishing order in the frontier community. In the state capital Orozco and some of his soldiers offered at least a semblance of resistance to the mutineers. Rojas and some of his followers managed to retire outside of the city to continue their efforts in behalf of Vázquez.

The situation seemed so grave that Abraham González hurriedly left Mexico City for his troubled state capital where he found Orozco quiet. Eulogists praise this evidence of Orozco's loyalty and charge that the conduct of the government later forced him to rebel. Critics contend that the situation was not yet favorable to his rebellion, partly because the commander's resignation had not been formally accepted. Despite the fact that the central government's leaders were concerned about Orozco's intentions (going so far as to instruct Francisco Villa, after ascertaining his loyalty, to watch Orozco), he was provided with one hundred carbines and fifty thousand cartridges for use in reestablishing order.

The Vazquista rebellion which burst forth in full force in February served as the stalking-horse for Orozco. On February 2, in the Santa Rosa Cemetery on the outskirts of Chihuahua City, Professor Braulio Hernández, a revolutionary leader who had resigned as Secretary-General of Chihuahua, and some associates signed a revolutionary manifesto. Charging that the Madero government had betrayed its program, these supporters of Emilio Vázquez called for "land and justice." The garrison of Casas Grandes rebelled in favor of Lic. Vázquez and took possession of the town. In a number of

[14] Magaña, *Emiliano Zapata,* II, 163-64.

communities in Chihuahua, Durango, and Coahuila supporters answered the call.

On February 17, Emilio Vázquez issued a manifesto in San Antonio accepting the provisional presidency offered him by the rebels in Chihuahua. However, in an effort to avoid any involvement with American authorities, he denied that he had organized or directed the armed movements. Four days later he telegraphed Madero, asking him to resign. The President answered the demand with a stinging rebuke.

If I occupy this post, it is by the freely indicated will of the majority of the Mexican citizens. [In that election] you were one of my opponents and only obtained an insignificant minority. It should have made you understand that the Mexican people had no preference for you and that they disapproved of your dismal conduct in the Secretariat of Government. In that post you abused the trust which I, as Chief of the Revolution, placed in you.

Madero concluded with a slap at the insurgent leader for still remaining in San Antonio. "No revolution triumphs when it cannot count on national opinion and when its chief, instead of exposing his life, . . . remains sheltered from all risk and under the protection of a foreign flag." [15] Ambassador Wilson, not enthusiastic about the Vazquista rebellion, even recommended that "in our as well as Mexican interests he should either be expelled from American territory or under [a] liberal interpretation of [the] neutrality laws be imprisoned." [16]

On the morning of February 27, Ciudad Juárez, after a brief exchange of shots, fell to the Vazquistas. The opposition newspaper *El Mañana* greeted the news with the laconic comment that "history repeats itself." [17] A few days later, on March 3, Orozco disavowed the Madero government and rose in rebellion with the personnel at his command. Francisco Villa clashed with Orozco's forces on the outskirts of Chihuahua and was forced to withdraw. Governor González took refuge with the government forces under Villa. Orozco notified the Vazquistas

[15] Emilio Vázquez to Madero and reply, Feb. 17 and 21, 1912, AdeM.
[16] Wilson to State Dept., Feb. 27, 1912, SDF, 812.00/2943.
[17] *El Mañana,* March 1, 1912.

that he was with them. A commission from the rebels at Ciudad Juárez hurried to Chihuahua City to confer with Orozco.

Although Pascual Orozco had been the valiant of the Madero revolution and although his rebellion was declared on the grounds that Madero had not fulfilled the pledges of the Plan of San Luis Potosí, there is reason to believe that personal considerations and other influences had their effect. Unquestionably, the taciturn northern revolutionary and his loquacious father were dissatisfied with the financial and other rewards which had come to them following the revolution. Orozco had sought the governorship of Chihuahua, and his failure to receive it was a blow to his ambition and to his father's vanity. Panegyrists have called Orozco the "soul of the revolution," but he was without a conspicuous position in the new regime. Instead, he received the secondary post in command of irregular forces in Chihuahua. There is evidence that in their state of dissatisfaction father and son succumbed to the blandishments of conservative influences. The evidence is naturally circumstantial, but nonetheless impressive.

The conservative elements recognized the impossibility of restoring their power through one of their own group; a champion from the revolution who could control the masses and at the same time serve their purposes was needed. Orozco appeared to meet the requirements. He had been amenable to conservative influences during the closing days of the Madero armed movement. Now, as he moved toward rebellion against Madero, Orozco was friendly with the Creels and Terrazas, land and cattle barons of Chihuahua. Gonzalo Enrile, a key figure in this rebellion, had held a minor consular post under Díaz, and was reputed to be the intermediary between the insurrection and the unseen powers financing it. Orozco's newspaper support consisted of two papers supported financially by Creel and of two or three minor journals. The rebel leader received funds from the Mining Bank of Chihuahua, reportedly by direction of conservative interests.[18]

[18] Letcher to State Dept., May 10, 1912, SDF, 812.00/3930; Puente,

Indirect confirmation of these indications of conservative backing was contained in a report by Ambassador Wilson. He related that Oscar Braniff, a conservative, had told him that the "movement led by Orozco is financially supported by the best elements in Mexico." [19] Consul Letcher in Chihuahua gave unquestioned credence to this view of the Orozco rebellion. He reported that as soon as the movement started, "all the members of the old party rushed foward to aid him [Orozco] to save the state." He concluded that "the Revolution is the result of intrigue pure and simple, and takes advantage of the ignorance of the people. It is fostered and backed by the wealthiest men of the State." [20]

A revolutionary Junta had been established, Emilio Vázquez was acknowledged as provisional president, and Orozco was designated military commander. Regardless of the shadowy forces behind the movement, Orozco could count on popular support. In addition, his situation was favored by his post as commander of the irregulars and by the military prestige which he enjoyed among his subordinates. With almost six thousand men Orozco shortly controlled the state of Chihuahua. On March 8 a rebel vanguard departed for Jiménez to the southeast. The ultimate goal was the conquest of the nation's capital and the resignation or deposition of Madero.

The rebellion profoundly disturbed Madero's government. It meant the defection of six thousand troops possessed of considerable military supplies and the loss of control in Chihuahua. President Madero called on the nation to support the government which it had elected. The administration requested suspension of constitutional guarantees in the troubled area, increase of the army to sixty thousand men, and authorization for a twenty-million-peso loan to meet the expenses of the campaigns in Chihuahua and Morelos. The administration obtained its requests only after delay caused by tumultuous

---

Pascual Orozco, pp. 14-20; Figueroa Domenech, *Veinte meses de anarquía,* p. 107.

[19] Wilson to State Dept., April 26, 1912, SDF, 812.00/3732.

[20] Letcher to State Dept., March 20, 1912, SDF, 812.00/3424.

sessions in the unruly Congress. The press contributed to the difficult situation by sensational reports.

Ambassador Wilson's conduct tended to magnify the calamities which confronted the harassed administration. He directed a circular to American nationals advising those in areas considered dangerous or isolated to leave. This recommendation was published in the press creating considerable excitement. Mr. Wilson called the Diplomatic Corps together to discuss means of defending lives and property. In that connection the American diplomat requested five hundred rifles and ammunition for the defense of the American colony. On March 22, on behalf of the American Colony Committee, he requested one thousand Krag-Jorgenson rifles and two hundred and fifty thousand cartridges. The following day he quadrupled the amount of ammunition requested. Three days later he endorsed the request of two "wealthy and responsible" Americans who desired to order an additional thousand rifles and a million cartridges. The military supplies requested appeared excessive under the circumstances, and the State Department declined to accede.[21]

Panic spread throughout Mexico City. Civilian volunteers began to drill in preparation to defend the capital against possible attack. The Madero administration transmitted to the State Department evidence on the activities of Emilio Vázquez, but the American government replied that the exile's conduct did "not seem to warrant arrest." [22] The Secretary of War, General González Salas, resigned his post and was designated as commander of a large column being formed to combat the rebellion in the north. President Madero went to the station to bid him farewell and to wish the troops success.

González Salas established his base at Torreón. He an-

[21] Wilson to State Dept., March 15, 22, 23, and 25, 1912, SDF, 812.113/218, 241, 242, and 251.

Early in May the Mexican government deported two Americans charged with traffic in arms, also allegedly for the defense of the American colony, under the name of the Tampico News Co. Two directors of this company were members of the circle associated with Ambassador Wilson.

[22] State Dept. to Mexican Embassy, March 20, 1912, SDF, 812.00/2970.

nounced amnesty for revolutionists who submitted within eight days. The government commander had about six thousand men, approximately the same number as was available to Orozco, and thirty cannons. Between March 15 and March 19 several encounters and skirmishes took place in the one hundred and forty miles between Jiménez, the rebel base, and Torreón. On March 23 federal forces were defeated by revolutionists under José Inés Salazar at Corralitos, only twenty-odd miles from Jiménez.

Federal field headquarters had been established at Conejos, a rail center located fifty-five miles northwest of Torreón. The main federal force was divided into three sections, one each under Generals Trucy Aubert, Joaquín Téllez, and González Salas, and the northward move was begun. Although a unified attack was projected, the columns were not in communication. Near Rellano, about thirty-five or forty miles from the rebel base at Jiménez, the insurgents attacked the train convoy of the section under González Salas. A locomotive loaded with dynamite which was launched by the rebels disrupted the federal convoy causing confusion and panic. Some federal soldiers rebelled under enemy attack. González Salas, wounded, regrouped his disorganized forces and began the return journey to Torreón during which the defeated commander took his own life. Trucy's column reached the scene too late to retrieve the situation. Before withdrawing to Torreón he launched a hurried attack on Jiménez which prevented an immediate rebel march to the south.

The defeat and the suicide of the federal commander caused a sensation. Although the federals had suffered only three hundred casualties, the press exaggerated the setback giving it the proportions of a disaster. Ambassador Wilson reported that "it is generally believed now that the government is likely to fall." [23] Small wonder that there were those who found some basis for Orozco's boasts that he would take Torreón and proceed to the capital. Actually the rebels' military success had not been outstanding. Operations conducted against

[23] Wilson to State Dept., March 29, 1912, SDF, 812.00/3430.

Orozco had been inefficient, uncertain, and costly. The insurgent leader, flush with victory, proclaimed a revolutionary plan in which Madero was denounced, a program was announced, and a method for selecting an interim president, after occupation of the capital, was indicated. Expressly, but not by name, Orozco withdrew his recognition of Emilio Vázquez as provisional president. Although a division had appeared in the insurgent ranks, Emilio Vázquez continued to claim the provisional presidency and on the last day of March sent Madero the following telegram: "If you hand over the power to the Revolution, . . . peace, tranquility, justice, liberty, and progress will return immediately to the country." [24]

Madero's only answer was to dispatch more troops to battle the insurgents. On March 24, Victoriano Huerta was named Commander of the Northern Division. It was reported that the appointment had been suggested by General García Peña, Secretary of War. Madero was not enthusiastic about naming the man who had escorted Porfirio Díaz to Veracruz and who had conducted himself so questionably in Morelos. The conditions of the moment and the approval of Rafael Hernández and even of Gustavo Madero decided the matter.[25] While Huerta was organizing his forces and dispatching men and equipment to the north, skirmishes and encounters continued north of Torreón. Francisco Villa captured Parral, a railroad center flanking the rebel base of Jiménez, and arrested General José de la Luz Soto, but successive counterattacks by the insurgents finally forced federal evacuation of the town.

The forces of Villa and Trucy regrouped in April at Bermejillo, about twenty-five miles from Torreón. Huerta arrived from the capital with the last convoy on April 12. He set up his headquarters in Torreón and announced amnesty for those rebels submitting within fifteen days. The commander of the Northern Division did not hurry. He prepared his operations carefully, concentrating available manpower. The major por-

[24] Magaña, *Emiliano Zapata*, II, 180-81; Amaya, *Madero y . . . revolucionarios*, pp. 380-90.

[25] Bonilla, *El régimen maderista*, p. 13*n*.

tion of the force of nine thousand men was comprised of federal soldiers, but respectable numbers of rurales from the frontier states, including Villa and his men, formed part of the army. Huerta was assisted by an able staff including the talented artillery specialist Colonel Guillermo Rubio Navarrete.

Ambassador Wilson continued to act in a manner which tended to discredit and disturb the Madero government. On April 13 he suggested to the State Department the possibility of sending American troops to Chihuahua to protect American lives and property. If the Department agreed, Wilson thought he "should be instructed" to sound out the Mexican government! The State Department replied that it was "inopportune" to act on the suggestion. Nevertheless, since President Taft wished to remove the Mexican question as an issue in the American presidential campaign, Wilson was instructed to communicate a note to the Mexican Minister of Foreign Affairs in which the United States gave notice that it "expects and must demand that American life and property within the Republic of Mexico be justly and adequately protected" and that "this government must hold Mexico and the Mexican people responsible for all wanton and illegal acts." President Madero replied that his government could not be responsible for the acts of the rebels in the form indicated in the American note.[26]

Early in May Huerta began to move north along the railroad line from Bermejillo. In possession of Parral, Orozco had delayed launching an attack on Torreón. Apparently he had waited in the hope of obtaining additional munitions and supplies. These were not forthcoming, and the rebel commander had lost valuable time and a golden opportunity. In addition, the rebel movement was losing its unity. At this point Emilio Vázquez belatedly entered Mexico. He hoped to bridge the gap between the rebellion in the north and that in the south. At Ciudad Juárez he declared himself provisional president. Although he had begun the original uprising and

[26] Wilson to State Dept., April 13, 1912, SDF, 812.00/3690; Huntington Wilson to American Embassy, April 14, 1912, SDF, 812.00/3593A.

his revolutionary reputation and grievances against the administration had been useful early in the movement, neither Orozco's personal political ambitions nor the ideological purposes of his backers permitted continued support of Emilio Vázquez. Responsible rebel leaders, including Orozco and Enrile, promptly repudiated the pretender who, after being held virtually a prisoner in Ciudad Juárez, returned to El Paso, his political life ended.[27]

Opportunity gone and unity shaken, the Orozco rebellion was seriously handicapped by insufficient supplies and equipment for the number of men available. The closing of the American frontier to shipment of such supplies destroyed any hope of remedying this situation. The military liquidation of the Orozco rebellion had become inevitable; the campaign was comparatively short considering the man power and the area involved. Huerta dispatched Villa and his men as an advance guard. This unit defeated the rebels on May 9 at Tlahualilo, less than twenty-five miles northeast of Bermejillo, thereby clearing the right flank for the main column advancing northward. The first real encounter between the main forces occurred on May 12 on the plains of Conejos, thirty miles north of Bermejillo. It was real temerity for Orozco to accept field battle with the federal forces lacking as he did disciplined troops and equipment, especially good, well-handled artillery. The courage of his men was to no avail against the federal batteries at Conejos.[28]

The revolutionaries retreated northward, and Orozco began to concentrate his strength at Rellano. As they went, the rebels tore up the railroad tracks and destroyed bridges, so the federal army advanced slowly, repairing the damage done by the retreating insurrectionists. The encounters of Tlahualilo

[27] Consul Edwards to Secretary of State, May 8, 1912, and Consul Letcher to Secretary of State, May 10, 1912, SDF, 812.00/3841 and 3930.

[28] The first defeat for the Orozco forces was the signal for intensified activity by the League for Social Defense. This capital political group was composed of elements of the old regime led by García Granados. They harassed and tried to discredit the administration. Delegates of the League went to the rebel camp to hold "peace" talks.

and Conejos were isolated actions, but they helped to concentrate the enemy on the main battlefield. Huerta açcelerated his northward advance, and Orozco had to accept battle if he were going to block the way to the state capital. On May 22 and May 23 the second battle of Rellano was fought. Both sides suffered heavy losses, but the federals won a decisive victory credited to the effective and extensive use of artillery. The rebels left over five hundred dead and wounded on the lost battlefield and retreated toward Jiménez.

An American consular official reported that the "battle of Rellano and its results will have a determining effect on the rebellion . . . They [the rebels] were entirely dislodged . . . and retired to Jiménez with spirits broken."[29] Even Ambassador Wilson, slow to accept the reports of decisive federal victory, reported that the "rebels are badly demoralized." Consistent with his practice of counterbalancing any favorable reports, he added that "conditions in Oaxaca [are] serious." [30]

Despite harassing operations and skirmishes the rebels were not able to prevent Huerta's army from reaching Jiménez. Characteristically, at this point Huerta dispatched forces under Villa and General Rábago to occupy Parral to protect the west flank and the rear of the main column as it proceeded northward. This detail disposed of, Villa and his men rejoined the main force preparing to advance toward Bachimba, approximately one hundred miles to the northeast and only thirty-five miles from Chihuahua City.

It was in Jiménez that an incident occurred which caused Villa's removal from the fighting. There, some of Villa's soldiers expropriated a beautiful mare. The owner protested to General Huerta who ordered the animal returned. When Villa disobeyed the order, he was arrested, and General Huerta ordered him to be shot summarily. The prisoner was already standing before a wall and the execution squad had been formed when Colonels Raúl Madero and Rubio Navarrete

[29] Letcher to State Dept., June 28, 1912, SDF, 812.00/4357.

[30] Wilson to State Dept., May 2 and 31, 1912, SDF, 812.00/4008 and 4090.

successfully interposed their influence so that General Huerta suspended the execution. A telegraphic exchange brought an order from Madero that Villa be brought to the capital for trial on the charge of insubordination.[31]

The Northern Division continued its northward advance. The efforts of the rebels were limited to delaying tactics. Early in July the forces of Orozco made a stand in the Canyon of Bachimba, were defeated and dislodged, and fell back to Chihuahua City. Even this city, which they had held for four months, was now untenable, and the insurgents had to remove to Ciudad Juárez on the frontier. The campaign was nearing an end. Just after mid-August, Ciudad Juárez fell to the federal forces. The rebel army had been conquered for all practical purposes, and the remnants scattered into guerrilla bands. Ambassador Wilson reported the disintegration of the Orozco movement in characteristic terms: "These victories and this recovery of territory, while lending a temporary prestige to the national government, have apparently produced no other substantial results." [32]

Huerta, his command divided because of the changed conditions, returned grumpily to Mexico City. Honors bestowed by Madero failed to assuage his irritation, and the opposition press hailed him as a hero. Even so, the government's leaders, and particularly the president, were filled with optimism and confidence. The federal army had served loyally, and the administration's and the president's prestige had been reinforced, but the federal army had also recovered its lost prestige. At the same time the Madero revolution, as a military potential, had fallen into disrepute: Orozco had been squashed, and Villa emerged from the campaign dishonored. Madero had thrown himself into the arms of the federal army, and the victory over Orozco had given that army a moral and practical preponderance over the president.

[31] Pancho Villa was brought to the capital early in July. He was formally charged, tried, and convicted. In Nov., Villa was transferred to Santiago Tlaltelolco, and from there he escaped late the following month.

[32] Wilson to Secretary of State, Aug. 28, 1912, SDF, 812.00/4899.

The conservative elements did not consider their cause beaten. They turned next to support the movement headed by Félix Díaz. This stocky, swarthy son of the famed guerrilla brother of Porfirio Díaz had been favored by his uncle. Shortly after being trained in the Military College, he obtained a seat in the Chamber of Deputies. The ambitious young man aspired to be governor of Oaxaca, but this aspiration represented a challenge to the Científicos. General Díaz punished his nephew's audacity by sending him on a diplomatic assignment to Chile. Later, having restored himself to his uncle's favor, he became inspector of police in the Federal District.

This was his position when the Díaz government was overthrown. The nephew of the fallen dictator believed himself entitled to the succession, but he resumed his seat in the Chamber until the new legislature was installed in September, 1912. Then, when Governor Benito Juárez Maza of Oaxaca died, he contended against Miguel Bolaños Cacho for the vacant post, but was defeated. After his partisans there had undertaken a brief, unsuccessful uprising, Félix went to Veracruz to organize a rebellion against the government. He sought and obtained his discharge from the army, and this should have alerted the government. Actually, the administration was suspicious of his intentions, but no proceedings were instituted because of lack of proof. At dawn on October 16, Félix Díaz rebelled against the government. He was supported by the 21st Battalion and a fraction of the 19th. Within a few hours the rebels were in control of the city and had captured its commander. It was hoped that the fleet and the balance of the forces would second the movement. However, Commodore Azueta took charge of the flotilla, replaced suspect officers with trustworthy personnel, and kept the vessels loyal, their guns trained on the rebels. Despite this, as the beginning of a rebellion, the Díaz movement had been brilliant.

In the inevitable revolutionary plan Díaz attacked the administration and endeavored to justify his movement. Here was projected no socio-economic revolution, but rather the promise to "impose peace by means of justice." He called on all desirous of contributing to a rebirth of an "era of peace and concord" to join with him, for "it is no longer possible to bear in silence so many ills as the evil administration, product of the revolutionary movement of 1910, has originated and continues causing in the Republic." Specifically, he accused the government of "the most cruel abuse of authority," which he pictured as threatening property, honor, and life. The irritations of the federal army were detailed in a pointed effort to attract its support. Díaz told the Mexican people that "I promise only peace for which I will work and fight . . . All the material benefits and the exercise of liberty will come by themselves as a natural fruit of that peace, of order in the economy, and of calm and impartial justice for all." [33]

The rebellion stimulated conservative opinion in the capital. The opposition press hailed the army as the nation's salvation, and for a few days the salutation "Felices días" (happy days) enjoyed considerable vogue in military circles. The American Consul in Veracruz reported that Díaz offered "all possible guarantees for life and property" and that "local sentiment [is] pro Díaz and against the government." [34] Although the Chamber of Deputies rejected a motion of censure proposed by Moheno, seventy-eight deputies, about one third of the membership, felt that the situation required a demonstration of their support of the administration. Accordingly, they signed a resolution indicating their disposition to lend "aid with the object of sustaining the legitimacy of the constituted government" and their willingness "to adopt all means which should be necessary for the quick and effective reestablishment of peace in the Republic." [35]

In the midst of the difficult situation Madero remained tranquil and confident. When the *cuartelazo* of Félix Díaz was reported, Madero was said to have remarked, "Better and bet-

[33] Ribot, *Félix Díaz,* pp. 10-12.
[34] Oct. 16, 1912, SDF, 812.00/5281.
[35] Palavicini, *Mi vida revolucionario,* p. 126.

ter. In this way we will finish with the last of Porforismo." [36] The President ordered General Joaquín Beltrán to concentrate forces near Orizaba and then to proceed to retake Veracruz. Detachments were dispatched from the surrounding districts. The army organized, but awaiting supplies and artillery, General Beltrán established his headquarters at Tejería, a station on the Mexican Railroad, sixteen kilometers from the port which was his objective.

The foreign consuls in Veracruz, led by American Consul William Canada, requested an interview with the federal commander. Late in the afternoon on October 19 they conferred with him on the outskirts of Tejería. The diplomats requested that bombardment of the port and fighting in the streets be avoided. Since Beltrán indicated that he was only following orders, the consuls requested that he transmit their request to the Secretary of War. The Secretary approved of the General's conduct and directed that no concessions be granted. The following day General Beltrán notified Consul Canada that the port "will be taken by force of arms." [37] Mayor Félix Leycegui of Veracruz requested that all means be taken to avoid harm to noncombatants among the city's fifty thousand inhabitants.

Félix Díaz hoped and expected that the army would support his uprising. He confined himself within the port city and made no offensive moves. There was no echo in the country. Nevertheless, General Beltrán did not attack, and the government impatiently tried to prod him to action. Perhaps the delay represented the vacillation of the army or the desire of Beltrán to gauge which way the wind was blowing. The General attributed it to his careful preparations. Artillery had to be brought from Orizaba and strategically located, and, as he reported, "in order to attack I have to surround." [38] Yet it did not take long to foresee the inevitable failure of the rebellion. Mr. Schuyler, who was in charge of the American Em-

[36] Calero, *Política mexicana,* p. 92.
[37] Schuyler to State Dept., Oct. 21, 1912, SDF, 812.00/5306.
[38] Beltrán, *Plaza de H. Veracruz,* pp. 84-85.

bassy during the absence of Ambassador Wilson, sensed the situation. On October 20 he reported that

Díaz has apparently lost much of his prestige in the last twenty-four hours. On Thursday he was the hero of the hour, but his failure to follow up his advantage lost him the support of many people who are ready to espouse his cause openly just as soon as they are sure it will be successful. The attitude of the army is one of waiting.[39]

General Díaz tried to win over the federal force besieging Veracruz. To the very last moment he continued to believe that the attackers would desert. On October 20 he wrote a confidential message to General Beltrán:

I ask you to think seriously on the just nature of the cause . . . I have placed myself on the side of the army so that its personnel of worth . . . should occupy their proper places . . . I am in the position of being able to serve as the common banner between both contenders . . . Choose the conduct which you judge most correct, and your letter will be saved, destroyed, or returned as you yourself indicate.[40]

General Beltrán, in the presence of his staff, replied indicating that the "valor and obligation of . . . a general" dictated his conduct.[41]

The following day General Díaz renewed his efforts to convince the federal general to associate with him "for the good of the Fatherland and to end the fratricidal war. If the situation were reversed, I would have joined with you for the same sacred object." In a handwritten postscript signed "Félix" the seduction effort continued: "[I make] one last effort, Joaquín. The Fatherland will reward us with its applause as soon as we restore the peace which it wants so much internally and the prestige which it had in the concert of nations." [42]

On October 21, General Beltrán notified the diplomatic

39 *Ibid.*, pp. 89-90.
40 *El Imparcial*, Jan. 16, 1913.
41 Beltrán, *Plaza de H. Veracruz*, pp. 108-9.
42 *Ibid.*, pp. 110-11.

corps and the Mayor of Veracruz that there would be a period of twenty-four hours before an attack. He also directed an appeal to Díaz to surrender. General Díaz refused, indicating that there "does not remain other recourse than that of defending the city to the last."[43] Mayor Leycegui telegraphed Madero requesting an extension of the "armistice" on the grounds that there had not been sufficient time to place noncombatants in a safe place. Madero answered with the recommendation that all possible precautions be taken, but indicated that the attack must begin. The capture of the port "is indispensable for public order and prestige of the government."[44]

At six A.M. on the twenty-third of October the federal artillery opened fire. By eight o'clock a five-pronged infantry attack had entered the city. The attackers numbered between two and three thousand while the defenders counted on approximately a thousand soldiers and an equal number of volunteers. General Beltrán was "utterly surprised to note the lack of military preparations for the protection of the city. I expected to find wire entanglements, ditches, and entrenchments."[45] Within a few hours the plaza was captured and Félix Díaz had been arrested.

In eight days the rebellion, so auspiciously started, was ended. The failure was so complete that adherents of the rebel leader propagated a series of excuses to explain the disaster: that Beltrán had betrayed an agreement with Díaz to join the movement; that Beltrán had been bribed to remain loyal to the government; and that Beltrán had attacked under the cover of a white flag. Although the federal commander emphatically and convincingly denied these allegations, the charges were repeated by the press and echoed by Ambassador Wilson and Consul Canada.[46] The truth of the matter was that Félix Díaz had sluggishly paralyzed his own revolution

[43] *Ibid.*, p. 94.
[44] Ribot, *Félix Díaz*, pp. 115-16.
[45] *La Opinión* (Veracruz), Nov. 5, 1912.
[46] Wilson, *Diplomatic Episodes*, p. 245; Canada to State Dept., Nov. 27, 1912, SDF, 812.00/5662.

by awaiting defections and had inadequately prepared to defend the city he had won.

To judge the prisoners an extraordinary court martial was convened in Veracruz on October 24. Charges of rebellion were brought against twenty-three persons. Before the court martial Félix Díaz assumed all responsibility for the rebellion, and the defense spoke of the illegality of the proceedings and the extreme penalties demanded (death for four of the prisoners and ten-year sentences for eleven others). Some of Madero's associates, who attributed the frequency of uprisings to the leniency of the government, considered the time ripe to make an example. However, the President felt that Félix Díaz's "own words discredit and finish him . . . Why should I stain myself by killing a man who has committed suicide morally?" [47] Madero's policy was one of faith in the law and adherence to the law.

A series of delegations approached the President regarding the fate of the rebel leader. To a group of students Madero stated that the authorities judging Díaz were those who ought to resolve his fate. Several Progressive Constitutional party members demanded the immediate execution of Díaz. Madero stated that "it is not vengeance but justice which the Nation seeks." He assured his visitors that "if until now I have been gentle and kind, waiting for the disturbers of the peace to turn their steps and accept the democratic system which my government has established, henceforth I will be inexorable." [48] The bloodthirsty demand of these delegations, who, it was charged, were government inspired, served to awaken public sympathy for the prisoners.

The court martial sentenced Félix Díaz and three officers to death and five others to varying prison sentences; it freed the remaining fourteen accused. A delegation of aristocratic ladies visited President Madero to plead for the life of Félix Díaz. Madero told them

I am no more than the executor of the law. Pardon from me would

[47] Vasconcelos, *Ulises criollo*, p. 409.
[48] Márquez Sterling, *Los últimos días*, pp. 318-19.

be as incongruous as vengeance. I did not advise Sr. Félix Díaz to rise in arms . . . Neither have I condemned him to death for his rebellious disloyalty. A court martial has judged him . . . If some legal action can save him, that should be put in operation. I will neither save nor execute him.[49]

The women withdrew, indignant and angry.

Legal proceedings were instituted to forestall the execution of the sentence. Pleas were submitted to the Judge of the District of Veracruz and to the Supreme Court in the capital requesting the issuance of an injunction on the grounds that Félix Díaz had resigned from the army before the uprising and that, therefore, he was not subject to military justice. The Supreme Court, presided over by Lic. Francisco Carbajal and dominated by members appointed by Porfirio Díaz, granted an injunction and sent telegraphic orders suspending the execution. It was suggested that Madero order that steps be taken to prevent the message from reaching the military authorities at Veracruz in time, but the President refused, as he expressed it, to proceed like Don Porfirio.[50]

[49] *Ibid.*, pp. 319-20.

Gen. Beltrán published a telegram, allegedly sent to him by President Madero, in which he was directed to submit the prisoners to a special court martial and apply the "supreme penalty before twenty-four hours." José Valadés and Alfonso Taracena, emphasizing certain peculiarities about the message, question the authenticity of the telegram. The death penalty within twenty-four hours was mandatory under Article 1171 of the Military Code.

If the challenged message is interpreted to mean that Madero was ordering execution prior to the time prescribed, why did the President, twenty-two hours later, advise Beltrán that a personal emissary would leave shortly for Veracruz? The emissary, Capt. Gustavo Garmendia, insinuated that "the palace" was displeased by the delay in carrying out the sentence. Unquestionably there were those in the government who felt this way.

Although Beltrán felt that Madero, or the government, was trying to prod him to act on his own responsibility, the evidence as well as Madero's nature argue against an illegal proceeding. General Beltrán declared on several occasions that the charge that "I had instructions from the government to shoot the prisoner . . . [is] a barefaced lie." Beltrán, *Plaza de H. Veracruz*, pp. 387-88; *La Prensa*, June 18, 1931; *La Opinión*, July 29, 1934.

[50] Fernández Güell, *El moderno Juárez*, p. 181.

The administration celebrated the defeat of Félix Díaz as a victory. Madero, confident in the legality of his position, was more optimistic than ever. Three rebellions with conservative support or instigation had failed. The federal army had remained at its post in the face of the attempted rebellion of Reyes, the call of Orozco, and the movement of Félix Díaz. These repeated efforts were intended, in part, to show the world that Madero was incompetent and unpopular. However, all three uprisings had been crushed, and the government seemed reasonably stable.

Nevertheless, the opposition was no less determined to conquer Madero and the revolution. Indeed, one observer concluded that "the defeat of General Díaz in Veracruz had no results, in reality, but to enliven the desires of all the enemies of the Madero regime that Sr. Madero should fall." [51] Opposition plotters were active from the moment of Félix Díaz's defeat. Word spread that an attempt would be made to free Díaz. The government accepted the bait and arranged for the transfer of the prisoner to the Federal District Penitentiary in Mexico City, which, Rodolfo Reyes later admitted, was "what was desired by us." [52] The reason the conspirators desired this move soon became apparent.

[51] Espinosa, Piña, and Ortiz, *La decena roja*, p. 73.
[52] *Excelsior*, July 2, 1930.

XVII. The Ten Tragic Days Begin

MADERO, in a message to Congress in September, 1912, declared that if

> a government such as mine . . . is not able to endure in Mexico, Gentlemen, we should conclude that the Mexican people are not fit for democracy and that we need a new dictator who, saber in hand, would silence all ambitions and would suffocate the efforts of those who do not understand that liberty flourishes only under the protection of the law.[1]

Was the President beginning to appraise the situation more realistically and to doubt the efficacy of his political touchstone in the Mexican environment? More likely, Madero, shaken and disturbed by his experience in office, was speaking rhetorically. He refused to believe that the situation could be so forbidding, that the Mexicans were not ready for democracy, and that a new dictator was needed, and he continued to view the situation confidently during the early weeks of 1913. He told visitors that peace would soon be restored.

The victories achieved over Orozco, Reyes, and Díaz seemed to give the President's conviction new force and his approach new justification. Actually, the situation was such that serious consideration was imperative. The army had not betrayed the Madero government, but was its conduct attributable to loyalty or to waiting for the right man and the right moment? On

[1] Madero, "Informe . . . el 16 de septiembre de 1912," in *Diario Oficial,* 122, No. 13, 137-49.

this force the regime was almost completely dependent. The opposition press and leadership continued to harass the administration. Landowners, at first scornful of Madero, became fearful lest he move more energetically toward land reform. More or less reinforcing this formidable opposition were others of conservative economic views including foreign business interests. One commentator sadly noted that "as a matter of fact, I do not know any large interest in Mexico which was exerting its influence to strengthen the Madero government." [2] Add to these conditions the restlessness of the masses and the dissatisfaction of the revolutionaries, and it becomes evident that the optimism of Madero and some of his close advisors was unjustified.

On all sides there was an atmosphere of unrest and apprehension. The Renovators met several times to discuss the situation. The revolutionary deputies resolved to visit the President to warn him of the gravity of the situation and to urge more radical reforms. It was late in January, 1913, when this group of deputies told Madero that "the Revolution goes to its ruin, dragging down the government emanating from it, simply because it has not governed with revolutionists." The delegation admitted that the counterrevolution was natural and logical, but "it was natural and logical also that the strongest, most popular government which the country has had should have been able to suffocate the counterrevolution. Nevertheless, the contrary has happened."

The Renovators declared that the counterrevolution aimed "to destroy the Plan of San Luis Potosí and to make the Revolution of 1910 pass into History as a sterile movement of men without principles who bloodied the soil of the Fatherland and overwhelmed it in misery." [3] They argued that the government's error was the belief that the counterrevolution could be defeated by force alone. They insisted that the continued and complete support of public opinion was needed and that the excesses of the opposition press had contributed

[2] Bell, *Political Shame,* p. 219.
[3] Secretaría de Gobernación, *Memoria . . . ,1913-16.*

to the government's loss of prestige as had the hybrid nature of the government itself.

To the gloomy evaluation and the suggestion of radical reforms of men and measures Madero replied that the Renovators were wrong in their fears and that nothing bad was going to happen. He expressed his opinion that the government enjoyed the support of the army and the people. When Deputy Eduardo Hay insisted that the President was badly informed and that the moment was of great gravity, Madero reproached the group for its fears and doubts.

The drift of the times caused concern in other revolutionary quarters. In the north, Governor Carranza of Coahuila invited the governors of Chihuahua, Sonora, San Luis Potosí, and Aguascalientes to join him in a hunting party in December, 1912, in the hills near Saltillo. Governor Cepeda of San Luis Potosí attended personally, while the others sent representatives. The hunting party was followed by a reception and dinner at a leading hotel in Saltillo. Carranza addressed the gathering. He noted that Madero's government was passing through very critical circumstances and expressed his feeling that the policy of transaction and weakness was compromising the ideals and interests of the revolution. He urged that the governors of revolutionary origin unite to face whatever difficult situation might arise. The enemies of Carranza allege that he was preparing to rebel against Madero but that events in Mexico City disrupted his plans. Supporters of the governor, with equal vigor, defend his conduct, asserting that his only purpose was to defend Madero and, more important, the revolution. Regardless of his ultimate intention—and evidence of a plot is lacking—Carranza's activity was additional proof that distressing conditions existed. Pessimistically the editor of *Nueva Era* remarked that it took courage to declare oneself a Maderista.

The conservative elements intensified their efforts to harass, discredit, and destroy the Madero regime. The opposition press relentlessly hammered away. *El Mañana* shouted that "now is the time to save the Fatherland . . . A resignation would work the miracle . . . We urge it without rest."[4] Ambassador Wilson, returned from a leave, poured forth a flood of words in his reports depicting in the most somber and lurid terms the inadequacy of Madero's government. On January 7 he reported that the "situation is gloomy, if not hopeless."[5] About a month later his campaign of pessimism reached a crescendo in a thirteen-page letter! Ambassador Wilson felt it necessary to tell his superiors that

> in the foregoing portrayal of the existing political conditions in Mexico, I must beg the Department to believe [!] that I am activated solely by the desire to discharge the obligation incumbent upon me . . . and that it would be far more pleasurable to report differently if a due regard for the truth and fidelity to the character of my mission would permit.[6]

The tenor of Mr. Wilson's reports was such that Secretary of State Philander C. Knox felt compelled to transmit a confidential memorandum to President Taft in which, citing examples, he noted

> an increasing pessimism in the reports of the American Ambassador upon the political situation in Mexico which appears to the Department to be unjustified, if not, indeed, misleading . . .
>
> [Some of the reports] might almost be characterized as indicating an intention on the part of the Ambassador to force this government's hand in its dealing with the Mexican situation as a whole. The apparent disagreement between the Ambassador and the Department being so fundamental and serious that the Department feels it would err if it did not bring the matter pointedly to your notice.[7]

Not content with casting aspersions on the Madero government, Ambassador Wilson, through the veil of mounting personal aversion, saw Madero as a callous eccentric and tyrant, capable of the greatest perfidies and infamies. The opponents of the regime, by contrast, appeared to the American diplomat

[4] *El Mañana,* Jan. 14 and 24, 1913.
[5] Wilson to Secretary of State, Jan. 7, 1913, SDF, 812.00/5823.
[6] Wilson to Secretary of State, Feb. 4, 1913, SDF, 812.00/6068.
[7] Knox to President Taft, Jan. 27, 1913, SDF, 812.00/7229A.

as wise, patriotic, and disinterested gentlemen. In mid-January, Wilson reported, on the basis of a rumor forwarded by Consul Canada in Veracruz, that the Madero government planned a "sham revolutionary uprising" in order "to kill Félix Díaz and his companions in prison." [8] This report was at variance with the Madero policy of forgiveness and with the very nature of the Mexican Executive. In view of Félix Díaz's role in the subsequent rebellion, the Ambassador's agitated concern for his safety was perhaps more than coincidental.

Even more suggestive were Wilson's veiled comments to the Cuban Minister. Márquez Sterling related his conversation with the American diplomat in a report to his government dated January 20, 1913:

> He [Wilson] affirmed, "I do not expect that the situation will improve, but I think that it has to get worse . . ."
>
> "Then," I asked him, "you do not have confidence in the constituted government?"
>
> Mr. Wilson delayed briefly to organize his ideas.
>
> "Those words you have spoken, Minister, are very strong," he answered me slowly. "For now, all I can say is that I have many doubts . . ."
>
> "Do you believe, Ambassador, that the fall of President Madero's government is near?"
>
> Mr. Wilson hesitated before answering me. "Its fall will not be easy, but neither is it impossible!" [9]

The conservative opposition talked of when, not whether, Madero would fall. Actually there were two elements in the conspiracy. Members of the old Científico faction had their gaze fixed on General Gerónimo Treviño, who, while not of their group, enjoyed army prestige. The second group included: Rodolfo Reyes, political manager for his father General Bernardo Reyes; General Manuel Mondragón, representing Félix Díaz; General Gregorio Ruiz; and Don Cecilio Ocón. The gestation of the plot occurred in Havana, and the first tangible result was the transfer of Félix Díaz to Mexico City.

[8] Wilson to State Dept., Jan. 14, 1913, SDF, 812.00/5865.
[9] Márquez Sterling, *Los últimos días*, pp. 336-39.

Ocón conspired ceaselessly, promoting meetings of the discontented, sustaining the opposition press, and conferring with army officials. The Catholic party was aware of the plotting, and individual members participated. General Huerta, who was being treated for eye trouble in the sanitarium of Dr. Aureliano Urrutia, a clerical supporter and adviser of the General, was approached by several Reyist supporters who, with the doctor, helped to prepare him for his role. The disgruntled militarist undoubtedly was only a latent participant at this stage.

The conspirators met in the house of General Mariano Ruiz in the capital suburb of Tacubaya. A number of army officers attended these sessions as plans of rebellion were formulated. No less than eight plans were projected. The blow was originally planned for the first day of the year but was postponed until February 5. When it was then discovered that Vice-President Pino Suárez was absent from the city, a further postponement to Tuesday, February 11, was necessitated. Definite word that the government knew of their plans prompted an emergency meeting on Saturday night, February 8, at which it was decided to strike early the next day. The conspirators were so confident of success that they had wine and food at Tacubaya with which to celebrate.

The government did have several warnings of the impending uprising.[10] Indeed, rumors, precise as to dates, names of individuals involved, and regiments compromised, were current in the capital. Madero believed the reports exaggerated and met warnings with indifference. He regarded the stories which were circulating as a normal aspect of Mexican politics. But Gustavo, on hearing the reports, hurried back to Mexico City from Monterrey, where he had gone preparatory to his departure for Japan. Accompanied by a friend, he spent Saturday night covering the city, collecting information and confirming the reports and rumors.

It was typical of the Mexican Revolution that the blow

[10] *El Estandarte* (Oaxaca), Dec. 23, 1917.

which destroyed its first government should come in Mexico City, the capital, so alien and antagonistic to the Revolution that it was to destroy and absorb Revolutionary leaders time and again. It was typical that the city should callously be turned into a battleground. And it was typical that Madero should entrust his fate and that of his government to Huerta, an unscrupulous inebriate, who proceeded to betray that trust.

The preparations for the *cuartelazo* had been worked out carefully in great detail. The immediate objective was to free Bernardo Reyes and Félix Díaz who were to serve as leaders of the movement. In the predawn hours of Sunday morning, February 9, the movement began simultaneously in the Tlalpam and Tacubaya suburbs. In the former place three hundred students of the Military School of Aspirants, an institution of military instruction founded by Díaz, participated. From the barracks of Tacubaya came three hundred dragoons of the 1st Cavalry Regiment and four hundred men of the 2d and 5th Artillery Regiments. This force, with some additions from barracks in the city proper, divided into two columns. One section headed for the Military Prison of Santiago Tlaltelolco where General Reyes was incarcerated. The guard offered no resistance, and Reyes, who had been advised of the change of date, was ready and walked out of the prison. Other prisoners, seeking to escape in the confusion of the moment, rioted and set fire to the building. More than a hundred were killed in the resulting melee.

This column then advanced to the Penitentiary. After a cannon had been set up near the building, the release of Félix Díaz was demanded. The prison director telephoned the Minister of Government for instructions and was ordered to resist. However, with only twenty men available to defend the prison, the director concluded that resistance was impossible and yielded. Félix Díaz, unadvised that the date of the rebellion had been advanced, was in the midst of shaving when his rescuers arrived. He completed this before joining his comrades in a march on the National Palace which was scheduled to be in the possession of the other column.

The second column, composed of Aspirants and part of the 1st Cavalry, had indeed taken possession of the National Palace. Gustavo Madero, arrived at the Zócalo (or main plaza), had been recognized and captured. Also a prisoner was Minister of War García Peña, who had been slightly wounded when he tried to restore the National Palace to government control. When General Lauro Villar, Military Commander of the Plaza, discovered the situation, he quickly recruited some loyal forces and recovered the government building. Two hundred and thirty-two Aspirants were arrested, Gustavo Madero and García Peña were released, and loyal personnel were placed in charge of the Palace. By his energetic and courageous conduct General Villar had disrupted the plans of the rebellion. He prepared to defend the Palace: federal troops were stationed on the roof; in the plaza, from one end to the other in front of the building, soldiers of the 11th Battalion took up positions; and in the doorways were placed two mortars and six machine guns.

The column headed by General Reyes, Félix Díaz, and Ruiz left the Penitentiary and headed for the center of the city. The rebel forces occupied a series of parallel streets which lead into the Zócalo. Then the first group of rebels led by General Ruiz entered the plaza approaching the central door of the National Palace, which they believed to be in the hands of the Aspirants. General Villar and Adolfo Bassó, Intendant of the National Palace, with drawn pistols forced the obese General Ruiz to surrender.

A few moments later General Reyes appeared at the head of some soldiers. Villar called on him to halt and surrender, but the rebel leader continued to advance. The order to fire was given, and General Bernardo Reyes went down in a hail of bullets. His son Rodolfo recorded that he told his father it was necessary to halt in view of the changed situation. His father, who "was as if enchanted," answered fatalistically: "The column should stop, not I. What has to be, should be at once!" Rodolfo concluded that his father "had the fever of desperation, of humiliation, of grief, and of despair. [He] ceaselessly hoped that death would come to free him."[11] General Reyes seemed determined not to survive another failure.

The beginning of the firing was the signal for a battle of about ten minutes between the loyal forces defending the Palace and the rebels in the porticos, buildings, and streets on the west side of the plaza. Many civilians were caught in the deadly crossfire. When the firing ceased, almost as abruptly as it had begun, the plaza presented a desolate aspect. More than four hundred persons, the overwhelming majority civilians, had been killed and nearly a thousand had been wounded. General Villar had been wounded in the left collarbone, a circumstance which would necessitate naming a new federal commander. Reyes had been killed, and Félix Díaz led his rebel forces away from the main plaza with the Ciudadela fortress as their objective.

Meanwhile, at Chapultepec Castle, President Madero had been advised of the events of the early hours of the morning. When he was informed that the National Palace was once again in the hands of loyal forces, he was determined to go there considering it his proper place in the situation. Mounted on a beautiful horse and escorted by the presidental guard and the cadets of the Military College, Madero proceeded down the Paseo de la Reforma in the direction of the National Palace. Although of nervous, emotional temperament, the President once again demonstrated his composure in moments of emergency. He rode calmly down the main boulevard, smiling and waving to persons along the way who cheered the valiant executive. The presidential party had reached the end of Juárez Avenue, near the National Theater, when heavy firing was heard from the direction of the National Palace. It was decided to await the results of the battle in the Zócalo. Since scattered shots were coming from adjacent buildings, one of which killed a policeman a few steps from the President, the presidential party took refuge in the Daguerre Photo Shop. With Madero were Ministers Hernández, Bonilla, and Ernesto Madero and General Huerta.

[11] R. Reyes, *De mi vida*, I, 193, 236-39.

Word was received that the rebel attack on the Palace had been repulsed, and Madero prepared to continue to his destination. A crowd gathered outside the shop, and the President appeared on the balcony to receive an ovation. He remounted and then proceeded to the National Palace. The first problem to be faced was that of naming a replacement for the wounded Villar. Against his own better judgement and despite a deep aversion, Madero, apparently on the advice of Minister of War García Peña, named General Victoriano Huerta as Military Commander of the Plaza to organize the defense and to direct the attack on the rebels.[12] When the loyal Villar learned that Huerta was to be his replacement, he cautioned the new commander, "Much care, Victoriano, much care." [13]

The rebels had withdrawn from the Zócalo, but they left a small group of Aspirants in the towers of the Cathedral. These remained there, isolated, for two days. Finally, disguised by Cathedral priests, the Aspirants managed to escape. The main nucleus of the rebels reassembled near the Statue of Charles IV where Juárez Avenue meets the Paseo. From that point they moved south toward the Ciudadela. The rebels occupied the four streets leading to the fortress, setting up artillery and machine guns, and, shortly before noon, the Ciudadela was surrendered to them.

The old fortress, which recently had served as a combination arms plant, armory, and warehouse, is a long, single-story building with walls more than four feet thick. Surrounded by broad streets, it dominated the immediate area except for Belem prison to the southeast. At the south was a small space enclosed by an iron fence which separated the area from some private houses. To the west was Artillery Park and some pri-

[12] Gen. García Peña, vehemently denying responsibility, claimed that the appointment was made over his strenuous objections. He alleged that Madero told him that "Papacito [Francisco, Sr.] y Gustavo" were responsible. Bonilla, *El régimen maderista,* p. 56.

[13] *La Opinión,* July 29, 1934.

In the light of Huerta's subsequent conduct, one commentator observed that "Madero was overthrown by the bullet which wounded Villar." Lamicq, *El dolor mexicano,* p. 65.

vate houses, and to the northeast was the Garden of Carlos Pacheco. The fortress is an historic landmark. In the time of Juárez the building was occupied by rebels during the uprising of General Negrete, but General Sóstenes Rocha recaptured it and suffocated the rebellion in a few hours.

In 1913, by all accounts, the Ciudadela was less able to resist assault than in 1871. Porfirio Díaz had modified the formidable solid walls by adding a number of windows. The fortress no longer dominated the city, which had grown, especially to the west. Although they had captured supplies with the Ciudadela, the rebels enclosed in the fortress apparently were doomed to perish in time or by force. The government could obtain reinforcements and maintain a tight blockade. It held the initiative. Rodolfo Reyes admitted that "I do not understand the military arts, but I gather that . . . [had the federals placed their artillery properly,] the Ciudadela would have been swept [by fire]. Then [they] would have been able to capture it by assault."[14]

Nevertheless, there followed ten days of military sham. It was a ten-day lugubrious farce with terror, suffering, and death for countless noncombatants and with extensive property damage. Federal artillery was badly placed and ineffectively employed. Loyal troops were sent to be slaughtered by the entrenched defenders who received supplies from the outside despite federal "encirclement." The bloody hoax was played to the last card with a callous disregard for innocent sufferers.

After taking the fortress the rebels deployed on the flat roof which had a thirty-nine-inch-high railing. Since the anticipated assault was not immediately forthcoming, the insurgents were able to place their guns in the streets. An artificial calm followed the eventful morning. The streets of the capital were deserted except for small groups of people who restlessly gathered on corners. At the National Palace, Madero notified the governors that an unsuccessful revolt had occurred and that order had been reestablished. His conclusion was premature as the report of the loss of the Ciudadela soon revealed.

[14] R. Reyes, *De mi vida,* II, 23.

As soon as the true situation was ascertained, Madero began consultation with his cabinet. These counsellors confirmed the appointment of Huerta, agreed to call Rubio Navarrete from Querétaro to take command of federal artillery, and discussed requesting from the Permanent Commission of Congress extraordinary financial and war powers. The government telegraphed nearby detachments to concentrate in the city for service against the rebels. The cabinet suggested that Madero seek safety outside of the city, and it was proposed that Minister Bonilla visit the northern governors to seek reinforcements and possible refuge for the administration, if that should become necessary. Madero decided to go to Cuernavaca to bring General Angeles and his forces back to the capital.

Before the President left Mexico City, two unpleasant episodes occurred. In a garden beside the executive office within the National Palace, General Ruiz and fifteen Aspirants were executed. Although there is some confusion as to who ordered the act, there is no doubt that General Huerta hastened to carry it out. It has been suggested that his conduct was motivated by a desire to demonstrate his loyalty and silence the protests against his appointment or to silence Ruiz who knew of his contacts with the rebel leaders.[15] The second episode involved mob attacks on the establishments of the opposition press which popular opinion indignantly blamed for inciting the rebellion. The mob tried to sack and burn the offices of *El País, La Tribuna, The Independent Herald,* and *El Noticioso Mexicano.* Opposition elements alleged that the mob was incited and led by members of the Porra.

Madero departed for Cuernavaca in an open car around 3 P.M. He was accompanied by his aides, Captains Federico Montes and Gustavo Garmendia, Deputy Alejandro Ugarte, stenographer Elías de los Ríos, and Alfredo Alvarez. The President reassured his companions that they would reach Cuernavaca safely. At Tres Marías they encountered a military

[15] Bonilla, *El régimen maderista,* p. 57; Alessio Robles, *Historia política de la Revolución,* p. 30; De Bekker, *Huerta,* pp. 20-21; Arenales, *El combate,* p. 26.

repair train with a seventy-five man escort. Madero agreed to complete his trip in greater security on the train.

In the caboose of the southward-moving train conversation gradually turned to the uprising in the capital. Madero confidently predicted it would be quashed as soon as he could gather adequate forces. When Captain Garmendia recommended that, once the rebels were defeated, they should all be shot, Madero laughingly brushed this advice aside with, "Do not worry Garmendia, all will be arranged properly." This prompted Alvarez to ask Madero whether he thought that if he were to fall into the enemies' power, they would pardon him. Madero dryly replied in the negative. A long, meaningful silence followed. Some of his companions expressed concern about the naming of Huerta as Military Commander. Madero admitted that the nomination was a compromise of the moment not to his liking and indicated that, on his return, Huerta would be replaced.[16]

At Cuernavaca, General Angeles was waiting at the station, and a long conference with him followed in the Bellavista Hotel. It was agreed that Angeles would mobilize his forces and order them to the capital. Alvarez reported that Madero also discussed a plan whereby Angeles would replace Huerta as Commander. Both the army officer and the President agreed that Madero's obligation was to remain in his office while the military crushed the revolt. They prepared to return to Mexico City the following day.[17]

Sunday evening the government ordered the mobilization of all nearby forces and telegraphed several zonal chiefs and governors to concentrate all available forces at a point near the capital. That night a quiet that stirred anxiety prevailed over the city. Only the cars of the Red Cross and White Cross slowly traversed the streets. The American Embassy quickly was converted into a center of mercy. Unfortunately, the Ambassador's activities were not confined to such laudable efforts. His conduct during the Ten Tragic Days prompted Márquez

[16] *La Opinión,* July 29, 1934.

[17] Alvarez, *Madero y su obra,* p. 14; Mena Brito, *Felipe Angeles,* p. 43.

Sterling to label the American Embassy a "center of conspiracy." [18]

Ambassador Wilson's reports during these trying times were dominated by criticisms of the government and contained errors or distortions of fact favorable to the rebellion. At 5 P.M. on the first day of the uprising Wilson reported that the "National Palace is the only place still loyal to Madero." That afternoon a representative of Díaz had called to ask the Ambassador to urge Madero to resign to avoid bloodshed. Wilson reported that "I stated that I was unable to take any action as he had no credentials and that I would not assume any responsibility except with the approval of the entire Diplomatic Corps." [19]

Later, with the approval of the "entire" corps—though Wilson mentioned only Cólogan (Spain), von Hintze (Germany), and Stronge (Great Britain) coming to the Embassy—he telephoned the Minister of Foreign Affairs to inquire "categorically" whether the government could provide protection for foreigners. Although the Minister promised to do what he could, Wilson reported that he was "unable to get any satisfaction." [20] A similar request for guarantees was submitted by an embassy clerk to the rebel chiefs.

The city awakened on Monday morning to a profound silence. Commercial houses remained closed. February 10 was the second day of waiting, of expectancy. That day an interview occurred between Félix Díaz and a commissioner for General Huerta in the pastry shop El Globo, located in the center of the city. Apparently an interview between the principals was arranged for the following day. In his messages that day Ambassador Wilson indicated that he was aware that "negotiations [are] being carried on with General Huerta," and reported the fantastic claim that "practically all of the local state authorities, police, and *rurales* have revolted to Díaz." [21]

[18] Márquez Sterling, *Los últimos días*, pp. 379-80.
[19] Wilson to State Dept., Feb. 9, 1913, SDF, 812.00/6057 and 6058.
[20] *Ibid.*
[21] Wilson to State Dept., Feb. 10, 1913, SDF, 812.00/6075 and 6077.

That evening the President returned to the capital with more than a thousand men under General Angeles. Rurales had arrived from Celaya and San Juan Teotihuacán, and the new arrivals were deployed along the Paseo, the western end of the government line. Madero found matters in very much the same state as when he had departed for Cuernavaca. The Permanent Commission of Congress had voted the Executive plenary powers in the branches of Finance and War. Rumors of the El Globo conference seemed to confirm Gustavo's belief that Huerta was part of the conspiracy and strengthened Madero's determination to replace him. When the matter was discussed in the cabinet, objections were raised to elevating Angeles over men of higher rank. In view of this obstacle and Huerta's effusive protestations of loyalty, Madero unwisely desisted in the matter. Angeles was placed in charge of the "western" sector.

De la Barra, motivated, he said, by "patriotism and humanity," wrote the President a letter in which he offered to serve as intermediary between the government and the revolutionaries in order to find a peaceful solution. Madero replied that he was not disposed to treat with the rebels.[22] The day ended with the streets deserted and an attack against the rebels anticipated momentarily. Ambassador Wilson, in unofficial notes to Minister Lascuráin and to Félix Díaz, requested that bombardment be conducted so as to cause as little damage as possible to the residential area of the city.[23]

Tuesday, the city was in a state of siege. The rebels, during the almost two days of waiting, had occupied all the buildings around the Ciudadela, with an advance guard holding the building of the Y.M.C.A. Finally, about 10 A.M. the long-awaited government attack began with a terrible cannonading. This firing was vigorously answered by the rebels. The city reverberated to the roar of cannon, the staccato rattle of machine guns, and the bark of rifle fire. Many grenades exploded in San Francisco and adjacent streets, and windows and electric

[22] *Revista de Revistas,* Feb. 23, 1913.
[23] Wilson, *Diplomatic Episodes,* p. 255.

lights were damaged by the rain of cold shot. A large number of the curious were killed and injured.

The federals attacked the fortress from four sides throwing various assaults against the enemy. For eight hours the battle raged. Contact was broken off at 6 P.M. The day's fighting ended with little change in the situation and no apparent advantage to either side, though the rebels had managed to take and hold the Park of Engineers. Casualties, dead and wounded, exceeded five hundred. That night a frightful silence followed the din of battle. It was broken only by occasional machine-gun bursts.

At 10.30 A.M. on Tuesday morning, barely a quarter of an hour after the federal offensive began, General Huerta and Félix Díaz conferred in the house of Enrique Cepeda on Nápoles Street in Colonia Roma. Cepeda served during the Decena Trágica (Ten Tragic Days) as the emissary between Huerta and the American Embassy and between Huerta and the rebels in the Ciudadela. At this conference the downfall of Madero was sealed, the decision as to when it would occur being reserved by Huerta. The first fruit of the deal was forthcoming late that afternoon when a force of loyal rurales was ordered to advance in the open down Balderas Street. The rebel machine guns on the Ciudadela and the YMCA cut the close formation to ribbons.[24]

President Madero remained optimistic. Forces continued to arrive from neighboring states. Rubio Navarrete, from Querétaro, declared his loyalty, and was placed in command of the government's artillery. He assured the President that the Ciudadela would fall the following day. *El Imparcial,* which had recently become a government publication, announced that the administration, supported by six thousand soldiers as compared with fifteen hundred rebels, was sure of victory.[25] Madero was confidently looking ahead. He told Vasconcelos that:

> When this is all over, I will change the cabinet. My ministers are

[24] Bonilla, *El régimen maderista,* p. 66.
[25] *El Imparcial,* Feb. 11, 1913.

very honorable, but I need more active [and] . . . younger men.

This situation will be resolved in a few days. Then we will remake the government. We must triumph because we represent the good.[26]

[26] Vasconcelos, *Ulises criollo,* p. 432.

XVIII. Ambassador Wilson Takes a Hand

ON THE THIRD DAY of the rebellion Henry Lane Wilson reported that "public opinion, both native and foreign, as far as I can estimate, seems to be overwhelmingly in favor of Díaz [!]" He underestimated federal strength, exaggerated the size of the rebel force, and complained of indiscriminate firing and extensive damage to property. Because of the possibility that the turbulent conditions might continue the Ambassador offered a startling proposal.

> I am convinced that the Government of the United States in the interest of humanity and in the discharge of its political obligations should send hither instructions of a firm, drastic and perhaps menacing character to be transmitted personally to the Government of President Madero and to the leaders of the revolutionary movement.
>
> If I were in possession of instructions of this character or . . . with general powers in the name of the President [!] I might possibly be able to induce a cessation of hostilities and the initiation of negotiations having for their object definite peace arrangements.[1]

Secretary Knox replied that the President was not convinced of the desirability of such instructions "at the present time," because they might precipitate intervention and because "drastic representations might radically affect the issue of military supremacy" for which the United States government did not

[1] Wilson to State Dept., Feb. 11, 1913, SDF, 812.00/6086 and 6092.

wish to become in any degree responsible.[2] That effect was precisely what Wilson, under the guise of humanitarian considerations, apparently desired to accomplish.

Early Wednesday morning (February 12), the firing was resumed, but it was largely localized in the area of the Ciudadela, where the heaviest fighting involved possession of the 6th District Police Headquarters on the corner of Victoria and Revillagigedo Streets. During the early hours of the day the rebels held the location, and fire from there disabled three federal cannons. Late in the morning, after a terrific fight, the federal forces captured the building and, capitalizing on this advantage, advanced along Revillagigedo Street to the Garden of Carlos Pacheco. However, heavy direct fire forced withdrawal from this advanced position. Other attacks were launched from the east, along the Arcos de Belem, and from the south. The former effort resulted in a costly advance to the front of the prison. The latter attack gained a few hundred feet.

As a result of the attack from the south, on which the rebels trained their cannon, a breach was opened in the northwest corner of Belem Prison, which housed five thousand prisoners. There was a mad scramble to take advantage of the situation. Many inmates were killed, some were recaptured and taken to the Penitentiary, and a number escaped or joined the rebels in the Ciudadela. At midday the fighting stopped while some of the foreign diplomats endeavored to arrange a neutral zone, but about four in the afternoon the firing began again and lasted until the early hours of the following morning.

The city was a frightening place. On many streets there were no lights, and there was a lack of police and other public services. The bodies of persons who had died of illness or wounds in the combat zone were beginning to decompose. Corpses were piled in the streets, immersed in petroleum, and burned in the hope of avoiding an epidemic. Articles of prime necessity began to be in short supply, and prices rose to fabulous heights. The government's soldiers were on short rations

[2] Knox to Wilson, Feb. 12, 1913, SDF, 812.00/6092.

during the first two days of fighting, and Gustavo Madero with his own funds purchased ten thousand sandwiches daily to feed the loyal soldiers.[3]

On the fourth day there was additional circumstantial evidence of the underlying plot. Rubio Navarrete, after conferring with Huerta on the preceding evening, told Madero that he wanted to modify his optimistic predictions. Now he said that the walls of the fortress were so thick that he would be able to do very little with the equipment at hand. Ambassador Wilson was active on Wednesday making similar representations both to the government and to the rebels. According to his report, Wilson, in the name of the diplomats who accompanied him, protested against the continuance of hostilities and the loss of American life and property and indicated that since the President of the United States was concerned, "vessels have been ordered to the various ports . . . [and] marines would be landed if necessary and brought to this city to maintain order and to afford protection to the lives and properties of foreigners."[4]

Despite his instructions, the Ambassador was employing an approach of a "menacing character" as leverage against the government. His interpretation of the reaction to his statement was again characteristic of his biased perspective. He had visited the National Palace about 11 A.M. with the German and Spanish Ministers. After he had made his statement, Wilson felt that the "President was visibly embarrassed." The Ambassador reported that Madero "tried to fix the responsibility on Díaz" and informed them that the government was taking steps which would end the rebellion by the following night. "These statements made no impression on me or my colleagues." The American diplomat insisted on a cessation of hostilities while representations were made to Díaz. Madero granted this request. The diplomats returned to the American Embassy where they were joined by the British Minister. The four men then visited Díaz at the Ciudadela. Wilson, as might

[3] Lamicq, *Madero*, p. 79.
[4] Wilson to State Dept., Feb. 12, 1913, SDF, 812.00/6112.

have been anticipated, was favorably impressed. "My colleagues and I were pleased with the frankness as well as [with] the humane views expressed by General Díaz." He noted with satisfaction that "he [Díaz] received us with all the honors of war." [5]

Thursday (February 13) was a day of terrific bombardment which continued into the night. One bomb from the Ciudadela hit a door of the National Palace. General Angeles's federal batteries, located near the National Railroad Station, caused considerable damage in the residential areas, but the shelling of the Ciudadela caused it little damage. The reason was not difficult to discover. The location of the federal batteries was such that the angle of trajectory did not permit hits on the walls. In addition, the cannon used were firing shrapnel grenades which could only penetrate the roof or harm exposed personnel.[6]

The rebels tried to take the tower of the Church of Campo Florida, but the federal forces repelled them inflicting heavy losses in an hour-long battle. The positions at the end of the day were about the same, but the radius of rebel activity seemed slightly extended. The government continued to concentrate more troops. Among the reinforcements arriving that day were one hundred men bringing two million cartridges from Veracruz.

The bombardment continued on Friday (February 14) with varying intensity. Federal forces fought their way almost to the door of the Y.M.C.A., but were forced to withdraw. The government felt stronger because General Rivera was reported coming to the capital from Oaxaca with nine hundred men and General Blanquet had arrived from Toluca with the 29th Battalion. The latter had wired affirming his loyalty on the tenth, but rumors continued to circulate about his intentions.

[5] *Ibid.*

[6] If further proof that the operations were not sincere is needed, it may be found in two reports by Col. Rubio Navarrete. "Informes rendidos 16 y 18 de febrero por el Comandante General de Artillería, Col. Guillermo Rubio Navarrete, al General Comandante Militar," cited in Amaya, *Madero y . . . revolucionarios*, pp. 429-31.

Instead of entering the capital, Blanquet encamped at Tlaxpana on the outskirts of the city.

The main events of Friday were in the diplomatic rather than in the military realm. The government was concerned about the prolongation of hostilities and the threat of international complications. Therefore, Madero agreed to accept the mediatory services of Spanish Minister Cólogan and of de la Barra. The preceding evening de la Barra had spoken with General Angeles regarding the location of some cannons near the British Legation, and in the course of the conversation had touched on the possibility of reaching an accord. Angeles reported the conversation to President Madero who invited de la Barra to the National Palace at 10 A.M. on Friday. De la Barra was authorized to speak to Generals Díaz and Mondragón regarding an armistice to permit civilians to leave the danger zone and to permit discussions aiming at resolution of the conflict. De la Barra arrived at the Ciudadela and had to wait briefly while Minister Cólogan made an unsuccessful effort with similar objectives.[7]

The peace emissary pointed out to the rebel chiefs the difficult situation and the international danger. Díaz and Mondragón repeated what they had told Minister Cólogan, namely, that the *sine qua non* for negotiations was the prior resignations of President Madero, Vice-President Pino Suárez, and the cabinet.[8] After the hour-long interview, de la Barra reported the result of his mission to Madero, who indicated to him that for no reason was he disposed to give up. The President discussed the situation with members of his cabinet. The majority present, excepting Bonilla and Jaime Gurza, favored resignation to avoid the foreign intervention implied in Ambassador Wilson's remarks.

Madero decided to telegraph President Taft to obtain the truth. In his message he indicated: that Americans would be

[7] After the visit to the Ciudadela, Cólogan told the Cuban Minister that Díaz "seems a little weak to me. However, the Ambassador [Wilson] will not pay any attention when I tell him about it." Márquez Sterling, *Los últimos días,* p. 394.

[8] *Revista de Revistas,* Feb. 23, 1913.

in no danger if they left the firing zone for other parts of the capital or its suburbs; that the government accepted full responsibility for property damage; and that the administration was taking all measures to insure the least damage possible and the early termination of the situation.

> It is true that my country is experiencing at present a terrible trial. The disembarcation of American forces would only make the situation worse. Through a lamentable error the United States would do a horrible wrong to a nation which always has been a loyal friend. [It] would tend to make more difficult the reestablishment in Mexico of a democratic government similar to that of the great American nation. I appeal to the sentiments of equity and justice which have been the rule of your Government and which undoubtedly represent the feelings of the great American people.[9]

This message dispatched, Madero told his cabinet that he would not resign for any reason. Referring to the telegram to President Taft, he optimistically remarked, "Now you will see how the intrigues of this evil ambassador are dealt with." [10]

However, the activities of Wilson continued. That very morning Minister of Foreign Affairs Lascuráin visited the American Embassy. The Ambassador "endeavored to impress on him the fact that public opinion, both Mexican and foreign, was holding the Federal Government responsible for these conditions" and urged him "to take some immediate action that would lead to discussions." Wilson suggested the desirability of calling the Senate and arranging an armistice. The American diplomat noted with satisfaction that Lascuráin was "profoundly impressed with what he believes to be the threatening attitude of our government and intimated to me in confidence that he thought the President ought to resign." [11]

Apparently, Wilson's suggestion bore fruit. At four in the afternoon a dozen senators gathered at the home of Senator Camacho. Minister Lascuráin attended and discussed the situ-

[9] Secretary Knox to American Embassy, Feb. 15, 1913, SDF, 812.00/6172C.

[10] Bonilla, *El régimen maderista,* p. 71.

[11] Wilson to State Dept., Feb. 14, 1913, SDF, 812.00/6153.

ation, particularly the threat of American intervention. Desiring a broader base of support for any action taken, the group decided to call a general meeting of the Senate for 7 A.M. the next morning. Lascuráin furnished a formal request in the name of the executive department.

Ambassador Wilson also endeavored to persuade some of his colleagues in the diplomatic corps to bring pressure for Madero's resignation. He requested the British, German, and Spanish Ministers to come to the Embassy in the early hours of the morning of February 15 "to supplement the work done with Mr. Lascuráin in . . . [the] interview Friday morning." [12] After his colleagues had arrived, the American diplomat gave full play to his obsessions and fears: that Madero was incompetent; that sacking by mobs was imminent; and that the hordes from Morelos would enter the city. Although the country was reasonably calm while the capital was enveloped by fighting, Wilson tried to make it appear that the nation was aflame with rebellion. He expressed his conviction that the federal army was disloyal to Madero. As a result of the two-hour session, the diplomats, as Wilson expressed it, developed an "identity of opinion" to assume the responsibility for an unofficial request that Madero resign. The Spanish Minister was designated to make the recommendation to the Mexican President.[13]

Twenty-five senators gathered in the Chamber early on Saturday morning. Since they did not have a quorum, the group proceeded as in private meeting. During the four-hour session which followed, Minister Lascuráin spoke of the difficult international situation, and de la Barra recounted his unsuccessful mediation efforts. The senators agreed that it

[12] He claimed that "although only the representatives of the great powers have acted with me in these matters, we have the support of the entire diplomatic corps." Actually, general consultation was difficult, if not impossible, under existing conditions. Several Latin American diplomats, notably the representatives of Cuba and Chile, were not at all in accord with Wilson's conduct. Wilson to State Dept., Feb. 15, 1913, SDF, 812.00/6175 and 6176.

[13] Wilson, *Diplomatic Episodes,* pp. 262-63; Márquez Sterling, *Los últimos días,* pp. 380-83.

was necessary to save the national sovereignty through the resignations of the President and Vice-President. They named themselves as a committee, appointed two of their number to serve as spokesmen, and proceeded to the National Palace accompanied by Lascuráin.

The senatorial committee was preceded by Minister Cólogan. The Spanish diplomat made his representations on behalf of his colleagues. Madero replied that he was the constitutional president and that his resignation would involve the country in chaos. With dignity he said that he "did not recognize the right of diplomats to interfere in a domestic question" and that he would "die in defense of his rights as the legally elected president." [14] Madero refused to see the senators who had come on an analagous mission. Instead, they were met by several cabinet officers, including Ernesto Madero, who informed them that the President had left with the Secretary of War to visit positions of the government's forces.

Ernesto Madero told the senators that although he did not represent the President and could not speak for him, he felt that he ought to advise them of the following: that the government had sufficient forces with which to master the situation and within a few days to take the Ciudadela; that conditions in the Republic were satisfactory; and that the danger of American intervention was not considered serious. On this last matter, he noted, the President was awaiting a reply from President Taft. Still, the spokesmen for the senators emphasized the need for the resignations in view of the threat to national independence. After the meeting several of the senators addressed a crowd gathered outside the Palace. They urged support of the legislative power, with the apparent object of bringing pressure on Madero to yield in the face of impending United States intervention.[15]

That afternoon Wilson and the German Minister, von Hintze, visited the National Palace with the declared object of seeing General Huerta to arrange an armistice and other

[14] Wilson to State Dept., Feb. 15, 1913, SDF, 812.00/6175.
[15] De Bekker, *Huerta*, pp. 109-13.

humanitarian moves. The Ambassador's report contained some startling complaints and observations:

> Upon arrival at the Palace much to our regret [!] we were taken to see the President whom we (had) not asked to see. It was only after repeated requests that we were allowed to have an interview [with Huerta] and then only in the presence of Mr. Lascuráin . . . There was a noticeable effort to prevent our talking alone with General Huerta.[16]

Madero showed Wilson a telegram which he had sent President Taft relevant to the Cólogan audience and the threat of intervention. In it the Mexican Executive had charged that the American Ambassador had instigated the resignation suggestion and had expressed concern lest the diplomat disembark troops.[17] Nevertheless, Madero then tried to modify the diplomat's attitude through logic and considerateness. He agreed to the idea of a twenty-four-hour armistice to begin at 2 A.M. on the following morning (Sunday), but he was unsuccessful in his attempt to convince Wilson that conditions in the country were at variance with the diplomat's information. Later, through Lascuráin, he offered the American representative the safety of a residence in the suburb of Tacubaya. Wilson declined to accept the offer and reported that "the removal of the Embassy would be a calamity to the entire American colony. Americans cannot be advised to go to a safer place because there is none[!]"[18]

Saturday had not been a day of intense fighting, although the bombardment and machine-gun fire was continued. Early

[16] Wilson to State Dept., Feb. 15, 1913, SDF, 812.00/6178.

[17] Wilson branded the message "irregular, false, and misleading." Regarding Taft's reply, the Ambassador indicated that he would "appreciate [as a matter] of great importance . . . [that the President should] sharply rebuke the scarcely veiled attack on this Embassy." He passed on the opinion, attributed to de la Barra, that "Madero's final answer [regarding] resignation, will largely depend on the reply he received from President Taft. I gather he would or at least might resign in the face of a threat of immediate intervention." Wilson's objective and the means he considered suitable were quite clear. Wilson to State Dept., Feb. 15 and 17, 1913, SDF, 812.00/6176 and 6208.

[18] Wilson to State Dept., Feb. 15, 1913, SDF, 812.00/6174.

on Sunday people began to pour out of their houses in search of food. Those who had been caught in residences within the danger zone took advantage of the lull in the fighting to leave their homes for safer locations, but around two in the afternoon, without any warning, the cannonading was renewed. Many persons were injured by this sudden outbreak of hostilities. The government charged that rebel efforts to strengthen their positions necessitated these countermeasures. Henry Lane Wilson rushed to the National Palace to protest. Márquez Sterling, who was just leaving the building, reported that the "nervous and agitated" American diplomat blamed the government for advancing and taking "positions along the approaches to the Ciudadela." [19]

Only three hours earlier Wilson had reported confidentially to Washington that "General Huerta has indicated a desire to talk with me and I shall see him some time during the day . . . I hope for good results [from] this." [20] At midnight Huerta sent Wilson a message indicating that it would be impossible to keep the appointment, but that "he expected to take steps tonight towards terminating the situation." [21] Perhaps Huerta's inability to confer with the American Ambassador was due to the awkward situation in which he found himself that afternoon.

A loyal officer had heard a report that during the period of the armistice provisions were reaching the besieged rebels in the Ciudadela. He investigated and saw eighteen carts of provisions entering the fortress. The officer, Rubén Morales, reported the situation to Madero who called for General Huerta and demanded an explanation. Huerta at first sought

[19] Márquez Sterling, *Los últimos días*, p. 438.

[20] Wilson to State Dept., Feb. 16, 1913, SDF, 812.00/6180.

In his memoirs Wilson noted that he had desired to communicate with Huerta to have a battery moved. Enrique Cepeda conveniently was available to carry this request. Cepeda returned with word that Huerta desired a meeting. Wilson wrote that two further exchanges occurred. The former diplomat claimed unconvincingly that this incident "unduly magnified and falsely interpreted" constituted the only "evidence identifying the embassy with a conspiracy." Wilson, *Diplomatic Episodes*, pp. 273ff.

[21] Wilson to State Dept., Feb. 16, 1913, SDF, 812.00/6186.

to deny the report, but, confronted with an eyewitness, he admitted the truth of the allegation. He said that the rebels, lacking provisions, were dispersing and spreading the movement through the city. He told the President that if he were able, he would send the Felicistas (supporters of Félix Díaz) women and liquor in order that they should remain content and together. Then, on the day the fortress was surrendered, there would not be a single Felicista free in the city.

This logic was not very convincing, but Huerta insisted, and the subject was changed to the matter of attack. Since day assaults were producing no result, Morales suggested a night attack. Madero and Pino Suárez were enthusiastic. General Huerta brusquely asked whether there was not implied a lack of confidence in his ability when they insisted on a plan of which he disapproved. The federal commander rose and, placing his hands on Madero's shoulders, said, "You are in the arms of General Victoriano Huerta." [22] Later events exposed this statement as being the epitome of deceit, but the President was disarmed by the seeming sincerity of his commander.

On Monday the firing continued with more or less intensity. At the house of Senator Camacho a small group of legislators gathered, but were unable to agree on a course of action. Two of them, Senators Pimentel and Obregón, went to visit General Blanquet in Tlaxpana to explore his sentiments. General Blanquet indicated that Huerta had been there and that it would not be possible to successfully assault the Ciudadela because to do so the government would need ten thousand men. He suggested that they tell Huerta about the meeting of the senators. Pimentel and Obregón visited Huerta and told him that they thought it advisable that he speak with the President.

General Huerta sent Ambassador Wilson a message that he might "anticipate some action which will force Madero from power at any moment and that plans were fully matured." The diplomat reported that he asked no questions and made no suggestions "beyond requesting that no lives be taken except

[22] *El Estandarte,* Dec. 28, 1917.

by due process of law[!]" [23] Plans were indeed maturing. General Blanquet refused, apparently by prearranged plan, to place his battalion in the line of siege. Instead, that afternoon this force was assigned to the National Palace. Wilson correctly interpreted this as being part of Huerta's plan to move all "purely Maderista soldiers" outside of the Palace and to replace them with "soldiers upon whom he could depend." With good reason the Ambassador expected "important developments tomorrow." [24] He confided to the representative of Cuba that "tomorrow all will be over, Mr. Minister." [25] Years later, Henry Lane Wilson had the audacity to claim that "I did not for a moment suppose that a violent *coup d'état* would occur or that Madero would be subjected to more than the pressure of overwhelming circumstances." [26]

As the web of treachery closed in on Madero, an unforeseen development almost tore the well-laid plans to pieces. Gustavo Madero had been convinced from the beginning of the rebellion that General Huerta was implicated. He urged Francisco to replace Huerta as commander. When a friend, Deputy Jesús Urueta, whose house adjoined Cepeda's in Nápoles Street, reported the meeting of Huerta and Díaz, Gustavo, to no avail, tried to get his brother to act. By the evening of the seventeenth Gustavo felt that the situation called for direct action. Boldly, with drawn pistol, he made Huerta prisoner, amidst protestations of innocence and affirmations of loyalty by the General.

It was two o'clock in the morning when the President learned of this incident. He ordered that Huerta be brought to him, and the General was permitted to defend himself. Huerta argued that he did not wish to initiate a badly prepared attack exposing the President to a defeat, and he recalled that at the beginning of his successful campaign in Chihuahua also, his slowness had been criticized. Huerta swore that he was loyal

[23] Wilson to State Dept., Feb. 17, 1913, SDF, 812.00/6225.
[24] Wilson to State Dept., Feb. 17, 1913, SDF, 812.00/6235.
[25] Márquez Sterling, *Los últimos días*, p. 488.
[26] Wilson, *Diplomatic Episodes*, pp. 274-75.

and promised that the following day he would prove it. Madero apparently was impressed, for he granted the General twenty-four hours to supply the proof, but said that if the allowed time elapsed without result, he would be inclined to believe the charges. At Huerta's request, the President personally returned the General's pistol. Gustavo he reprimanded for acting on "impulse." [27]

Tuesday morning, rumors of a new armistice circulated through the city, but from the early hours of the morning firing continued to be heard. Around ten o'clock there began a determined bombardment of the National Palace area from the Ciudadela. After an hour the firing became weaker and weaker until intervals of nearly one-half hour would elapse between volleys. The fighting phase was grinding to a halt as though to permit deceit and treachery to occupy the center of the screen.

Early that morning Huerta invited the President of the Supreme Court, Francisco Carbajal, and a group of senators to his office. When Carbajal arrived, Huerta offered to place his forces at the disposition of the court. Lic. Carbajal answered that he did not represent the court and had no power to make agreements. At this juncture nine senators, men who were resolutely Anti-Maderista, arrived at Huerta's office. Senator Guillermo Obregón told the General of the visit to Blanquet and said he spoke for the Senate majority, which believed that the President's resignation was the only remedy for the grave threat which confronted the nation.

Huerta, in turn, complimented the senators for their patriotic sentiments and showed them Rubio Navarrete's report on the difficulties of bombing the Ciudadela, as well as opinions signed by some military men that it was not possible to take the fortress. The federal commander added that the government lacked the elements necessary to dominate the situation. He indicated that he wanted some of his military associates to hear what the senators had to say. The General and the legislators were ready to cooperate. The visitors desired Huer-

[27] Bonilla, *El régimen maderista*, p. 75.

ta's support for their recommendation to Madero to resign; General Huerta wanted the prestige and arguments of the legislators to solidify the ranks of his military associates behind him.[28]

Minister of War García Peña, General Blanquet, and several other officers were called to the office of the military commander. Senator Obregón repeated his routine. The Minister of War replied that he did not think it was possible for a group of senators to subvert the army, and asked Huerta if he was supporting the legislators' proposals. Huerta replied that he only was submitting their request for an audience with the President.

After some twenty minutes of waiting, Madero received the delegation in the Presidential Salon. In answer to the President's inquiry, Senator Obregón stated the object of the visit in a few, precise words: to repeat the recommendation of the Senate of February 15. Madero bitterly observed that he was not surprised that a group which had never wanted to see Porfirio Díaz leave the Palace would come to him with such a purpose. He declared that there was no reason for his resignation because the fears of foreign intervention were unfounded. In support of this contention Madero read them President Taft's reply to his telegram which he regarded as a firm pledge against intervention.[29]

Senators Enríquez and Castellot tried to assure the President that their action ought not to be considered as the product of an hostile attitude toward him or his administration.

[28] Toro, *La caída de Madero,* p. 50; De Bekker, *Huerta,* pp. 117-35.

[29] Taft called reports that orders had been given to land troops inaccurate. He considered that "fresh assurances of friendship to Mexico are unnecessary after two years of proof of patience and good will," but emphasized the "vital importance" of the early establishment of real peace. Secretary Knox to American Embassy, Feb. 17, 1913, SDF, 812.00/6223A.

Senator Obregón could not have been speaking for the Senate as a whole or even for the twenty-five senators who had participated on the fifteenth. No formal session had been held, and three of the original group had reneged when informed that there was no real threat of intervention.

Rather they had come to express an honorable and patriotic opinion. Madero reiterated his refusal to resign: "I will never resign. The people have elected me, and I will die, if necessary, in the fulfillment of my obligation." [30] He requested that Enríquez and Castellot remain in order to inform Huerta of the exchange of views and of the fact that there was no foreign danger. The military commander was called, and the two senators did as Madero had requested informing Huerta of the results of the conference that he might make them known to the other army officials. The President asked Huerta to explain his plans for that afternoon to the senators. The General protested his loyalty and indicated that at 3 P.M. the Ciudadela would be attacked. Madero asked, "Now do you see? General Huerta has his plans and is confident of good results. There is no reason for alarm." [31] The President was trying to use Huerta and the senators to bolster the regime.

It was nearing 1:30 P.M., the normal luncheon hour at the National Palace. General Huerta, Gustavo Madero, and several others had departed for a banquet at the Gambrinus Restaurant. Madero, some of his cabinet officers, and several aides were in a small room adjoining the Salon de Acuerdos conferring about supplies for the government's troops and for the civilian population. The conference was interrupted by the entrance of Lieutenant Colonel Jiménez Riveroll, of the 29th Battalion, who indicated that he had been sent by Huerta to report that General Rivera was arriving from Oaxaca in a rebellious attitude and that Madero should accompany him to a safe place.

The President was in the process of refusing to do so when a commotion was heard in the adjacent salon. Madero and the others hurried into the larger room. There they found Major Izquierdo and twenty-five to thirty soldiers of the 29th Battalion whom a loyal aide had tried unsuccessfully to order to leave. The two files of soldiers in their lead-colored uniforms with rifles tilted, each with two combat belts with shiny banks

[30] Márquez Sterling, *Los últimos días,* pp. 456-57.
[31] Bonilla, *El régimen maderista,* p. 78ff.

of cartridges, and each with a mattock hanging from his belt, seemed strangely out of place in the carpeted executive conference room.

The President stood, with his cousin Marcos Hernández (brother of the cabinet officer Rafael Hernández) at his side, facing Riveroll and Izquierdo. Behind the latter were the soldiers while grouped back of the President were his aides, cabinet officers, and others. Discarding all pretense, Riveroll indicated that he had come to arrest Madero on the order of Blanquet in agreement with Huerta. Madero challenged Blanquet's right to order his arrest. When Riveroll sought to seize the President, two of the latter's aides, Captains Gustavo Garmendia and Federico Montes, drew gleaming 38-caliber pistols. Captain Garmendia fired killing Riveroll.

Some of the soldiers, either because they heard Major Izquierdo order it or as an automatic reaction in the tense situation, discharged their guns. The windows rattled from the multiple explosion, the curtains fluttered, and the room was filled with a cloud of smoke and the acrid smell of burnt powder. On the floor were the bodies of Riveroll and Izquierdo and of the mortally wounded Marcos Hernández. Madero, brave to the point of temerity, proceeded to advance towards the confused, leaderless soldiers. Repeating the reassuring "Calm, boys, do not fire," he advanced close enough until he could dash past them to the door which led to another anteroom. While the platoon disbanded, Madero went to the rooms which faced the main plaza. From below, outside the Palace, came the cries of rurales who had been alarmed by the shots. The President appeared on the balcony and told them not to worry, that the incident was past, and that they should return to their posts.

Although advised to flee to safety, Madero insisted on searching for General Blanquet. The President still could not believe that he had been abandoned by all the military. Accompanied by several aides Madero rode the elevator down to the patio where he encountered General Blanquet. The General stood, pistol in hand, in front of elements of the 29th

Battalion. In a strong voice he said, "Surrender, Mr. President." Madero, in a high-pitched, irritated voice replied, "You are a traitor, General Blanquet." Blanquet affirmed, "You are my prisoner." The President protested, "It is the President of the Republic to whom you are speaking," but Blanquet only repeated the fact that Madero was a prisoner. Resistance futile, the defeated Madero was taken to the office of the military commander located in the same patio. The majority of the cabinet members, excepting two who escaped, were arrested about the same time.[32]

At the Gambrinus Restaurant, Gustavo Madero was attending a private party honoring the promotion of the President of the Chamber to the rank of general. General Huerta was also present. Shortly after 1:30 P.M. Huerta made a telephone call, apparently to confirm that everything had gone according to schedule at the Palace, and then excused himself. Twenty minutes later a platoon of soldiers appeared and arrested Gustavo, imprisoning him in a coatroom of the restaurant. General Angeles, who, despite a cease-fire order, continued to fire on the Ciudadela, also was arrested. Sarita and other members of the Madero family took refuge in the Japanese Legation.

General Huerta assumed command and so notified the American Embassy and President Taft. "I have the honor to inform you that I have overthrown this Government. The armed forces support me, and from now on peace and prosperity will reign."[33] Late that afternoon the bells of the Cathedral and of the other churches rang forth the news. As evening fell the people were pouring into the streets enjoying the freedom and safety so lacking for ten days. To the south the sky

[32] Most eyewitness accounts tended to agree that Capt. Garmendia killed Riveroll and that Capt. Montes fired at Izquierdo, who may have been in the soldiers' line of fire. All agree that Madero, who normally did not carry a weapon, did not draw a pistol. The description presented is based on three eyewitness reports: Rubén Morales in *El Estandarte,* Jan. 10, 1918; Federico Montes as recounted by Gen. F. L. Urquizo in Barragán Rodríguez, *Historia del ejército,* I, 53-61; and González Garza, *La Revolución mexicana,* pp. 405-08.

[33] Huerta to President Taft, Feb. 18, 1913, SDF, 812.00/6256.

was aglow—a mob had set fire to the building of *Nueva Era*, the leading Maderista newspaper. Still to be formalized were the relations between Huerta and the rebels.

Ambassador Wilson was ready to assist in this matter. Earlier that day the American diplomat had jumped the gun on the coup exposing his familiarity with the plan. At noon he reported to Washington that "the supposition now is that the Federal Generals are in control of the situation." [34] The arrest of Madero, unexpectedly delayed, did not occur until an hour and a half later!

That evening the American representative invited Generals Huerta and Díaz to the Embassy. Huerta arrived accompanied by Lieutenant Colonel J. Mass and Enrique Cepeda. Díaz was attended by Rodolfo Reyes and several others. Protracted discussion followed, and, finally, after thirty minutes of private exchange between the principals, the Pact of the Ciudadela was signed. Rodolfo Reyes later justified the signing at the American Embassy on the basis that it was "neutral ground." [35] After agreement was achieved, Wilson told several colleagues, who were gathered outside the conference room, that everything was arranged. When Félix Díaz reentered the room, the Ambassador cried out, "Long live General Díaz, saviour of Mexico!" After introductions and a reading of part of the agreement, the generals were ushered out.[36]

By this pact it was decided that Congress would be convened, a new cabinet would be named (with considerable voice in the matter for Díaz), and General Huerta would serve as provisional president in which capacity he would support Díaz's candidacy for the permanent presidency. Ambassador Wilson reported that he "stipulated" three agreements which

[34] Wilson to State Dept., Feb. 18, 1913, SDF, 812.00/6249.

[35] R. Reyes, *De mi vida*, II, 29.

[36] Márquez Sterling, *Los últimos días*, pp. 473-74.

Wilson miscalculated badly. He thought that Félix Díaz had won, but the situation was made to order for Huerta. Recognizing Wilson's partiality for Díaz, the author of Huerta's "memoirs" has the General remark, "Wilson was my friend by carom." Piña, *Memorias de . . . Huerta*, pp. 8-9.

were not reduced to writing: release of Madero's ministers, freedom of the press, and joint action of Díaz and Huerta to preserve order in the city. It is to be noted that Wilson made no stipulation regarding the persons of Madero and Pino Suárez, at the least a serious error of omission. The contents of the arrangement were quite astounding in view of the fact that Madero had not yet resigned and was still alive! [37]

In subsequent years Wilson repeatedly denied any responsibility for the overthrow of Madero, but the evidence proved conclusively that the diplomat was aware of the plot and sympathized with and encouraged and abetted its promoters, even to the point of providing embassy facilities for their agreement. One observer, considering how narrowly Madero missed winning, concluded that "the least value which can be assigned to the unfortunate influence of the American Ambassador is still sufficient to have turned the scale." [38]

Wilson candidly informed the State Department that

> I have been assuming considerable responsibility in proceeding without instructions in many important matters, but no harm has been done [!] and I believe [that] great benefits have been achieved for our country and especially for our countrymen in Mexico . . . [whose] interests will receive just consideration . . . Our position here is stronger than it is have ever been.[39]

After Huerta and Díaz had left the Embassy, one of the diplomats inquired what would be the fate of "poor" Madero. "Oh," allegedly answered Wilson, "They will put Señor Madero in a madhouse where he should always be kept. As for the other [Pino Suárez], he is nothing but a scoundrel. So, if they kill him, it will be no great loss." The Chilean representative protested that "we must not allow it," but Wilson declared that "we must not meddle in the domestic affairs of Mexico[!]" [40]

[37] Wilson to State Dept., Feb. 18, 1913, SDF, 812.00/6264.

[38] Bell, *Political Shame*, p. 416.

[39] Wilson to State Dept., Feb. 18, 1913, SDF, 812.00/6264.

[40] Gruening, *Mexico*, pp. 568ff.; Márquez Sterling, *Los últimos días*, pp. 473-74.

The quotations from pages 568 and 570 of *Mexico and Its Heritage*, by Ernest Gruening (copyright 1928, by The Century Company), are used with the permission of Appleton-Century-Crofts, Inc.

XIX. *Martyr for Mexican Democracy*

CONSERVATIVE ELEMENTS in the capital lauded the "patriotic action" of General Huerta. The opposition press jubilantly celebrated the establishment of the new government. *El País* announced that "Maderism has been tumbled noisily and tragically never to be born again." *El Mañana* solemnly affirmed that "it was inevitable, it was fated." And *El Imparcial* sounded the tocsin of vengeance against the deposed governmental leaders for real, rumored, and imagined offenses:

Fortunately there is no contradiction between political aims and the demands of justice which requires that responsible officials should be punished . . . Those guilty of . . . crimes ought to suffer the legal consequences of their acts. Justice ought to be severe, cold, and inexorable with them.[1]

The followers of Félix Díaz demanded that four prisoners, including Francisco and Gustavo Madero, be turned over to them. However, Francisco Madero and Pino Suárez were essential to Huerta's plan to legalize his position. Therefore, he delivered only Gustavo Madero and Adolfo Bassó, Superintendent of the National Palace, to the Felicistas, as evidence of his good faith. Late on the night of the eighteenth Gustavo was taken by car to the Ciudadela. There, around two in the morning, General Mondragón decreed his death.

The President's brother was forced with blows and pushes

[1] *El País*, Feb. 20, 1913; *El Mañana*, Feb. 21, 1913; *El Imparcial*, Feb. 23, 1913.

to the door leading to the patio. Bleeding, his face distorted by blows, his clothes torn, Gustavo tried to resist that frenzied, drunken mob of nearly one hundred persons. Holding desperately to the frame of the door he appealed to that sea of faces reflecting the madness of mob violence. Referring to his wife, children, and parents, he pleaded with them not to kill him. His words were greeted by jeers and laughter. One of the crowd pushed forward and, with the mattock from his rifle or the point of a sword, picked out the prisoner's good eye. The blinded Gustavo uttered a single mournful cry of terror and desperation. After that, he made no more sounds, but covering his face with his hands turned toward the wall.

The mob laughed and jeeringly referred to the victim as a "coward" and a "whiner" and as "Ojo Parado." Prodding and sticking him with mattock and sword points and dealing him blows with fists and sticks they forced him to the patio. Gustavo moved, stumbling, without uttering a word. An assailant pressed a revolver to his head. The hand holding the weapon was unsteady and slipped, and the shot tore Gustavo's jaw away. He was still able to move a short distance, falling, at last, near the statue of Morelos which, inappropriately, was silent witness to this scene. A volley of shots was fired into the body. By lantern light it was ascertained that Gustavo Madero was dead. One of the crowd fired yet another shot into the body explaining drunkenly that it was the *coup de grâce*. The assassins proceeded to sack the body, and Gustavo's enamel eye was extracted and circulated from hand to hand.[2]

Some time later another car brought Adolfo Bassó to the same patio. Valiantly, his eyes fixed on the stars, he faced his execution. The pretext for Bassó's death was that, as Superintendent of the Palace and participant in its defense, he was responsible for the deaths of the rebels killed in the main plaza on February 9. The first day of the new regime had dawned stained with blood.[3]

[2] Taracena, *Madero: Vida*, pp. 587-89; Mena Brito, *Felipe Angeles*, pp. 70-74; Piña, *Memorias de . . . Huerta*, pp. 4-10.

[3] Rodolfo Reyes unconvincingly charged that Huerta's associates were

Ambassador Wilson, more concerned with such matters as Huerta's "satisfactory assurances" regarding guarantees of public order, unconcernedly accepted Huerta's explanation that Gustavo Madero had been killed by soldiers "without orders." The diplomat did feel that it was necessary to add that General Huerta told him that "the President and Gustavo Madero had tried to assassinate him twice and held him a prisoner for one day." The following day Wilson noted that "so far no other execution than those reported . . . have come to the knowlèdge of the Embassy," and added that Huerta had assured him that "every precaution was being taken to guard" Madero and Pino Suárez.[4] Secretary Knox informed Wilson that the shooting of Gustavo had "caused a most unfavorable impression here. The President is gratified to believe that there is no prospect of injury to the deposed President or Vice-President." [5]

Huerta's desire to legalize his position by means of having the deposed executives resign protected them initially. Late on the afternoon of the eighteenth the General released the cabinet officials of the former government, ostensibly in compliance with Wilson's request, but actually to convince Madero of Huerta's honorableness and of the advisability of complying with his resignation request.

The following morning a notice in the newspapers invited the members of the Chamber of Deputies to assemble at 10 A.M. to review the situation. Since not enough members to form a quorum appeared, those present held a private meeting to exchange ideas. It was suggested that the ushers be dispatched to bring the supplementary representatives who, although they could not participate actively, would create the semblance of a quorum. This was done, and at 4 P.M. the

---

responsible for the murders and that the Ciudadela location was chosen to place responsibility on the Felicistas. *De mi vida*, II, 40-52.

[4] Wilson to State Dept., Feb. 19 and 20, 1913, SDF, 812.00/6271 and 6277.

[5] Knox to American Embassy, Feb. 21, 1913, SDF, 812.00/6294A.

Chamber declared itself in permanent session to deal with the question of the resignations.

Early that morning a commissioner from Huerta, General Juvencio Robles, had visited the prisoners to demand their immediate resignations. General Robles told Madero that if they resigned, their lives would be guaranteed but that otherwise they would be exposed to any and all consequences. The deposed President apparently believed that the proposal was made in good faith, but he was evasive, seeking to bargain for the most favorable conditions. General Robles withdrew while Madero and his fellow prisoners, Pino Suárez and General Angeles, discussed possible bases for an arrangement.

It was agreed to ask Huerta for the following assurances in return for the resignations: that constitutional order in the states would be respected and the existing governors permitted to remain in their posts; that the friends and supporters of Madero would not be molested for political reasons; and that Madero, his brother Gustavo (the news of his death was being kept from Francisco), Pino Suárez, Angeles, and their families would be taken to Veracruz by special train to embark for exile. Madero realized that there was not sufficient guarantee that Huerta would fulfill his part of the bargain. Therefore, a fourth condition was added as follows: that the Ministers of Japan and Chile would accompany the prisoners to Veracruz after having received the resignations to exchange for a letter in which Huerta would accept the conditions. The prisoners hoped that the intervention of the diplomats would give the arrangements solemnity and a better chance of receiving compliance. Shortly afterwards Pedro Lascuráin arrived. Informed of the proposed bases for the resignations, he left to advise Huerta.

As the prisoners were being served the midday meal, Lascuráin returned with Ernesto Madero and Minister Hevia Riquelme of Chile. He indicated that Huerta had accepted the conditions. By 1 P.M. the joint resignation had been drafted. Pino Suárez argued for the inclusion of a phrase indicating that they had been obliged to resign by force. The intermediaries tactfully persuaded him that lives were involved and that such terminology would be impolitic under the circumstances. The final text of the resignation read:

Citizen Secretaries of the Honorable Chamber of Deputies: in view of the events which have developed since yesterday in the Nation and for the greater tranquility of it, we make formal resignation of our posts of President and Vice-President, respectively, to which we were elected.—We affirm the necessary. Mexico, February 19, 1913—Francisco I. Madero—José María Pino Suárez.[6]

The intermediaries, with Lascuráin in possession of the resignation, went forthwith to obtain Huerta's letter.

Later that afternoon Minister Márquez Sterling of Cuba, accompanied by Cólogan of Spain, came to the Palace to interview Huerta about the welfare of the prisoners. They met Chilean Minister Hevia Riquelme there, and he informed them about the resignations. Unable to see Huerta, all three went to visit Madero. At this meeting Madero accepted the offer of the cruiser *Cuba* for his departure from Mexico, and Márquez Sterling agreed to accompany the prisoners to the station and from there to Veracruz. Although the departure was scheduled for 10 P.M., the Cuban diplomat agreed, at the instance of Madero, to return earlier.

True to his word Márquez Sterling arrived at eight o'clock. The suite where the prisoners were detained consisted of three large rooms and a smaller one. The first served as a dining room for the prisoners. The second, which led to the patio, had been the Palace superintendent's office. Near the door stood a sentinel. To the right of the guard was the drawing room with several cots on which the prisoners slept. Madero, smiling, greeted the diplomat. Speaking thoughtfully, he remarked to the Cuban: "A President who, elected for five years, is overthrown in fifteen months has only himself to blame. The reason is that he did not know how to sustain himself. That will be the judgment of history if it is just." Sitting down, he added, "Minister, . . . if I again govern my country, I will

[6] Taracena, *Madero: Vida*, pp. 601-2; González Garza, *La Revolución mexicana*, pp. 410-12.

surround myself with determined men who would not be of 'intermediate colors'... I have committed great errors... Already it is late." [7]

Implicit in Madero's words to Márquez Sterling, as well as in other remarks made during his imprisonment, was his determination not to give up the struggle, but to continue it in exile. He definitely was thinking in terms of a new revolution against the usurpers. Francisco inquired of Gustavo's whereabouts. When no one answered, Madero declared that if his brother was not in the station that night, he would not leave. The Cuban, skirting the truth, emphasized that it was Madero who had to be saved under the existing circumstances.

Suddenly the shadow of doubt flashed across Francisco's face as he asked where was the letter from Huerta. Ernesto Madero, who, with Vázquez Tagle, also was visiting the prisoners, offered to try to find out. Ernesto returned with the alarming news that Lascuráin was going before Congress to present Madero's resignation. Madero, very much agitated, sent Manuel Vázquez Tagle to request that the resignations not be submitted until the prisoners were on the boat at Veracruz.

At 8:45 P.M. Lascuráin, tall and bespectacled, had appeared before the Chamber. The resignations were submitted, but some liberal deputies were disinclined to accept them. After several speakers, who were close to Madero and his government, urged acceptance on the grounds that the safety of the prisoners and their families was at stake, the resignations of Francisco Madero and Pino Suárez were approved by votes of 123-4 and 119-8 respectively. Vázquez Tagle arrived after the resignations had been offered and reported to Madero that he had been too late to comply with his mission.

Madero urged Vázquez Tagle to return to the Chamber and to request that Lascuráin not resign the interim presidency until the prisoners had departed. At 10:24 P.M. Lascuráin, as Minister of Foreign Relations, had been declared Interim President. He closed the session of Congress and opened the

[7] Márquez Sterling, *Los últimos días,* p. 500.

new one. After taking the oath of office, Lascuráin appointed Huerta as Minister of Government. When, at 11:20 P.M., Lascuráin resigned as Interim President, Huerta automatically assumed the executive power. Pedro Lascuráin had been President for fifty-six minutes. Madero's emissary arrived too late once again.[8]

When the prisoners learned of these developments, Madero's optimism flagged, and Pino Suárez feared an attack on their persons if they were left alone that night. Shortly thereafter an officer advised Márquez Sterling that the ten o'clock departure had been cancelled. For security and in case another hour for leaving was set the Cuban diplomat agreed to spend the night with the prisoners. Madero resignedly predicted that "the train will not leave at any hour." [9]

The former President arranged three chairs to serve as a bed for their guest. Pino Suárez laughingly observed that the Cuban probably never had expected to find so hard a bed in diplomacy. Madero, forgetting the concern of the moment and entering into the spirit of the exchange, said that time would make the Minister forget the hardship of the night, but begged him not to report to his government that in Mexico diplomats had to carry beds in their pocket! After the Cuban took off some of his garments, Madero continued the banter by exclaiming how slovenly their guest was and proceeded to fold the clothes neatly. Before going to sleep, Francisco expressed his desire to know where Gustavo was.

Márquez Sterling reported that, as the first light of dawn penetrated the room, Pino Suárez began a whispered monologue with him. It was as though he was arguing with himself:

They will never dare to touch General Angeles . . . As for us, we seem to be in the death house, do we not? Nevertheless, what is

[8] Lascuráin later asserted, in a sworn statement, that Huerta had pledged the freedom of the prisoners and that the resignations were not dependent on any conditions being fulfilled. In addition, he declared that Madero's requests, which he attributed to the failure of Gen. Huerta to provide the promised letter, came too late to be complied with. Maldonado, *Los asesinatos,* pp. 49-53.

[9] Márquez Sterling, *Los últimos días,* pp. 507-8.

dangerous is our liberty, not our existence. Our imposed resignation provokes revolution. To kill us would be equivalent to decreeing anarchy. I do not agree with Sr. Madero that the people will overthrow the traitors, rescuing their legitimate rulers. What the people will not consent to is that they should shoot us.

The speaker seemed to distrust his own logic, and the pessimism that dwelled within came to the surface.

What have I done to them that they should try to kill me? Politics have given me nothing but sorrows and deceptions. Believe me, I have wished only to do good . . . to respect the life and feeling of the citizens, to comply with the laws, and to exalt democracy . . . Is this the reason that they lead to the scaffold two honorable men who do not hate, intrigue, deceive, or profit? [10]

At 10 A.M. Márquez Sterling was still with the prisoners. Madero found it hard to believe that their lives were in danger, but Pino Suárez was more pessimistic. With a poetic sense of the tragic, but without recrimination, the unfortunate Vice-President lamented: "The same hatreds pursue me as the President, but without the compensation of his honors and glory. My fortune has to be sadder than yours, Sr. Madero." [11] Madero felt that they ought to seek the protection of the law, but his comrade believed that the only efficacious protection could come from the diplomatic corps. Márquez Sterling, before departing, promised to do what he could in the latter direction and to have the families of the two men initiate legal action in their behalf.

The choice between resignation and the lives of the prisoners had been a deceptive one. Once the resignations had been submitted, the lives of the prisoners were in great danger. The train which was to carry them to safety had been cancelled on the ground that it was feared a rescue might be attempted. This excuse was fortified by the announcement of General José Refugio Velasco, military commander in Veracruz, that he would continue to regard Madero as the legitimate executive until the Senate legalized the existing situation.

[10] *Ibid.*, pp. 510-17.
[11] *Ibid.*, p. 520.

Madero's request that General Angeles be in charge of the escort to Veracruz also aroused suspicions.

Real and feigned concern over such matters was symptomatic of the fact that the group which had come to power considered a freed Madero a serious threat to their position. Rodolfo Reyes frankly admitted that "Madero and Pino Suárez . . . were, [and] no one denies it, an indisputable danger for us . . . He who says that he thought of freeing them is lying."[12] The author of Huerta's "memoirs" declared that the new executive knew, from second hand, of "the tenacity of Madero and his faith in the triumph of the revolution" and that he "feared that one day he [Madero] would overthrow me [Huerta]."[13]

Although there was concern for the prisoners' safety in many quarters, it was natural that the families affected would be most apprehensive. Madero's wife, mother, and sisters left no stone unturned in their desperate effort to save their loved one and his associates. Madero's parents addressed a note to the diplomatic corps begging its members to interpose their good offices to obtain guarantees for the lives of the prisoners, and the distraught mother also composed the following telegram to President Taft:

Mexico, D.F. February 20, 1913

I pray you to intercede in order that the agreement made with my son Francisco, Jr., Pino Suárez, and his friends by General Huerta to permit them to go to Europe may be carried out. Their lives are in danger . . . They have a right to liberty because they are honorable men and this was the expressed condition on which he resigned, as is known to some of the foreign diplomatists who intervened in the matter. I address you as a mother in trouble who appeals to the only person whose influence can save the life of her son and assure him his liberty.

Mercedes G. de Madero[14]

[12] R. Reyes, *De mi vida,* II, 93-94.

[13] Joaquín Piña, the author of Huerta's "memoirs," was a journalist and an intimate associate of Huerta. While obviously he was not recording Huerta's exact words, he probably accurately reported Huerta's attitude on significant issues. Piña, *Memorias de . . . Huerta,* pp. 6-9.

[14] SDF, 812.00/M26/12.

Several foreign diplomats, alarmed by the danger to the prisoners, made energetic respresentations in their behalf. Most active in this respect was the representative of Cuba, Manuel Márquez Sterling. On February 19 the Cuban Minister wrote to Ambassador Wilson, in the latter's capacity as dean of the diplomatic corps, suggesting that the corps initiate steps "to avoid the useless sacrifice of the life of Sr. Madero," and he offered the use of the cruiser *Cuba,* anchored in Veracruz, as a transport to take the deposed executives into exile.[15]

Considering the feverish efforts of some of his colleagues, it is astounding that Ambassador Wilson would later blandly claim that "so far as I know, only one of my colleagues, Mr. Riquelme, the Chilean Minister, who was on intimate terms with the Madero family, felt concern for the future of the ex-President."[16] Márquez Sterling continued to urge united action by his fellow diplomats. The Japanese Minister, Hurigutchi, provided refuge in his nation's legation for the Madero family and carried their appeals to the diplomatic corps. The representatives of Brazil and Spain, though the latter followed Wilson's lead very closely, interviewed General Huerta in regard to the prisoners. Ambassador Wilson, accompanied by the German Minister, von Hintze, also visited the new executive, but his representation in behalf of the prisoners was not very energetic.

Petitions in behalf of the prisoners were not limited to those of the diplomats. José Vasconcelos called Wilson on the telephone on February 19, but the Ambassador assured him that there was no reason for concern, that Madero was in no danger, and that he would leave on a special train.[17] Deputy Luis Manuel Rojas, Grand Master of the Grand Lodge of the Valley of Mexico to which Madero and Pino Suárez belonged, invoked the bonds of Masonry to aid the prisoners. On February 20 he cabled President Taft as follows: "As Brother Mason I ask you to intervene in some way to protect the endangered

[15] Márquez Sterling, *Los últimos días,* pp. 483-84.
[16] Wilson, *Diplomatic Episodes,* p. 285.
[17] Vasconcelos, *Ulises criollo,* p. 438.

lives of F. I. Madero and J. María Pino Suárez."[18] The following day he visited Ambassador Wilson, also a Mason, with the same object. Concern for the prisoners was not restricted to the Mexican capital. A large number of state legislators in Texas wired the State Department urging that "every legitimate step be taken to save [the] life of former President Madero."[19]

Henry Lane Wilson was the key figure in the minds of those who desired to protect the prisoners. Wilson failed to perform the role that was intended for him. On February 19 he reported that General Huerta had asked his advice about whether "it was best to send the ex-President out of the country or place him in a lunatic asylum." Wilson replied that he "ought to do that which was best for the country." It was the following day that Wilson, accompanied by the German Minister, visited Huerta and "unofficially requested that the utmost precaution be taken to prevent the taking of his [Madero's] life or the life of the Vice-President except by due process of law[!]."[20] The State Department, apparently startled by these dispatches, promptly sent the Ambassador the following message marked "Confidential and Urgent":

> General Huerta's consulting you as to the treatment of Madero tends to give you a certain responsibility in the matter. It moreover goes without saying that cruel treatment of the ex-president would injure, in the eyes of the world, the reputation of Mexican civilization, and this Government earnestly hopes to hear of no such treatment and hopes to hear that he has been dealt with in a manner consistent with peace and humanity.
>
> Without assuming responsibility you may in your discretion make use of these ideas in your conversations with General Huerta.[21]

Not only by his government but also by his fellow diplomats and by Madero's family and friends the American representa-

[18] *La Prensa,* Feb. 12, 1933.

[19] Morris Sheppard to Secretary Knox, Feb. 21, 1913, SDF, 812.00/6295.

[20] Wilson to State Dept., Feb. 19 and 20, 1913, SDF, 812.00/6271 and 6277.

[21] State Dept. to Wilson, Feb. 20, 1913, SDF, 812.00/6271.

tive was urged to use his influence with the new government. On February 19 Márquez Sterling and the Japanese Minister brought the note of Madero's parents to the diplomatic corps to the American Embassy. The Cuban diplomat supported the Maderos' request for action by the corps, but Wilson said that that would be impossible. He specified that the ministers could interview Huerta on the matter individually but that they could not act in the name of the entire corps.[22]

The following afternoon, February 20, Sara Pérez de Madero, accompanied by her sister-in-law Mercedes, called at the American Embassy to deliver Madero's mother's telegram to President Taft and to request the intercession of the Ambassador. Of the four persons present during the interview—Mrs. Wilson accompanied her husband—only Sra. Madero recorded the conversation in detail. This was done in an interview with an American journalist more than three years after the exchange with Wilson took place, and under these circumstances it is doubtful that the "detail" could include more than general ideas and impressions. Nevertheless, the interview unquestionably made a singular impression on Sara Madero, and she has sworn to the correctness of the account. In addition, the general ideas attributed to Wilson correspond quite closely with his remarks to other persons and with his concepts as gleaned from his reports and other writings.[23]

The conversation with Wilson was conducted in English, and Sra. Madero was impressed by the Ambassador's brusque-

[22] Márquez Sterling, *Los últimos días,* pp. 487-88.

This attitude contrasted sharply with Wilson's activity and concern for the safety of the prisoners Félix Díaz and Bernardo Reyes in January and for de la Barra during the Decena Trágica. Wilson to State Dept., Jan. 14, 1913, SDF, 812.00/5865; Wilson, *Diplomatic Episodes,* pp. 269ff.

[23] Sra. Madero gave her account of the conversation with Ambassador Wilson in an interview with Robert Hammond Murray, correspondent in Mexico for the New York *World.* In 1927, Sra. Madero attested to the correctness of the interview before the American Vice-Consul in Mexico City. Gruening, *Mexico,* pp. 570-72.

Márquez Sterling met the Madero women as they were about to leave the Embassy, and Sra. Madero told him about the interview. The Cuban's report of Sra. Madero's immediate impressions parallels the tone of her statement to Murray. Márquez Sterling, *Los últimos días,* pp. 545-47.

ness. She told him that the reason for the visit was to seek protection for the lives of the prisoners. Wilson asked what she wanted him to do. Sra. Madero asked him to use his influence "to protect the lives of my husband and the other prisoners." The diplomat replied, "That is a responsibility that I do not care to undertake." Madero's wife gave Ambassador Wilson her mother-in-law's telegram to be forwarded to President Taft, and, though Wilson felt that it was unnecessary to send the message, at Sra. Madero's insistence he agreed to do so.

The American diplomat told Sra. Madero that her husband's downfall was due to the fact that he did not know how to govern and "that he never wanted to consult with me . . . You know, Madam, your husband had peculiar ideas." Apart from declaring that her husband had high ideals, Sra. Madero avoided any argument on this point and proceeded to ask for the same protection and assurance for the life of the Vice-President as she had asked for that of Madero. She reported that Ambassador Wilson impatiently replied that "Pino Suárez is a very bad man. I cannot give any assurance for his safety. He is to blame for most of your husband's troubles. That kind of man must disappear." Sra. Madero told him that Pino Suárez had a wife and six children who would be destitute in the event of his death, but, she claimed, Wilson merely shrugged his shoulders.

The Ambassador told her that Huerta had consulted him on what should be done with the prisoners. "I told him that he must do what is best for the interests of the country." At this point Mercedes Madero, interrupting, exclaimed, "Why did you say that? You know very well . . . that they are going to kill them!" Without answering, Wilson turned to Madero's wife, observing, "You know that your husband is unpopular. The people were not satisfied with him as President." If that was true, Sra. Madero asked, why was there any objection to his going into exile? Wilson replied, "You need not worry. The person of your husband will not be harmed." He told her that he knew the coup was going to happen and, therefore, had suggested that Madero resign. If that was so, Sra. Madero asked, why had he not warned her husband? Wilson bluntly stated, "That would not have been good policy, because then he would have prevented it." [24]

Despite the concern of the American government, some of his diplomatic colleagues, and Madero's family, there is no evidence, aside from several notes on minor matters, that Ambassador Wilson took steps beyond the two interviews with Huerta already described. Perhaps this was because, as he claimed, he did not realize that the lives of the prisoners were in real danger, perhaps it was because he was preoccupied with other matters. The American representative was busy condemning the old government, praising the new one, and urging its recognition. Apparently Wilson was more concerned about recognition than about humanity.

On February 20 he noted that "a wicked despotism has fallen" and that the installation of the new government had taken place "amid great popular demonstrations of approval." Later that evening he reported that the new government was "evidently secure" and requested that the department provide him with immediate instructions regarding recognition. He recommended that the department take into consideration "that the Provisional Government takes office in accordance with the Constitution and precedents." A further justification for recognition, and a good example of the criteria guiding the Ambassador, was reported two days later: "The atmosphere here is now entirely friendly and Americans are receiving more consideration than ever in the history of Mexico." [25]

The impatient Wilson did not wait for instructions. On the evening of February 20, "in view of the extreme urgency of the situation and in the absence of instructions," he assembled the diplomatic corps to discuss recognition. His excuse for this move was an invitation from Huerta to meet him at a formal reception at the Palace the following day at noon. Wilson

[24] Gruening, *Mexico*, pp. 570-72.

[25] Wilson to State Dept., Feb. 20 and 22, 1913, SDF, 812.00/6277, 6287, and 6326.

reported that his colleagues agreed with him that recognition was imperative to enable the new government to impose its authority and to reestablish order. The diplomats agreed to attend the function at the Palace. The following day, at the gathering in the Salon of Ambassadors, Wilson read a statement as dean of the corps, noting that he had been informed "that Your Excellency has assumed the high position of Interim President of the Republic, in accordance with the laws that exist in Mexico" and offering "our sincere congratulations." Huerta expressed his appreciation with appropriate phrases.[26] That evening, February 21, Wilson sent a circular telegram to all American consular officials advising them of the situation and instructing them "in the interest of Mexico [to] urge general submission and adhesion to the new government, which will be recognized by all foreign states today."[27] There was no foundation for this last assertion!

Shortly after the reception for the diplomatic corps Huerta met with his cabinet. The fate of the prisoners was discussed, and, apparently, it was decided to subject them to prosecution. The Subsecretary of Government was instructed to investigate what bases existed for legal action. On the afternoon of the following day another session was held, and Huerta advised his ministers that the prisoners were to be transferred to the Penitentiary of the Federal District. After the meeting, but with some of the ministers still present, Huerta advised Colonel Luis Ballesteros, an army officer, that he was to take charge of the prison and would be held responsible for the prisoners.

Two rurales officers, Major Francisco Cárdenas and Lieutenant Rafael Pimienta, were selected to transfer the prisoners. What additional instructions were given these officers and who gave them are matters which cannot be ascertained with certainty. However, according to the account attributed to Cárdenas, he was given a more important assignment than the mere transfer of the prisoners by General Blanquet, Military

[26] *La Prensa,* Feb. 12, 1933.
[27] SDF, 812.00/6325.

Commander of the Plaza. At the Ministry of War, the Secretary, General Mondragón, confirmed the arrangements, and Cárdenas received the impression that Huerta and the cabinet approved. Indeed, this account alleged that Cárdenas received personal confirmation from Huerta. Cecilio Ocón, who had prepared Pimienta for his role, was to arrange various details—the cars and a simulated rescue attack on the party.[28]

Meanwhile, in the Intendancy of the National Palace the prisoners lived in an atmosphere of deepening gloom. An occasional visitor, the writing of a letter, and the changing of the guard were the only interruptions of the slowly passing time. Pino Suárez's letter to Deputy Serapio Rendón of Yucatán offers a glimpse of the prisoners' thoughts during those long hours:

Dear Serapio,

Excuse that I should write you with pencil . . . As you know, we have been obliged to resign our respective posts. However, that does not mean that we are safe. God will have the final word. I urge you, if something bad happens to me, to try to console my wife. The poor woman has suffered a great deal. You know how much we have loved each other.

I refuse to believe that they would harm us after the humiliation of which we have been victims. What would they gain . . .?

It is said that tomorrow we will be taken to the Penitentiary . . . The President is not so optimistic as I am [regarding the prospect of the move] for last night on retiring he told me that we would never leave the Palace alive. I guard my fears in order not to dishearten him . . . But will they have the stupidity to kill us? You know, Serapio, that they would gain nothing for we would be greater in death than we are today in life . . .

José Ma. Pino Suárez[29]

Word of the death of Gustavo, which Madero heard from the lips of his mother late in the morning or early in the afternoon of February 22, left the former-President disconsolate with grief and filled with gloom. When the prisoners went to bed

[28] Mellado, *Crímenes del Huertismo,* pp. 30-35.
[29] De Bekker, *Huerta,* pp. 175-77.

that night at ten o'clock, Angeles noted that Madero buried his head beneath his blanket and believed that he was crying for Gustavo.

About twenty minutes after the prisoners had retired, Colonel Joaquín Chicarro entered the suite followed by Major Cárdenas. The prisoners were ordered to get up, and Angeles demanded to know what was transpiring. Chicarro told him that Madero and Pino Suárez were being transferred to the Penitentiary. As they dressed hurriedly, Madero wanted to know why they had not been notified before, but the question remained unanswered. Madero embraced Angeles before leaving the room, but Pino Suárez, who had reached the patio before he realized that he had not bid the General farewell, waved his hand and shouted, "Good-bye, my General." [30]

Madero was directed to a closed automobile while Pino Suárez was told to enter a Peerless parked near by. Each car had a chauffeur, and there was an aide in the front seat of the Peerless. Cárdenas and another officer guarded Madero while Pimienta had a similar assistant in the car with Pino Suárez. The two cars moved slowly out of the National Palace. At the door of the Penitentiary of the Federal District Madero prepared to leave the car, but Cárdenas ordered him to wait. Cárdenas got out of the car and spoke with a person who came out of the Penitentiary.[31]

After a few moments, Cárdenas returned to the car and ordered the chauffeur to take the road along the north side of the prison. According to some accounts Madero said nothing after entering the car, but some say that he demanded to know why they were being taken beyond the door of the Penitentiary. Cárdenas reportedy told him that they were going to the "back door" to avoid arousing curiosity. The cars turned right and stopped near the middle of the east wall. All the outside lights of the prison were turned on, a fact

[30] Márquez Sterling, *Los últimos días*, p. 571.

[31] One investigator believed that this person might have been Col. Ballesteros. However, in the account attributed to Cárdenas, the person was said to be Cecilio Ocón. Maldonado, *Los asesinatos*, p. 11; P. González Blanco, *De . . . Díaz a Carranza*, p. 106.

which circumstantially points to complicity by the new prison director.

The prisoners were ordered out of the cars and shot by their escort, Cárdenas was charged as being principally responsible for the death of Madero and Pimienta for the death of Pino Suárez. The escort riddled the cars with bullets to provide evidence of an "attack," and then the bodies were brought into the Penitentiary. An autopsy revealed that Madero had died of two bullets which entered his head. Pino Suárez had died of three head wounds, but there were five other bullets in his body.[32] Madero, who refused to murder, was the first Mexican president to be assassinated. Although the ultimate responsibility for the murders is difficult to place,[33] the deaths tended to discredit the Huerta administration and the Ciudadela movement.

It was not until the morning of February 24 that the bodies were handed over to the families for burial. With no pomp the remains of the late President were transported in an electric funeral car to the French Cemetery for interment. The police directed that the coffin remain closed, but it was opened slightly to insert a crucifix at the instance of the widow. That evening Sra. Madero, accompanied by her late husband's parents and sisters and by Ernesto Madero and his family, departed for Veracruz where they embarked for Havana. Emilio, Alfonso, and Raúl Madero fled to the United States.

[32] Maldonado, *Los asesinatos*, pp. 12-13; *La Prensa*, Feb. 12, 1933.

[33] While the actual assassinations were committed by the escort, the trail of responsibility led to the office of the Commanding General of the Plaza and the War Department. Huerta never was cleared completely of the charge of complicity. The failure of the cabinet members to resign when they learned of the deaths or to pursue the guilty placed the group in an unfavorable light. *El Universal*, Oct. 7, 1915, Nov. 9, 12, 14, and 28, 1917, and March 4, 1926; *Excelsior*, Feb. 23 and 25 and March 3, 1926.

XX. The Revolution Goes On

THE GOVERNMENT released an official version of the death of the prisoners. It was stated that the convoy transferring the prisoners to the Penitentiary had been attacked and the prisoners were shot while trying to escape. Hardly anyone believed the official account. Some of the ministers, deciding to investigate the affair, ordered Cárdenas to appear, but they learned from the Secretary of War that he had left the city on orders. Later he was promoted by Huerta. Although the administration promised action, no official investigation was undertaken and no punishments were meted out.[1]

Despite the heinous crime the political change continued to be celebrated in some quarters. *El Mañana,* less than a week after the double murder, observed that its work "has ended," while a Catholic daily reported that there had been a demonstration by women at La Soledad Church in Oaxaca "to give thanks to the august patroness for having conceded the sal-

[1] When the federal army was defeated in 1914, Cárdenas fled from Mexico to Guatemala disguised as a mule driver. After the successful armed movement of Obregón against Carranza, the Maderistas hoped for justice. The Pro-Madero Committee brought charges against Pimienta and Cárdenas. The latter was taken prisoner and interned in Guatemala City after the Obregón government requested his extradition. However, before Guatemalan President Estrada Cabrera could comply with the request, Cárdenas committed suicide on Nov. 30, 1920.

Pimienta, by then a general officer, was charged formally in Nov. 1920. In his preliminary statements he asserted that his companion on the night of Feb. 22, Agustín Figueras, was responsible for the death of the prisoner. Pimienta was indicted and consigned to a military court which proceeded to absolve him. In Dec., 1923, he arose in rebellion in the state of Mexico in connection with the de la Huerta movement and was killed.

vation of the Republic."[2] However, the assassinations shocked Mexico City, and resentment because of them was reported from other sections of the country. A wave of indignation swept the United States. Only Ambassador Wilson, lacking in sensitivity and political acumen, remained unruffled and indifferent.

On February 23 de la Barra gave the diplomatic corps the official version of the deaths and promised a full investigation. Wilson reported that the tragedy had produced no effect and that he was disposed to accept the government's account. Having thus disposed of this issue to his own satisfaction, the Ambassador urged that the State Department inform the American public "of the friendly disposition of this Government towards the United States and of the activity it is displaying in restoring order." What the American representative most desired was to obtain recognition of the Huerta regime. However, Secretary Knox informed him on February 25 that "for the present" formal recognition was not to be accorded "except upon specific instructions from the Department to do so." Within a few hours a nettled Wilson asked the Department to be "more specific" and warned of "embarrassment in our transactions and perhaps the loss of some vantage ground already taken."[3]

Apparently Wilson considered it necessary to explain his conduct and justify his policy. He submitted the following information for the consideration of the President and the Secretary of State:

> That the government of Madero during its entire existence was anti-American and that neither appeals nor veiled threats affected it in its incomprehensible attitude; that during the last three and perhaps six months of its existence it presented the aspect of a despotism infinitely worse than that which existed under General Díaz; that though the new government resulted from an armed revolution . . . it nevertheless assumed office according to the usual constitutional precedents . . .; that the new Administration is evi-

[2] *El Mañana,* Feb. 28, 1913; *El País,* Feb. 26, 1913.

[3] Wilson to State Dept., Feb. 23 and 24; Knox to American Embassy, Feb. 25; and Wilson to State Dept., Feb. 25, 1913, SDF, 812.00/6323, 6353, 6379A, and 6380.

dently approved and accepted by Mexican public opinion and especially by the more respectable part thereof . . . and . . . by the foreign elements . . .; that anti-American sentiment has almost entirely disappeared; and that the new government is showing decided pro-American proclivities . . .

Moved by these considerations . . . I am endeavoring in all possible ways and frequently on my own responsibility to aid this Government to establish itself firmly and to procure the submission and adhesion of all elements in the Republic.[4]

Among the steps Wilson took was another message directing American consuls to exert themselves ceaselessly to obtain the general submission the Ambassador desired. However, American public opinion, aroused by the shocking crime, could not be ignored, and two days later Secretary Knox advised Wilson that practically the entire American press was distressed by the tragedy and "treated as inadequate the explanations of the Huerta regime," which "cannot expect to escape public suspicion."[5] The Secretary of State urged a policy of circumspection and suggested the propriety of some modification of the Ambassador's telegram to all consular officials.

Henry Lane Wilson was not to be discouraged or deterred from his purpose. He discounted disturbances and spoke of general adhesion to the new regime and of peace being "general throughout the Republic." On March 1, Wilson precipitously reported that Carranza had submitted to the provisional government and concluded that the "outlook is for greater peace in the Republic than has been known for years." Four days later he confidently predicted that "Carranza's rebellion" would be put down.[6] These optimistic reports were intended to encourage a favorable decision on the question of recognition. Because of public opinion and the fact that President-Elect Woodrow Wilson would shortly assume the office, the Taft administration preferred to maintain a *status quo* attitude toward the Mexican situation.

[4] Wilson to State Dept., Feb. 26, 1913, SDF, 812.00/6394.

[5] Knox to American Embassy, Feb. 28, 1913, SDF, 812.00/6431A.

[6] Wilson to State Dept., Feb. 27 and 28 and March 1 and 5, 1913, SDF, 812.00/6412, 6433, 6447, and 6505.

After the new government had taken office in the United States, Ambasador Wilson continued to defend his conduct, to report favorably on the situation, and to advocate recognition. On March 12 he submitted a detailed report to Secretary of State Bryan explaining his action during and after the Decena Trágica. Although the substance of this report was drawn from his telegrams of those ten days, the Ambassador did expand on some of his ideas. He attacked the Madero government, which, he charged, had degenerated rapidly into "a despotism of the worst character accompanied by the worst possible evidences of corruption, incompetence, impotency, inefficiency and nepotism." And, as though these charges were not enough, Wilson described the late President as follows:

> Madero came to power as an apostle of liberty, but he was simply a man of disordered intellect who happened to be in the public eye at the psychological moment... In the last days of his government... his mental qualities, always abnormal, developed all the characteristics of that dangerous form of lunacy of which the best example in ancient times is a Nero and in modern times a Castro.[7]

Regarding the President's death, Ambassador Wilson asserted that the tragedy was, to him, unexpected. He declared that, under the circumstances, everything possible had been done to save Madero's life. "If I had been in the slightest degree apprehensive of any intention on the part of the government to deal foully with the ex-President, I might have been more agitated and more vehement, but not more active." Inclined to credit the official version of the incident or to ascribe it to a subordinate military conspiracy to which the government was not a party, Wilson explained his public acceptance of the official version as the only course open to him and as "the surest method of arresting hasty judgment and of allaying that singular and perverse sentimentality which frequently leads to the commission of greater crimes as punishments for lesser ones." He cynically noted that, besides, regardless of how revolting the crime, he could not see the reason for American concern and agitation over the death of two Mexi-

[7] Wilson to State Dept., March 12, 1913, SDF, 812.00/6840.

cans "relegated to private life by their resignations." [8] Wilson had no doubts as to the legal constitution of the Huerta government and recommended recognition on the grounds of "expediency and interest."

The Ambassador, in his telegraphic reports, sought to minimize the nature and extent of the revolt against Huerta and to describe favorably the degree of the government's control over the country. His opinions were frequently contradicted by the reports of American consuls. Early in March, while Wilson was busily reporting confidence in the new administration and the prospect of peace, Consul Philip Hanna at Monterrey advised the State Department that the state of Coahuila was in rebellion. On March 8, Wilson, with questionable concern, stated that his "only fear" was that there would be a "general slaughter of Carranza's forces by the federals." Three days later, with a zest that belied his reported anxiety, he telegraphed that Carranza had been defeated near Saltillo with a loss of between "fifty to one hundred" and was driven to Monclova where he "is now being surrounded and his forces in all probability will be dispersed." In contrast, the consul at Ciudad Porfirio Díaz reported three days later that Carranza's success at Monclova was unquestionable and that his forces were increasing in number.[9]

Ambassador Wilson continued to recommend the recognition of Huerta's provisional government. He reported such action as taken by Spain, France, Austria, Hungary, Japan, Italy, Germany, Portugal, China, Belgium, Norway, Russia, and several other nations. Time and again he urged similar action by the United States on "the high grounds of international polity, American interests, and for the procurement of peace and order in Mexico." As time passed and the Wilson administration refused to follow the course indicated, the Ambassador reported that the failure to recognize was causing a rising tide

[8] *Ibid.;* Wilson, *Diplomatic Episodes,* p. 286; *Investigation of Mexican Affairs* (Senate Document 285, 66th Congr., 1st sess.), p. 2278.

[9] Wilson to State Dept., March 8 and 11, 1913; Consul Luther Ellsworth to State Dept., March 14, 1913, SDF, 812.00/6571, 6631, and 6693.

of bitterness and resentment and that it was impossible for the Embassy to transact any kind of business with the government.[10]

The new American President and the Ambassador had the same last name, but there the similarity ended. They differed in background and personality and on criteria for policy. Henry Lane Wilson held Woodrow Wilson's and Secretary of State Bryan's knowledge of Mexico and the situation there in utter contempt. President Wilson, in turn, distrusted his representative in Mexico. Therefore, he sent William Bayard Hale and other agents to Mexico. The presence of these agents, whose reports tended to confirm and increase the President's suspicions regarding the Ambassador, was resented bitterly by Henry Lane Wilson. This situation was mutually intolerable, and, on July 8, 1913, Ambasador Wilson was recalled to Washington for "consultation." On his arrival in New York the diplomat, "for the purpose of arousing public opinion," gave reporters an outline of conditions in Mexico, which he later pompously described as "furnishing the first true picture." [11]

His clique in Mexico swamped the State Department with telegrams and even sent a delegation armed with a thirty-nine-page pamphlet to Washington to defend the Ambassador. Nothing could save him.[12] Secretary Bryan informed Wilson that the President had decided to accept his resignation. Early in October, Henry Lane Wilson returned to private life, but the reaction to his conduct lingered with deleterious effect on Mexican-American relations.

Ambassador Wilson, by his conduct and reports, had harassed and tended to discredit the Madero government. Unquestionably, his attitude helped to deprive the administration of

[10] Wilson to State Dept., April 9 and July 11, 1913, SDF, 812.00/7066 and 8027.

[11] Wilson, *Diplomatic Episodes*, p. 312.

[12] Cook, *Facts Submitted by American Colony to President Wilson;* Stephenson, *John Lind of Minnesota*, p. 214.

Ambassador Wilson attributed his removal to partisan politics and alleged that Woodrow Wilson's Mexican policy was a factor in the German decision to precipitate a European war! *Diplomatic Episodes*, p. 335.

public confidence, to weaken it, and to encourage the opposition. During the Decena Trágica the American representative placed himself in opposition to the Madero government and abetted the conspiracy to overthrow it. Wilson was charged with complicity in the murders of Madero and Pino Suárez to the extent that they were committed with his knowledge, if not his consent. His extraordinary activity in behalf of the Huerta government lent color, if not substantiation, to the charge. Direct responsibility never has been proven, but the American diplomat cannot escape moral responsibility because he failed to employ his influence to prevent the double tragedy. An energetic, unequivocal warning by Wilson would have rendered resort to the *ley fuga* most unlikely. In any event, Venustiano Carranza officially charged the American Embassy with a large part of the responsibility for the state of affairs in Mexico,[13] and the opinion persisted to cast a shadow on the relations between the two nations for years.

Woodrow Wilson was distressed by the existence of the Huerta government, a dictatorship which had come to power through violence. It was to the Mexican problem that he first applied his concept of a foreign policy based on explicit moral considerations. He refused to recognize the new government and sent John Lind as his personal representative to the troubled nation. Lind's mission was to arrange for the diplomatic elimination of Huerta, the end of the civil war, the holding of free elections, and the accomplishment of the reforms which would satisfy the desires of the Mexican people. Huerta was obdurate, and Wilson, regarding his conduct as defiance, permitted arms to be shipped to those who, under Carranza, were fighting to destroy the Huerta regime.

Within two days after he had assumed the provisional presidency with the approval of the Chamber of Deputies, Huerta had been recognized by the army, by twenty-three of the twenty-seven governors, and by the Supreme Court. When the news of the assassinations spread, discontent became vocal

[13] "Manifesto to the Nation," June 11, 1915, in Secretaría de Gobernación, *Memoria . . . 1913-16,* p. 341.

and opposition took form. The deaths of Madero and Pino Suárez provided a mighty banner for the revolutionary movement against the Huerta regime, which aimed to restore constitutional government under revolutionary control.

Groups in Sonora, Durango, Chihuahua, Coahuila, Zacatecas, and Sinaloa assumed a hostile attitude. On March 26, Venustiano Carranza issued the Plan of Guadalupe under which he rejected the government of Huerta and launched an armed rebellion to reestablish constitutional government. In Sonora, Governor Maytorena refused to recognize Huerta and requested a leave from the local congress. Subsequently, the state legislature disavowed Huerta, and Benjamín Hill and Alvaro Obregón took the lead in military preparations in that state. Francisco Villa launched a rebellion in Chihuahua in memory of Francisco Madero. In other areas irregular forces of Maderista origin arose to defy the provisional government. And, in the south, Zapata continued to rebel, carrying on high the banner of agrarian reform.

Huerta, faced by the hostility of the American government and the swelling tide of opposition, was obsessed by his political insecurity. He resorted increasingly to terrorism and violence. Several deputies, including Pino Suárez's friend Serapio Rendón, perished, presumably murdered. Governors Antonio Hidalgo (Tlaxcala), Rafael Cepeda (San Luis Potosí), Alberto Fuentes D. (Aguascalientes), and Abraham González (Chihuahua) were arrested. The last-named was brutally slain when his captors threw him under the wheels of a moving train.

On September 23, 1913, Dr. Belisario Domínguez of Chiapas rose in the Senate and asked the upper chamber to depose Huerta, who, he said, was haunted by the ghost of Madero to the point of insanity, which alone could explain the policy of terror.[14] On October 7 the courageous doctor disappeared. When members of Congress tried to protest, Huerta closed the national legislature by force of arms, arresting many of its members. He usurped the legislative and judicial powers and

[14] Lamicq, *Criollos, indios y mestizos,* pp. 125-32.

ruled an unveiled dictatorship with a terroristic program. Harassed in the south, his armies suffering defeats in the north and northwest, and faced by the persistent and determined opposition of Woodrow Wilson, Huerta finally resigned in July, 1914.

If Francisco I. Madero in life had inaugurated the first phase of the revolution, in death he divided Mexico politically and militarily and ushered in, indeed provided the immediate justification for, the united war against Huerta. The bitterness, the warfare, and the chaos were not to end with the downfall of Victoriano Huerta. The unity of opposition became the disunity of victory. More violence was to follow and more blood was to be spilled, but in the process a revolutionary program was to evolve.

Francisco Madero's detractors have described him as everything from a misguided visionary to a mentally unbalanced person, while his followers have proclaimed his as a redeemer and an apostle. Actually he was a sincere, well-intentioned idealist. His conduct was influenced by a generous, emotional, and overly optimistic, overly enthusiastic nature. In his private life his conduct was exemplary and temperate in an environment characterized by intemperance. Driven by a compulsion compounded of humanitarian and patriotic considerations, Madero sacrificed the comforts and glowing prospects of his private life to enter the arena of politics.

In a few brief months he was catapulted from relative obscurity to the top level of political action and prominence. Through his book, his correspondence, his political organizing, and his campaigns, he contributed to the awakening of his country and laid the foundation for popular response to and support of the revolution which followed. His was an amazing demonstration of energy, courage, and determination. Madero the candidate was truly the "Apostle of Democracy."

The armed movement which Madero began marked the close of an era and the inauguration of a profound social and political revolution. By his political and military action Madero set in motion the forces of discontent which were to carry the

Mexican Revolution far beyond what the man from Coahuila desired or even contemplated. As the leader of an armed rebellion Madero was adequate, if not outstanding, and he did provide the revolution with a visible head and what little unity and cohesion it possessed. Instead of pushing the revolution to complete victory, Madero compromised at Ciudad Juárez. That the revolution was halted before its complete triumph was obtained—indeed, before a solid foundation in terms of unity and program had been created—was due to the leader's humanitarianism, to his hope to legalize the situation and to follow a policy of conciliation and cooperation with all factions, all interests, and all Mexicans, and to the deleterious conservative influence of some members of Madero's family.

Madero's administration was brief and difficult. It has been said that he failed as a man of government. He suffered from lack of political experience, and his relatives, with some exceptions, were like a dead-weight anchor on the ship of state. Madero tried to compromise with those who would not compromise, to reconcile the irreconciliable. He vacillated, torn between his democratic ideals and techniques sanctioned by tradition and recommended by his followers and the exigencies of the situation. He not only believed in political democracy but made an earnest, reasonably consistent effort to apply it. Francisco Madero tried to embark on a new political way of life without the existence or creation of a new political environment. Mexico was not ready for political democracy, nor was that the urgent need of her people. Madero visualized that as the immediate goal and as the means for a gradual accomplishment of other reforms. He did not lack energy or will, but rather intuition and understanding of the Revolution which he had initiated and of which he became the symbol. Madero failed to sense the urgent necessity and widespread demand for immediate, far-reaching change.

Despite these limitations his efforts were well-intentioned and his accomplishments not to be overlooked. Labor enjoyed freedom, agrarian reform was studied, and humble beginnings of change initiated; education was promoted, and democratic principles were applied. These efforts and results were not inconsiderable in the light of the overwhelming difficulties which confronted his government: the press antagonistic, the conservatives entrenched and opposed; the foreign elements distrustful; and the revolutionaries divided and demanding. Armed rebellions discredited the administration while absorbing its energies and resources and threatening its very existence. The discharge of the insurgent forces, a mistaken policy opposed by the revolutionists, made the government dependent on the federal army. The uprisings increased that dependence. Madero was at the point of overcoming his enemies and, many believe, was moving or would have moved in the direction that the Revolution demanded when treachery cut short his regime.

With his death Francisco Madero achieved once more unquestioned greatness and success. Madero's assassination was regarded by the insurrectionists as a blow at the Revolution. His martyrdom accomplished, at least for a time, what he had been unable to do while alive: unite all the revolutionists under one banner. Pino Suárez was correct when he predicted that destroyed Madero and he would achieve greater stature. Under the halo of martyrdom all Madero's errors, faults, and limitations were forgotten. Remembered were his ideals, his virtues, and his sacrifice. "Like all apostles . . . they hated him unto death and glorified him unto immortality." [15]

[15] Seoane, *Méjico,* p. 13.

Bibliography

Abbreviations

AdeAV	Archive of Antonio F. Villarreal
AdeGG	Archive of Federico González Garza
AdeM	Archive of Francisco I. Madero
AdeRC	Archive of Ramón Corral
AdeTD	Archive of Teodoro Dehesa
AdeV	Archive of José C. Valadés
AdeZ	Archive of Emiliano Zapata
CdeFFP	Correspondence of Félix F. Palavicini
CdelaB	Correspondence of Francisco L. de la Barra
CdeM	Correspondence of Francisco I. Madero
SDF	United States, State Department Files

Bibliography

The cornerstone of bibliographical compilations for the period of the Mexican Revolution is Ignacio B. Castillo's *Bibliografía de la Revolución mexicana* (Mexico City, 1918). Subsequent publications were included in Roberto Ramos's three-volume *Bibliografía de la Revolución mexicana* (Mexico City, 1931-40). In addition, the *Hispanic American Historical Review* contains three helpful compilations: C. K. Jones, "Bibliography of the Mexican Revolution," I, No. 4 (Nov., 1918), 480-81; Jones's "Hispanic American Bibliographies—Mexico, Nueva España," VI, No. 2 (May, 1921), 753-985; and H. I. Priestley, "Mexican Literature of the Recent Revolution," II, No. 2 (May, 1919), 286-311.

MANUSCRIPTS AND PRIVATE ARCHIVAL MATERIALS

Barra, Francisco L. de la, Archivo de. Used with permission of Col. Magaña Cerda.

Bonilla, Manuel, Jr. Memorias. Typed at Mazatlán, Jan. 31, 1925, and Dec., 1927. In possession of José C. Valadés. Manuscript.

Corral, Ramón, Archivo de. Published in *La Prensa* (San Antonio), 1937, and in *La Opinión* (Los Angeles), 1937.

Dehesa, Teodoro, Archivo de. In possession of José C. Valadés.

González Garza, Federico, Archivo de. Used with permission of owner.

Leyva, José María. Cuento de expedición a Baja California. In possession of José C. Valadés. Manuscript.

Madero, Francisco I., Archivo de. Located in home of the late Alfredo Alvarez. A selection of this correspondence has been published in *La Prensa* (San Antonio), 1931-38, and in *La Opinión* (Los Angeles), 1931-38, by José C. Valadés.

Madero, Francisco I., Correspondencia de. 4 vols. covering May-June, 1911. Biblioteca Nacional.

Muñoz Lumbier. Incidentes prerevolucionarios en Pachuca. In possession of José C. Valadés. Manuscript.

Palavicini, Félix F., Correspondencia de. Used with permission of Ing. Palavicini.

Rangel, J. M. Ricardo Flores Magón. In possession of José C. Valadés. Manuscript.

Valadés, José C., Archivo de. Used with permission of owner.

Villarreal, Gen. Antonio F., Archivo de. Published in *La Prensa* (San Antonio), 1934-35.

Zapata, Emiliano, Archivo de. Used with permission of Col. Magaña Cerda.

Government Documents

Barra, Francisco León de la. "Informe leído por el C. Presidente Interino de la República al abrirse el tercer período de sesiones del 25 Congreso de la Unión el 16 de septiembre de 1911," in Diario Oficial, 66, No. 14, 209-18.

—— Informe leído ante la Cámara de Diputados sobre los actos administrativos de su gobierno durante el período comprendido del 26 de mayo al 4 de noviembre de 1911. Mexico City, 1911.

Díaz, Porfirio. Informe que en el último día de su período constitucional da a sus compatriotas . . . 1880. Mexico City.

—— Informe que . . . 1888. Mexico City.

—— Informe que . . . 1892. Mexico City.

—— Informe que . . . 1896. Mexico City.

—— Informe que . . . 1900. Mexico City.

—— "Informe al H. Congreso de la República, el 16 de septiembre de 1904," in Diario de los debates de la Cámara de Senadores, 22 Congreso, 1 período. Mexico City, 1904.

—— "Informe al H. Congreso de la República, el 16 de septiembre de 1909," in Diario de los debates de la Cámara de Diputados del Congreso de los E. U. Mexicanos, 24 Congreso, 1 período, 2 Año. Mexico City, 1909.

—— "Informe leído . . . al Congreso de la Unión, el 16 de septiembre de 1910," in Diario Oficial, 60, 141 ff.

González, Manuel. Manifiesto que en el último día . . . da a sus compatriotas. Mexico City, 1884.

Huerta, Victoriano. Informe leído por el C. Presidente de la República al abrirse el segundo período de sesiones del 26 Congreso de la Unión, el 1 de abril de 1913. Mexico City, 1913.

Investigation of Mexican Affairs. Report and Hearing before a subcommittee on Foreign Relations, Senator Albert Fall presiding, pursuant to Senate Resolution 106, United States Senate, 66th Congress, 1st session. Senate Document No. 285. 2 vols. (Serial nos. 7665 and 7666). Washington, Government Printing Office, 1920.

Madero, Francisco I. "Informe leído por el C. Presidente de la República Mexicana al abrirse el cuarto período de sesiones del 25 Congreso de la Unión, el 1 de abril de 1912," in Diario Oficial, 119, No. 27, 405-13.

—— "Informe leído por el C. Presidente de la República al abrirse el primer período del 26 Congreso de la Unión, el 16 de septiembre de 1912," in Diario Oficial, 122, No. 13, 137-49.

Papers Relating to the Foreign Relations of the United States, 1910-1917. 8 vols. (Serial nos. 5945, 6183, 6367, 6598, 6786, 6955, 7127, 7331). Washington, Government Printing Office, 1918-26.

Secretaría de la Defensa Nacional. Documentos correspondientes a los sucesos y defensa de la "Ciudadela" por los Generales Manuel Mondragón y Félix Díaz durante los días del 9 a 18 de febrero de 1913. Archivo de la Defensa Nacional, D-041-12.

—— Relación de los CC. Aspirantes que fueron internados en la Penitenciaría del D. F. por haber defeccionado en febrero de 1913. Archivo de la Defensa Nacional, D-041-14.

Secretaría de la Economía Nacional, Dirección General de Estadística. Tercer censo de población. Mexico City, 1910.

Secretaría de Gobernación. Memoria de la Secretaría de Gobernación, 1913-16. Mexico City, Talleres Linotipos de Revista de Revistas, 1916.

Secretaría de Guerra y Marina. Campaña de 1910 a 1911: La 2 zona militar. Mexico City, Talleres de Departamento de Estado Mayor, 1913.

Secretaría de Hacienda. Cuenta de la Hacienda Pública Federal. Mexico City, 1913. Covers the period 1911-12.

—— Cuenta de la Hacienda Pública Federal. Mexico City, 1914. Covers the period 1912-13.

United States, Department of State, Archives. Files 812.00/322-9325 and 812.002/1-25. Washington, D. C.

OTHER PUBLISHED WORKS

Agrupación Pro-Madero. Reseña de las ceremonias conmemorativas, 22 de febrero de 1920, ed. by Executive Committee of Agrupación Pro-Madero. Mexico City, 1920.

Aguilar, Rafael. Madero sin máscara. 1st ed. Mexico City, Impr. Popular, 1911.

Aguirre Berlanga, Manuel. Revolución y reforma: Genesis legal de la revolución constitucionalista. Vol. I. Mexico City, Impr. Nacional, 1918.

Alessio Robles, Miguel. Historia política de la Revolución. 3d ed. Mexico City, Ediciones Botas, 1946.

—— Obregón como militar. Mexico City, Edit. Cultural, 1935.

Alvarez, Alfredo. Madero y su obra. Mexico City, Talleres Gráficos de la Nación, 1935. Documents.

Amaya, Juan Gualberto. Madero y los auténticos revolucionarios de 1910. Mexico City, 1946.

Amezcua, Gen. Genaro (ed.). México revolucionario a los pueblos de Europa y América, 1910-18. Havana, Impr. Espinosa, 1918. A collection of documents, speeches, and articles about the Zapata movement.

Aragón, Alfredo. El desarme del ejército federal por la revolución de 1913. Paris, Wellhoff at Roche, 1915.

Araquistain, Luis. La Revolución mejicana: Sus orígenes, sus hombres, su obra. Madrid, Cía. Ibero-Americana de Publicaciones, 1929.

Arenales, Ricardo (pseud. Emigdio S. Paniagua). El combate de la Ciudadela. Mexico City, Tip. Artística, 1913.

Baerlein, Henry. Mexico, Land of Unrest. 2d ed. Philadelphia, Lippincott, 1914.

Baker, Ray Stannard. Woodrow Wilson. 9 vols. Garden City, N.Y., Doubleday Page, 1927-39.

Bancroft, Hubert Howe. History of Mexico, 1516-1887. (Vol. V of History of the Pacific States of North America.) San Francisco, A. L. Bancroft, 1883-88.

Barragán Rodríguez, Juan B. Historia del ejército y de la revolución constitucionalista. 2 vols. Mexico City, Talleres de la Edit. Stylo, 1946.

Beals, Carleton. Mexico, An Interpretation. New York, B. W. Heubsch, 1923.

—— Porfirio Díaz, Dictator of Mexico. Philadelphia, Lippincott, 1932.

Becerra, Marcos E. Palavicini. Mexico City, Talleres Linotipos de El Hogar, 1924.

Bell, Edward I. Political Shame of Mexico. New York, McBride, Nast, 1914.

Beltrán, Joaquín. La toma de la Plaza de H. Veracruz. Mexico City, Herrero Hnos. Sucesores, 1930.

Bonilla, Manuel, Jr. Diez años de guerra: Sinopsis de la historia verdadera de la Revolución mexicana. 1st part, 1910-13. Mazatlán, Impr. Avendano, 1922.

—— El régimen maderista. Mexico City, Talleres Linotipos de El Universal, 1922.

Breceda, Alfredo. México revolucionario, 1913-17. Vol. I. Madrid, Tip. Artística Cervantes, 1920.

Brenner, Anita, and George R. Leighton. The Wind That Swept Mexico. New York, Harper, 1943.

Buletín del Primer Congreso Nacional Espiritista. Nos. 1-10, 13, Jan. 25 to March 29, 1906 and April 8, 1906.

Bulnes, Francisco. El verdadero Díaz y la Revolución. Mexico City, Eusebio Gómez de la Fuente, 1920.

—— The Whole Truth About Mexico: President Wilson's Responsibility. Translated by Dora Scott. New York, Mr. Bulnes Book Co., 1916.

Cabrera, Luis (pseud. Blas Urrea). Obras políticas. Mexico City, Impr. Nacional, 1921.

Calero, Manuel. Cuestiones electorales. Mexico City, Impr. de Ignacio Escalante, 1908.

—— Un decenio de política mexicana. New York, Middleditch, 1920.

—— El problema actual: La vice-presidencia en la república. Mexico City, Impr. de Ignacio Escalante, 1903.

Callahan, James Morton. American Foreign Policy in Mexican Relations. New York, Macmillan, 1932.

Callcott, Wilfred Hardy. Liberalism in Mexico, 1857-1929. Palo Alto, Calif., Stanford University Press, 1931.

[Carillo, Adolfo]. Memorias inéditas de don Sebastián Lerdo de Tejada. Brownsville, Texas, Tip. El Porvenir, 1893.

Casasola, Agustín V. Historia gráfica de la Revolución, 1900-40. Mexico City.

Case, Alden B. Thirty Years with the Mexicans. London, Fleming H. Revill Co., 1917.

Castillo, José R. del. Historia de la revolución social de México. Mexico City, 1915.

Cline, Howard. The United States and Mexico. Cambridge, Mass., Harvard University Press, 1953.

Colima, Federico de la. Madero y el Gral. Díaz. Mexico City, Edit. Guerra y Vázquez, 1913.

Comité Ejecutivo Electoral Antireeleccionista. Memorial presentado a la Cámara de Diputados pidiendo la nulidad de las elecciones. Mexico City, Impr. Idea Libre, 1910.

Cook, G. W. Facts Submitted by American Colony to President Wilson . . . Mexico City, 1913.

Creelman, James. Díaz, Master of Mexico. New York, Appleton, 1911.

—— "Interview with Porfirio Díaz," *Pearson's Magazine,* XIX, No. 3 (March, 1908), 241-77.

Cuevas, Mariano. Historia de la iglesia en México. Vol. 5. El Paso, Texas, Edit. Revista Católica, 1928.

DeBekker, Leander Jan. De cómo vino Huerta y cómo se fué: Apuntes para historia de un régimen militar. Mexico City, Libr. General, 1914.

Díaz Dufoo, Carlos. Limantour: Una victoria financiera. Mexico City, Eusebio Gómez de la Puente, 1910.

Didapp, Juan Pedro. Los Estados Unidos y nuestros conflictos internos. Mexico City, Tip. El Republicano, 1913.

Diego-Fernández, José. Méjico: Política experimental. Mexico City, Talleres Gráficos de la Nación, 1919.

Dillon, E. J. Mexico on the Verge. London, Hutchinson, 1921.

Doblado, Manuel. México para los Mexicanos: El presidente Huerta y su gobierno. Mexico City, Impr. de Antonio Enríquez, 1913.

Dromundo, Baltasar. Emiliano Zapata. Mexico City, Impr. Mundial, 1934.

Dunn, H. H. The Crimson Jester, Zapata of Mexico. New York, National Travel Club, 1934.

Espinosa, Gonzalo N., Joaquín Piña, and Carlos B. Ortiz. La decena roja. Mexico City, 1913.

Esquivel Obregón, T. Democracia y personalismo. Mexico City, Impr. A. Carranza e Hijos, 1911.

Estrada, Roque. La Revolución y Francisco I. Madero. Guadalajara, Impr. Americana, 1912.

Fábila, Manuel (ed.). Cinco siglos de legislación agraria en México, 1493-1940. Vol. I. Mexico City, 1941.

Fernández Güell, Rogelio. Episodios de la Revolución mexicana. San José, Costa Rica, Impr. Trejos Hnos., 1914.

—— El moderno Juárez: Estudio sobre la personalidad de D. Francisco I. Madero. Mexico City, Tip. Artística, 1911.

Fernández Rojas, José. De Porfirio Díaz a Victoriano Huerta, 1910-1913. 2d ed. Guadalajara, Tip. de la Escuela de Artes y Oficios del Estudio, 1913.

—— La Revolución mexicana de Porfirio Díaz a Victoriano Huerta. Mexico City, Edit. F. P. Rojas e Cía., 1913.

Ferrer de M., Gabriel. Vida de Francisco Madero. Mexico City, Secretaría de Educación Pública, 1945. Biblioteca Enciclopédica Popular, No. 80.

Figueroa Domenech, J. Veinte meses de anarquía. Mexico City, 1913. Second part of La Revolución y sus héroes (*See* González, Antonio P., etc.).

Flores Magón, Ricardo. Epistolario revolucionario e íntimo. 3 vols. Mexico City, Grupo Cultural Ricardo Flores Magón, 1925.

—— Sembrando ideas. Mexico City, Ediciones del Grupo Cultural Ricardo Flores Magón, 1923.

—— Semilla libertaria. 2 vols. Mexico City, Grupo Cultural Ricardo Flores Magón, 1923. Articles.

—— Tribuna roja. Mexico City, Ediciones del Grupo Cultural Ricardo Flores Magón, 1925. Speeches.

Fornaro, Carlo de. Carranza and Mexico. New York, Mitchell Kennerley, 1915.

—— Díaz, Czar of Mexico. New York, 1909.

—— México tal cual es. Philadelphia, International Publishing Co., 1909.

Galarza, Ernest. The Roman Catholic Church as a Factor in the Political and Social History of Mexico. Sacramento, Calif., Capital Press, 1928.

Garcia, Silvino M. Vibraciones revolucionarios. Mexico City, Impr. Victoria, 1916.

Gavira, Gabriel. Su actuación político-militar revolucionaria. 2d ed. Mexico City, Talleres Gráficos de A. del Bosque, 1933.

Godoy, José F. Porfirio Díaz, President of Mexico. New York, Putnam, 1910.

González, Antonio P., and J. Figueroa Domenech. La Revolución y sus héroes. 5th ed. Mexico City, Herrero Hnos. Sucesores, 1912.

González-Blanco, Edmundo. Carranza y la Revolución de México. Valencia, Edit. Prometeo, 1914.

González Blanco, Pedro. De Porfirio Díaz a Carranza. Madrid, Impr. Helénica, 1916.

González Garza, Federico. La Revolución mexicana: Mi contribución política-literaria. Mexico City, A. del Bosque, 1936.

González M., José (pseud. Luis C. Balderrama). El clero y el gobierno de México. Mexico City, Edit. Cuauhtémoc, 1927.

González Roa, Fernando. El aspecto agraria de la Revolución mexicana. Mexico City, Departamento de Aprovisionamientos Generales, Dirección de Talleres Gráficos, 1919.

—— Las cuestiones fundamentales de actualidad en México. Mexico City, Impr. de Secretaría de Relaciones Exteriores, 1927.

Goríbar, Benigno A. El Maderismo en cueros. Havana, Impr. del Avisador Comercial, 1913.

Gruening, Ernest. Mexico and Its Heritage. New York, Century, 1928.

Guerrero, Praxedis. Artículos literarios. Mexico City, Edición del Grupo Cultural Ricardo Flores Magón, 1924.

Gutiérrez de Lara, Lázaro. El pueblo mexicano y sus luchas por la libertad. Los Angeles, Citizen Print Shop, n.d.

Guzmán, Martín Luis. The Eagle and the Serpent. Translated by Harriet de Onís. New York, Knopf, 1930.

—— Memorias de Pancho Villa. Mexico City, Ediciones Botas, 1939.

Hackett, Charles Wilson. The Mexican Revolution and the United States, 1910-26. Boston, 1926. World Peace Foundation Pamphlet, IX, No. 5.

Hannay, David. Díaz. London, Constable and Co., 1917.

Hernández, Fortunato. Más allá del desastre. Mexico City, 1913.

Hernández Chávez, Salvador, and Alfonso López Ituarte. La angustia nacional. Mexico City, Impr. de A. López, 1913 (?).

Hernández Ferrer, Antonio. Mi juicio acerca la Revolución mexicana. Havana, López, Prado y Fernández, 1920. Speech at Tabasco, Jan. 16, 1920.

Hubner, Manuel Eduardo. México en marcha. Santiago, Edit. Zig-Zag, 1936.

Junco, Alfonso. Carranza y los orígenes de su rebelión. Mexico City, Ediciones Botas, 1935.

Kelly, Francis Clement. Blood-Drenched Altars. Rev. ed. Milwaukee, Bruce Publishing Co., 1935.

Lamicq, Pedro (pseuds. Pirra-Purra, Crater). Madero por uno de sus íntimos. El dolor mexicano. Criollos, indios y mestizos. Mexico City, Oficina Edit. Azteca, 1914. These three titles were first published separately and were later republished in a single volume.

Lara Pardo, Luis. De Porfirio Díaz a Francisco Madero: La sucesión dictatorial de 1911. New York, Polygot Publishing Co., 1912.

—— Madero: Esbozo político. Mexico City, Ediciones Botas, 1937.

—— La prostitución en México. Mexico City, 1908.

León, Nicolás. Compendio de la historia general de México. 2d ed. Mexico City, Herrero Hnos. Sucesores, n.d.

León Suárez, José. El conflicto mexicano. Buenos Aires, Gadola, 1914.

López-Portillo y Rojas, José. Elevación y caída de Porfirio Díaz. Mexico City, Librería Española, 1921.

McBride, George M. The Land Systems of Mexico. New York, American Geographical Society, 1923.

Madero, Francisco I. Estudio sobre la conveniencia de la construcción de una presa en la Cañon de Fernández. San Pedro, Coahuila, Impr. Benito Juárez, 1907.

—— "Mis memorias," in Anales del Museo Nacional de Arqueología, Historia y Etnografía. Mexico City, 1922.

—— El partido Nacional Antireeleccionista y la próxima lucha electoral: Su programa, sus trabajos, tendencias y aspiraciones. San Pedro, Coahuila, El Demócrata, 1910.

—— La sucesión presidencial en 1910. 3d ed. (1st ed. San Pedro, Coahuila, 1908. 2d ed. Mexico City, 1909). Mexico City, Libr. de Viuda de Ch. Bouret, 1911.

Madero y su obra. Mexico City, Talleres Gráficos de la Nación, 1934. Documents.

Magaña, Gen. Gilardo. Emiliano Zapata y el agrarismo en México. 3 vols. Mexico City, Edición de la Secretaría de Prensa y Propaganda del Partido Nacional Revolucionario, 1934-36. Vol. 3, published posthumously, was completed by Carlos Pérez Guerrero.

Maldonado, M. Calixto. Los asesinatos de los señores Madero y Pino Suárez. Mexico City, 1922.

Manero, Antonio. El antiguo régimen y la Revolución. Mexico City, Tip. La Europea, 1911.

—— Cartas políticas. Mexico City, Viuda de Ch. Bouret, 1913.

—— The Meaning of the Mexican Revolution. 1915.

—— Por el honor y por la gloria. 1916. Editorials.

Maqueo Castellanos, Estebán. Algunos problemas nacionales. Mexico City, Edit. Eusebio Gómez de la Puente, 1909.

María y Campos, Armando de. Múgica: Crónica biográfica. Mexico City, Cía de Ediciones Populares, 1939.

Márquez Sterling, M. Los últimos días del Presidente Madero: Mi gestión diplomática en México. Havana, Impr. El Siglo XX, 1917.

Martínez, Rafael (pseud. Rip-Rip) and Eduardo Guerra. Madero: Su vida y su obra. Monterrey, 1914.

Maytorena, José N. Algunas verdades sobre el General Alvaro Obregón. Los Angeles, 1919.

Melgarejo, Antonio D. Crímenes del Zapatismo. Mexico City, Impr. Antonio Enríquez, 1913.

Mellado, N. Guillermo. Crímenes del Huertismo. Mexico City, 1916.

Mena Brito, Bernardino. Carranza, sus amigos, sus enemigos. Mexico City, Ediciones Botas, 1935.

—— Felipe Angeles, federal. Vol. I. Mexico City, Publicaciones Herreros, 1936.

Mendieta y Núñez, Lucio. El problema agraria de México desde su origen hasta la época actual. Mexico City, Impr. Mundial, 1923.

Moheno, Querido. ¿Hacia dónde vamos? Mexico City, Talleres de I. Lara, 1908.

Molina Enríquez, Andrés. "Boletín de la Dirección General de Agricultura, Parte II," Revista de economía rural y sociológica. Mexico City, 1911.

—— Los grandes problemas nacionales. Mexico City, Impr. A. Carranza e Hijos, 1909.

—— La revolución agraria de México de 1910 a 1920. 5 vols. Mexico City, Talleres Gráficos del Museo Nacional de Arqueología, Historia y Etnografía, 1933-37.

Morales Hesse, José. El General Pablo González. Mexico City, 1916.

Núñez del Prado, G. Revolución de México: La Decena Trágica. Barcelona, 1913.

Obregón, Alvaro. Ocho mil kilometros en campaña. Paris, Librería de la Viuda de Ch. Bouret, 1917.

Orozco, Wistano Luis. Legislación y jurisprudencia sobre terrenos baldíos. 2 vols. Mexico City, 1895.

Ortiz Rubio, P. "Medio Siglo," in Luis G. Franco, Tres años de historia del ejército de México, 1930-32. Mexico City, Ramo de Guerra y Marina, 1945. Pamphlet No. 8.

—— La revolución de 1910. 2d ed. Mexico City, Ediciones Botas, 1936.

O'Shaughnessy, Edith. Diplomatic Days. New York, Harper, 1917.

—— A Diplomat's Wife in Mexico. New York, Harper, 1916.

Oviedo Mota, Alberto. Pasa a la verdad. Mexico City, Secretaría de Gobernación, Talleres Gráficos, 1920.

Palavicini, Félix F. Mi vida revolucionario. Mexico City, Ediciones Botas, 1937.

Pani, Alberto J. Una encuesta sobre educación popular. Mexico City, Depto. de Aprovisionamientos Generales, Dir. de Talleres Gráficos, 1918.

Parkes, Henry B. A History of Mexico. Boston, Houghton Mifflin, 1938.

Phipps, Helen. Some Aspects of the Agrarian Question in Mexico: A Historical Study. Austin, University of Texas, 1925. Studies in History No. 2515.

Pina, Joaquín. Memorias de Victoriano Huerta. Fort Bliss, Texas, 1915.

Ponce de León, Gregorio. El interinato presidencial de 1911. Mexico City, Impr. de la Secretaría de Fomento, 1912.

—— La paz y sus colaboradores. Mexico City, Impr. de Secretaría de Fomento, 1914.

Prida, Ramón. De la dictadura a la anarquía. 2 vols. El Paso, Texas, 1914.

—— From Despotism to Anarchy. El Paso, Texas, 1914. Abridged translation.

Priestley, Herbert I. The Mexican Nation, A History. New York, Macmillan, 1923.

Primer Congreso Nacional Espírita. Mexico City, Impr. de A. Carranza, 1906. March 31 to April 15, 1906.

Puente, Ramón. Pascual Orozco y la revuelta de Chihuahua. Mexico City, Eusebio Gómez de la Puente, 1912.

Quevedo y Zubieta, Salvador. El caudillo. Paris, 1909.

Ramírez Cabañas, Joaquín (pseud. Pérez Lugo). La cuestión religiosa en México. Mexico City, Centro Cultural Cuauhtémoc, 1926. Documents.

—— The Religious Question in Mexico. Mexico City, Centro Cultural Cuauhtémoc, 1926.

Ramírez Garrido, J. D. Desde la tribuna. Mexico City, Andrés Botas, 1916.

Resendi, Salvador F. La revolución actual. Mexico City, Viuda de Ch. Bouret, 1912.

Reyes, Bernardo. Defensa: Que por si mismo produce el General de División Bernardo Reyes acusado del delito de rebelión. Mexico City, Impr. Lacaud, 1912.

Reyes, Rodolfo. De mi vida: Memorias políticas. 2 vols. Madrid, Biblioteca Nueva, 1929-30.

Ribot, Hector. Félix Díaz en Veracruz: El movimiento revolucionario del 16 al 25 octubre 1912. Mexico City, Impr. la Calle de Humboldt, 1912.

Rippy, J. Fred. The United States and Mexico. New York, Knopf, 1934.

Rojas, Luis Manuel. La culpa de Henry Lane Wilson en el gran desastre de México. Vol. I. Mexico City, Cía. Edit. La Verdad, 1928.

Romero, Francisco. Porfirio Díaz. Mexico City, 1880.

Rubén García. El Antiporforismo. Mexico City, Talleres Gráficos de la Nación. 1935.

Sánchez Escobar, Rafael. Episodios de la Revolución mexicana en el sur. Mexico City, Talleres Tipográficos de la Casa de Orientación Para Varones, 1934.

—— El ocaso de los héroes. Mexico City, Talleres Tipográficos de la Casa de Orientación Para Varones, 1934.

Santillán, Diego Abad de. Ricardo Flores Magón, el apóstol de la Revolución social mexicana. Mexico City, Grupo Cultural Ricardo Flores Magón, 1925.

Senties, Francisco de P. La organización política de México: El partido Democrático. Mexico City, Impr. de Inocencio Arriola, 1908.

Seoane, Luis F. Méjico y sus luchas internas. Bilbao, Impr. de la Viuda e Hijos de Hernández, 1920.

Serrano, T. F. Episodios de la Revolución en México. El Paso, Texas, Modern Printing Co., 1911.

Sierra, Justo (ed.). México, su evolución social. 3 vols. Mexico City, 1900-1902.

Simpson, E. N. The Ejido: Mexico's Way Out. Chapel Hill, University of North Carolina Press, 1937.

Smith, Randolph W. Benighted Mexico. New York, John Lane Co., 1916.

Stephenson, George M. John Lind of Minnesota. Minneapolis, University of Minnesota Press, 1935.

Tablada, José Juan. La defensa social: Historia de la campaña de la División del Norte. Mexico City, Impr. del Gobierno Federal, 1913.

Tannenbaum, Frank. The Mexican Agrarian Revolution. Washington, D.C., The Brookings Institute, 1929.

—— Mexico, The Struggle for Peace and Bread. New York, Knopf, 1950.

—— Peace by Revolution. New York, Columbia University Press, 1933.

Taracena, Alfonso. Carranza contra Madero. Mexico City, Biblioteca de Los Andes, 1934.

—— Madero, el héroe cívico. Mexico City, Ediciones Xochitl, 1946. Vidas Mexicanas No. 29.

—— Madero: Vida del hombre y del político. Mexico City, Ediciones Botas, 1937.

—— Mi vida en el vértigo de la Revolución mexicana. Mexico City, Ediciones Botas, 1936.

—— La tragedia zapatista. Mexico City, Edit. Bolívar, 1931.

Thomson, Arthur. The Conspiracy Against Mexico. Oakland, Calif., International Press, 1919. Pamphlet.

Toro, Carlos. La caída de Madero por la revolución felicista. Mexico City, 1913.

—— La iglesia y el estado en México. Mexico City, Talleres Gráficos de la Nación, 1927.

Torrea, Juan Manuel. La Decena Trágica. Mexico City, 1939.

Travesí, Gonzalo G. La Revolución de México y el imperialismo yanqui. Barcelona, Casa Edit. Maucci, 1914.

Trowbridge, E. D. Mexico Today and Tomorrow. New York, Macmillan, 1919.

Turner, John Kenneth. Barbarous Mexico. Charles H. Kerr and Co., 1911.

Vasconcelos, José. Ulises criollo. 9th ed. Mexico City, Ediciones Botas, 1946.

—— Los últimos cincuenta años. Mexico City, 1924.

Vásquez, Emilio. La reelección indefinida. Mexico City, Impr. Ignacio Escalante, 1908. Originally published in 1890.

Vázquez Gómez, Francisco. Memorias políticas, 1909-13. Mexico City, Impr. Mundial, 1933.

Whetten, N. L. Rural Mexico. Chicago, University of Chicago Press, 1948.

Wilson, Henry Lane. Diplomatic Episodes in Mexico, Belgium and Chile. New York, Doubleday Page, 1927.

Zayas Enríquez, Rafael de. The Case of Mexico and the Policy of President Wilson. New York, A. and C. Boni, 1914.

NEWSPAPERS

El Antireeleccionista (Mexico City), 1909-10.

El Constitucional (Mexico City), 1910.

El Debate (Mexico City), 1909-11.

El Demócrata (Mexico City), 1911.

El Demócrata (San Pedro, Coahuila), 1906, 1908-9.

El Diario (Mexico City), 1911-13.

El Diario del Hogar (Mexico City), 1908-13.

El Dictamen (Veracruz), 1909.

El Estandarte (Oaxaca), 1917.

Excelsior (Mexico City), 1917-39.

El Gráfico (Mexico City), 1930.

El Hijo de Ahuizote (Mexico City), 1902.

El Imparcial (Mexico City), 1910-13, 1915-.

El Mañana (Mexico City), 1911-13.

Mexican Herald (Mexico City), 1907-13.

México Nuevo (San Antonio, Texas, and Mexico City), 1908-13, 1932.

El Monitor Democrático (San Antonio, Texas), 1911.

El Mosco (San Pedro, Coahuila), 1905.

El Nacional (Mexico City), 1909.

Nueva Era (Mexico City), 1912-13.

La Opinión (Los Angeles, Calif.), 1931-38.

La Opinión (Veracruz), 1911-12.

El País (Mexico City), 1910-13.

El Partido Democrático (Mexico City), 1909.

El Paso Morning Times (El Paso, Texas), 1906-11.
El Peninsular (Yucatán), 1909-10.
La Prensa (San Antonio, Texas), 1931-38.
Regeneración (Mexico City), 1900; (San Antonio, Texas), 1904; (St. Louis, Mo.), 1905-6; (Los Angeles, Calif.), 1908-11.
Regeneración (Mexico City), 1911.
La República (Monterrey, Nuevo León), 1908-9.
La Revista de Mérida (Mérida), 1909.
Revista de Revistas (Mexico City), Feb. 23, 1913.
Revolución (Los Angeles, Calif.), 1907.
San Antonio Express (San Antonio, Texas), 1910-11.
San Antonio Light and Gazette (San Antonio, Texas), 1910-11.
El Tiempo (Mexico City), 1908-9.
Todo (Mexico City), 1942.
La Tribuna (Mexico City), 1912-13.
El Universal (Mexico City), 1913-39.

Index

Index